IMAGE COMICS PRESENTS

MADAME
FRANKENSTEIN ™

MADAME FRANKENSTEIN

OR THE FEMININE MONSTROSITY

BY
JAMIE S. RICH
AND
MEGAN LEVENS

LETTERING AND BOOK
DESIGN BY CRANK!

LOGO DESIGN BY
STEVEN BIRCH @ SERVO

COVER ART AND CHAPTER BREAKS
BY JOËLLE JONES

COLOR AND TONES BY
NICK FILARDI

CREATED BY
MEGAN LEVENS & JAMIE S. RICH

SPECIAL THANKS TO
CHRISTOPHER MITTEN,
JOE BOWEN, ARON TIONGCO,
MEREDITH WALLACE, MONICA GARCIA,
DAVID BROTHERS, AND
ERIC STEPHENSON.

MEGAN LEVENS:
BUZZINGOVERBOMBSHELL.BLOGSPOT.COM
@SADMEGANGIRLS

JAMIE S. RICH:
CONFESSIONS123.COM
@JAMIEESRICH

CRANK!
CRANKCAST.NET
@CCRANK

ISBN-10: 1632151979
ISBN-13: 978-1-63215-197-1

IMAGE COMICS, INC.
Robert Kirkman – Chief Operating Officer
Erik Larsen – Chief Financial Officer
Todd McFarlane – President
Marc Silvestri – Chief Executive Officer
Jim Valentino – Vice-President

Eric Stephenson – Publisher
Ron Richards – Director of Business Development
Jennifer de Guzman – Director of Trade Book Sales
Kat Salazar – Director of PR & Marketing
Corey Murphy – Director of Retail Sales
Jeremy Sullivan – Director of Digital Sales
Emilio Bautista – Sales Assistant
Branwyn Bigglestone – Senior Accounts Manager
Emily Miller – Accounts Manager
Jessica Ambriz – Administrative Assistant
Tyler Shainline – Events Coordinator
David Brothers – Content Manager
Jonathan Chan – Production Manager
Drew Gill – Art Director
Meredith Wallace – Print Manager
Addison Duke – Production Artist
Vincent Kukua – Production Artist
Tricia Ramos – Production Assistant
IMAGECOMICS.COM

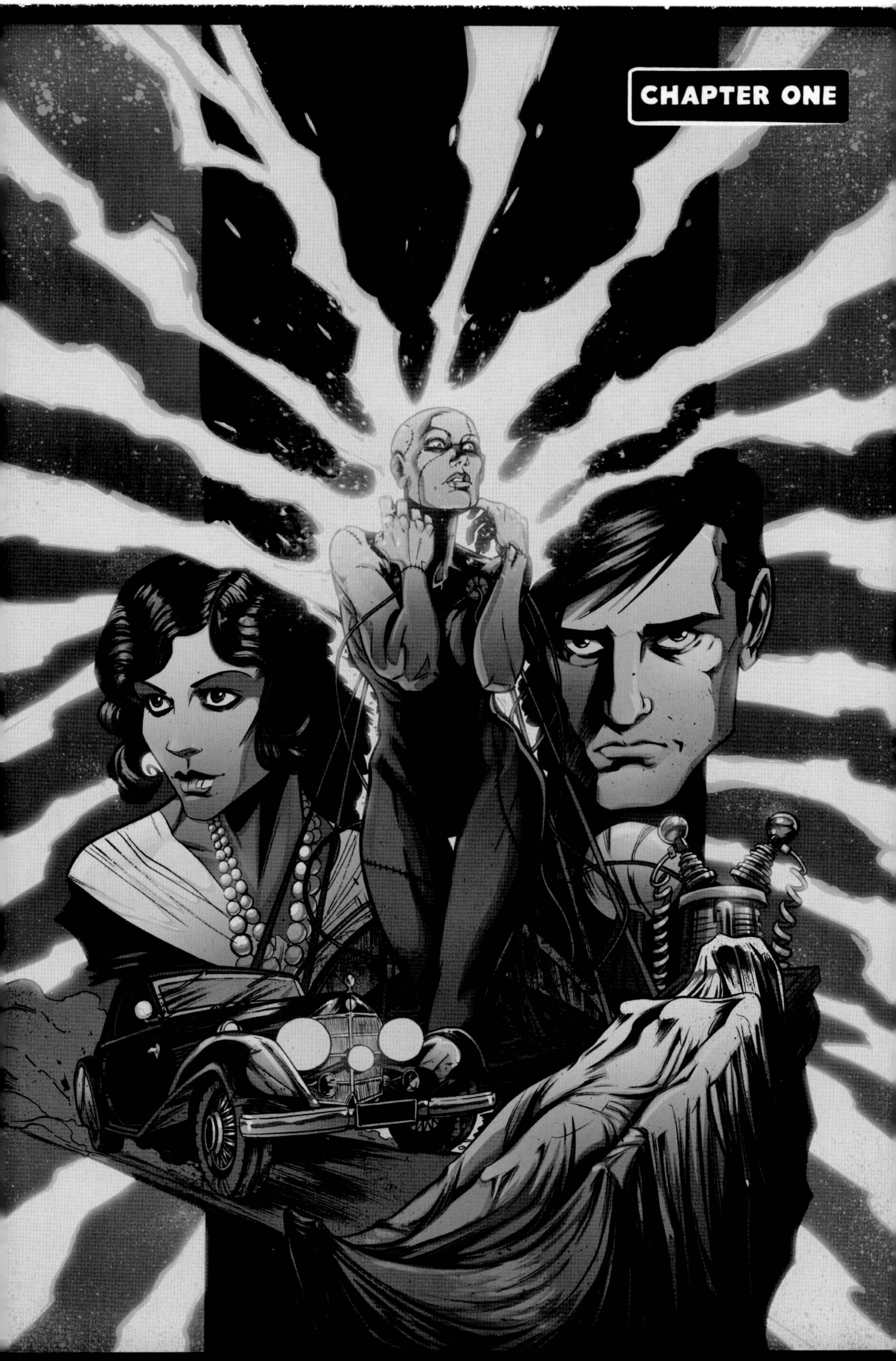
CHAPTER ONE

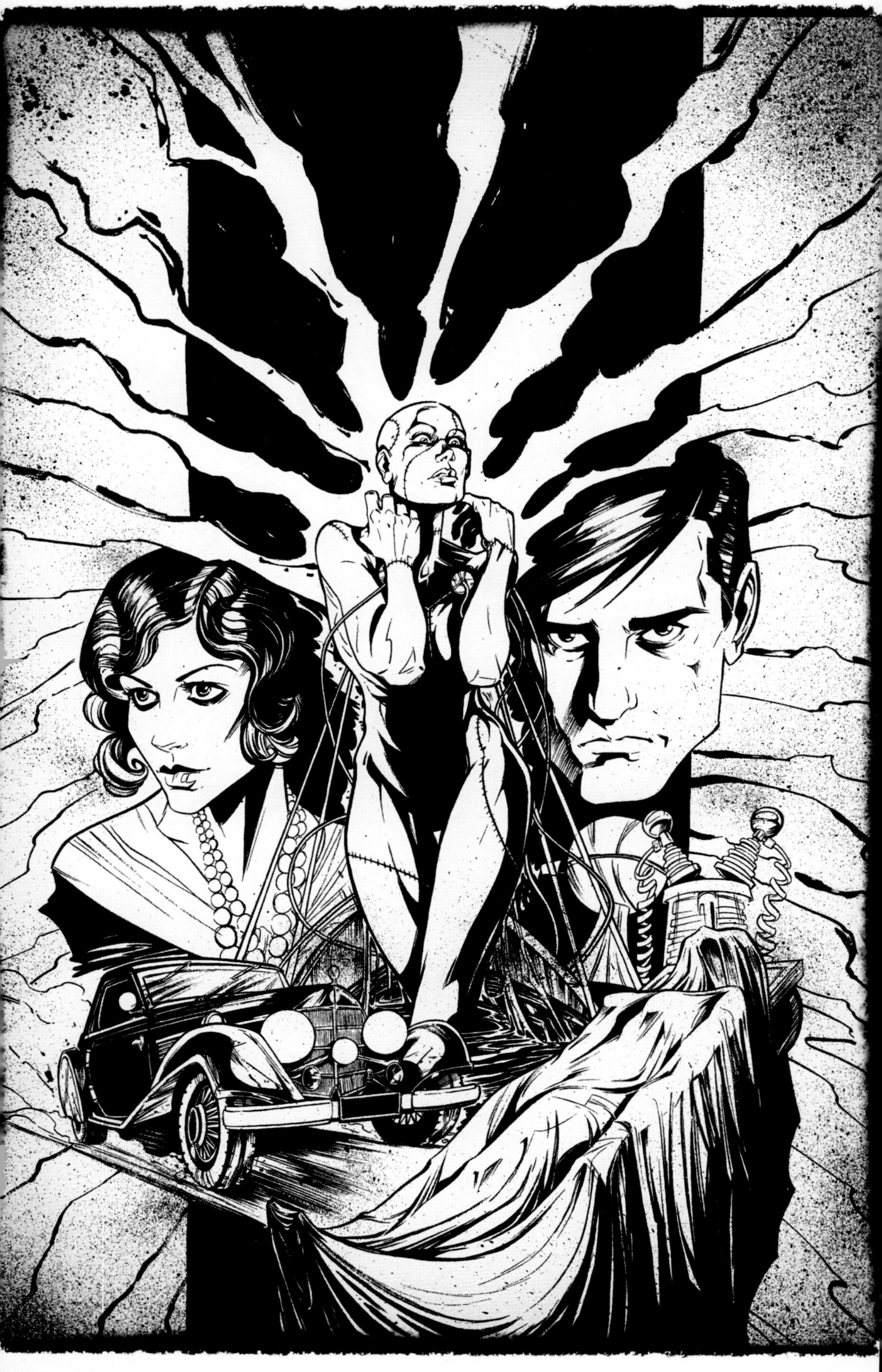

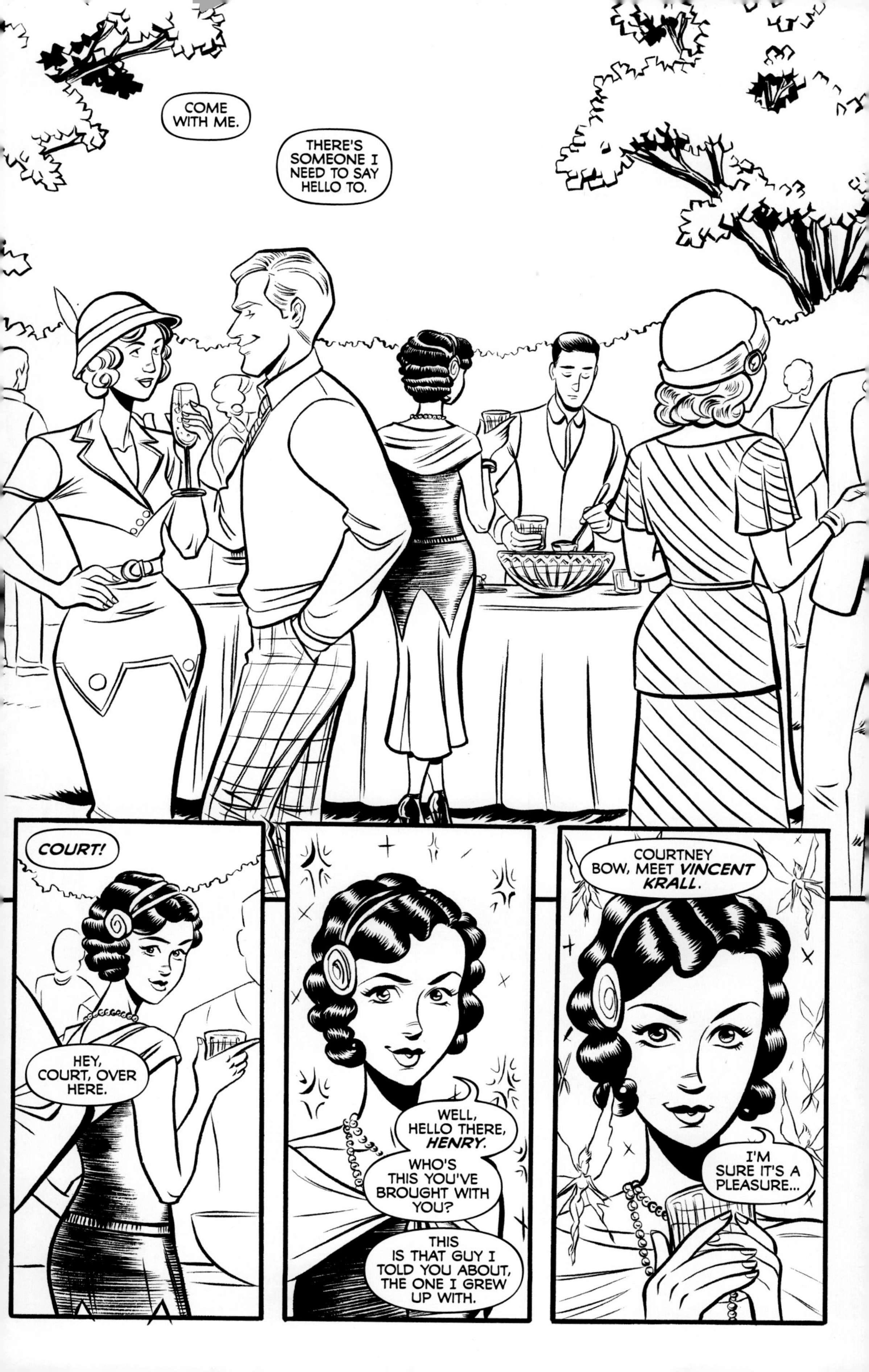
COME WITH ME.
THERE'S SOMEONE I NEED TO SAY HELLO TO.
COURT!
HEY, COURT, OVER HERE.
WELL, HELLO THERE, **HENRY**.
WHO'S THIS YOU'VE BROUGHT WITH YOU?
THIS IS THAT GUY I TOLD YOU ABOUT, THE ONE I GREW UP WITH.
COURTNEY BOW, MEET **VINCENT KRALL**.
I'M SURE IT'S A PLEASURE...

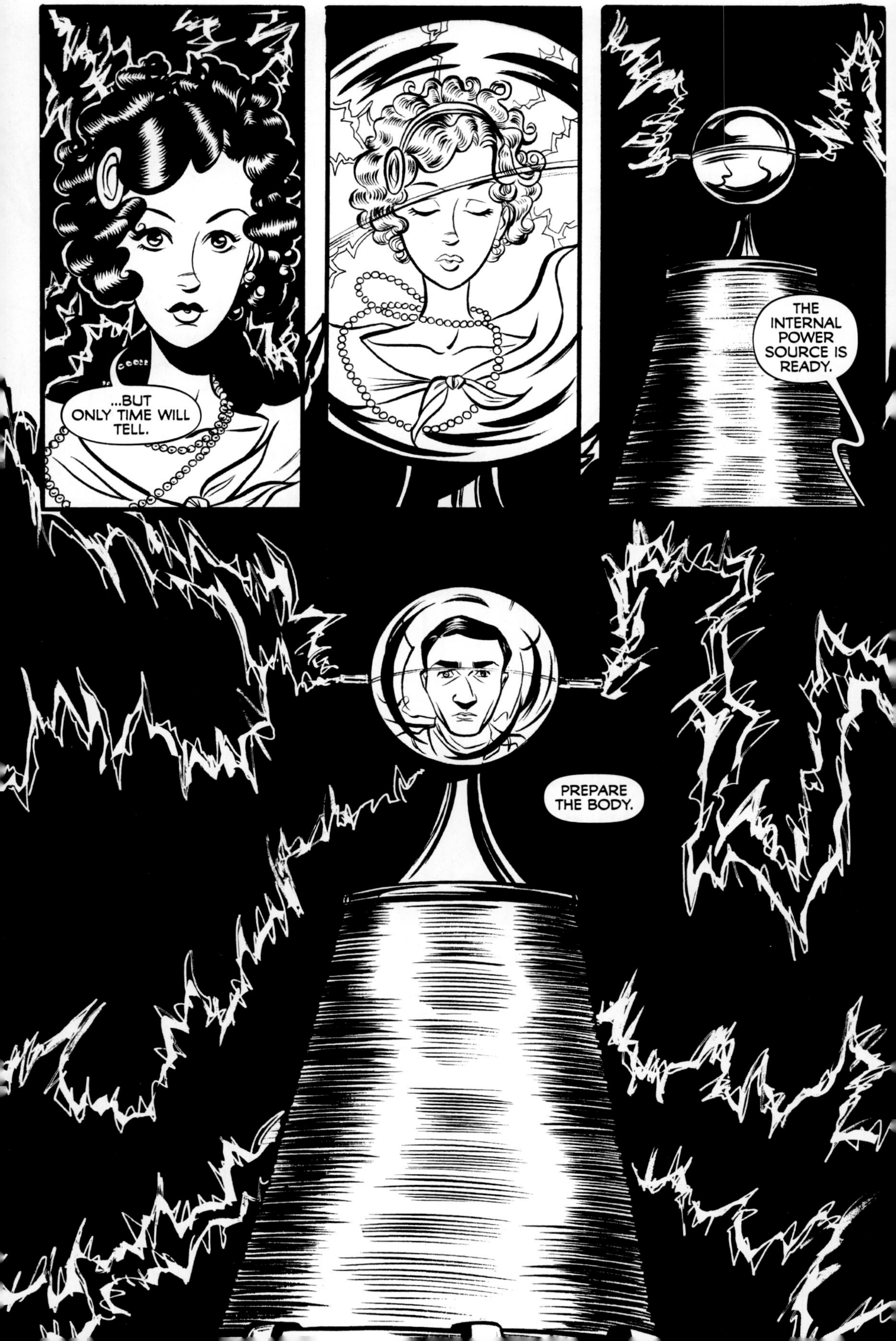
...BUT ONLY TIME WILL TELL.
THE INTERNAL POWER SOURCE IS READY.
PREPARE THE BODY.

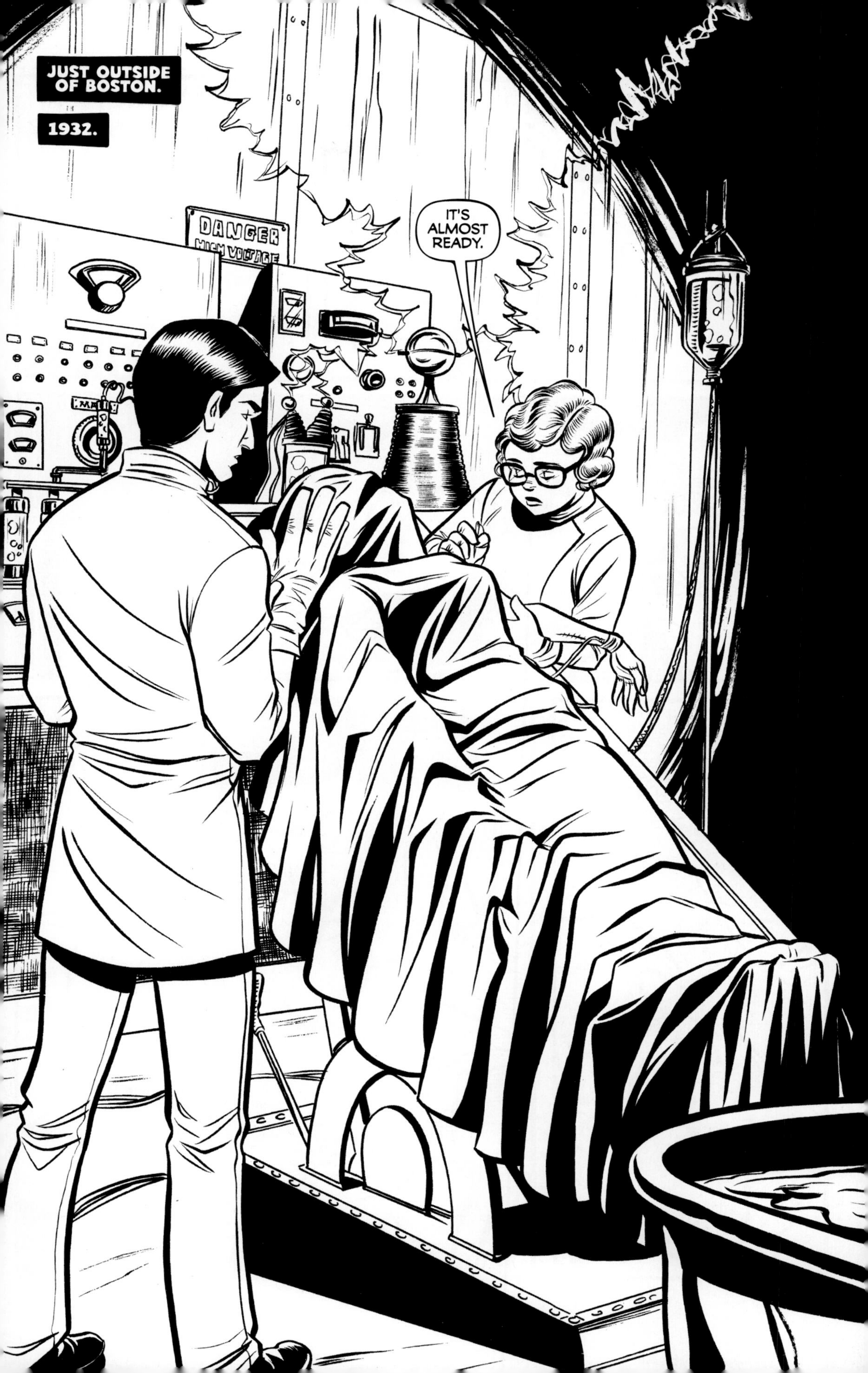
JUST OUTSIDE OF BOSTON.
1932.
DANGER HIGH VOLTAGE
IT'S ALMOST READY.

THIS ARM IS PROVING TRICKY.

HER ORIGINAL WAS BADLY MANGLED IN THE ACCIDENT.

I'M JUST GLAD THE HAND WAS PRESERVED SO THEY BOTH MATCH.

AND HER FACE.

SO PLEASED THAT HER FACE MOSTLY WENT UNHARMED.

THE FLESH IS WAXY, BUT IT STILL FEELS REAL.

THE CHEEKS ONLY NEED A LITTLE ADDITIONAL LIFE AND THE COLOR WILL RETURN.

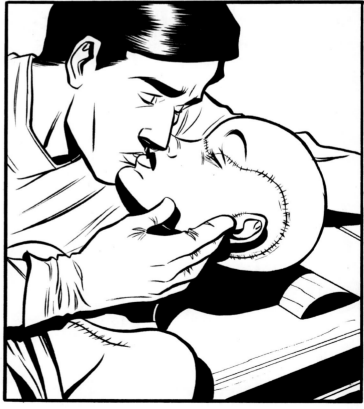

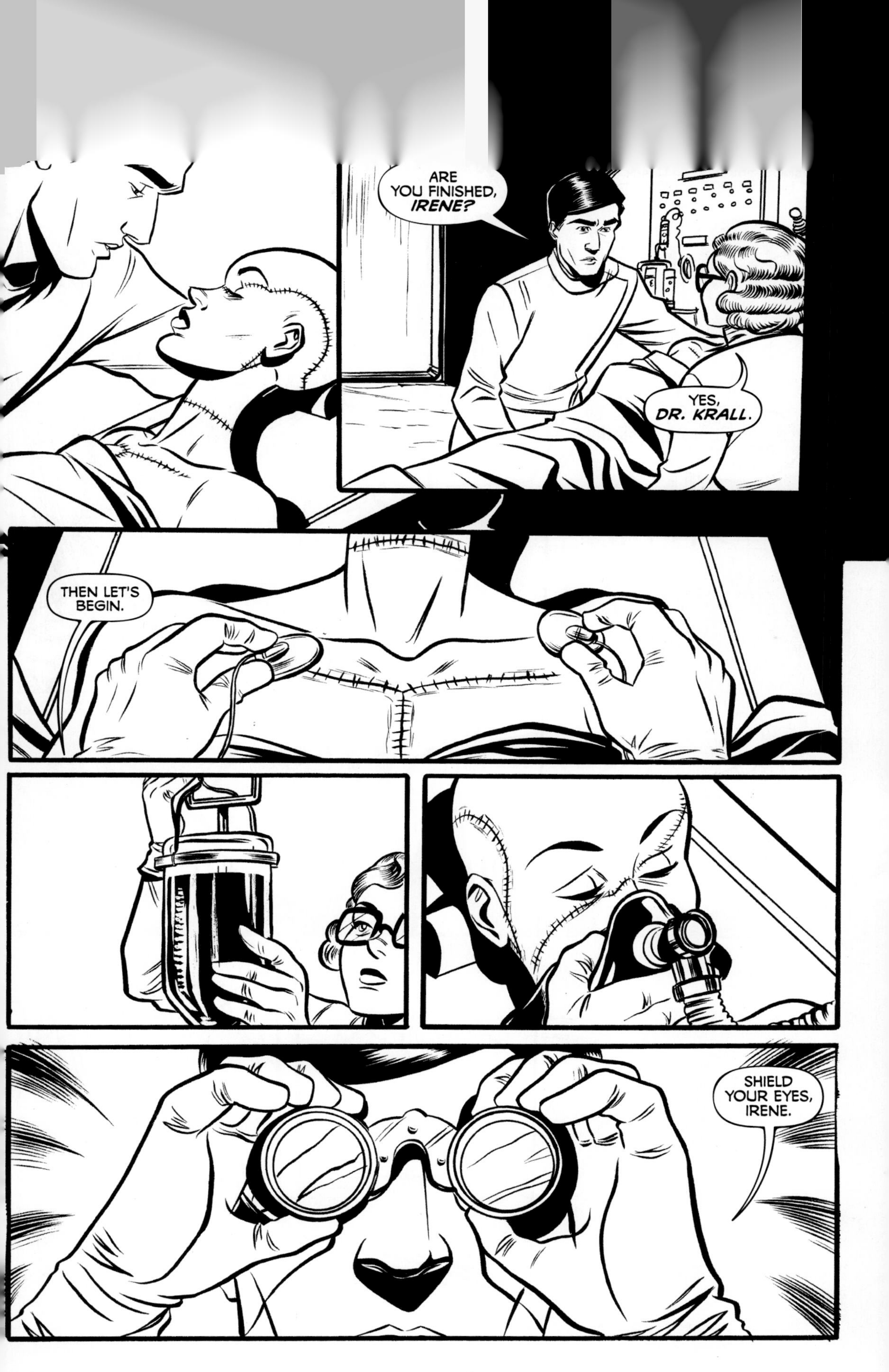
ARE YOU FINISHED, IRENE?
YES, DR. KRALL.
THEN LET'S BEGIN.
SHIELD YOUR EYES, IRENE.

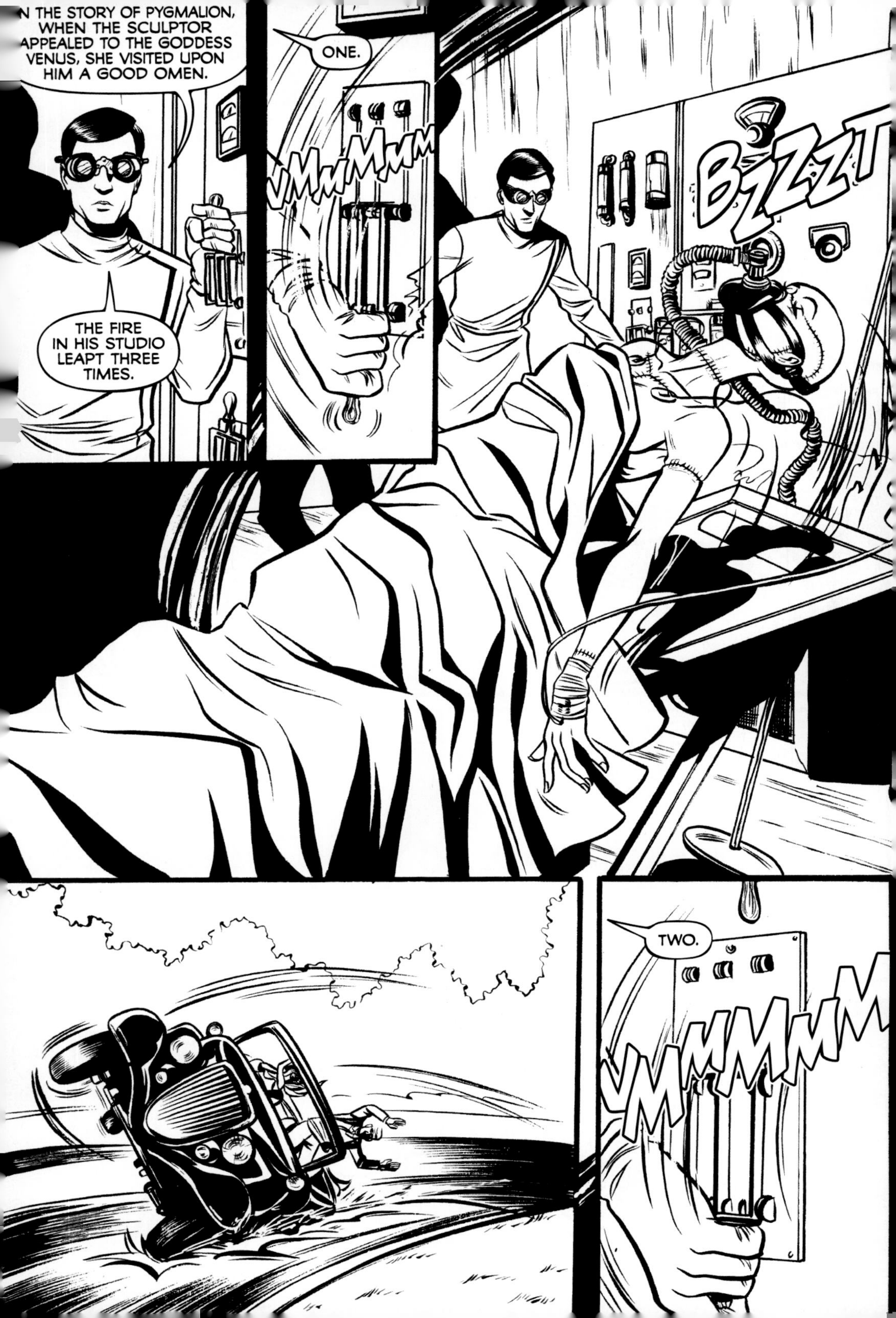
N THE STORY OF PYGMALION, WHEN THE SCULPTOR APPEALED TO THE GODDESS VENUS, SHE VISITED UPON HIM A GOOD OMEN.
THE FIRE IN HIS STUDIO LEAPT THREE TIMES.
ONE.
BZZZT
TWO.

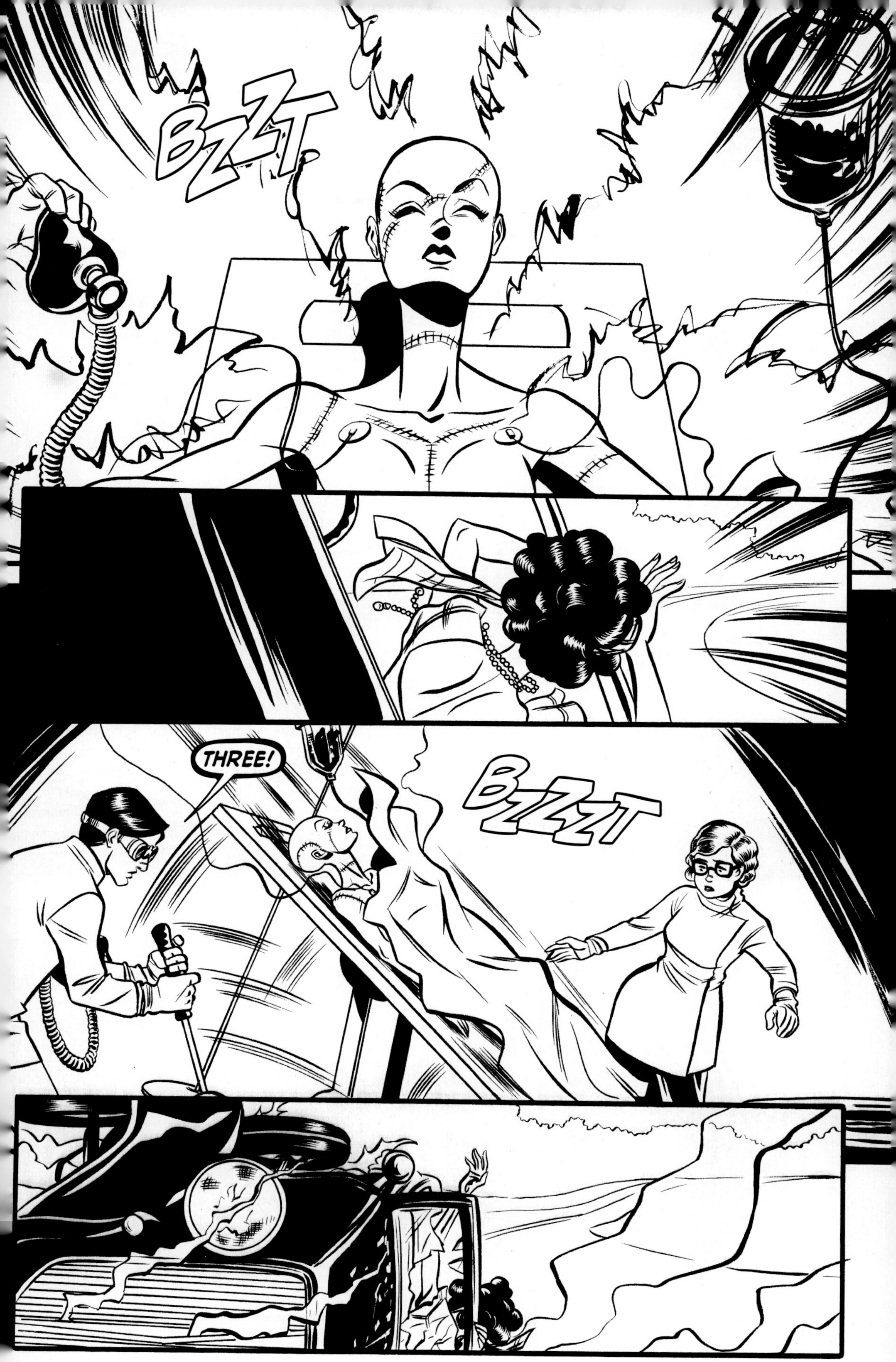
BZZT
THREE!
BZZZT

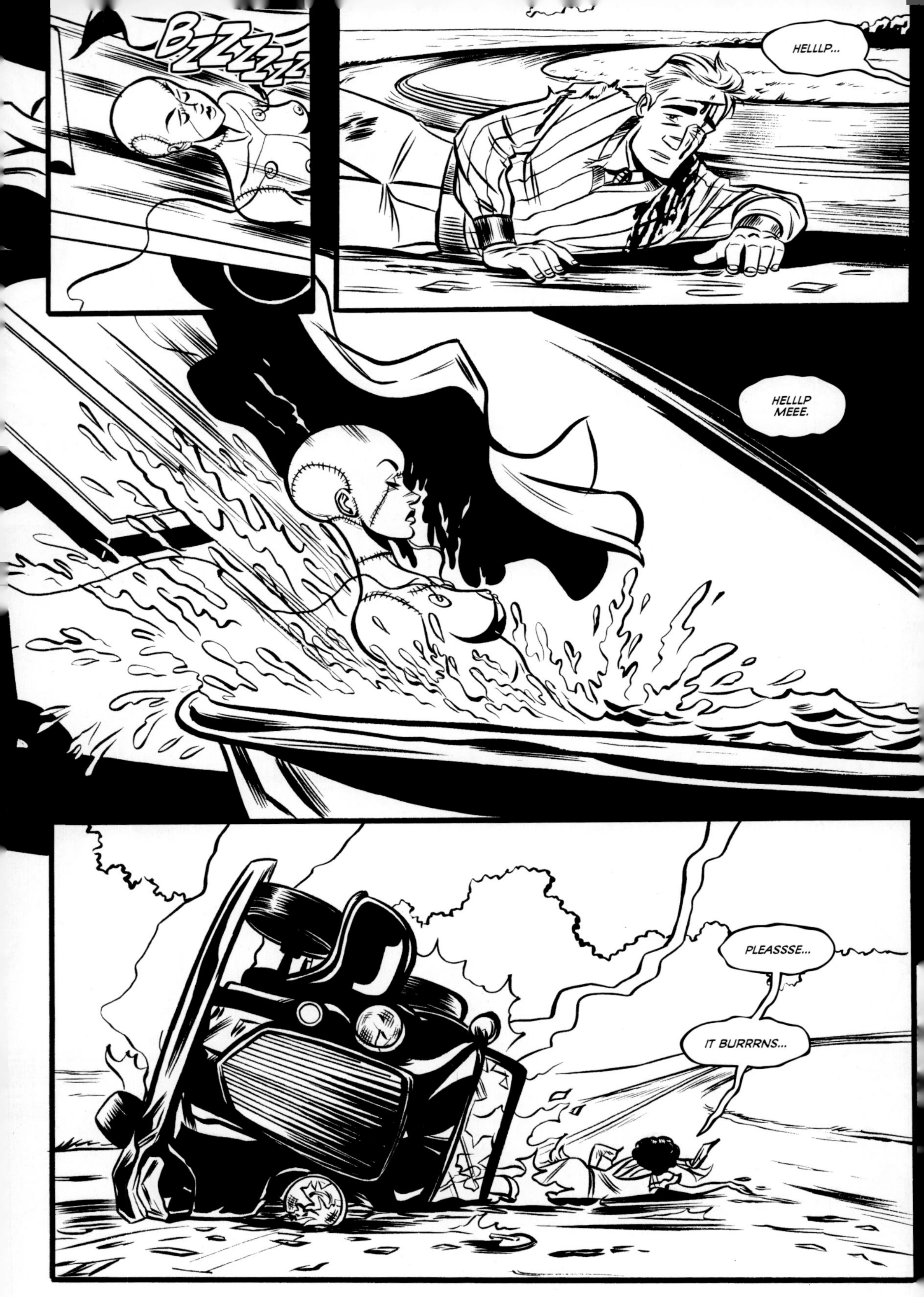
BZZZZZZ
HELLLP...
HELLLP MEEE.
PLEASSSE...
IT BURRRNS...

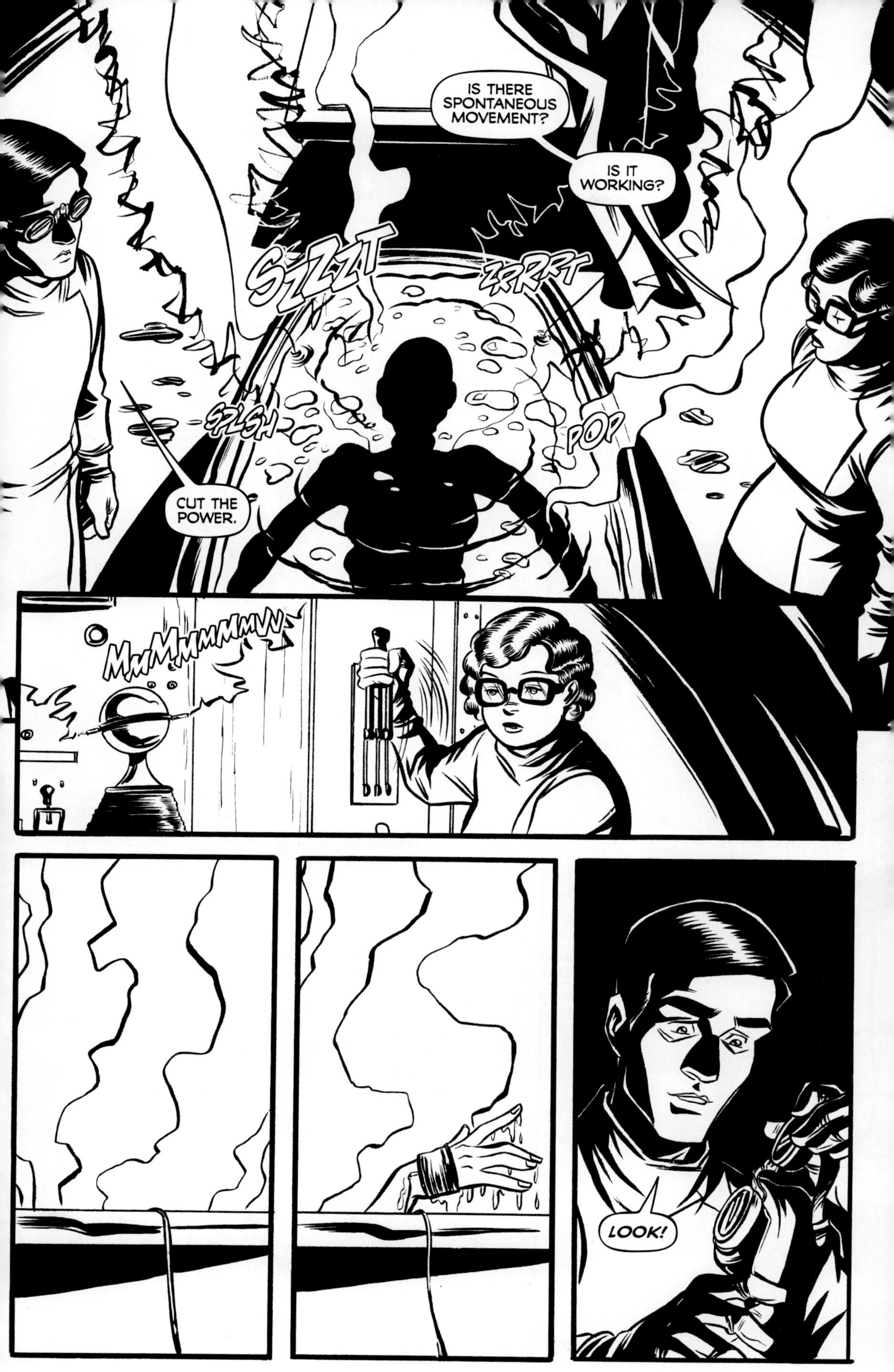
IS THERE SPONTANEOUS MOVEMENT?
IS IT WORKING?
SZZZT
ZRRRT
SPLSH
POP
CUT THE POWER.
MMMMMMMVV
LOOK!

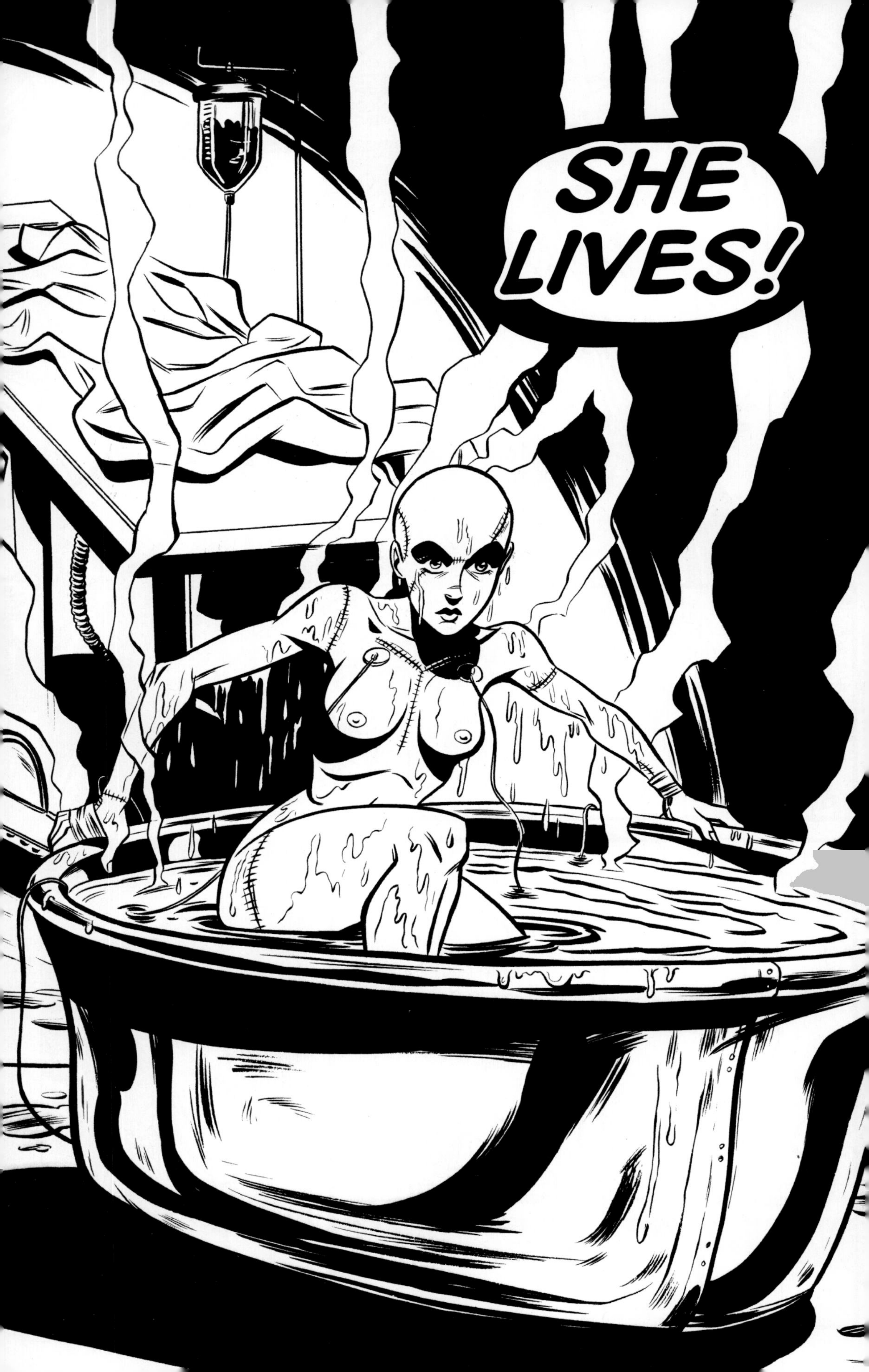
SHE LIVES!

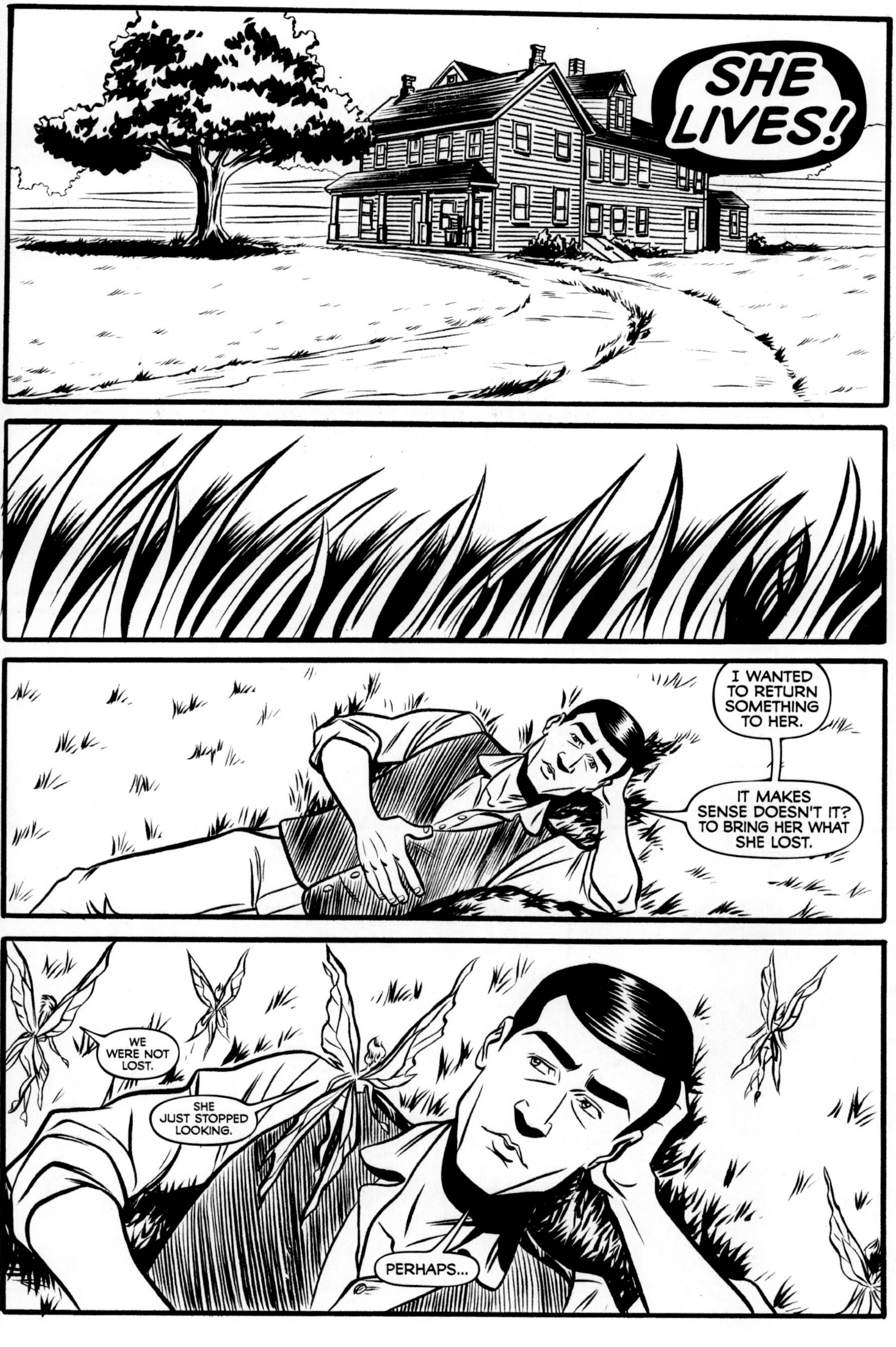
SHE LIVES!
I WANTED TO RETURN SOMETHING TO HER.
IT MAKES SENSE DOESN'T IT? TO BRING HER WHAT SHE LOST.
WE WERE NOT LOST.
SHE JUST STOPPED LOOKING.
PERHAPS...

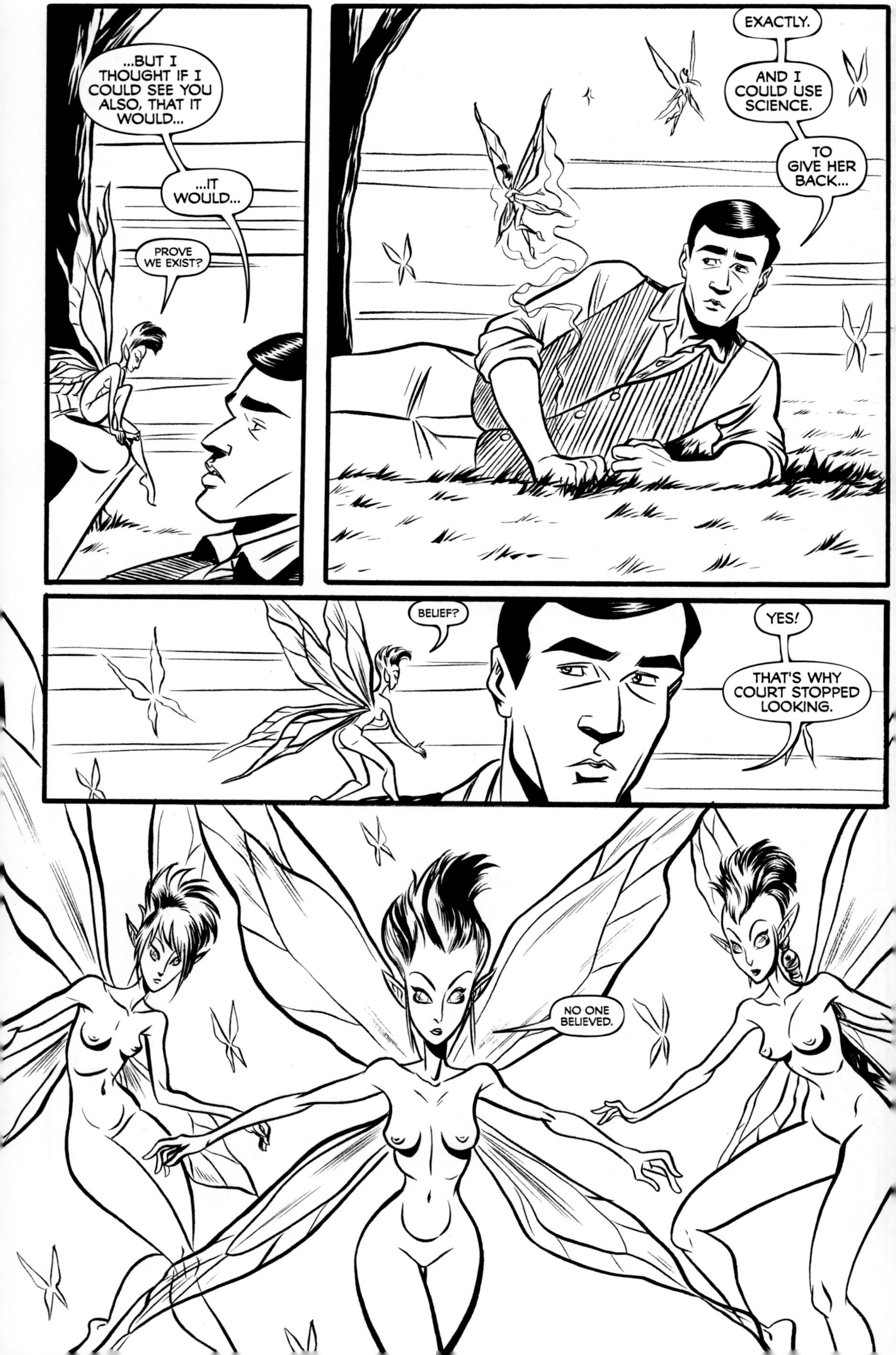
...BUT I THOUGHT IF I COULD SEE YOU ALSO, THAT IT WOULD...
...IT WOULD...
PROVE WE EXIST?
EXACTLY.
AND I COULD USE SCIENCE.
TO GIVE HER BACK...
BELIEF?
YES!
THAT'S WHY COURT STOPPED LOOKING.
NO ONE BELIEVED.

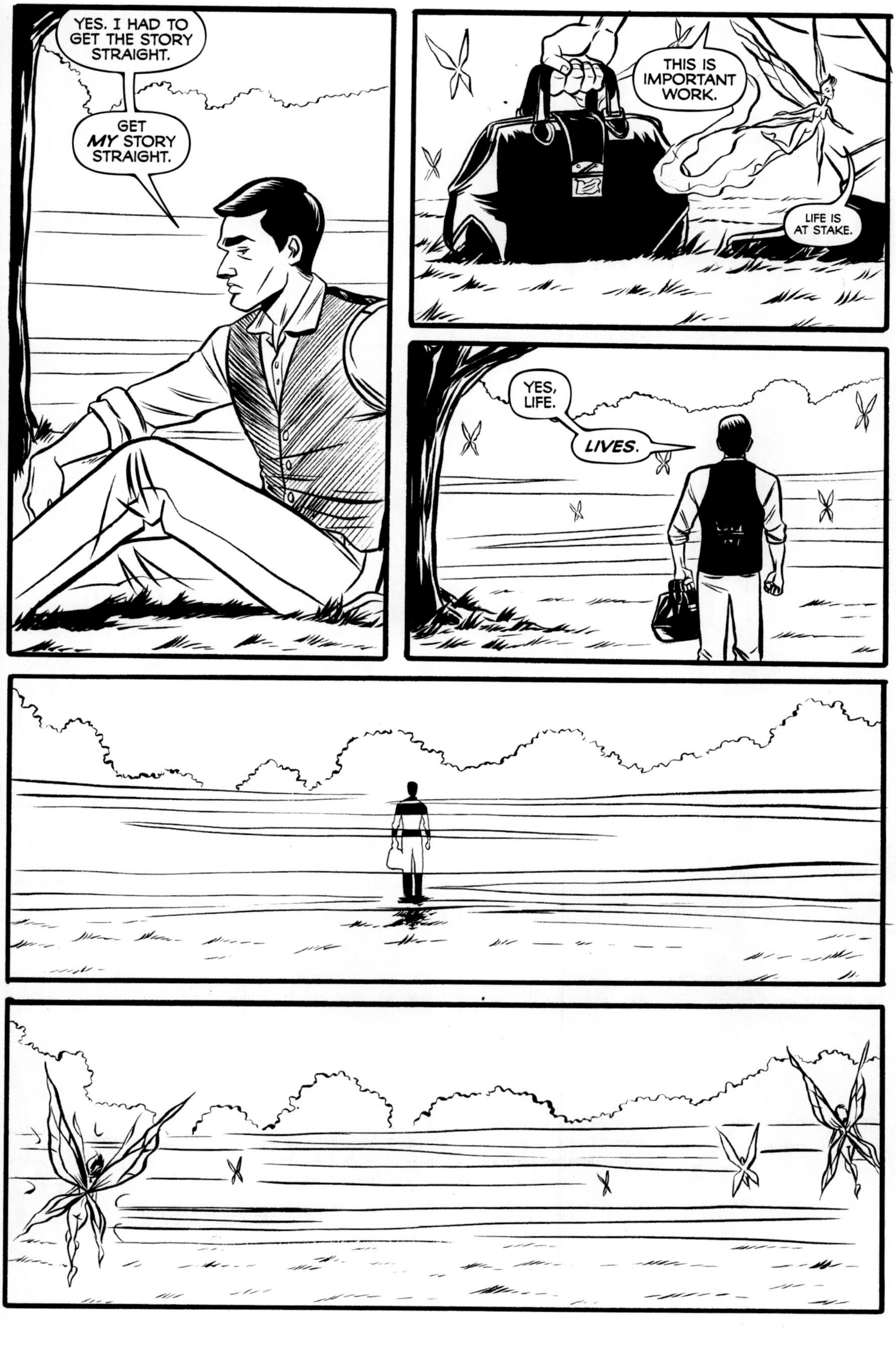
YES. I HAD TO GET THE STORY STRAIGHT.
GET MY STORY STRAIGHT.
THIS IS IMPORTANT WORK.
LIFE IS AT STAKE.
YES, LIFE.
LIVES.

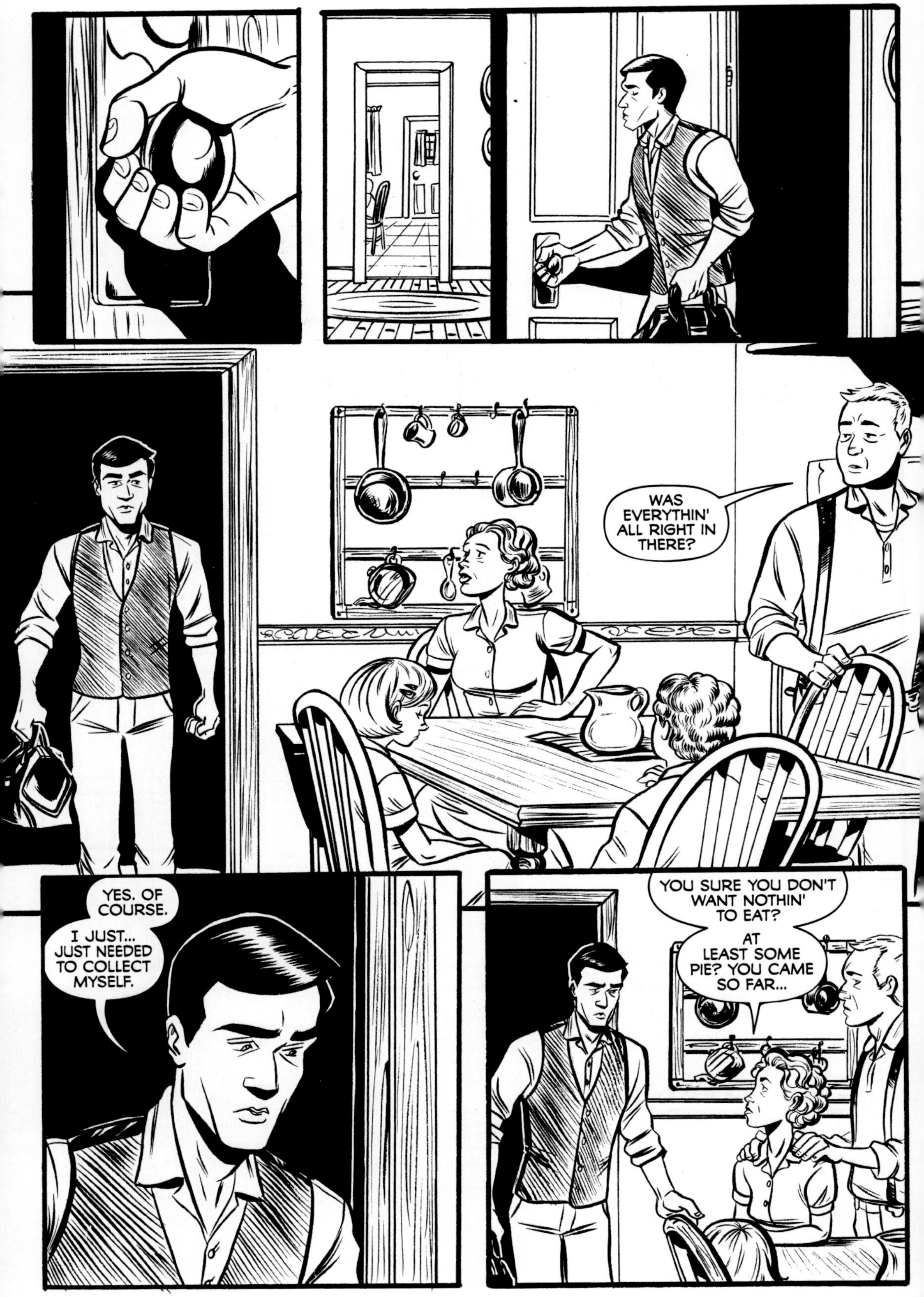
WAS EVERYTHIN' ALL RIGHT IN THERE?
YES. OF COURSE.
I JUST... JUST NEEDED TO COLLECT MYSELF.
YOU SURE YOU DON'T WANT NOTHIN' TO EAT?
AT LEAST SOME PIE? YOU CAME SO FAR...

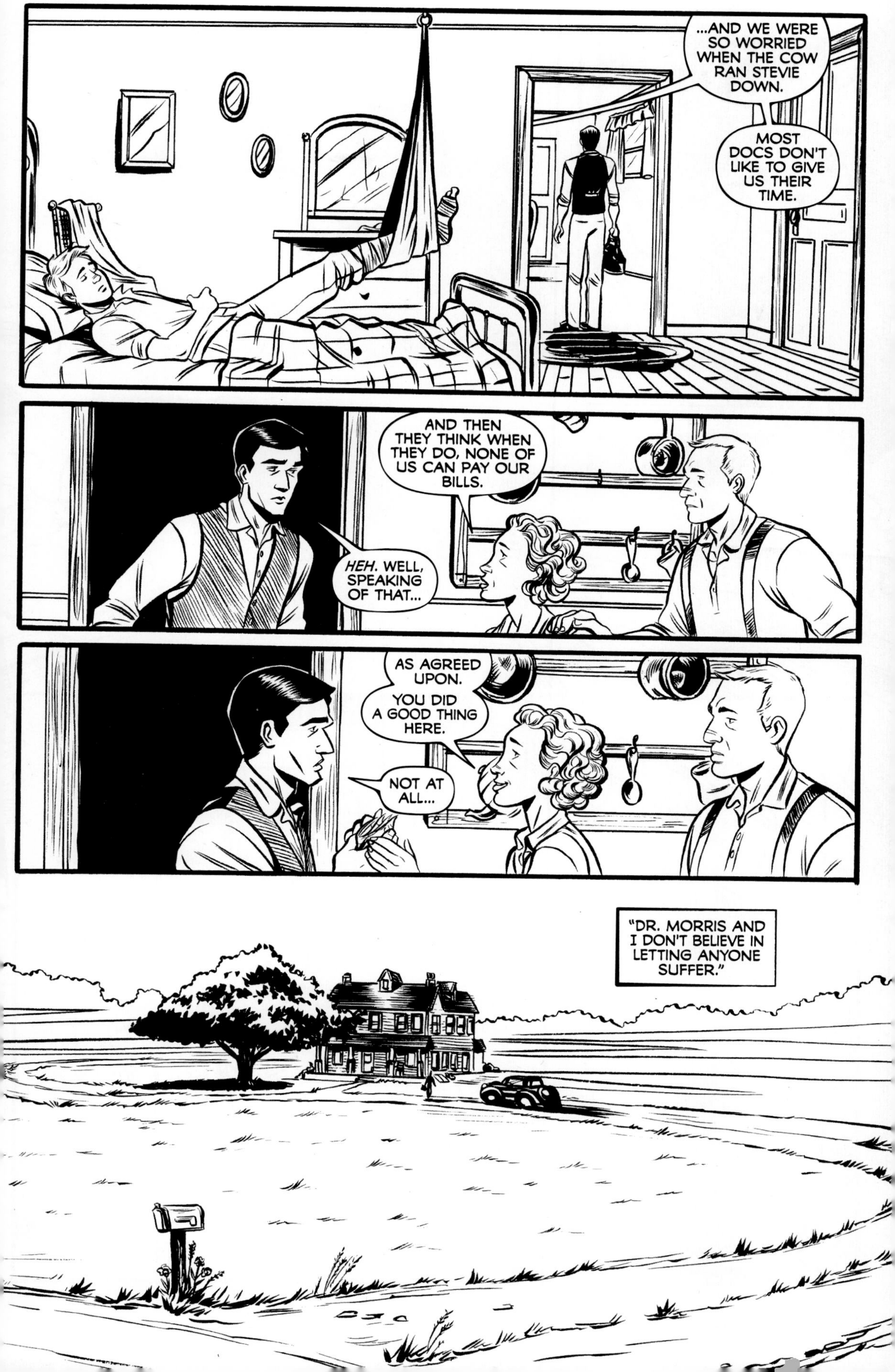
...AND WE WERE SO WORRIED WHEN THE COW RAN STEVIE DOWN.
MOST DOCS DON'T LIKE TO GIVE US THEIR TIME.
AND THEN THEY THINK WHEN THEY DO, NONE OF US CAN PAY OUR BILLS.
HEH. WELL, SPEAKING OF THAT...
AS AGREED UPON.
YOU DID A GOOD THING HERE.
NOT AT ALL...
"DR. MORRIS AND I DON'T BELIEVE IN LETTING ANYONE SUFFER."

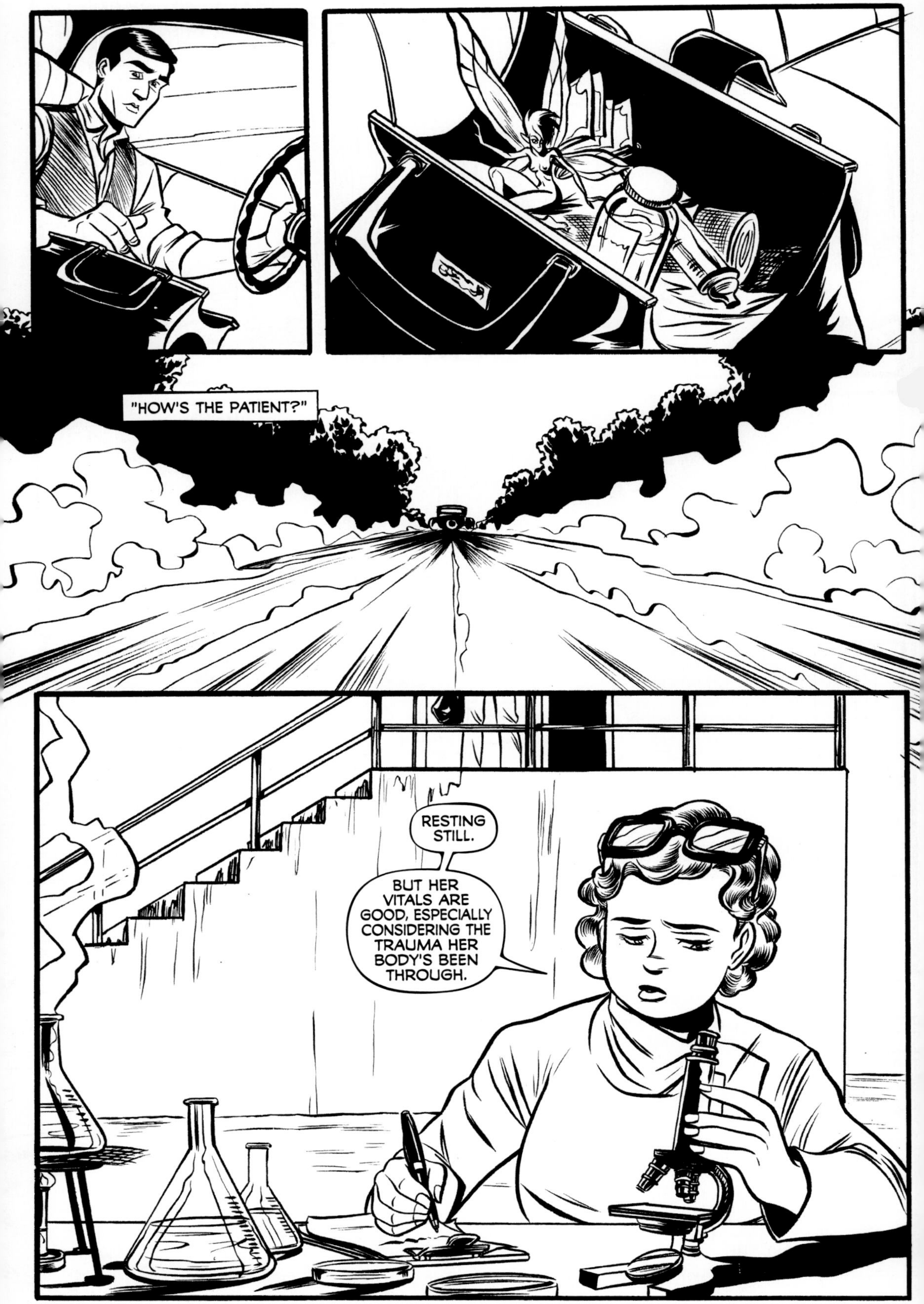
"HOW'S THE PATIENT?"
RESTING STILL.
BUT HER VITALS ARE GOOD, ESPECIALLY CONSIDERING THE TRAUMA HER BODY'S BEEN THROUGH.

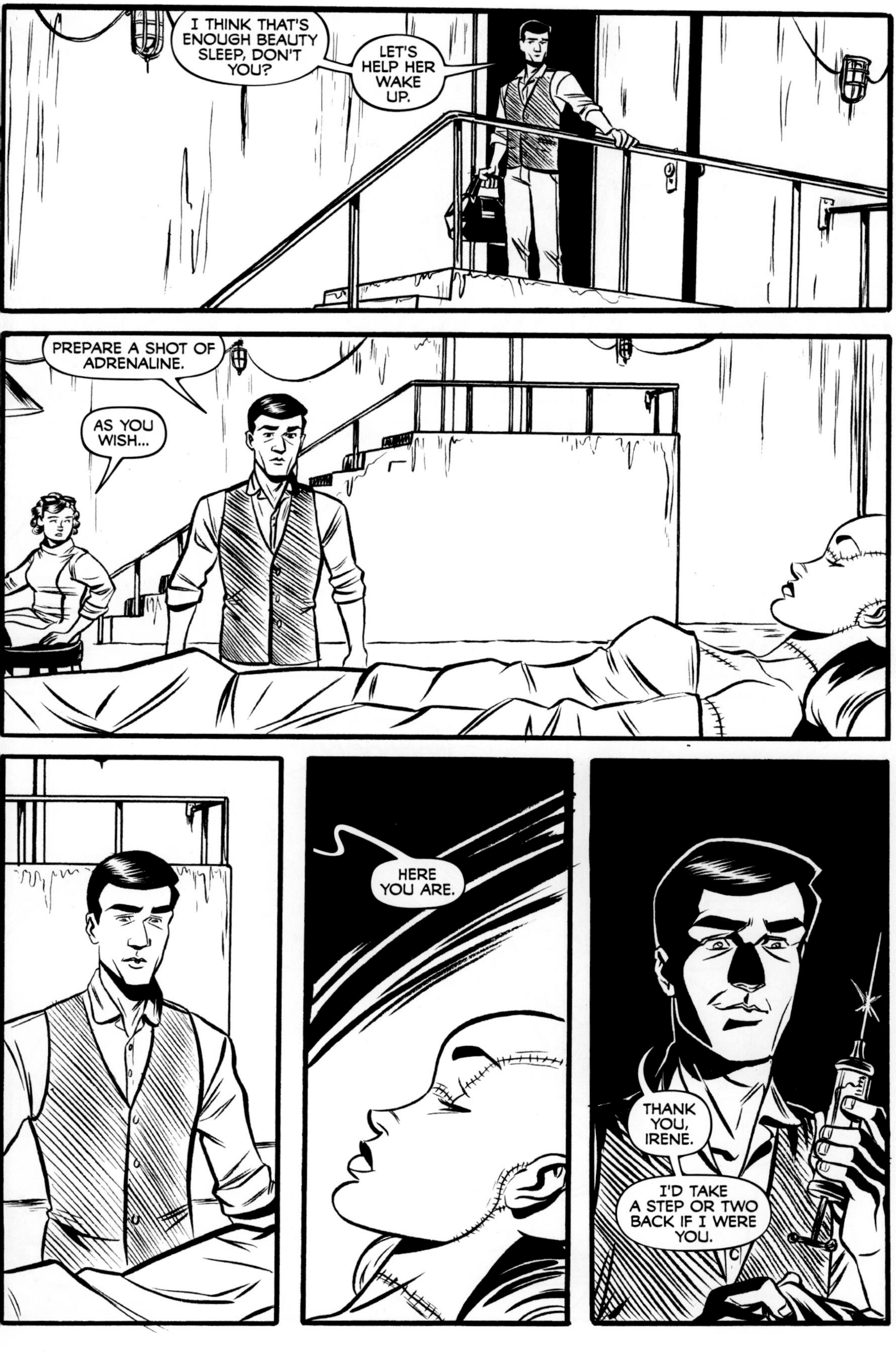
I THINK THAT'S ENOUGH BEAUTY SLEEP, DON'T YOU?
LET'S HELP HER WAKE UP.
PREPARE A SHOT OF ADRENALINE.
AS YOU WISH...
HERE YOU ARE.
THANK YOU, IRENE.
I'D TAKE A STEP OR TWO BACK IF I WERE YOU.

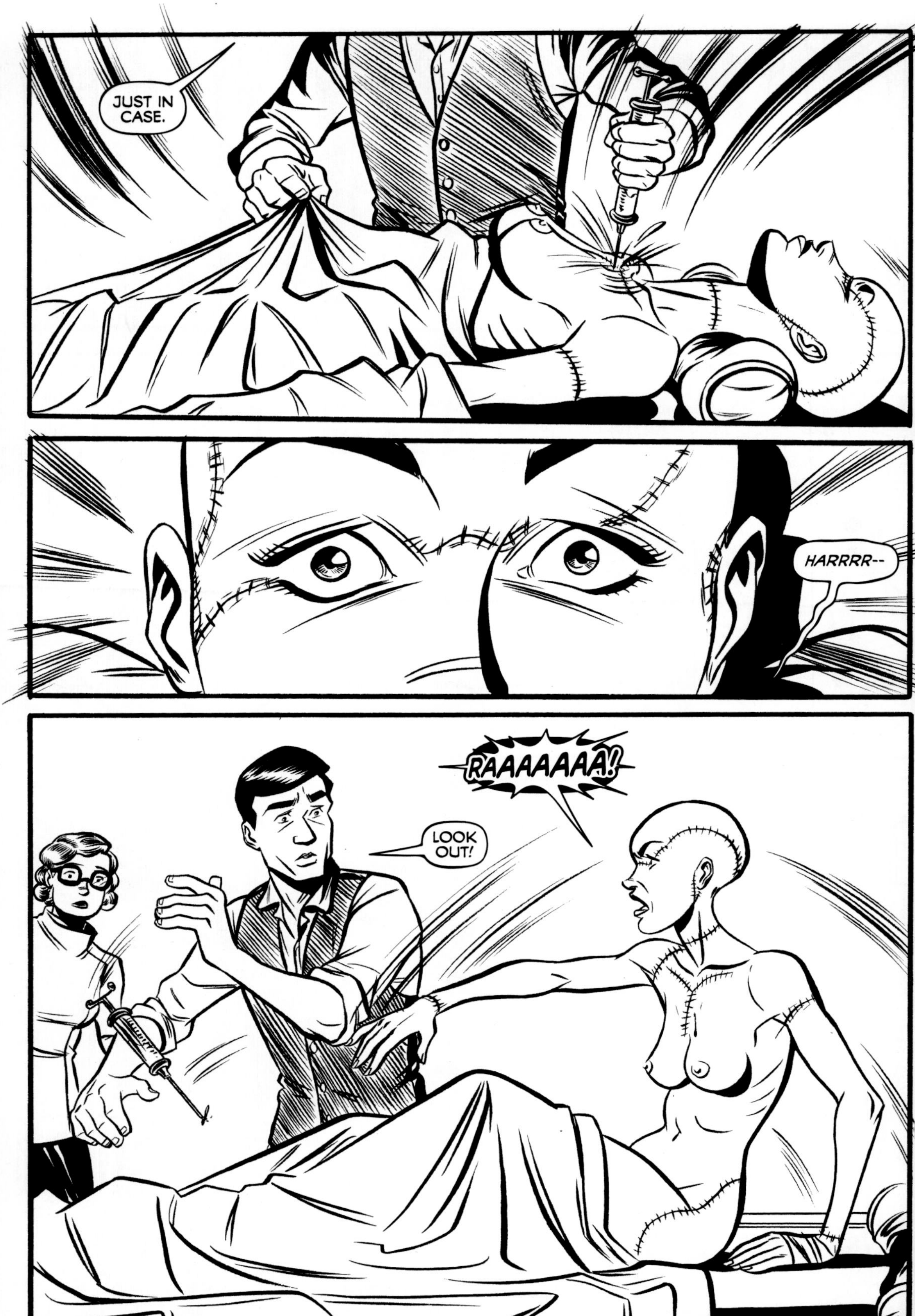
JUST IN CASE.
HARRRR--
RAAAAAAA!
LOOK OUT!

STOP HER!

IT'S TOO MUCH STIMULUS ALL AT ONCE.

SHE DOESN'T KNOW HOW TO PROCESS IT!

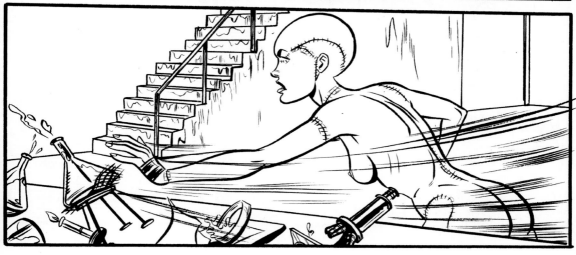

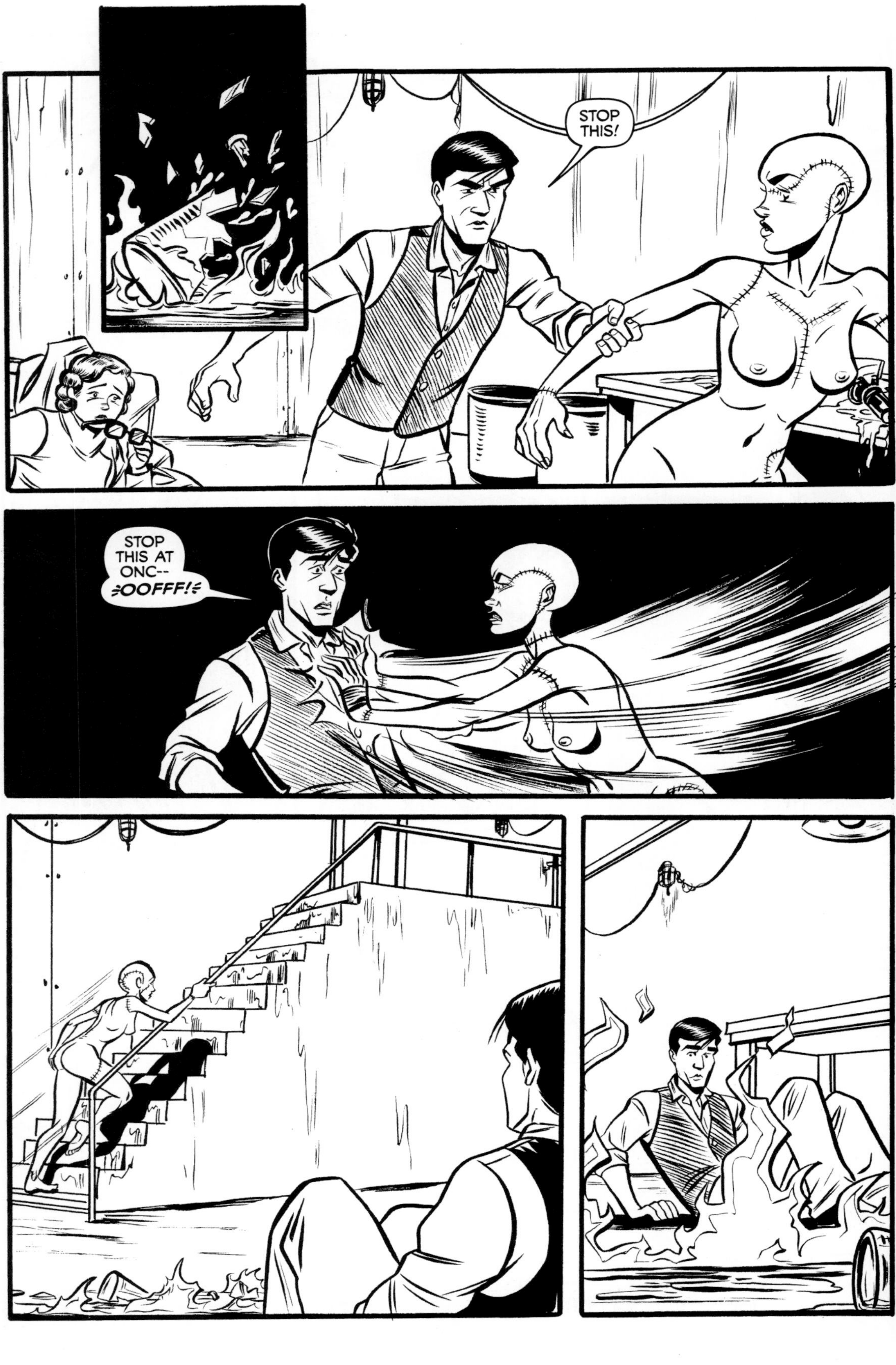

STOP THIS!
STOP THIS AT ONC-- OOFFF!

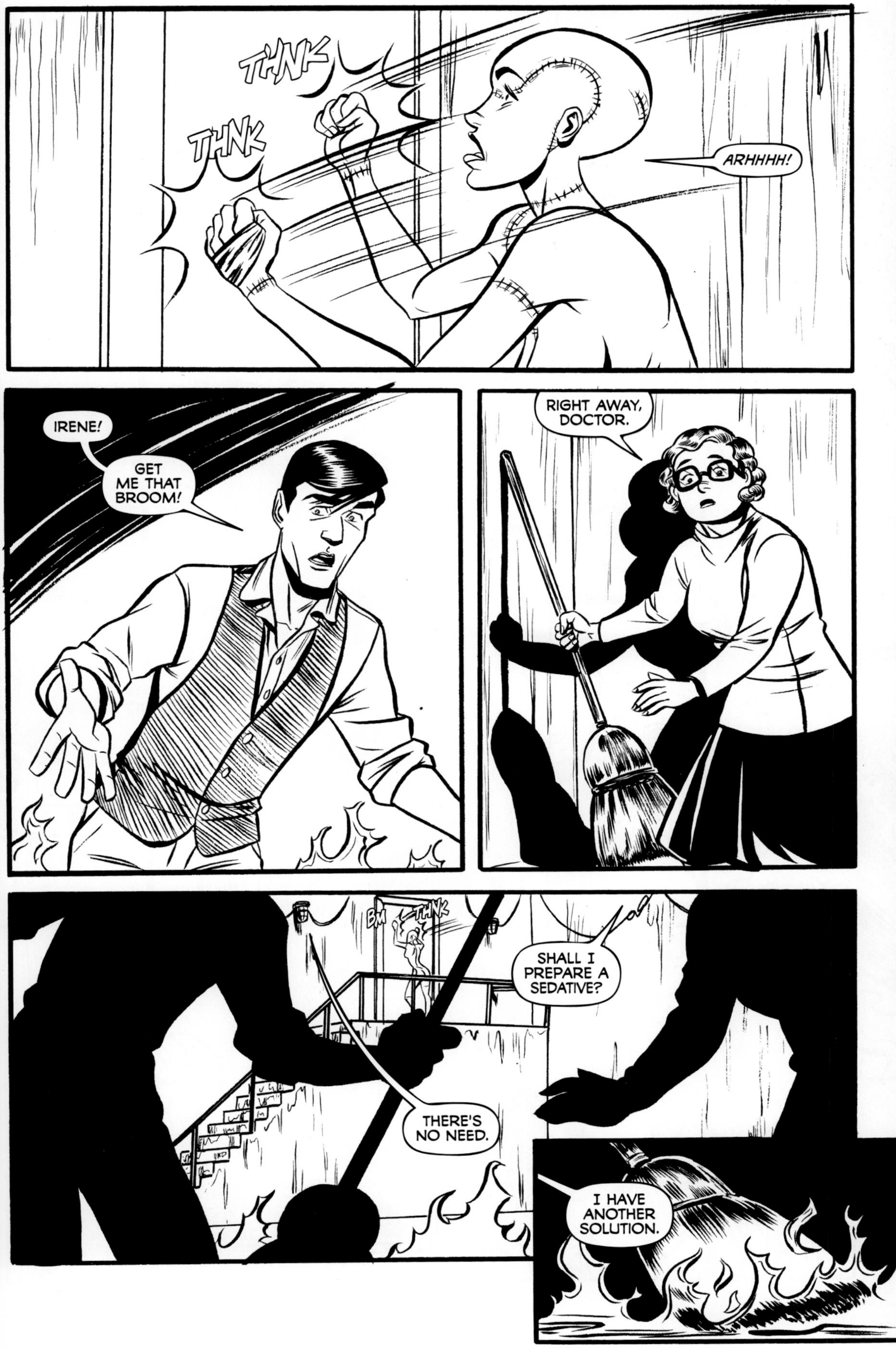
THNK
THNK
ARHHHH!
IRENE!
GET ME THAT BROOM!
RIGHT AWAY, DOCTOR.
BM THNK
SHALL I PREPARE A SEDATIVE?
THERE'S NO NEED.
I HAVE ANOTHER SOLUTION.

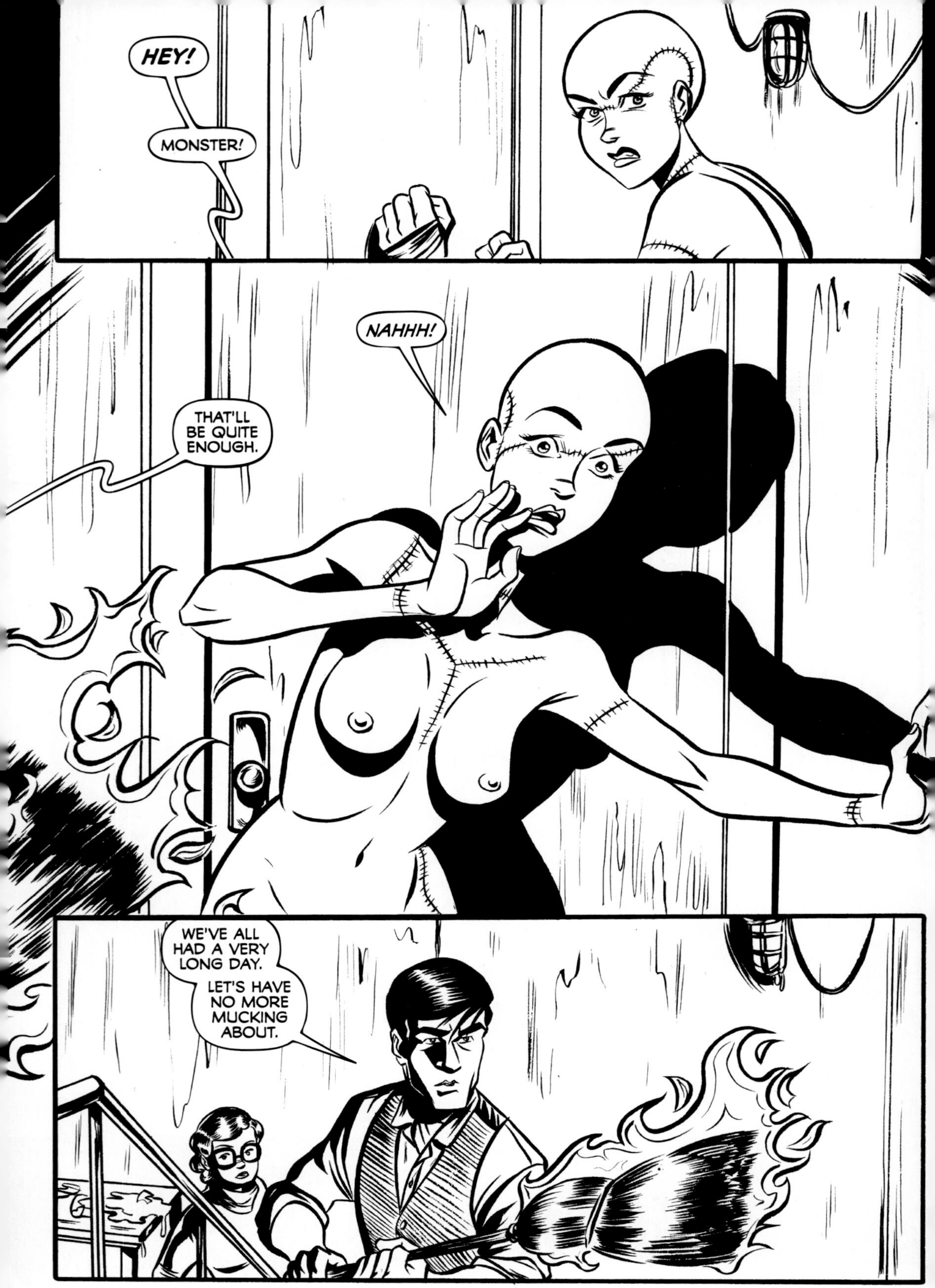
HEY!
MONSTER!
NAHHH!
THAT'LL BE QUITE ENOUGH.
WE'VE ALL HAD A VERY LONG DAY.
LET'S HAVE NO MORE MUCKING ABOUT.

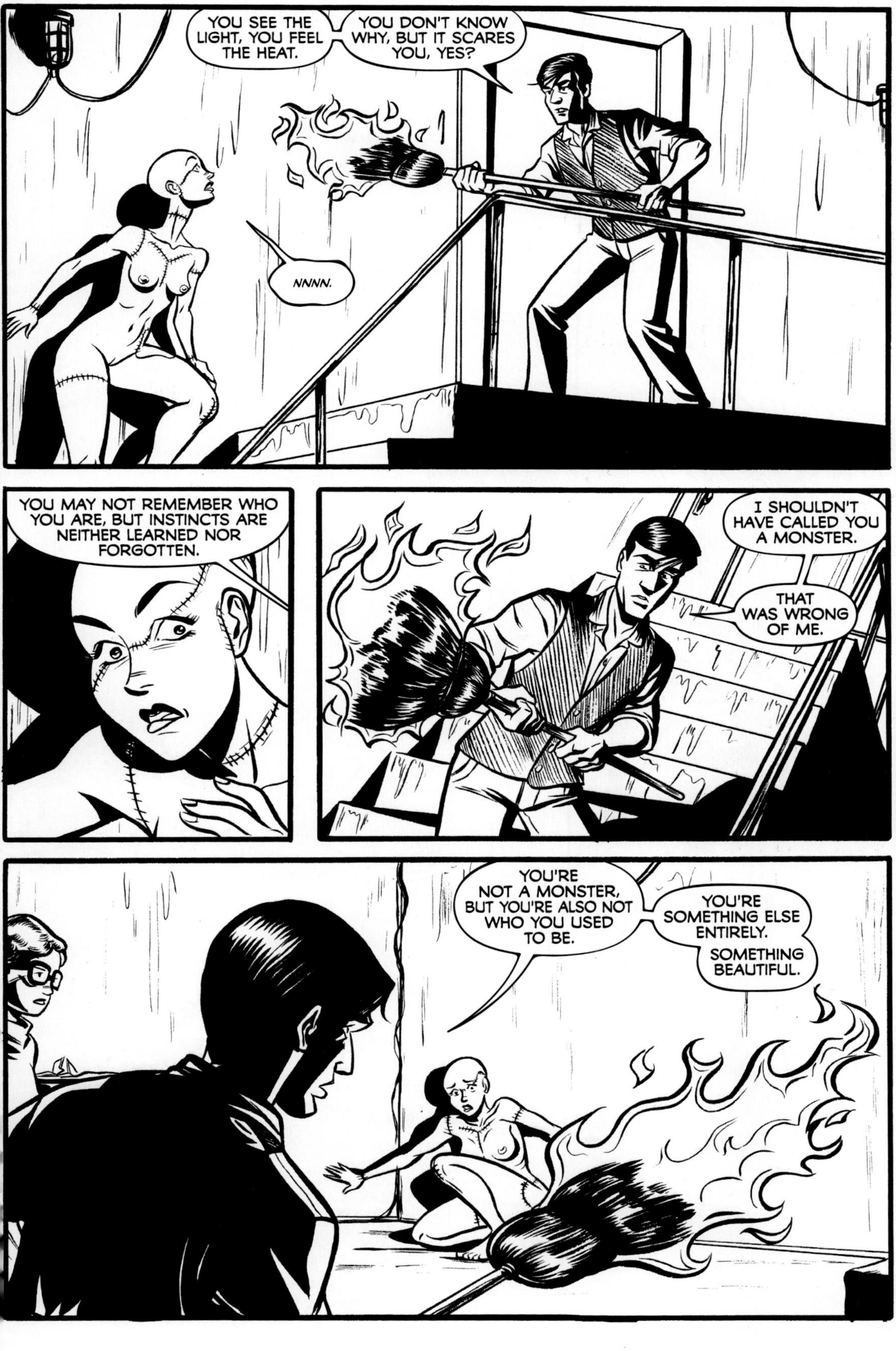
YOU SEE THE LIGHT, YOU FEEL THE HEAT.
YOU DON'T KNOW WHY, BUT IT SCARES YOU, YES?
NNNN.
YOU MAY NOT REMEMBER WHO YOU ARE, BUT INSTINCTS ARE NEITHER LEARNED NOR FORGOTTEN.
I SHOULDN'T HAVE CALLED YOU A MONSTER.
THAT WAS WRONG OF ME.
YOU'RE NOT A MONSTER, BUT YOU'RE ALSO NOT WHO YOU USED TO BE.
YOU'RE SOMETHING ELSE ENTIRELY.
SOMETHING BEAUTIFUL.

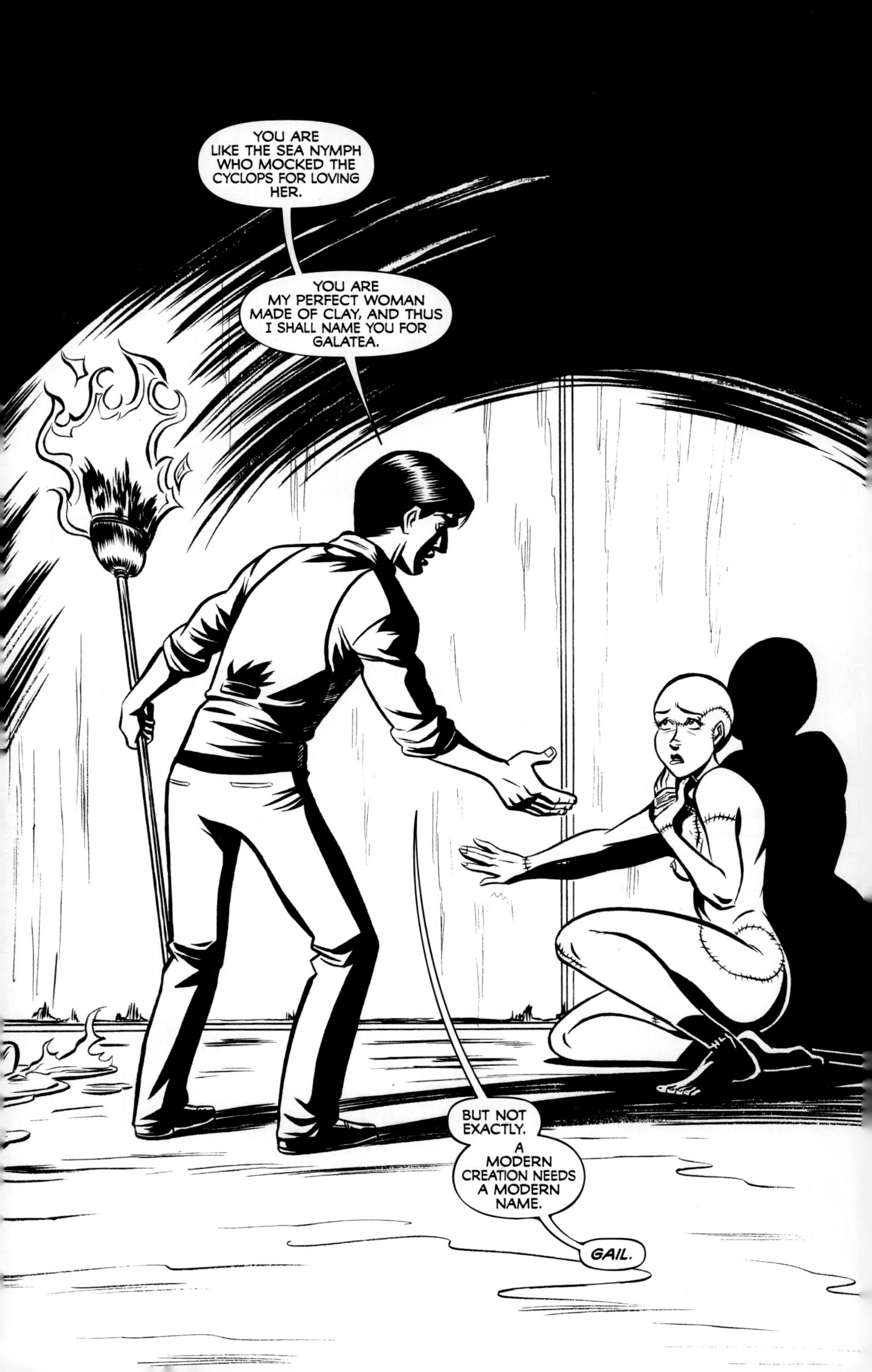
YOU ARE LIKE THE SEA NYMPH WHO MOCKED THE CYCLOPS FOR LOVING HER.
YOU ARE MY PERFECT WOMAN MADE OF CLAY, AND THUS I SHALL NAME YOU FOR GALATEA.
BUT NOT EXACTLY.
A MODERN CREATION NEEDS A MODERN NAME.
GAIL.

CHAPTER TWO

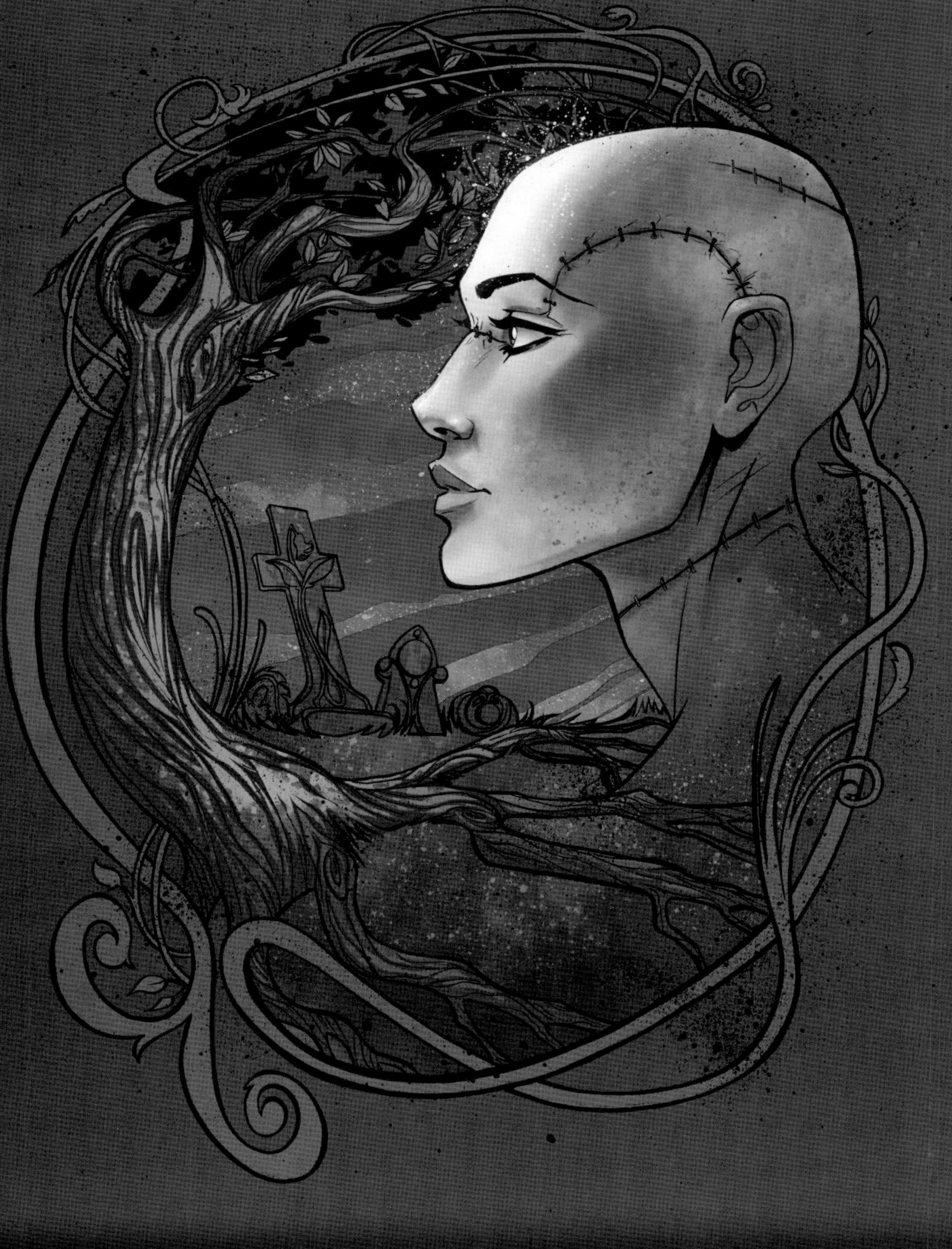

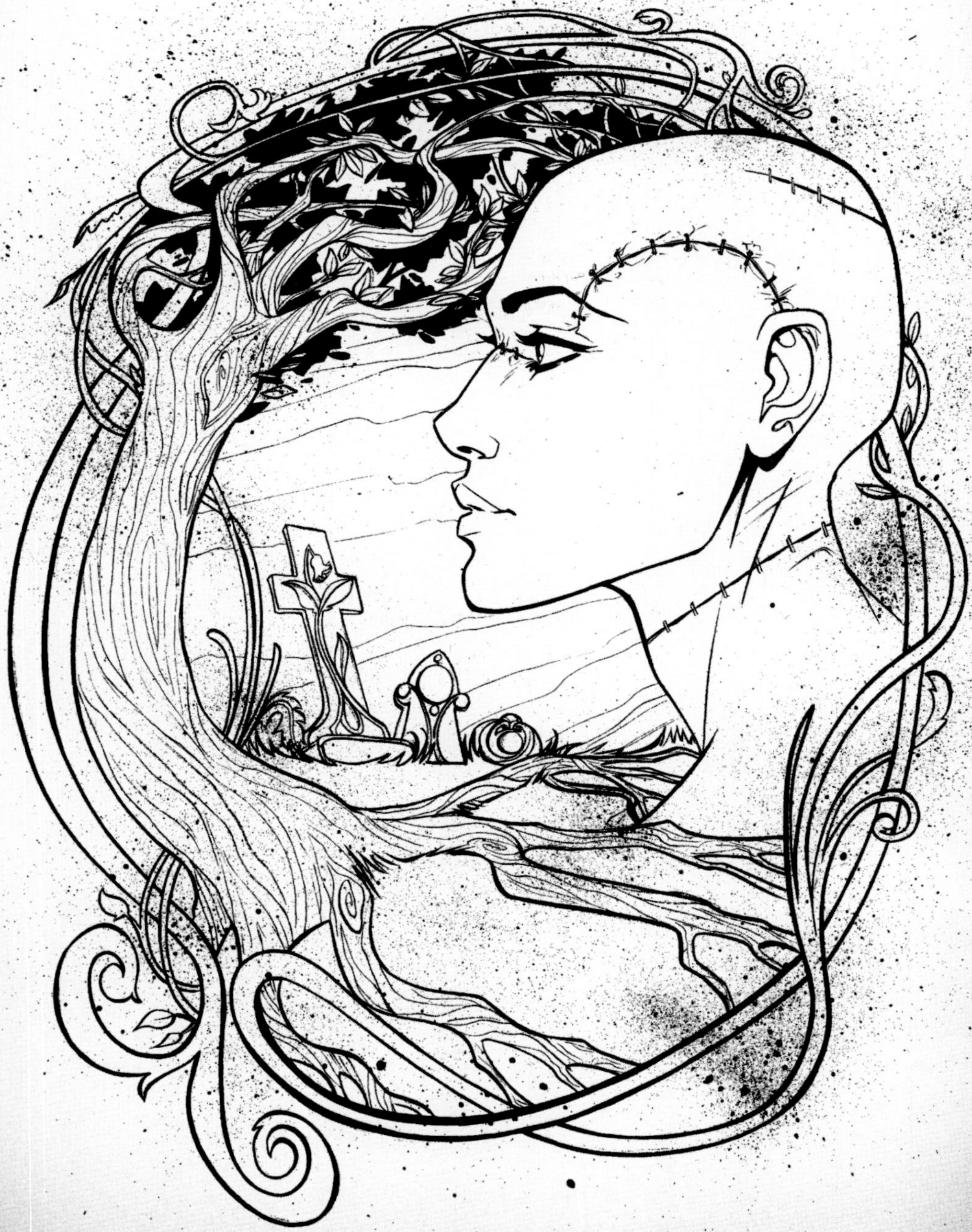

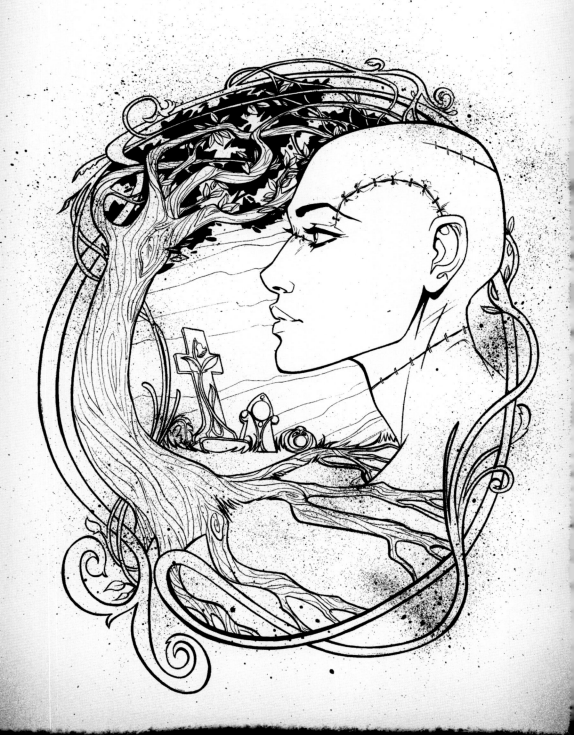

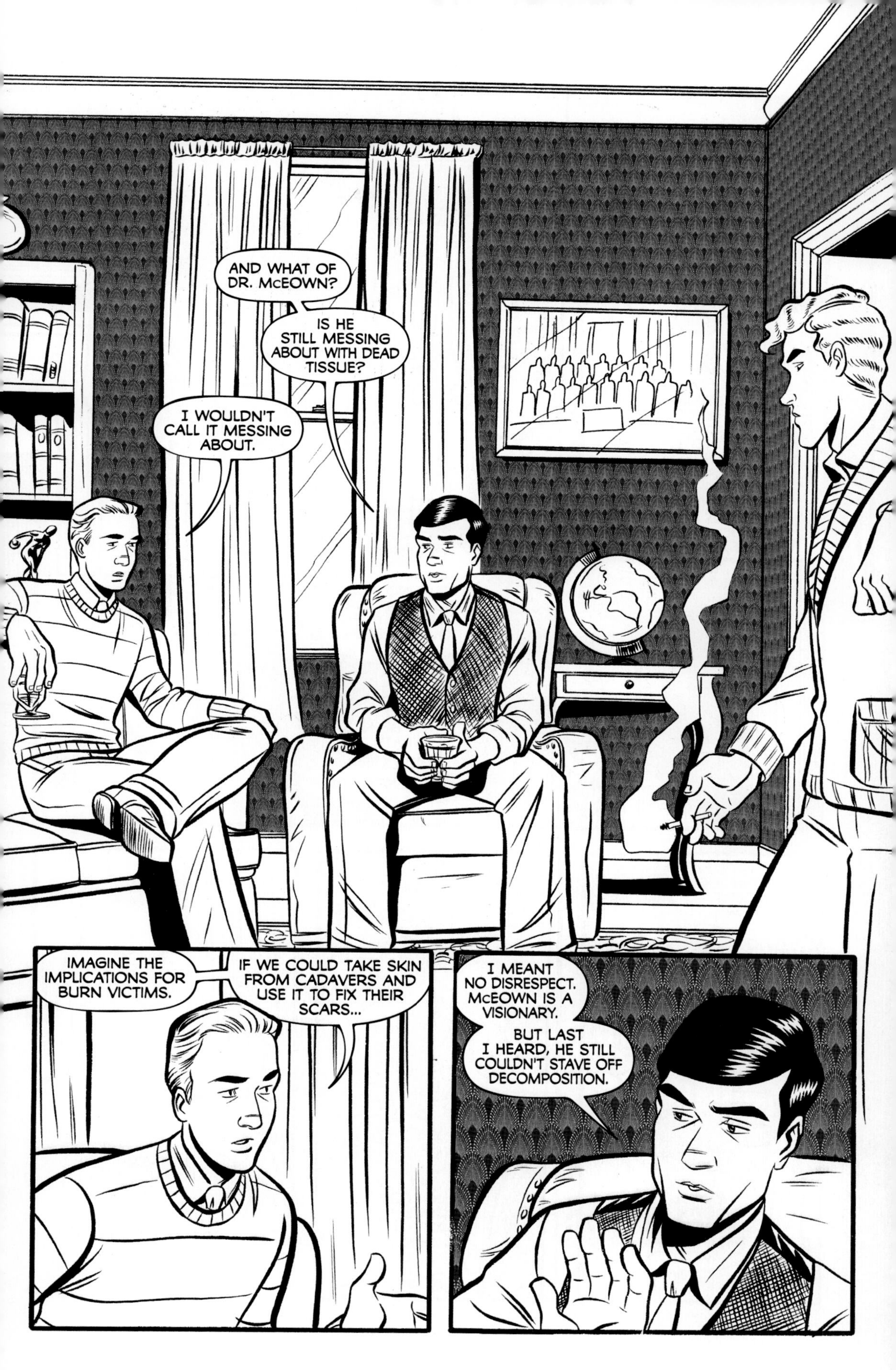

AND WHAT OF DR. McEOWN?
IS HE STILL MESSING ABOUT WITH DEAD TISSUE?
I WOULDN'T CALL IT MESSING ABOUT.
IMAGINE THE IMPLICATIONS FOR BURN VICTIMS.
IF WE COULD TAKE SKIN FROM CADAVERS AND USE IT TO FIX THEIR SCARS...
I MEANT NO DISRESPECT. McEOWN IS A VISIONARY.
BUT LAST I HEARD, HE STILL COULDN'T STAVE OFF DECOMPOSITION.

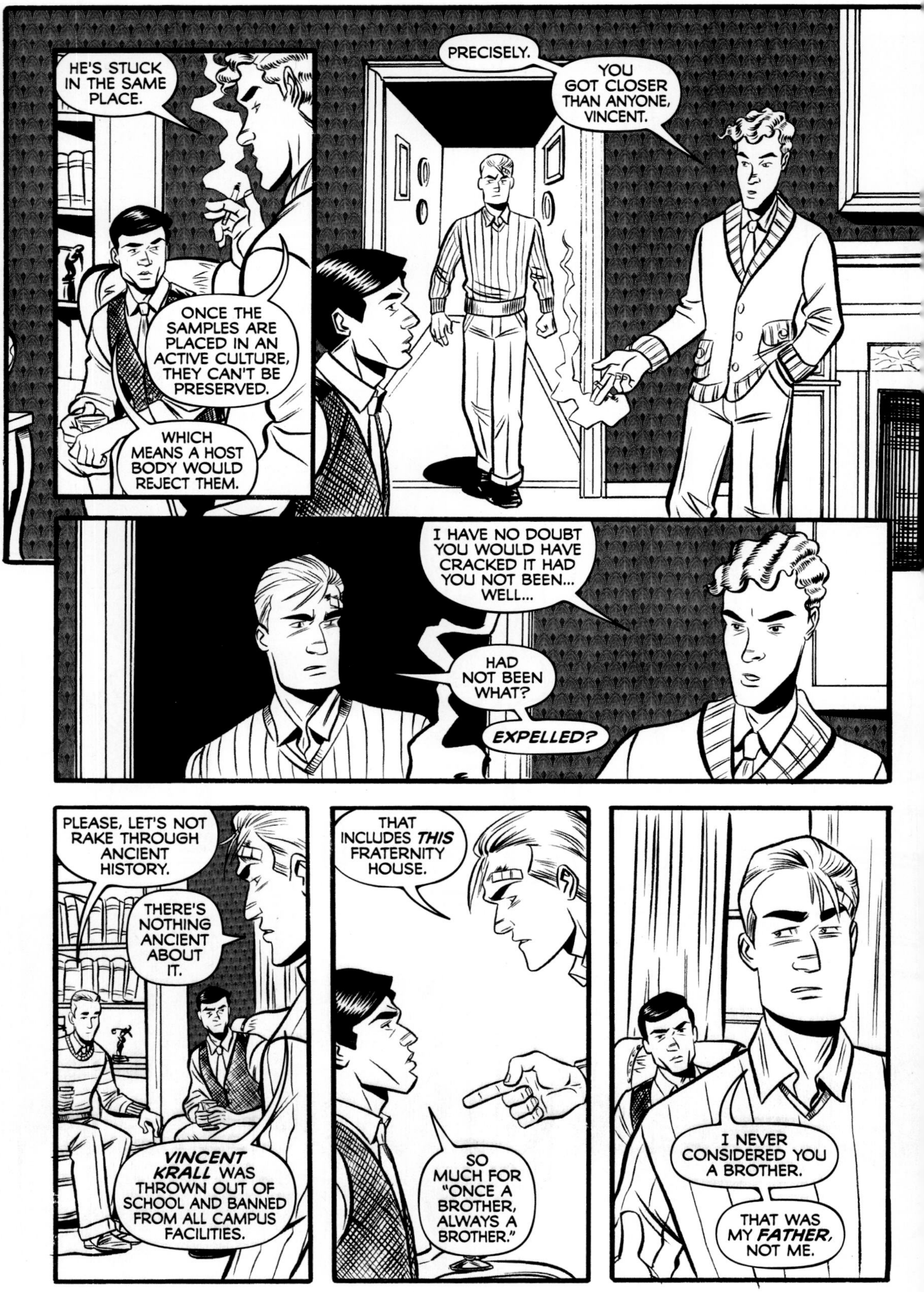
HE'S STUCK IN THE SAME PLACE.
ONCE THE SAMPLES ARE PLACED IN AN ACTIVE CULTURE, THEY CAN'T BE PRESERVED.
WHICH MEANS A HOST BODY WOULD REJECT THEM.
PRECISELY.
YOU GOT CLOSER THAN ANYONE, VINCENT.
I HAVE NO DOUBT YOU WOULD HAVE CRACKED IT HAD YOU NOT BEEN... WELL...
HAD NOT BEEN WHAT?
EXPELLED?
PLEASE, LET'S NOT RAKE THROUGH ANCIENT HISTORY.
THERE'S NOTHING ANCIENT ABOUT IT.
VINCENT KRALL WAS THROWN OUT OF SCHOOL AND BANNED FROM ALL CAMPUS FACILITIES.
THAT INCLUDES THIS FRATERNITY HOUSE.
SO MUCH FOR "ONCE A BROTHER, ALWAYS A BROTHER."
I NEVER CONSIDERED YOU A BROTHER.
THAT WAS MY FATHER, NOT ME.

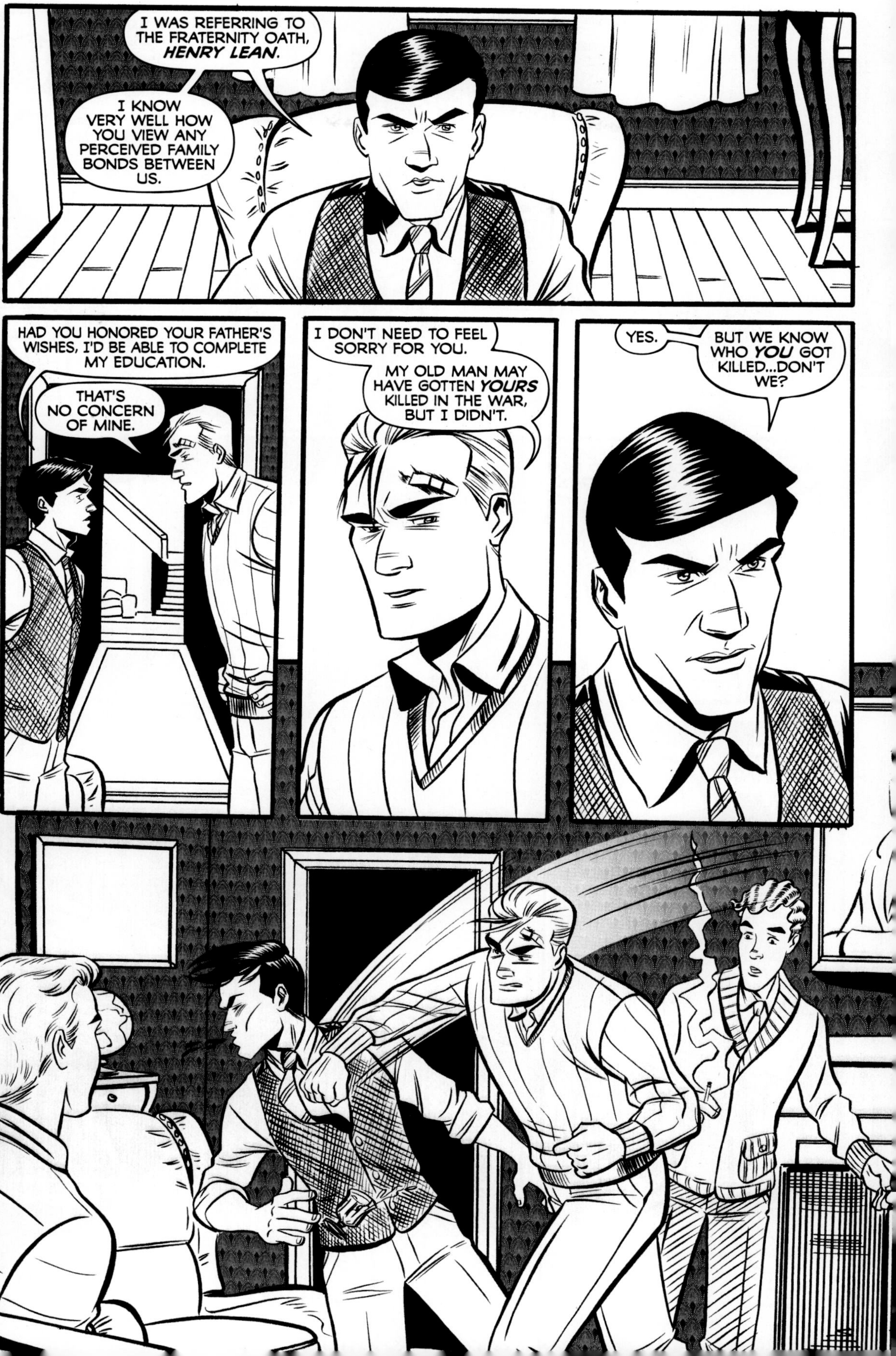

I WAS REFERRING TO THE FRATERNITY OATH, ***HENRY LEAN***.
I KNOW VERY WELL HOW YOU VIEW ANY PERCEIVED FAMILY BONDS BETWEEN US.
HAD YOU HONORED YOUR FATHER'S WISHES, I'D BE ABLE TO COMPLETE MY EDUCATION.
THAT'S NO CONCERN OF MINE.
I DON'T NEED TO FEEL SORRY FOR YOU.
MY OLD MAN MAY HAVE GOTTEN ***YOURS*** KILLED IN THE WAR, BUT I DIDN'T.
YES.
BUT WE KNOW WHO ***YOU*** GOT KILLED...DON'T WE?

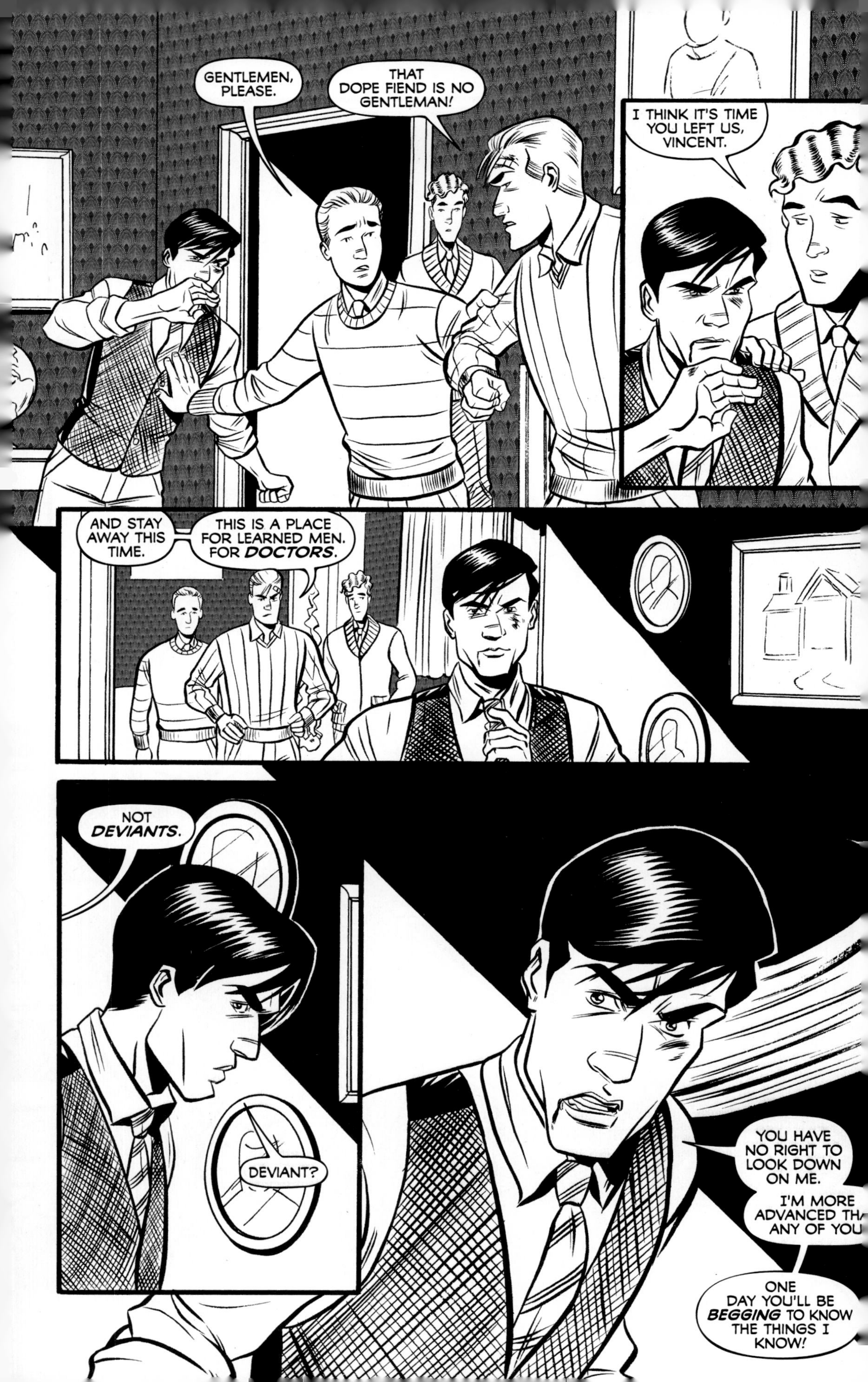
GENTLEMEN, PLEASE.
THAT DOPE FIEND IS NO GENTLEMAN!
I THINK IT'S TIME YOU LEFT US, VINCENT.
AND STAY AWAY THIS TIME.
THIS IS A PLACE FOR LEARNED MEN. FOR DOCTORS.
NOT DEVIANTS.
DEVIANT?
YOU HAVE NO RIGHT TO LOOK DOWN ON ME.
I'M MORE ADVANCED TH ANY OF YOU
ONE DAY YOU'LL BE BEGGING TO KNOW THE THINGS I KNOW!

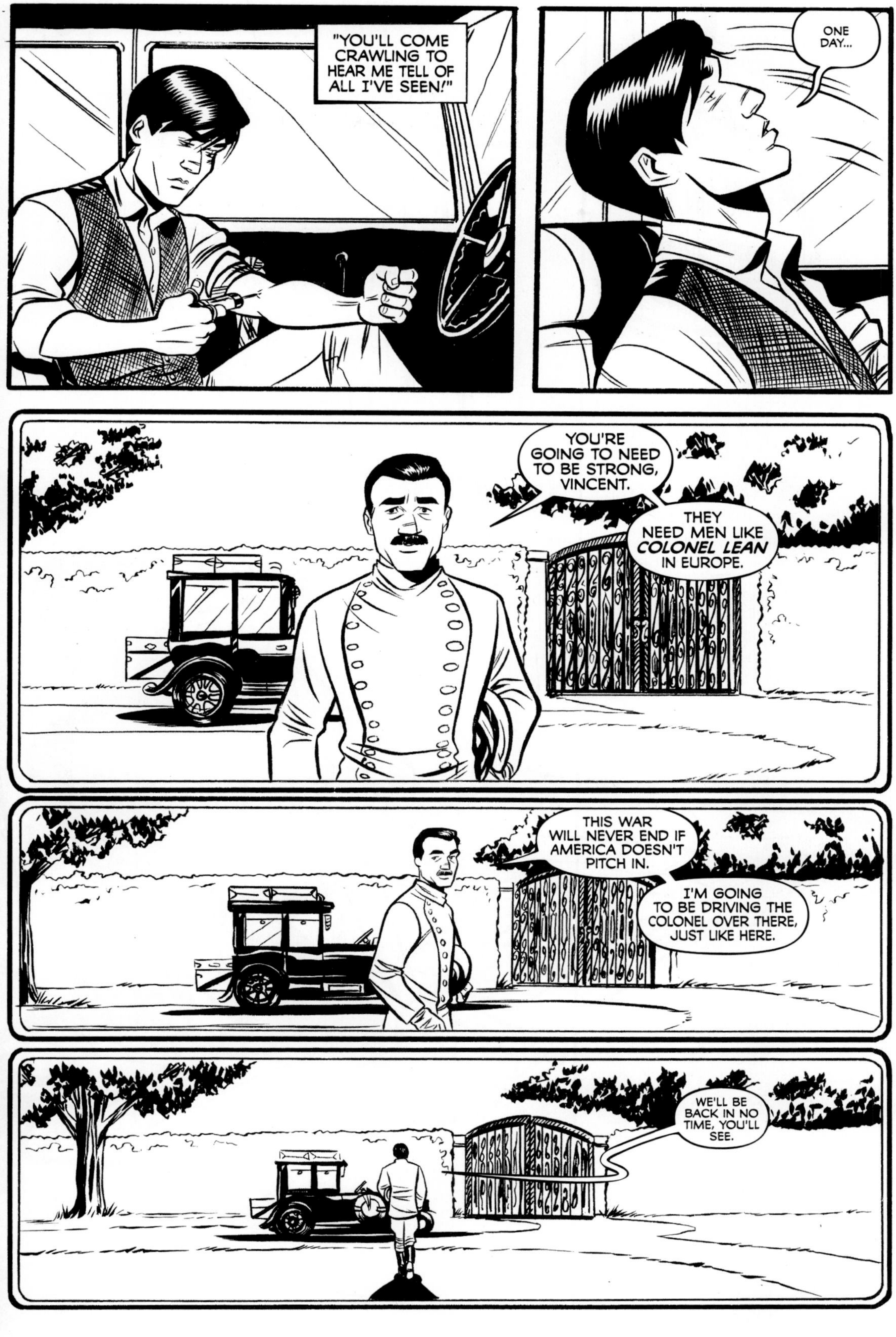
"YOU'LL COME CRAWLING TO HEAR ME TELL OF ALL I'VE SEEN!"
ONE DAY...
YOU'RE GOING TO NEED TO BE STRONG, VINCENT.
THEY NEED MEN LIKE *COLONEL LEAN* IN EUROPE.
THIS WAR WILL NEVER END IF AMERICA DOESN'T PITCH IN.
I'M GOING TO BE DRIVING THE COLONEL OVER THERE, JUST LIKE HERE.
WE'LL BE BACK IN NO TIME, YOU'LL SEE.

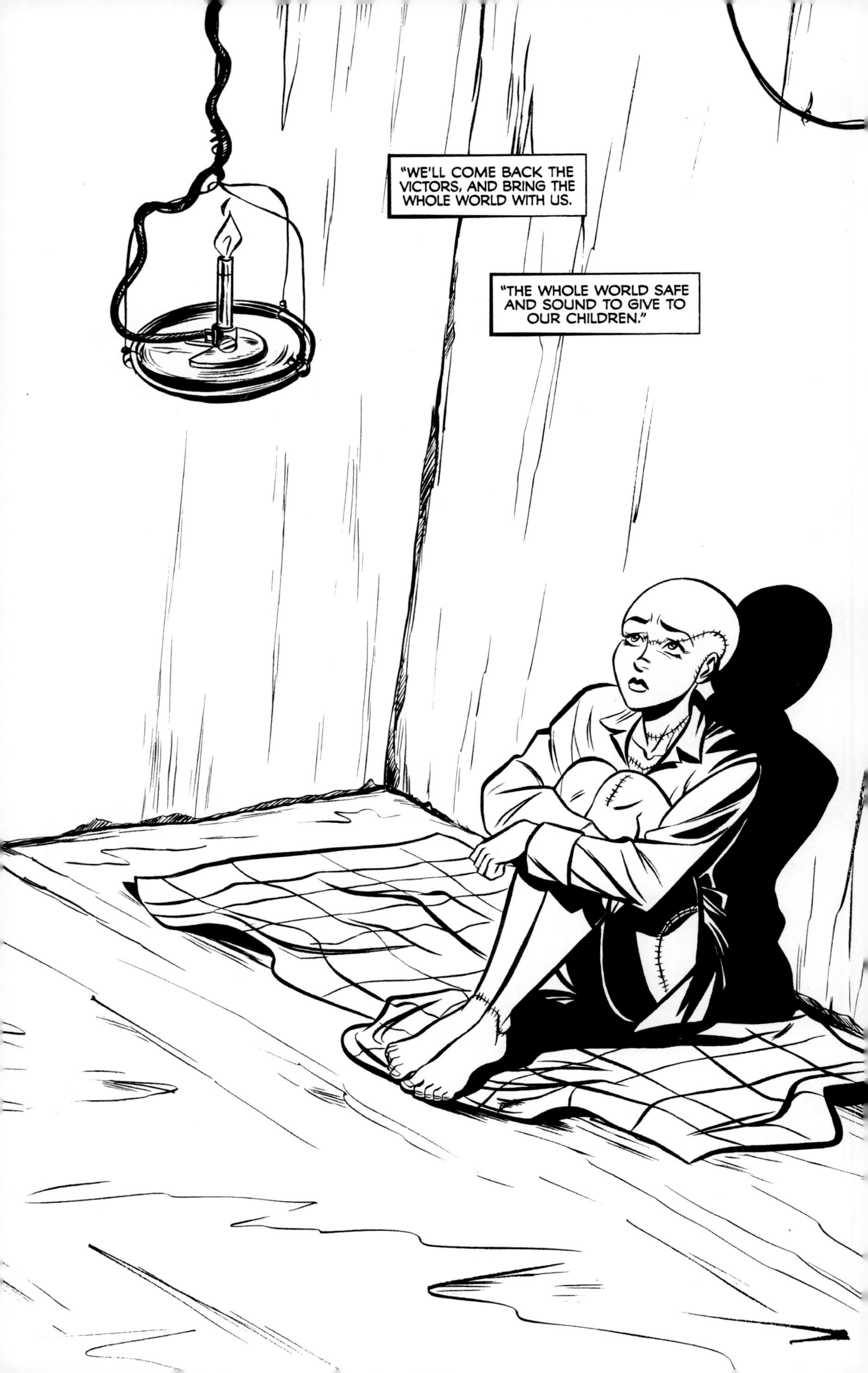
"WE'LL COME BACK THE VICTORS, AND BRING THE WHOLE WORLD WITH US.
"THE WHOLE WORLD SAFE AND SOUND TO GIVE TO OUR CHILDREN."

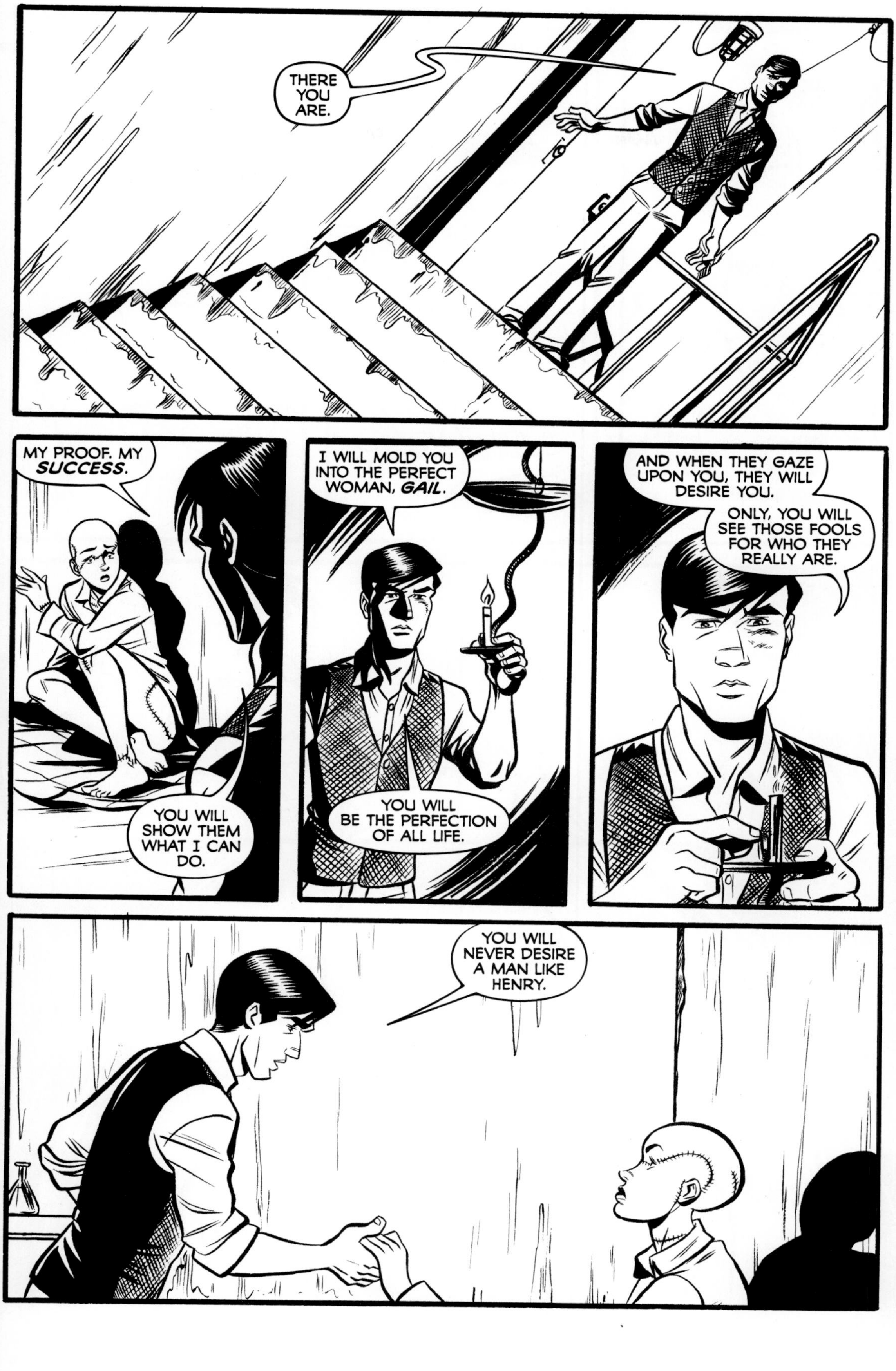

THERE YOU ARE.
MY PROOF. MY *SUCCESS*.
YOU WILL SHOW THEM WHAT I CAN DO.
I WILL MOLD YOU INTO THE PERFECT WOMAN, *GAIL*.
YOU WILL BE THE PERFECTION OF ALL LIFE.
AND WHEN THEY GAZE UPON YOU, THEY WILL DESIRE YOU.
ONLY, YOU WILL SEE THOSE FOOLS FOR WHO THEY REALLY ARE.
YOU WILL NEVER DESIRE A MAN LIKE HENRY.

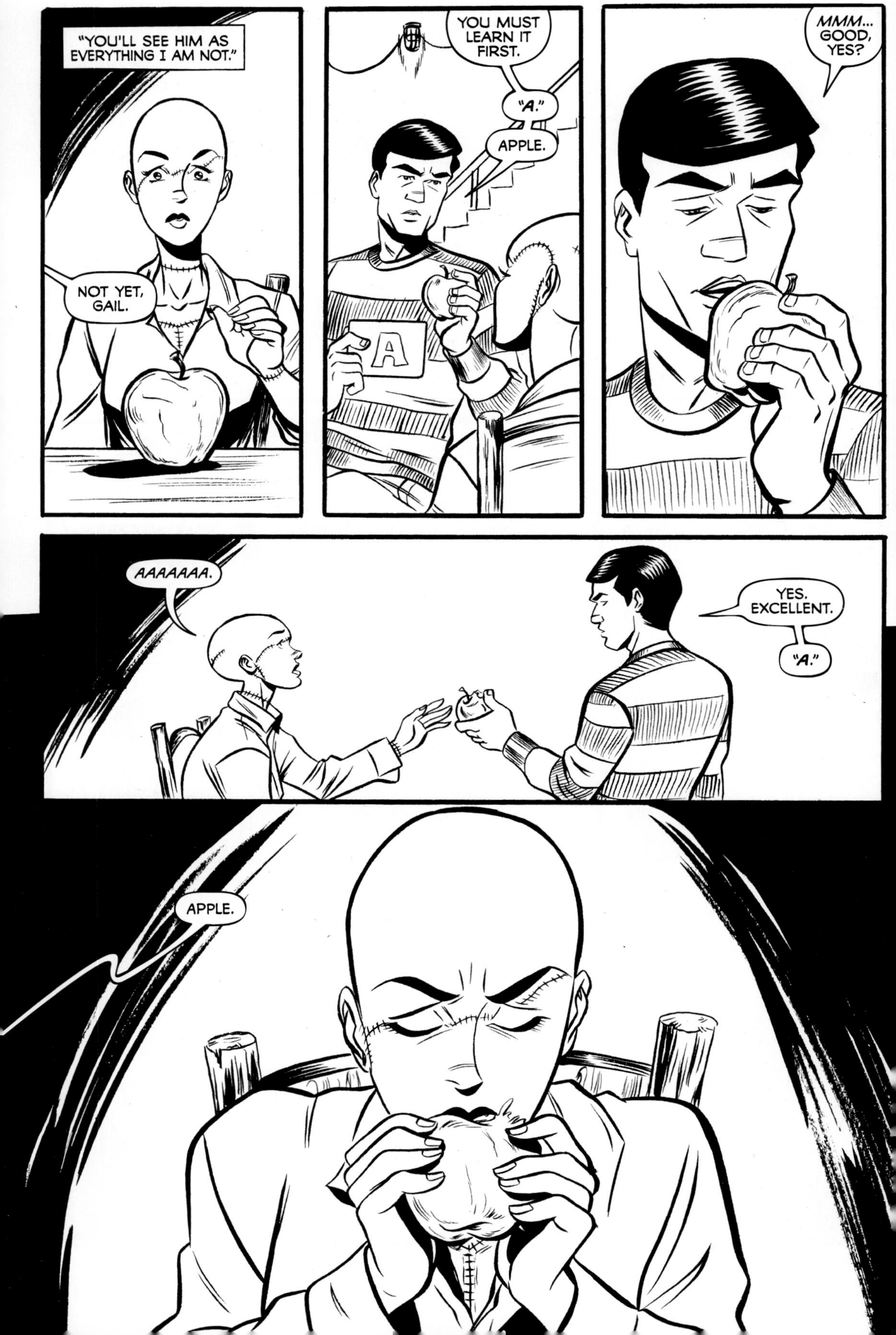
"YOU'LL SEE HIM AS EVERYTHING I AM NOT."
NOT YET, GAIL.
YOU MUST LEARN IT FIRST.
"A."
APPLE.
A
MMM... GOOD, YES?
AAAAAAA.
YES. EXCELLENT.
"A."
APPLE.

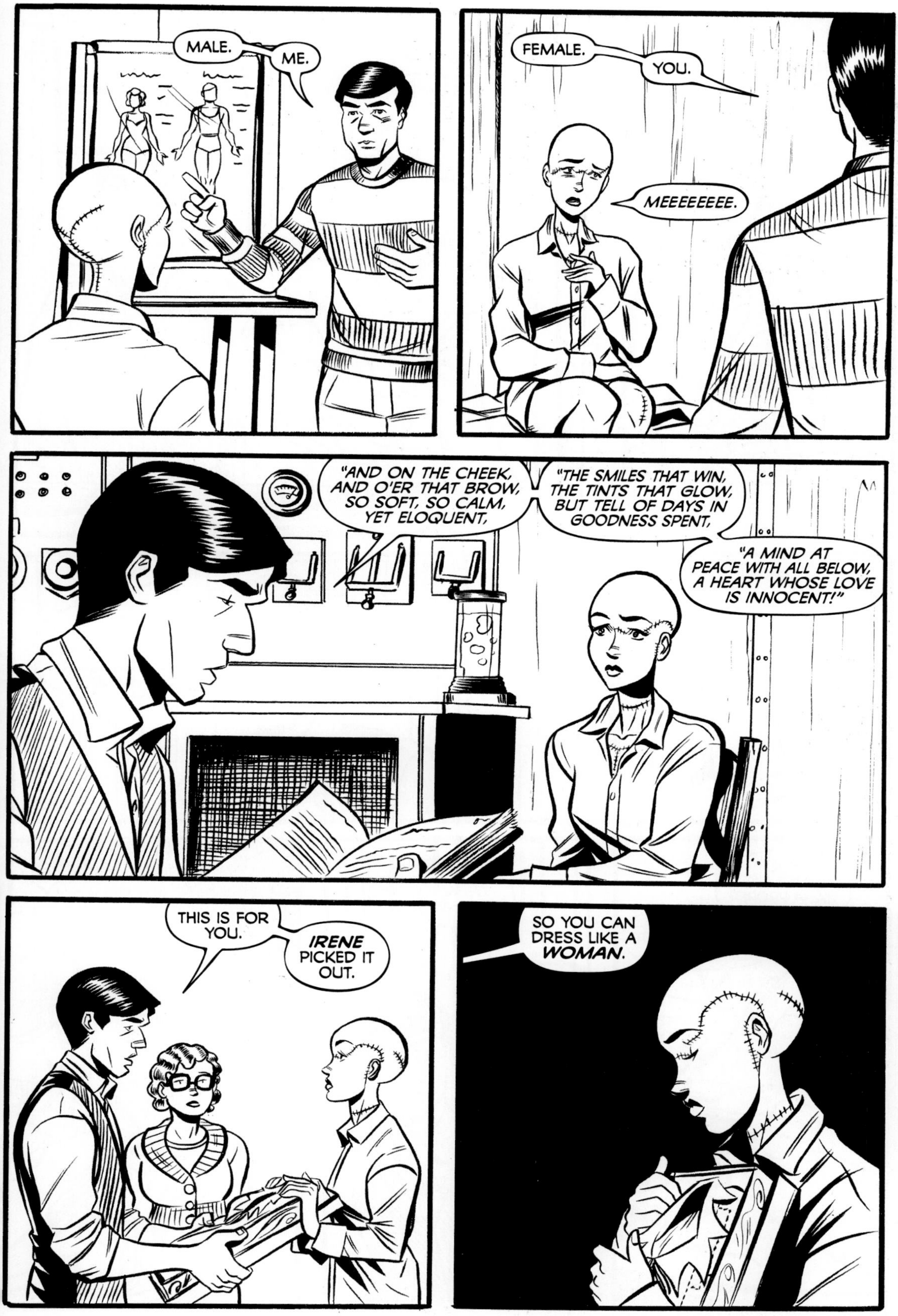
MALE.
ME.
FEMALE.
YOU.
MEEEEEEEE.
"AND ON THE CHEEK, AND O'ER THAT BROW, SO SOFT, SO CALM, YET ELOQUENT,
"THE SMILES THAT WIN, THE TINTS THAT GLOW, BUT TELL OF DAYS IN GOODNESS SPENT,
"A MIND AT PEACE WITH ALL BELOW, A HEART WHOSE LOVE IS INNOCENT!"
THIS IS FOR YOU.
IRENE PICKED IT OUT.
SO YOU CAN DRESS LIKE A WOMAN.

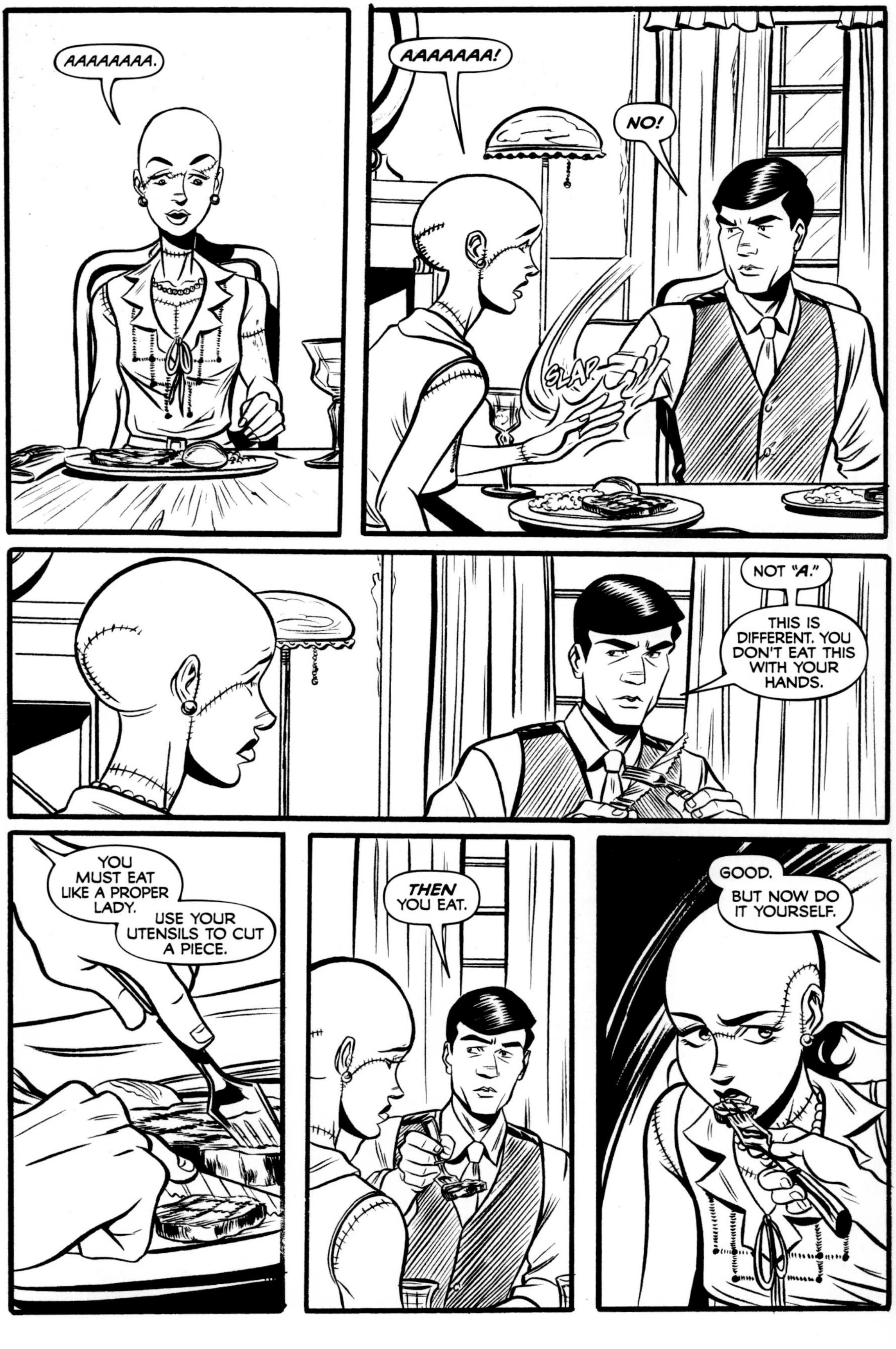
AAAAAAAA.
AAAAAAA!
NO!
SLAP
NOT "A."
THIS IS DIFFERENT. YOU DON'T EAT THIS WITH YOUR HANDS.
YOU MUST EAT LIKE A PROPER LADY.
USE YOUR UTENSILS TO CUT A PIECE.
THEN YOU EAT.
GOOD.
BUT NOW DO IT YOURSELF.

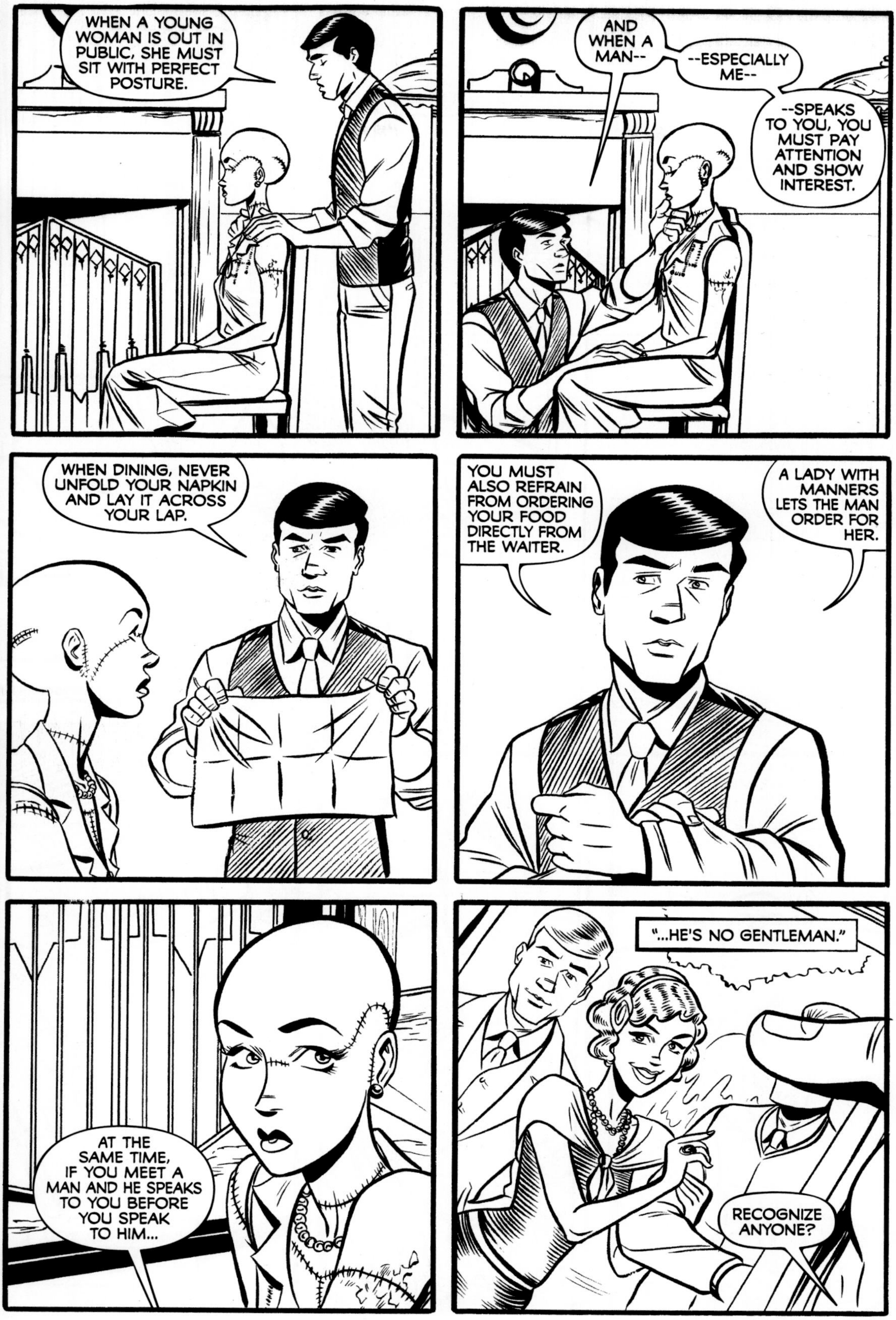
WHEN A YOUNG WOMAN IS OUT IN PUBLIC, SHE MUST SIT WITH PERFECT POSTURE.
AND WHEN A MAN--
--ESPECIALLY ME--
--SPEAKS TO YOU, YOU MUST PAY ATTENTION AND SHOW INTEREST.
WHEN DINING, NEVER UNFOLD YOUR NAPKIN AND LAY IT ACROSS YOUR LAP.
YOU MUST ALSO REFRAIN FROM ORDERING YOUR FOOD DIRECTLY FROM THE WAITER.
A LADY WITH MANNERS LETS THE MAN ORDER FOR HER.
AT THE SAME TIME, IF YOU MEET A MAN AND HE SPEAKS TO YOU BEFORE YOU SPEAK TO HIM...
"...HE'S NO GENTLEMAN."
RECOGNIZE ANYONE?

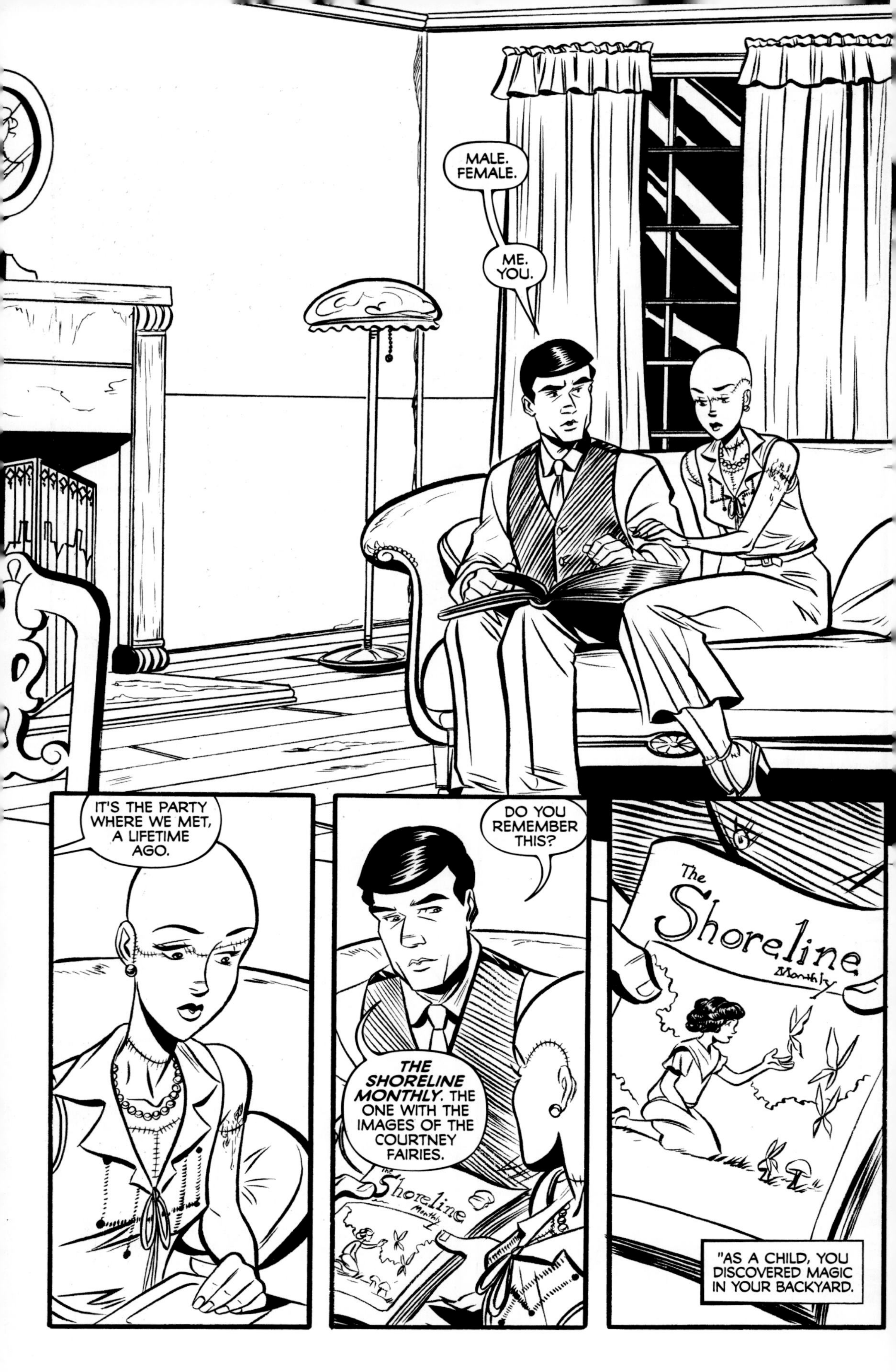
MALE. FEMALE.
ME. YOU.
IT'S THE PARTY WHERE WE MET, A LIFETIME AGO.
DO YOU REMEMBER THIS?
THE SHORELINE MONTHLY. THE ONE WITH THE IMAGES OF THE COURTNEY FAIRIES.
The Shoreline Monthly
The Shoreline Monthly
"AS A CHILD, YOU DISCOVERED MAGIC IN YOUR BACKYARD.

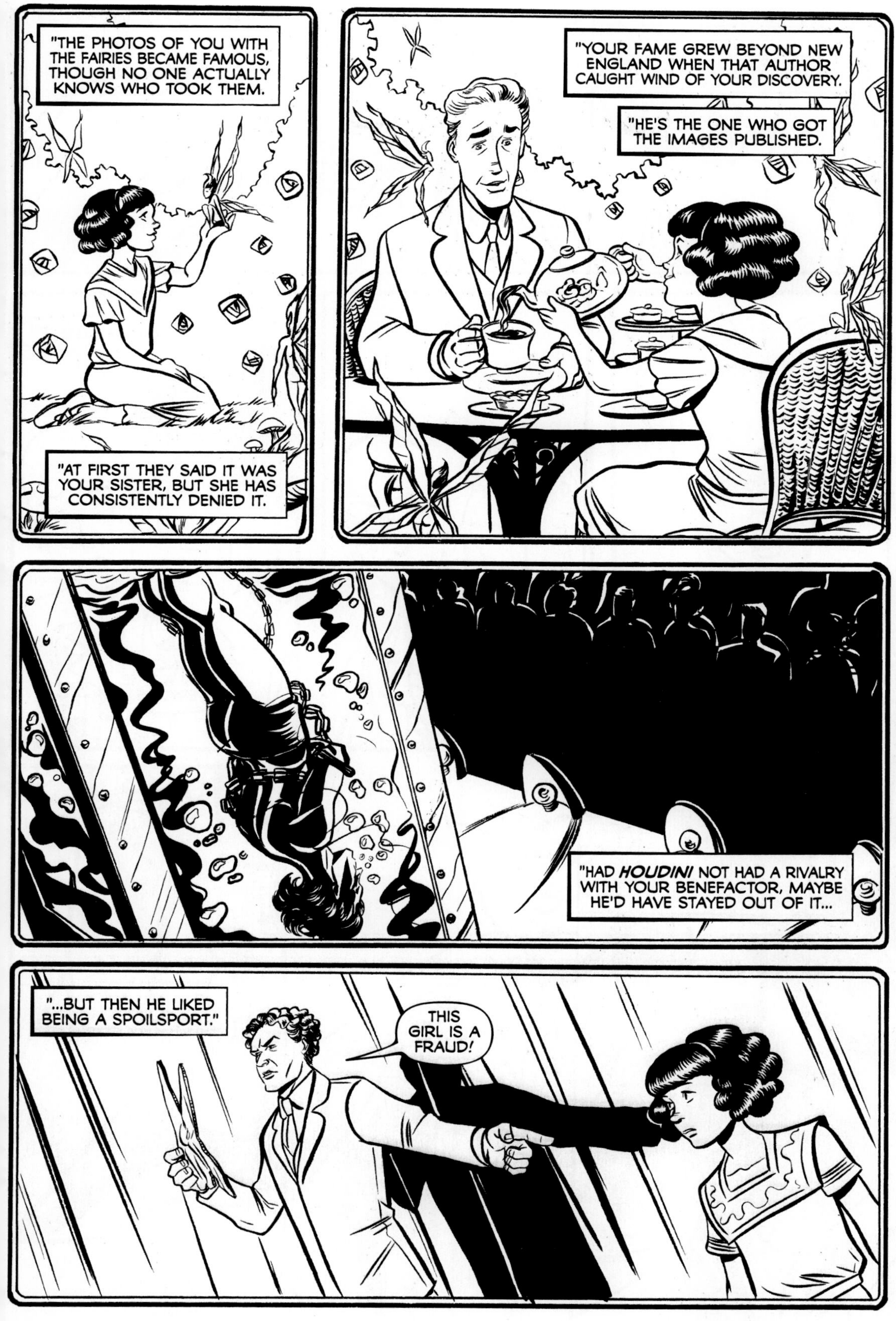
"THE PHOTOS OF YOU WITH THE FAIRIES BECAME FAMOUS, THOUGH NO ONE ACTUALLY KNOWS WHO TOOK THEM.
"AT FIRST THEY SAID IT WAS YOUR SISTER, BUT SHE HAS CONSISTENTLY DENIED IT.
"YOUR FAME GREW BEYOND NEW ENGLAND WHEN THAT AUTHOR CAUGHT WIND OF YOUR DISCOVERY.
"HE'S THE ONE WHO GOT THE IMAGES PUBLISHED.
"HAD HOUDINI NOT HAD A RIVALRY WITH YOUR BENEFACTOR, MAYBE HE'D HAVE STAYED OUT OF IT...
"...BUT THEN HE LIKED BEING A SPOILSPORT."
THIS GIRL IS A FRAUD!

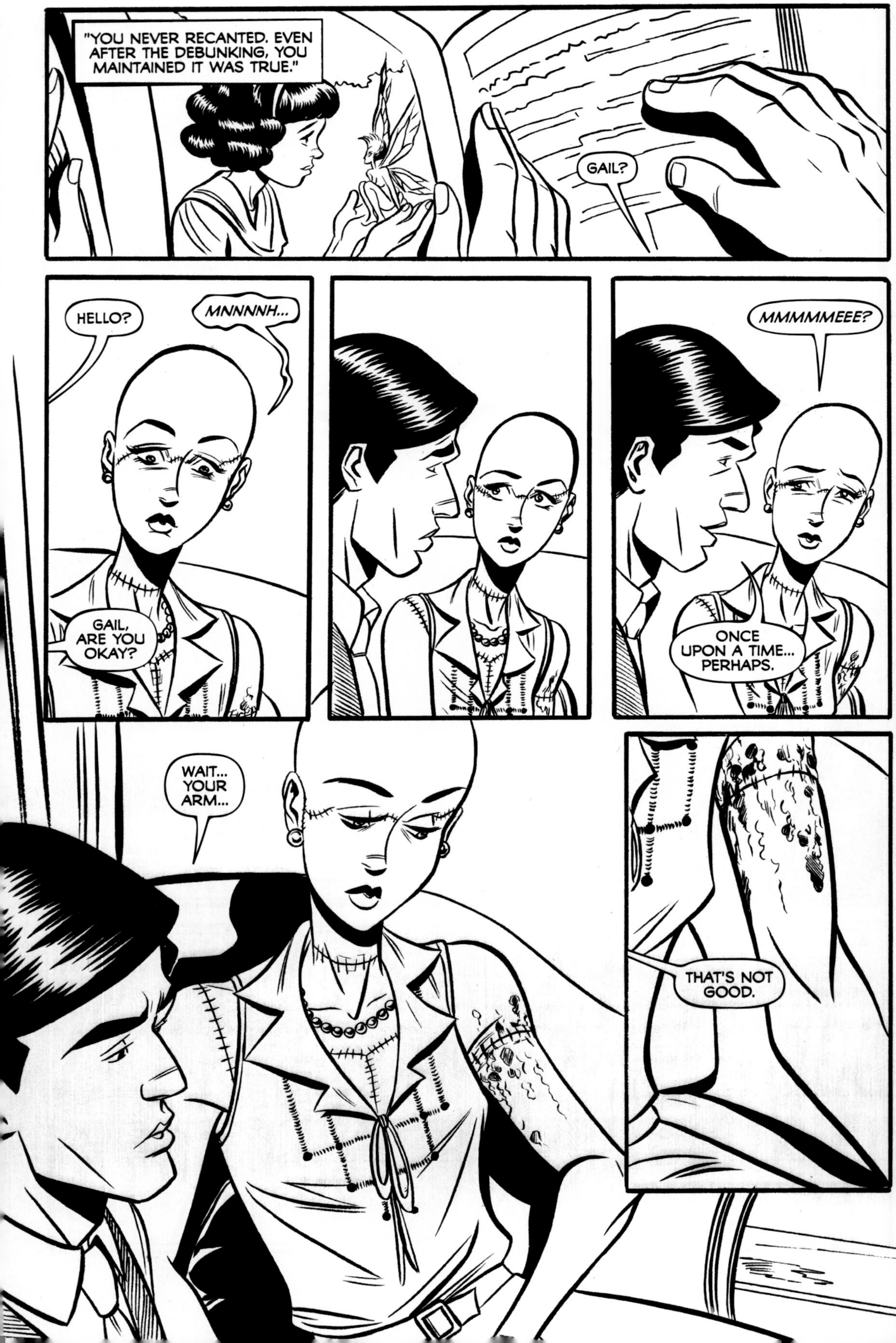
"YOU NEVER RECANTED. EVEN AFTER THE DEBUNKING, YOU MAINTAINED IT WAS TRUE."
GAIL?
HELLO?
MNNNNH...
GAIL, ARE YOU OKAY?
MMMMMEEE?
ONCE UPON A TIME... PERHAPS.
WAIT... YOUR ARM...
THAT'S NOT GOOD.

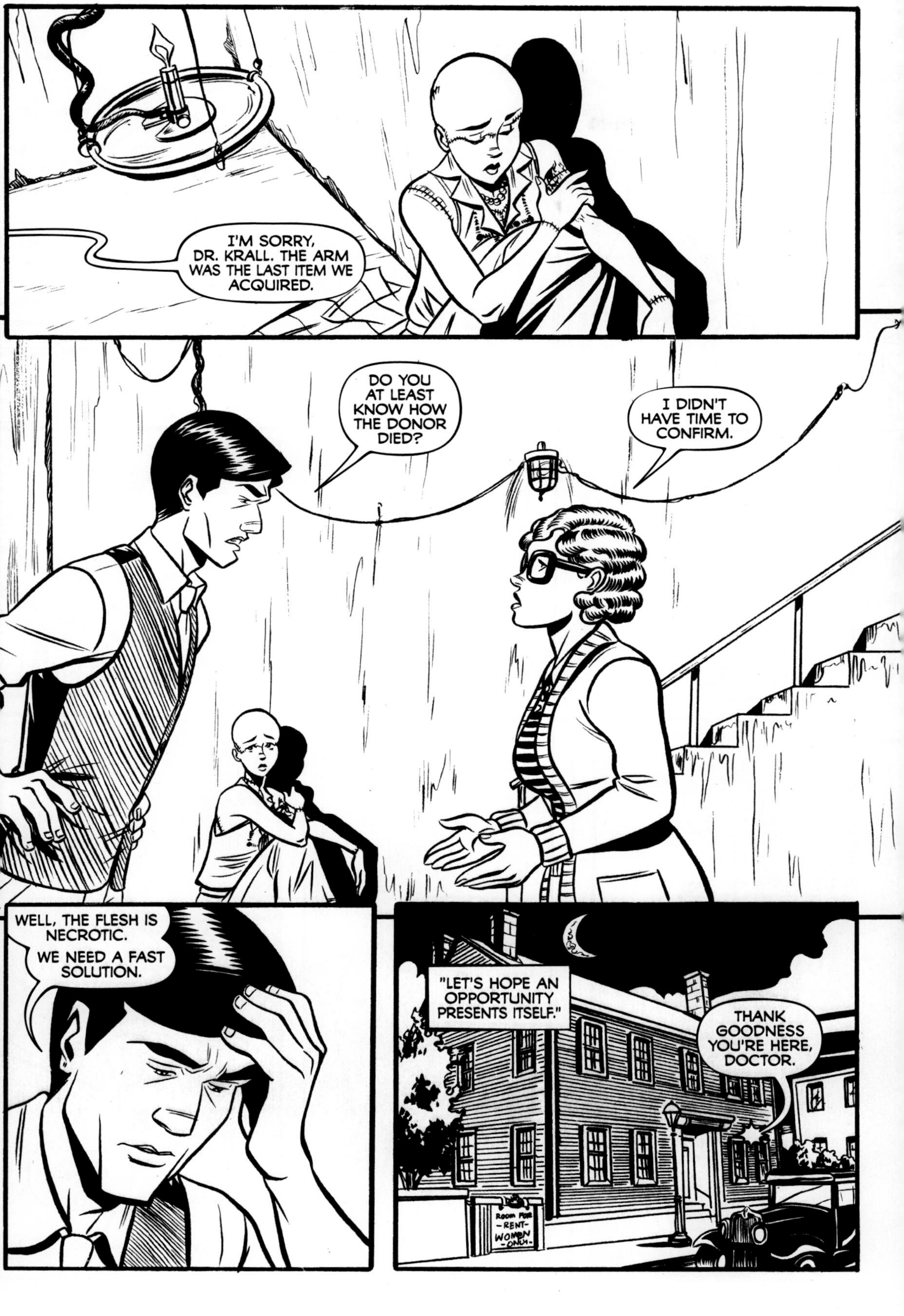
I'M SORRY, DR. KRALL. THE ARM WAS THE LAST ITEM WE ACQUIRED.
DO YOU AT LEAST KNOW HOW THE DONOR DIED?
I DIDN'T HAVE TIME TO CONFIRM.
WELL, THE FLESH IS NECROTIC.
WE NEED A FAST SOLUTION.
"LET'S HOPE AN OPPORTUNITY PRESENTS ITSELF."
THANK GOODNESS YOU'RE HERE, DOCTOR.
ROOM FOR -RENT- WOMEN -ONLY-

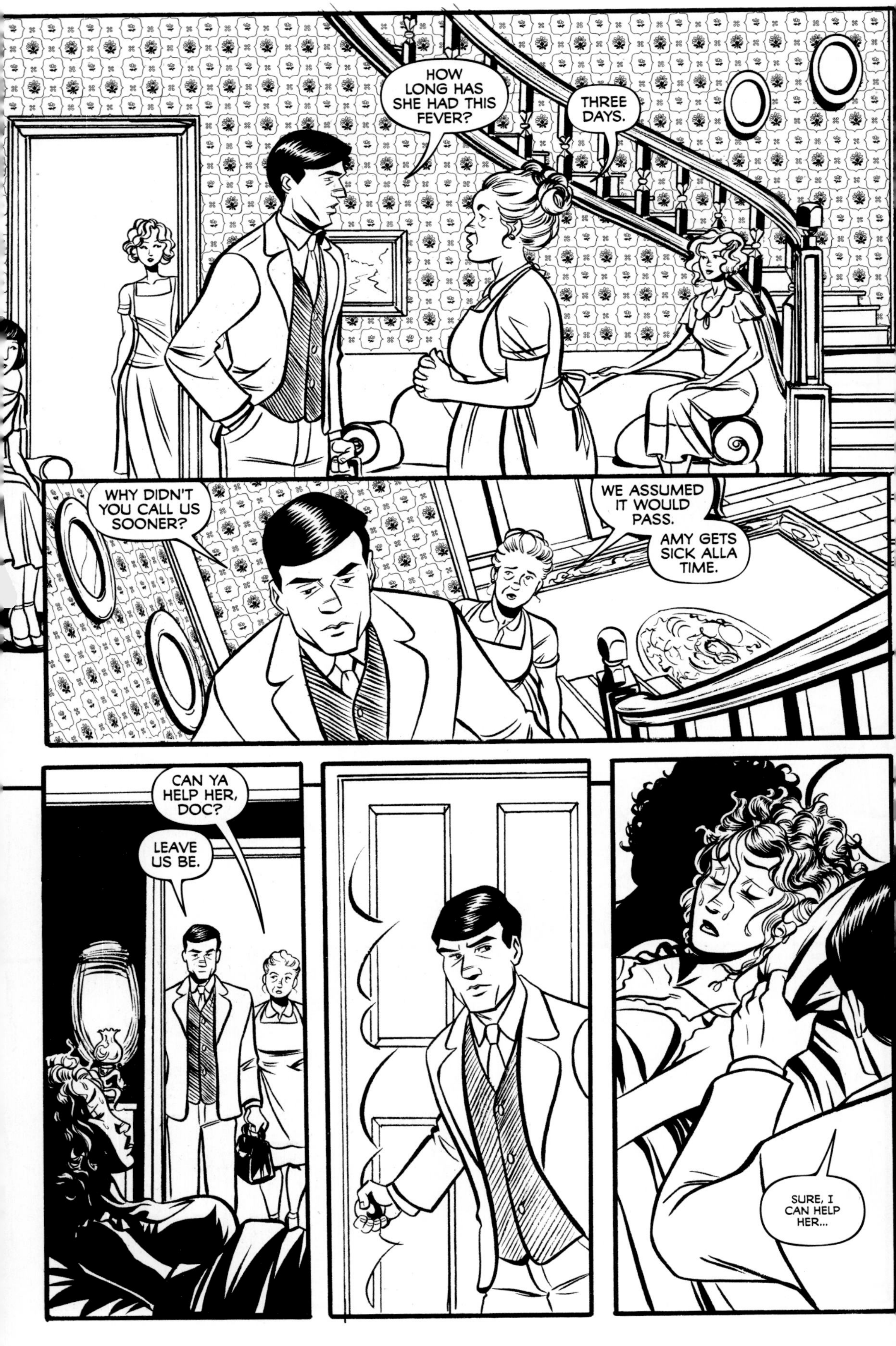
HOW LONG HAS SHE HAD THIS FEVER?
THREE DAYS.
WHY DIDN'T YOU CALL US SOONER?
WE ASSUMED IT WOULD PASS.
AMY GETS SICK ALLA TIME.
CAN YA HELP HER, DOC?
LEAVE US BE.
SURE, I CAN HELP HER...

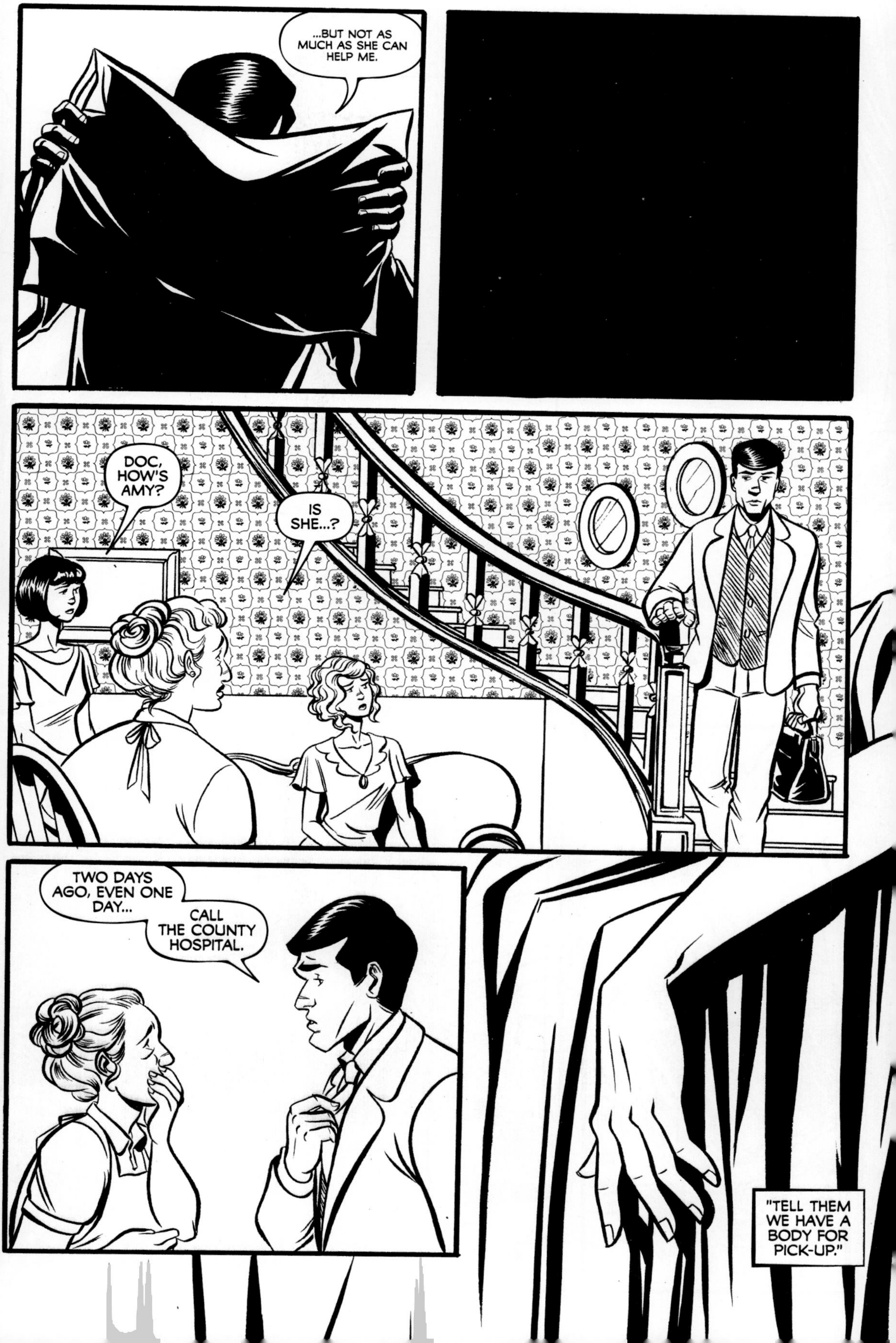

...BUT NOT AS MUCH AS SHE CAN HELP ME.
DOC, HOW'S AMY?
IS SHE...?
TWO DAYS AGO, EVEN ONE DAY...
CALL THE COUNTY HOSPITAL.
"TELL THEM WE HAVE A BODY FOR PICK-UP."

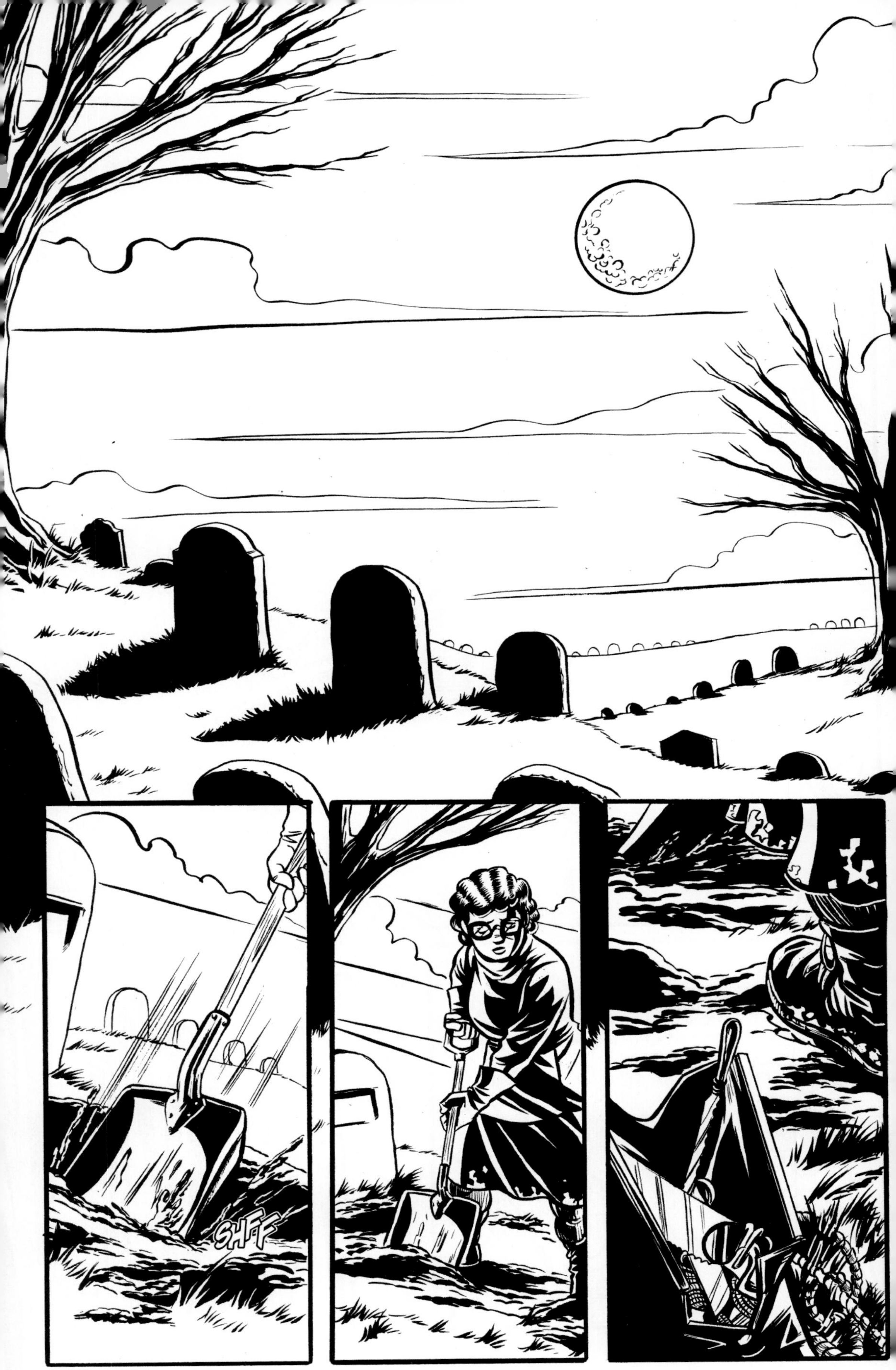
SHFF

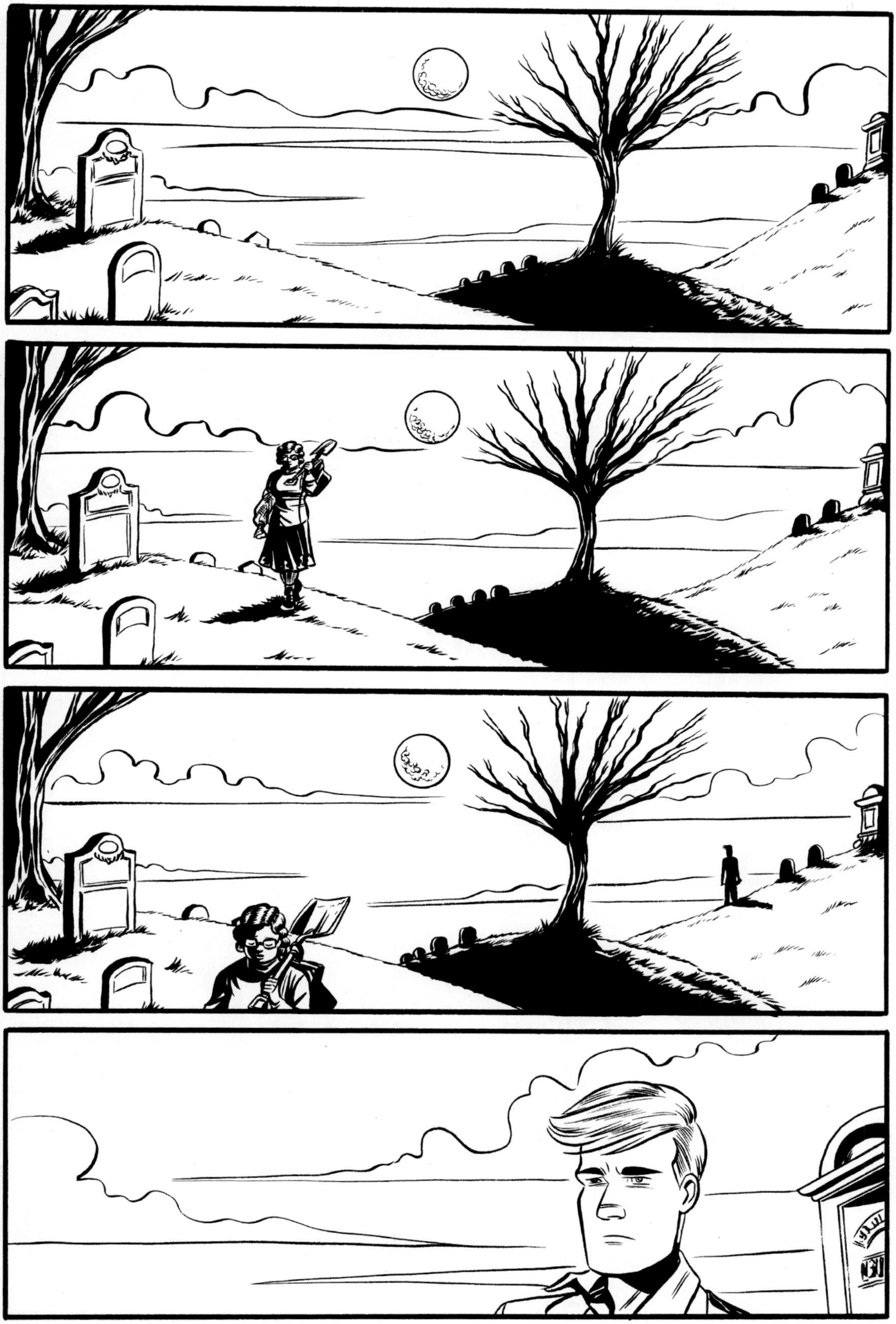

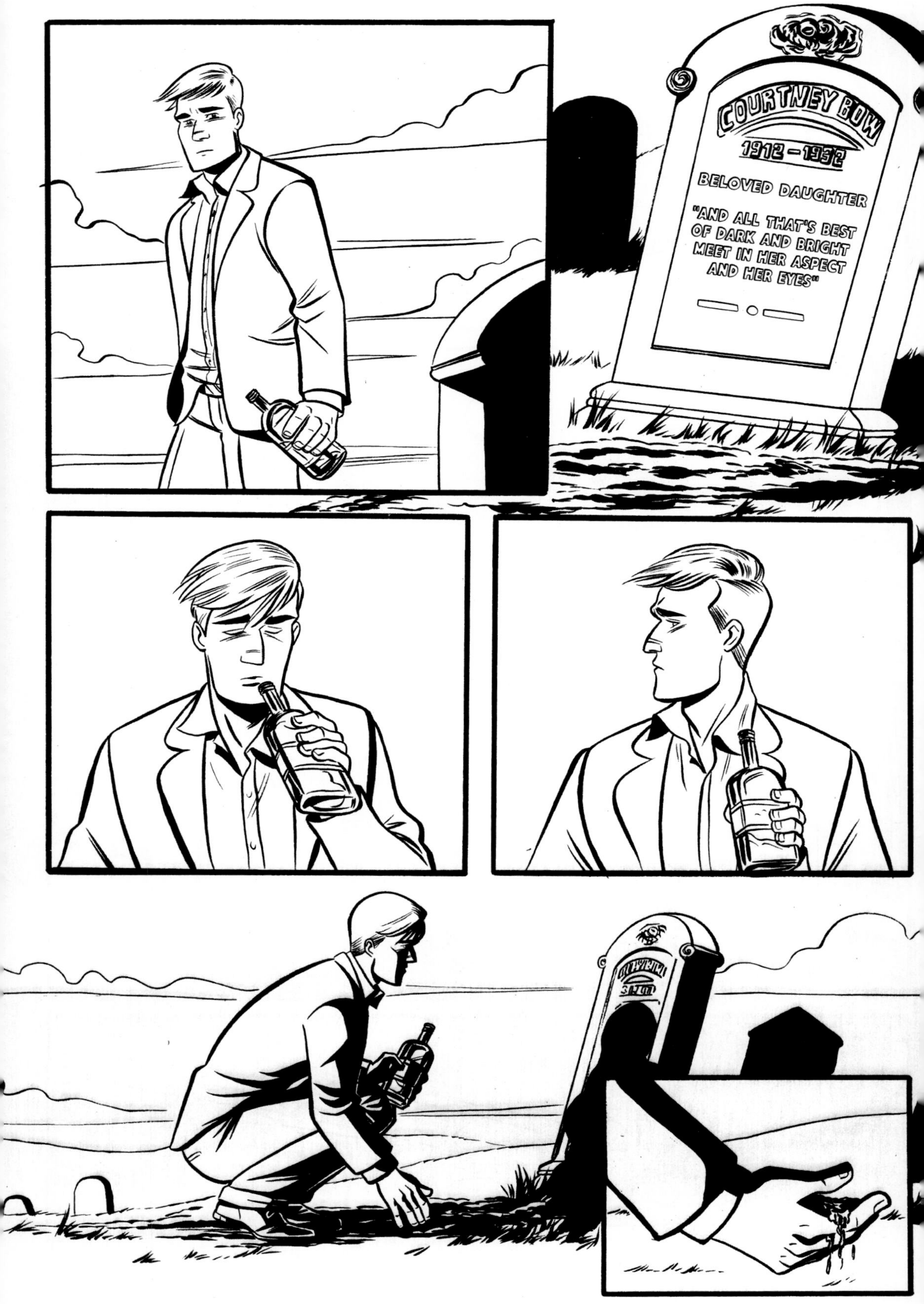
COURTNEY BOW
1912 – 1932
BELOVED DAUGHTER
"AND ALL THAT'S BEST
OF DARK AND BRIGHT
MEET IN HER ASPECT
AND HER EYES"

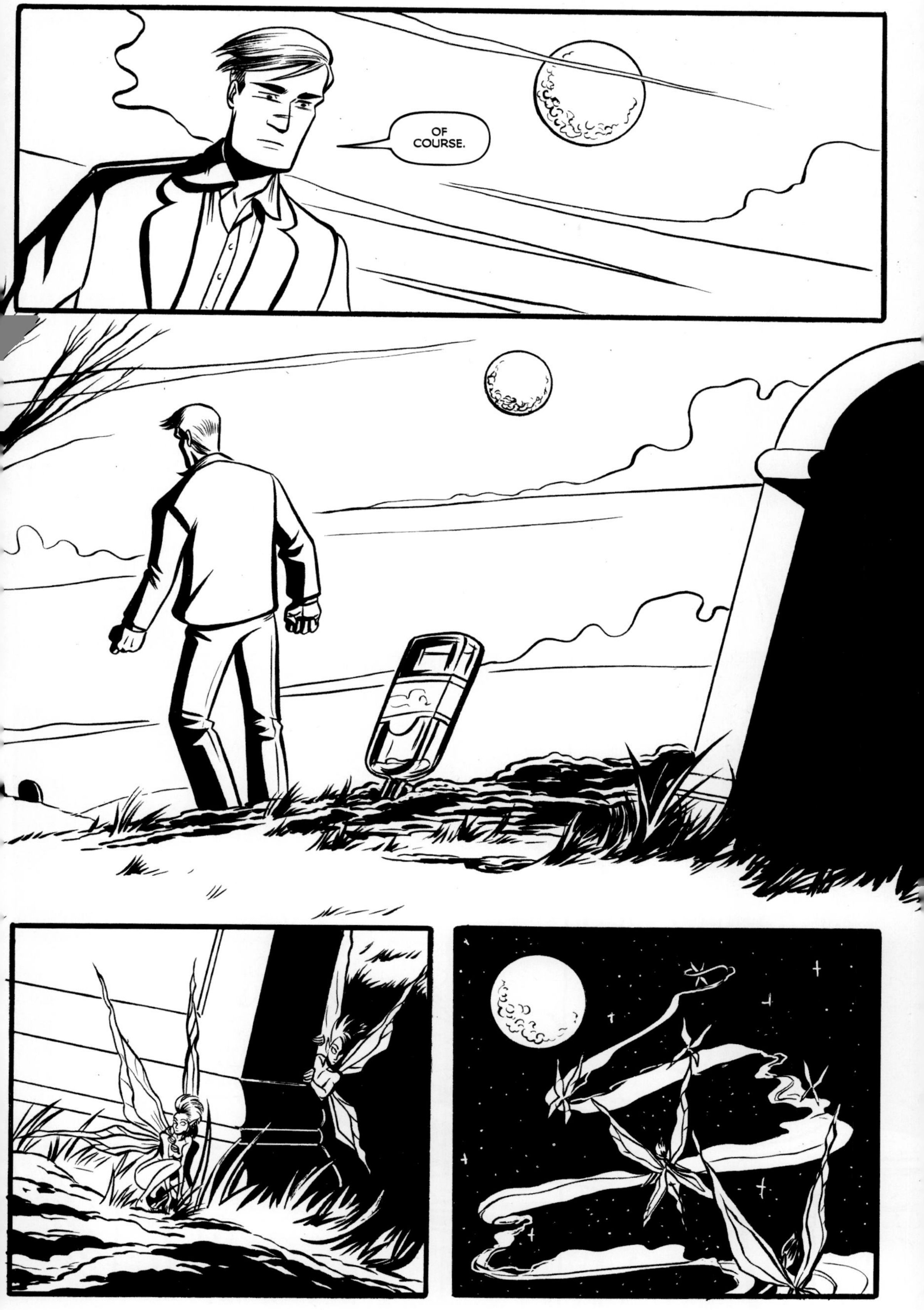
OF COURSE.

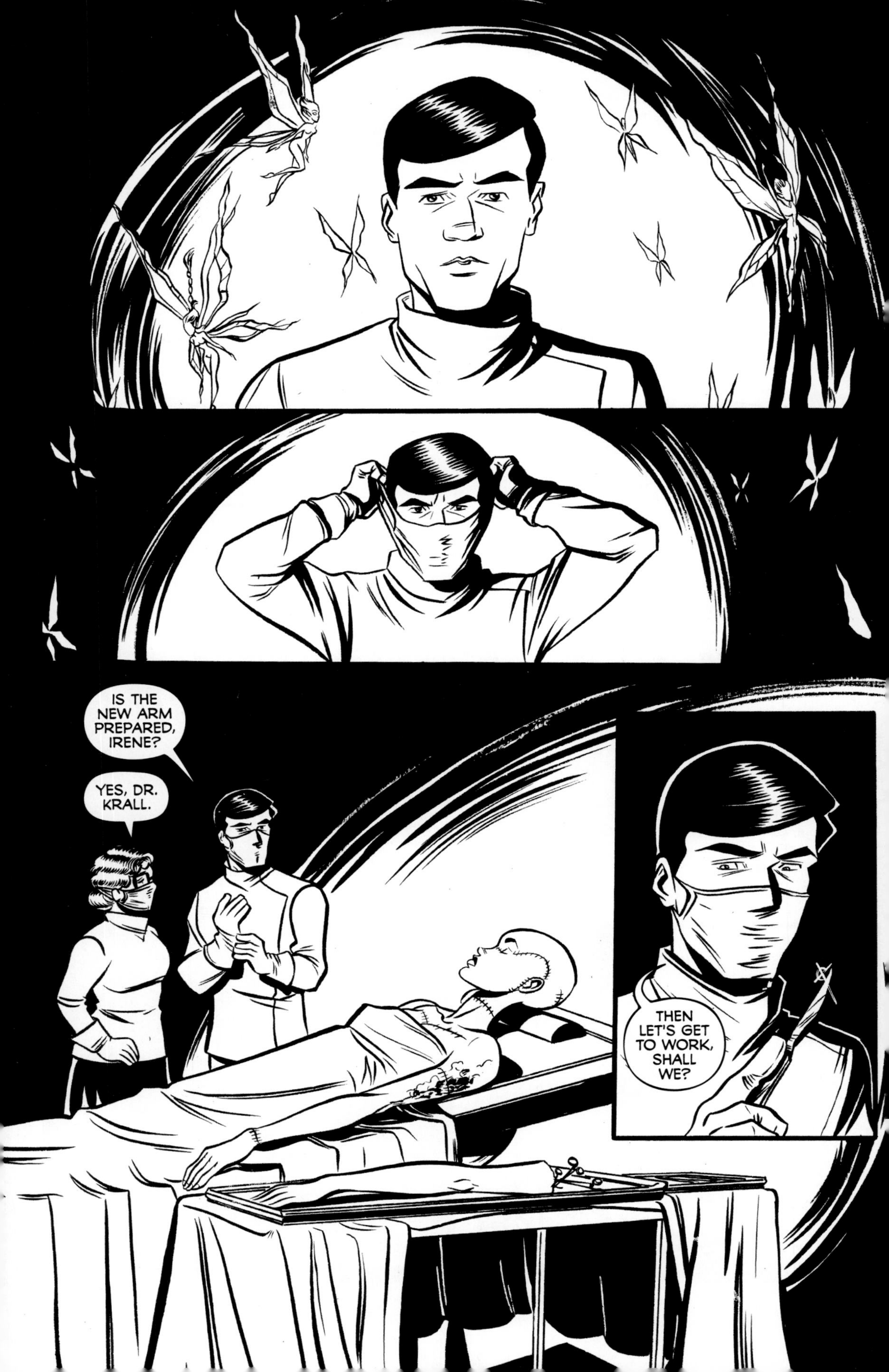
IS THE NEW ARM PREPARED, IRENE?
YES, DR. KRALL.
THEN LET'S GET TO WORK, SHALL WE?

CHAPTER THREE

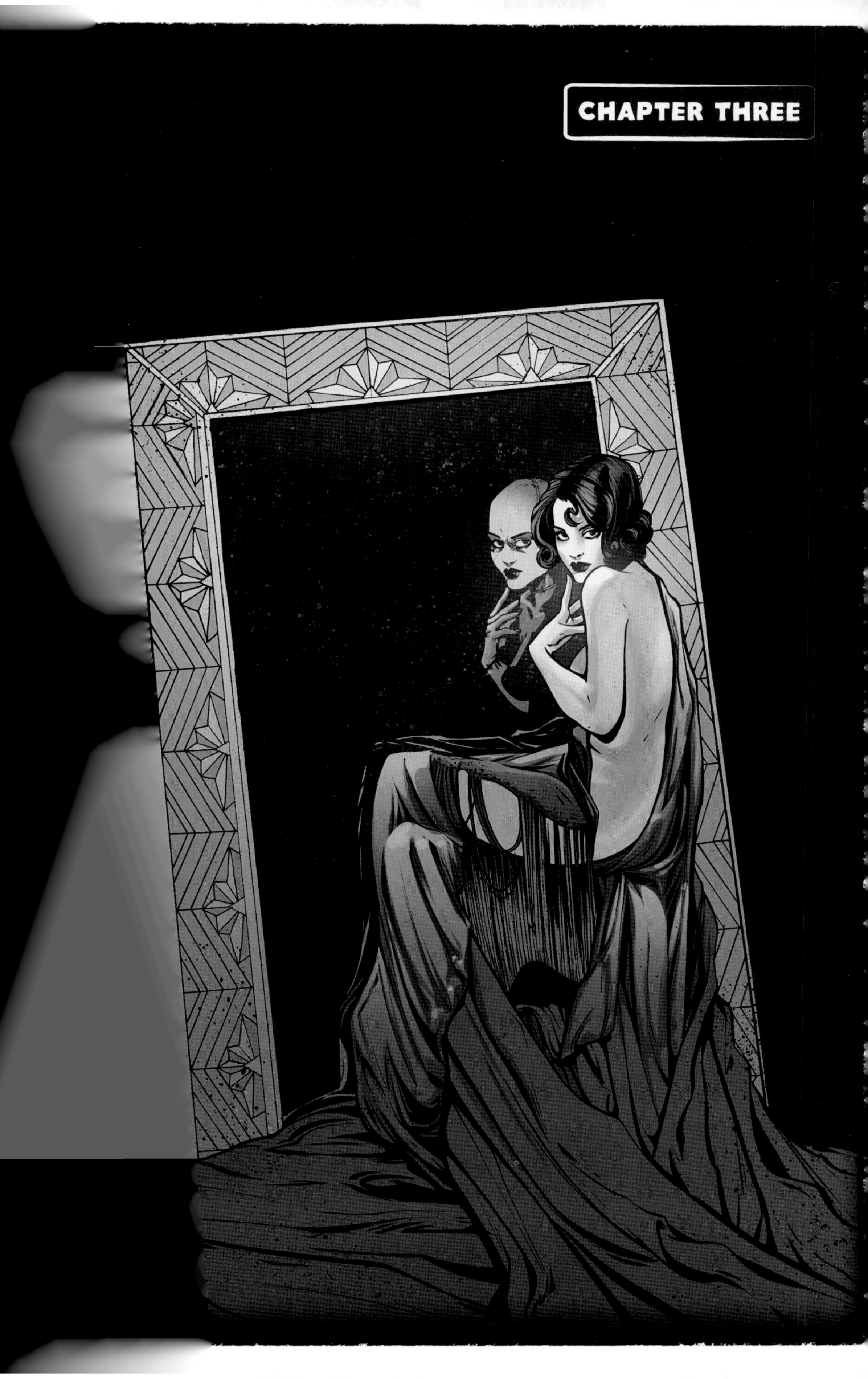

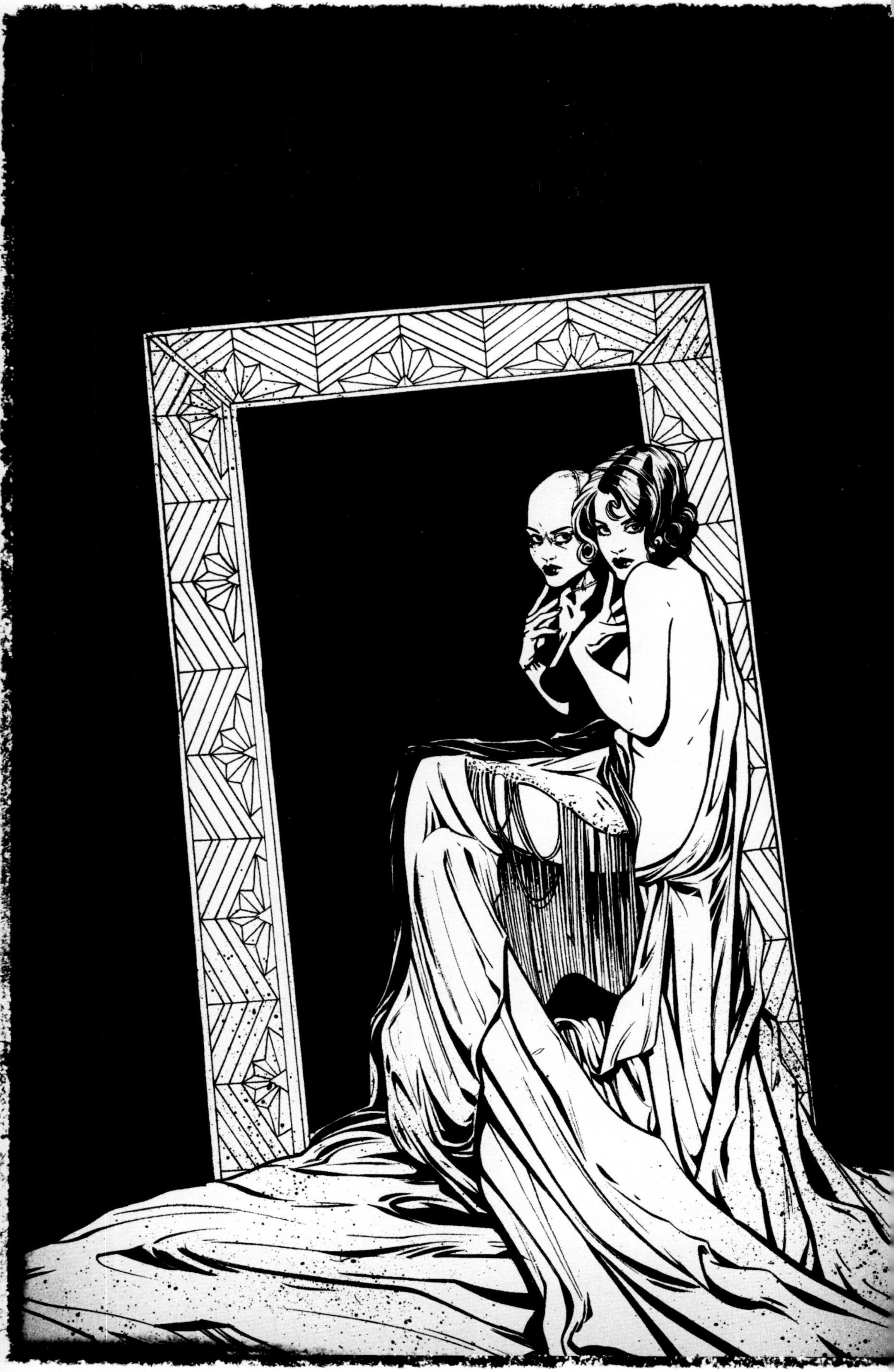

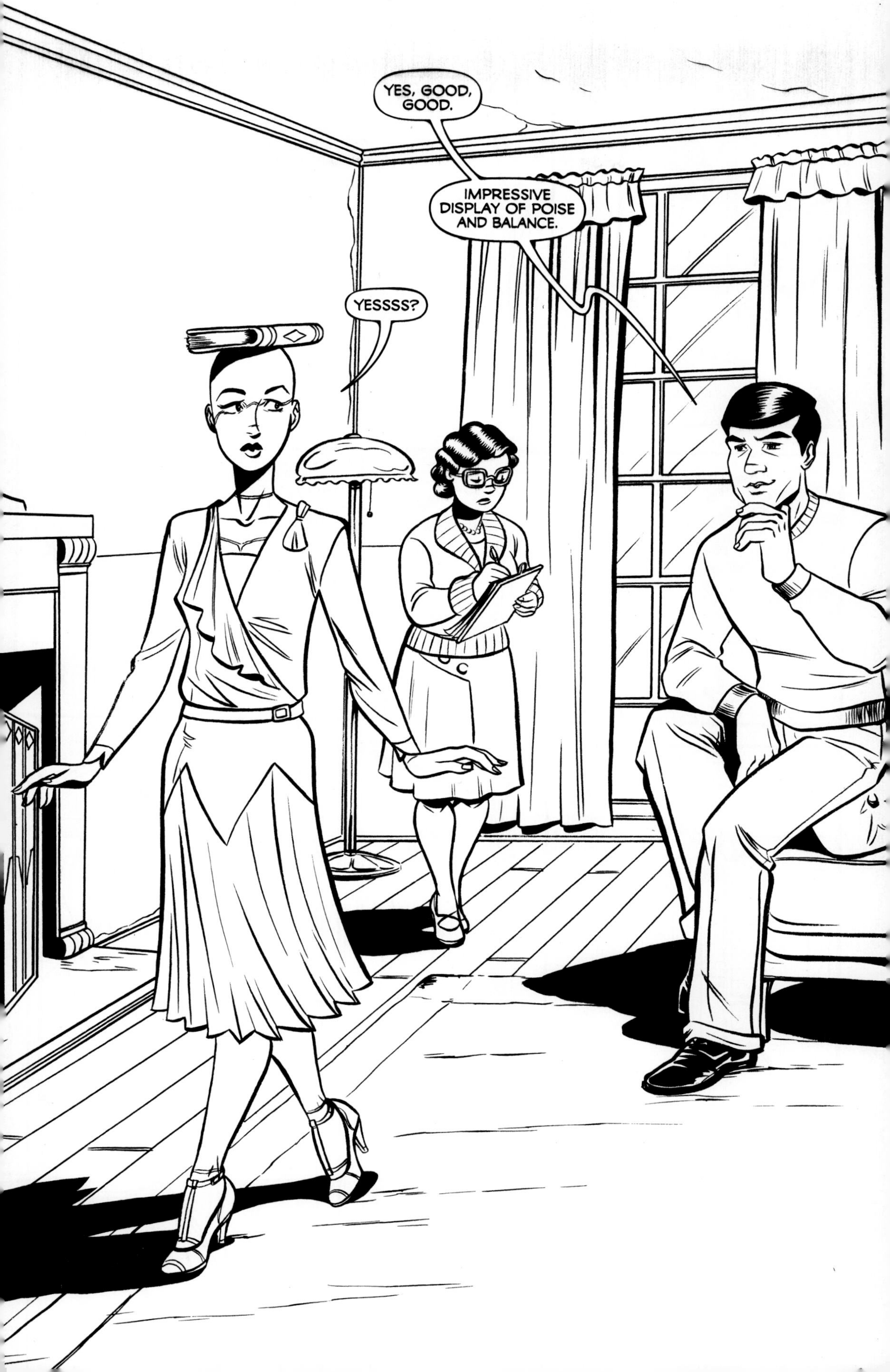
YESSSS?
YES, GOOD, GOOD.
IMPRESSIVE DISPLAY OF POISE AND BALANCE.

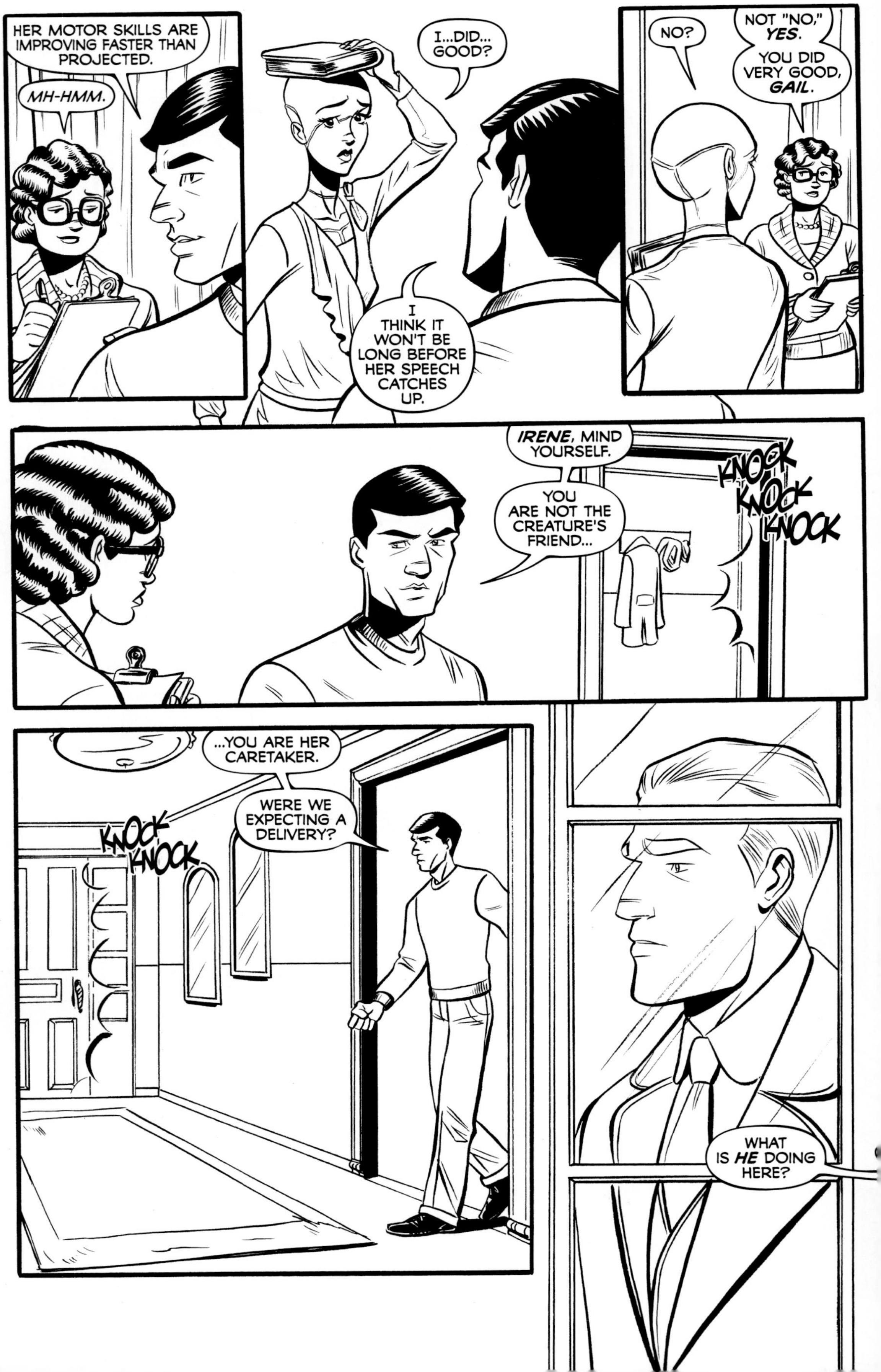
HER MOTOR SKILLS ARE IMPROVING FASTER THAN PROJECTED.
MH-HMM.
I...DID... GOOD?
I THINK IT WON'T BE LONG BEFORE HER SPEECH CATCHES UP.
NO?
NOT "NO," YES.
YOU DID VERY GOOD, GAIL.
IRENE, MIND YOURSELF.
YOU ARE NOT THE CREATURE'S FRIEND...
KNOCK KNOCK KNOCK
...YOU ARE HER CARETAKER.
WERE WE EXPECTING A DELIVERY?
KNOCK KNOCK
WHAT IS HE DOING HERE?

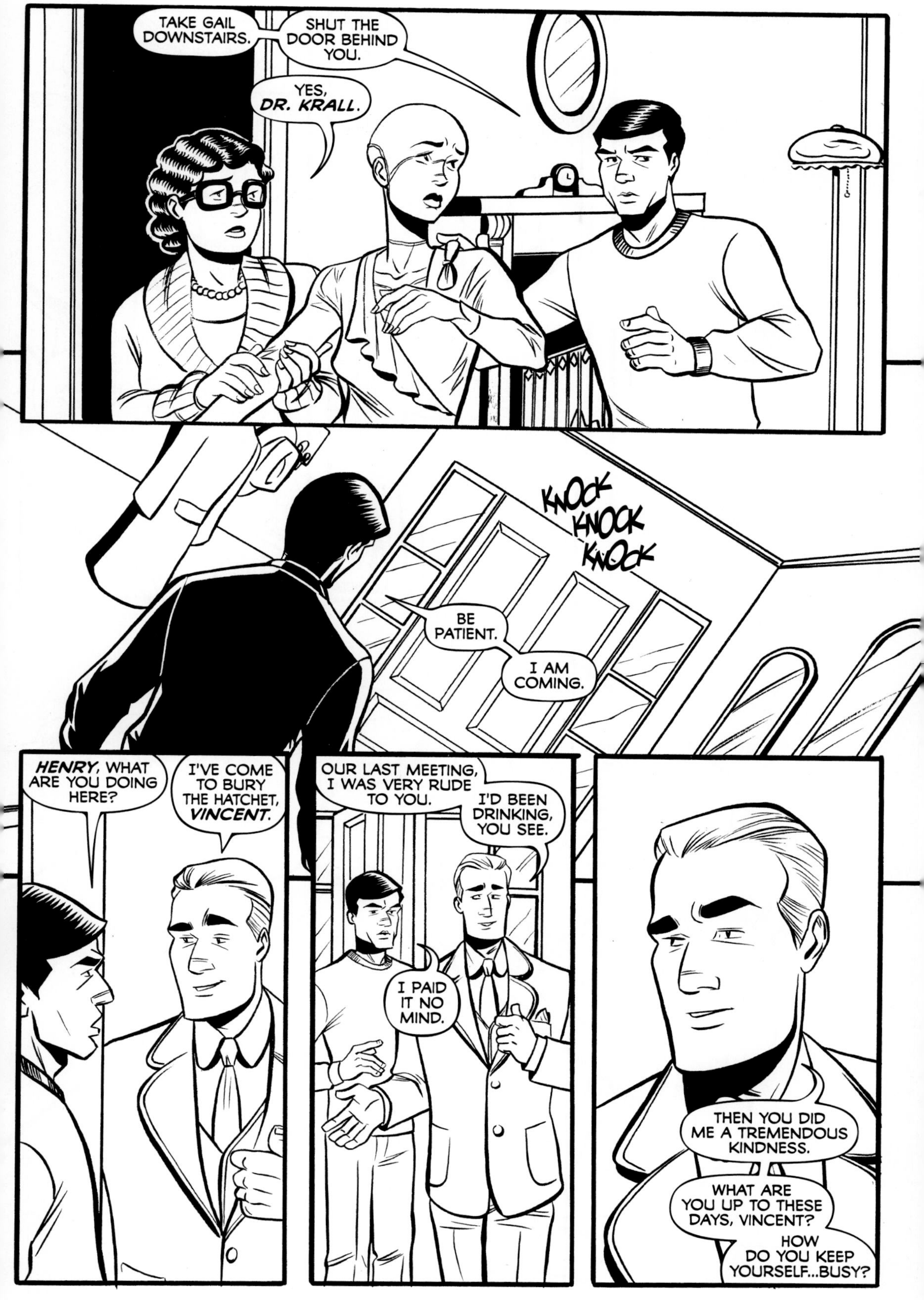

TAKE GAIL DOWNSTAIRS.
SHUT THE DOOR BEHIND YOU.
YES, DR. KRALL.
KNOCK KNOCK KNOCK
BE PATIENT.
I AM COMING.
HENRY, WHAT ARE YOU DOING HERE?
I'VE COME TO BURY THE HATCHET, VINCENT.
OUR LAST MEETING, I WAS VERY RUDE TO YOU.
I'D BEEN DRINKING, YOU SEE.
I PAID IT NO MIND.
THEN YOU DID ME A TREMENDOUS KINDNESS.
WHAT ARE YOU UP TO THESE DAYS, VINCENT?
HOW DO YOU KEEP YOURSELF...BUSY?

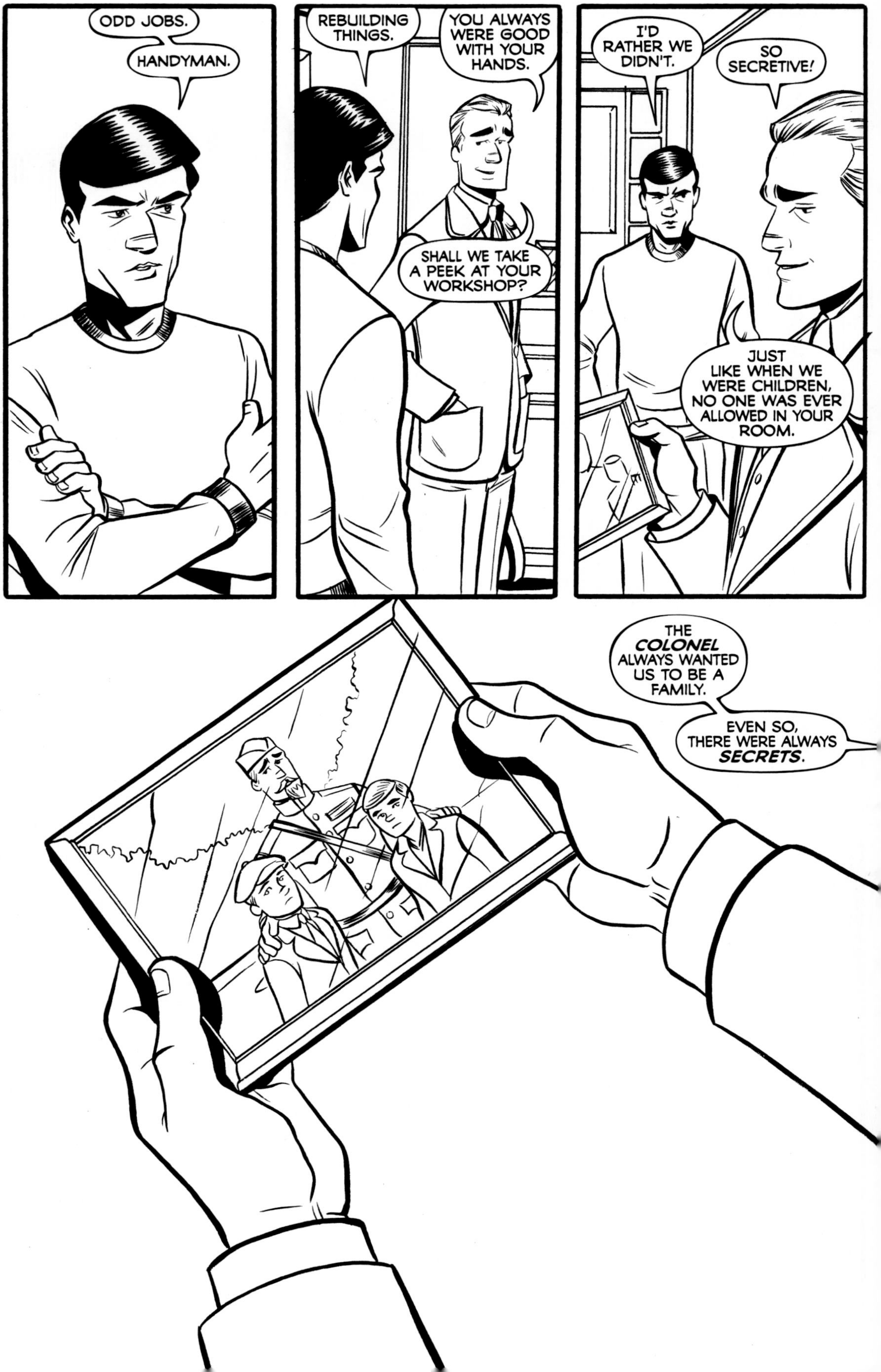

ODD JOBS.
HANDYMAN.
REBUILDING THINGS.
YOU ALWAYS WERE GOOD WITH YOUR HANDS.
SHALL WE TAKE A PEEK AT YOUR WORKSHOP?
I'D RATHER WE DIDN'T.
SO SECRETIVE!
JUST LIKE WHEN WE WERE CHILDREN, NO ONE WAS EVER ALLOWED IN YOUR ROOM.
THE *COLONEL* ALWAYS WANTED US TO BE A FAMILY.
EVEN SO, THERE WERE ALWAYS ***SECRETS***.

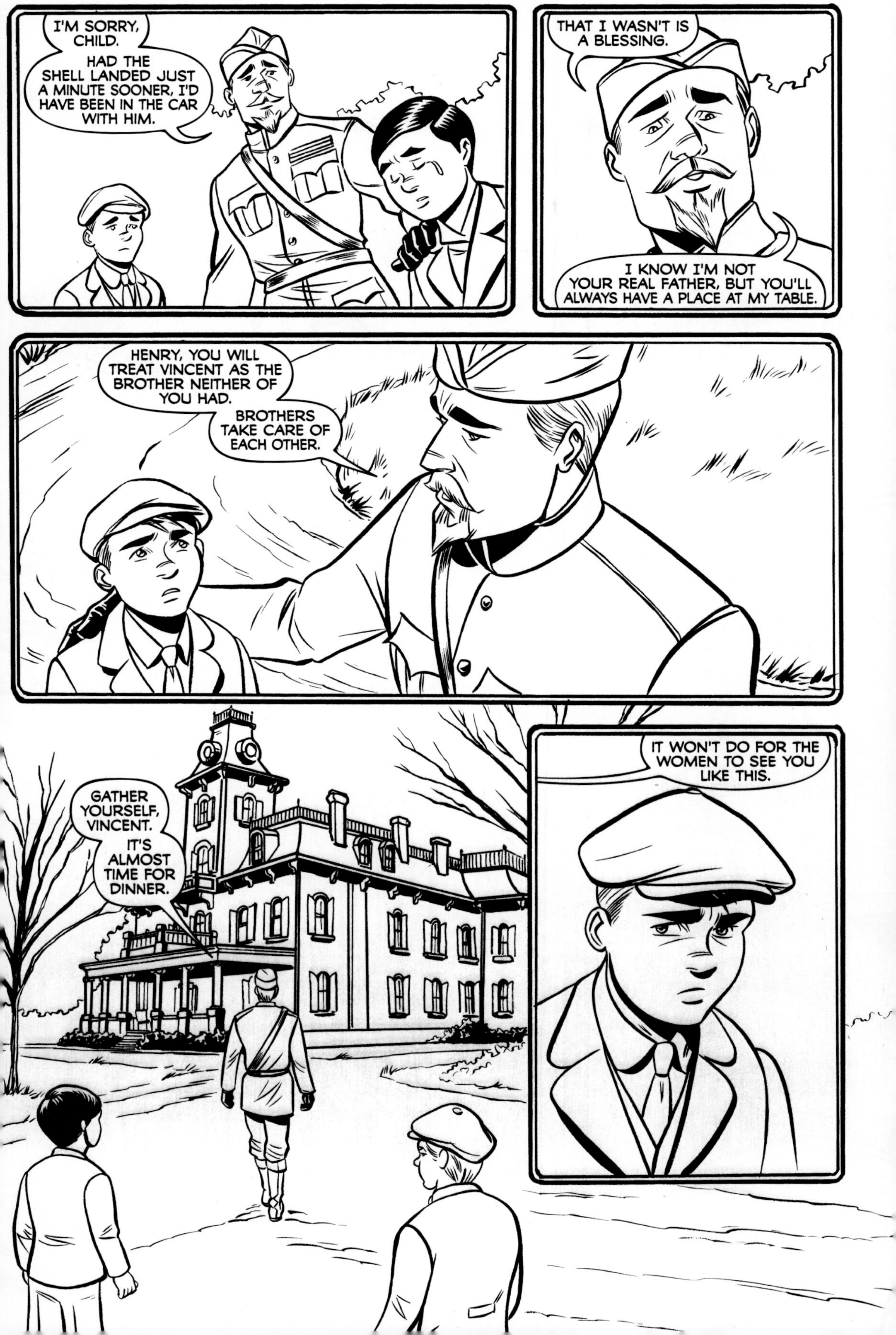
I'M SORRY, CHILD.
HAD THE SHELL LANDED JUST A MINUTE SOONER, I'D HAVE BEEN IN THE CAR WITH HIM.
THAT I WASN'T IS A BLESSING.
I KNOW I'M NOT YOUR REAL FATHER, BUT YOU'LL ALWAYS HAVE A PLACE AT MY TABLE.
HENRY, YOU WILL TREAT VINCENT AS THE BROTHER NEITHER OF YOU HAD.
BROTHERS TAKE CARE OF EACH OTHER.
GATHER YOURSELF, VINCENT.
IT'S ALMOST TIME FOR DINNER.
IT WON'T DO FOR THE WOMEN TO SEE YOU LIKE THIS.

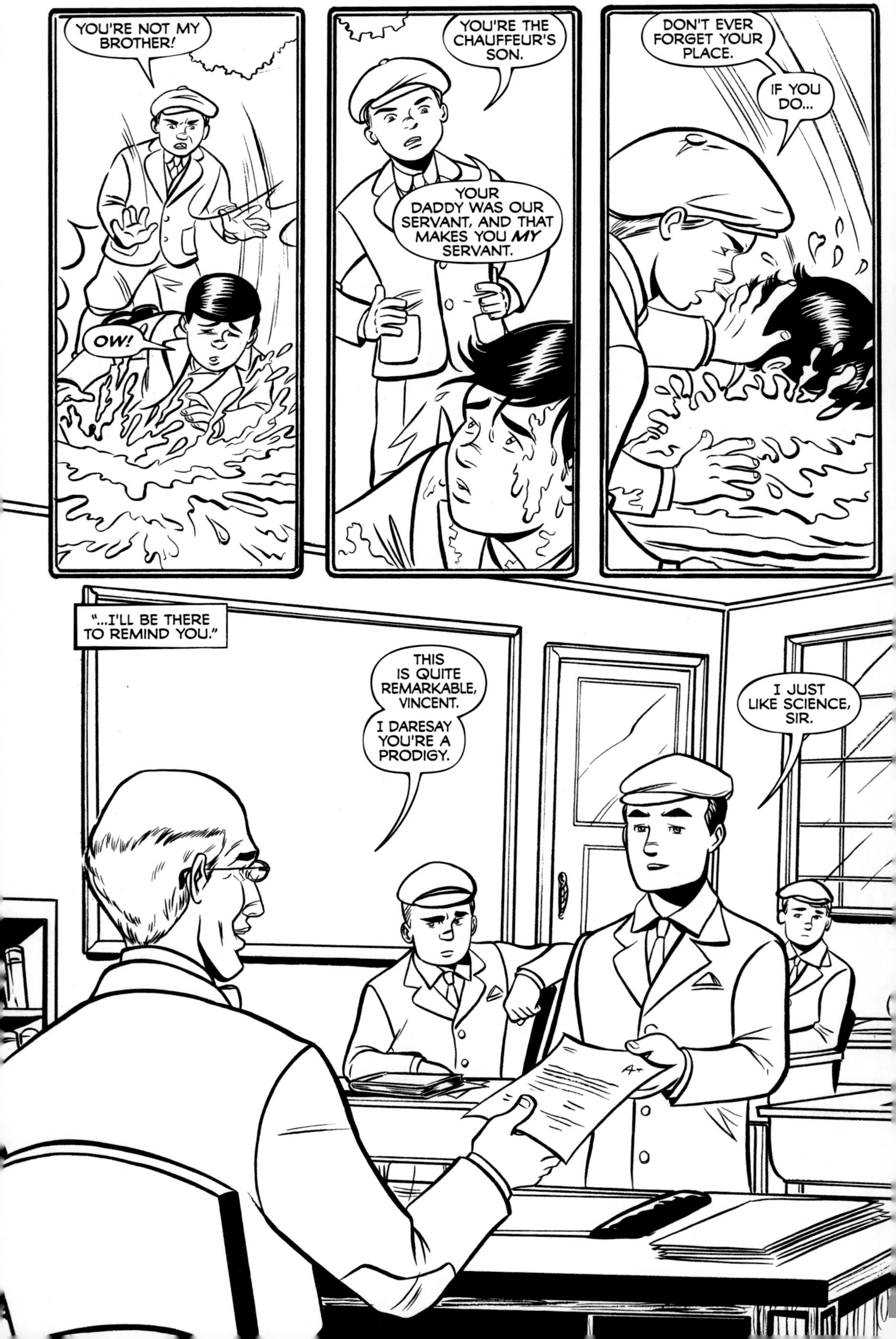
YOU'RE NOT MY BROTHER!
OW!
YOU'RE THE CHAUFFEUR'S SON.
YOUR DADDY WAS OUR SERVANT, AND THAT MAKES YOU *MY* SERVANT.
DON'T EVER FORGET YOUR PLACE.
IF YOU DO...
"...I'LL BE THERE TO REMIND YOU."
THIS IS QUITE REMARKABLE, VINCENT.
I DARESAY YOU'RE A PRODIGY.
I JUST LIKE SCIENCE, SIR.
A+

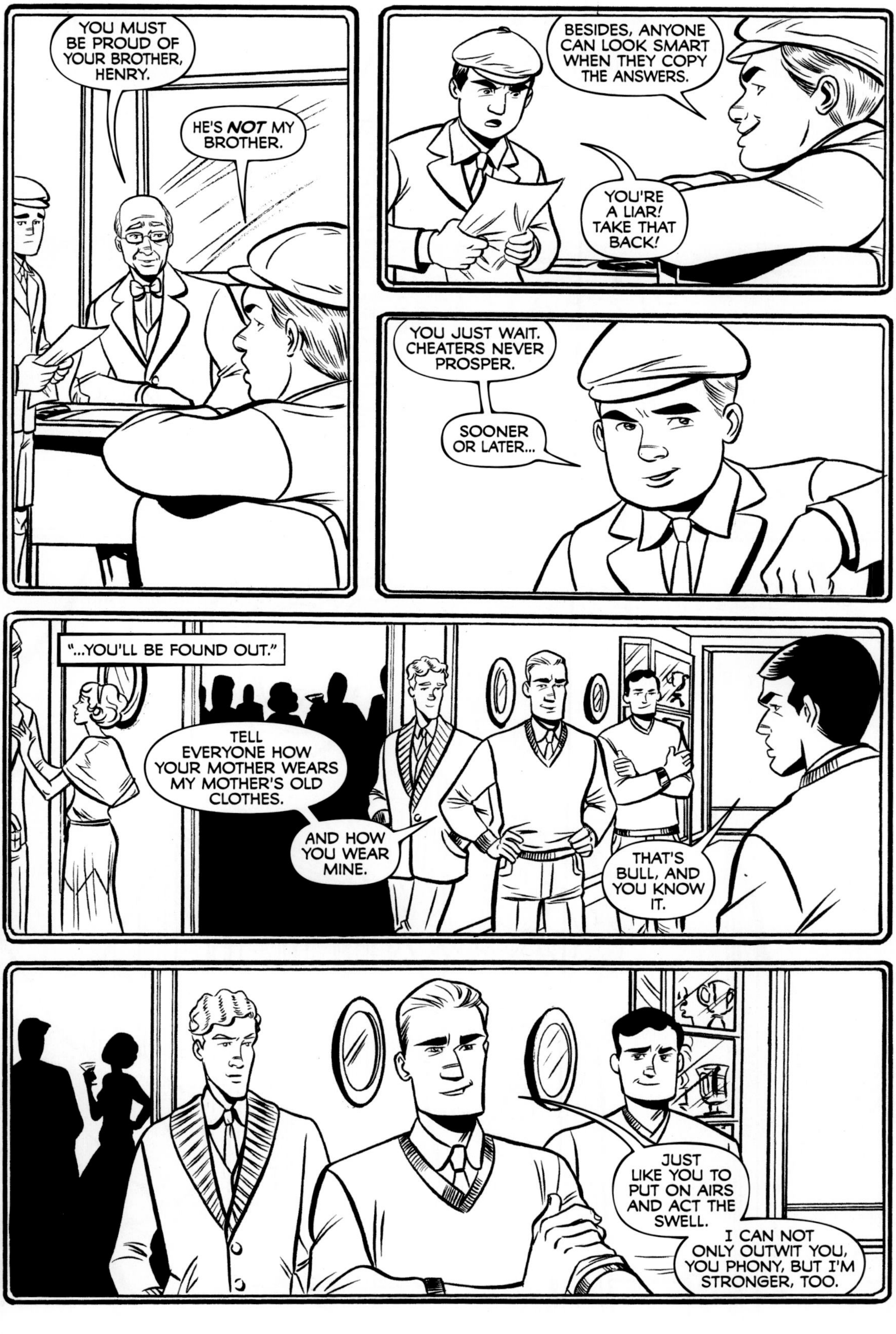
YOU MUST BE PROUD OF YOUR BROTHER, HENRY.
HE'S ***NOT*** MY BROTHER.
BESIDES, ANYONE CAN LOOK SMART WHEN THEY COPY THE ANSWERS.
YOU'RE A LIAR! TAKE THAT BACK!
YOU JUST WAIT. CHEATERS NEVER PROSPER.
SOONER OR LATER...
"...YOU'LL BE FOUND OUT."
TELL EVERYONE HOW YOUR MOTHER WEARS MY MOTHER'S OLD CLOTHES.
AND HOW YOU WEAR MINE.
THAT'S BULL, AND YOU KNOW IT.
JUST LIKE YOU TO PUT ON AIRS AND ACT THE SWELL.
I CAN NOT ONLY OUTWIT YOU, YOU PHONY, BUT I'M STRONGER, TOO.

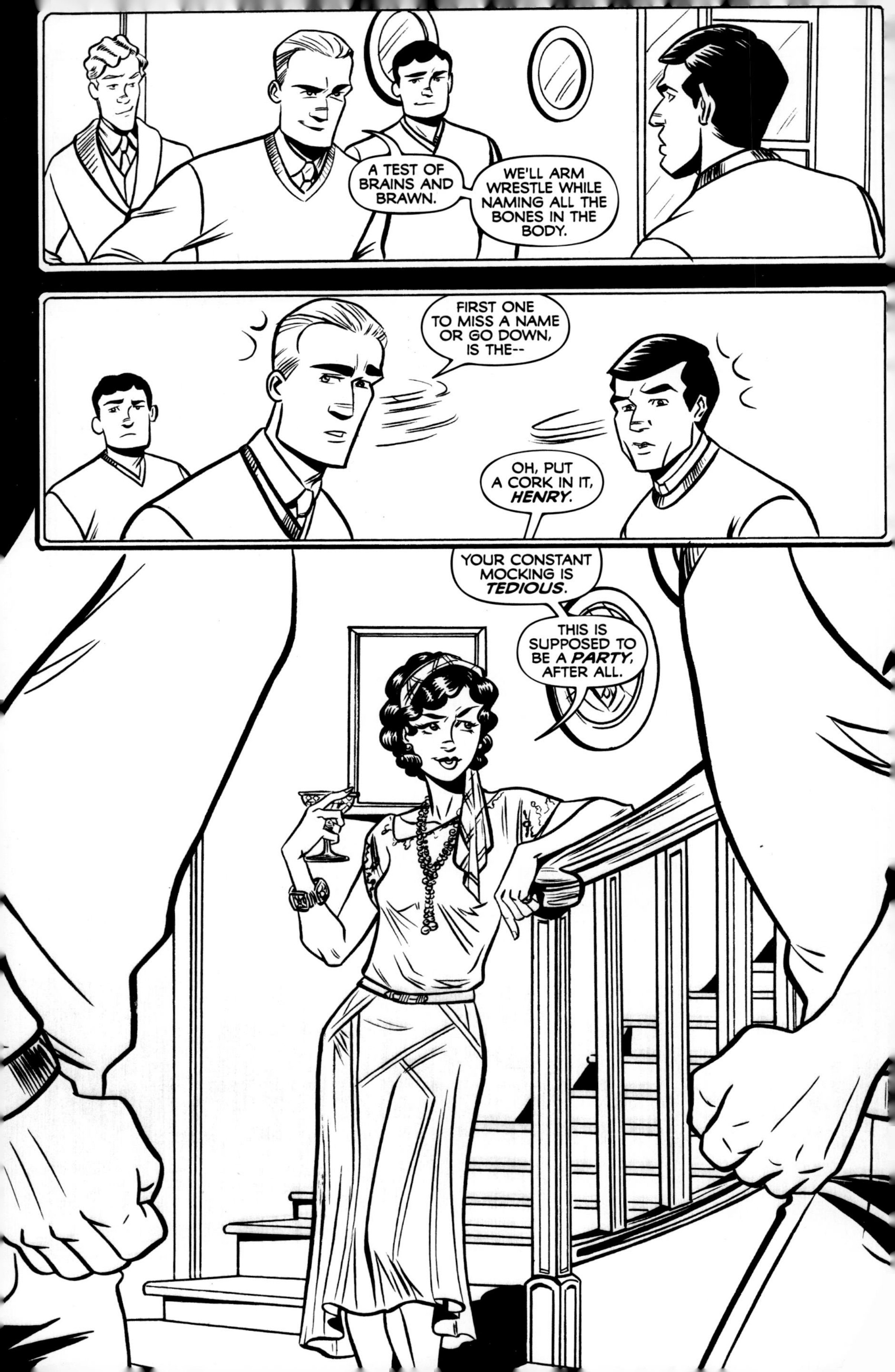
A TEST OF BRAINS AND BRAWN.
WE'LL ARM WRESTLE WHILE NAMING ALL THE BONES IN THE BODY.
FIRST ONE TO MISS A NAME OR GO DOWN, IS THE--
OH, PUT A CORK IN IT, *HENRY*.
YOUR CONSTANT MOCKING IS *TEDIOUS*.
THIS IS SUPPOSED TO BE A *PARTY*, AFTER ALL.

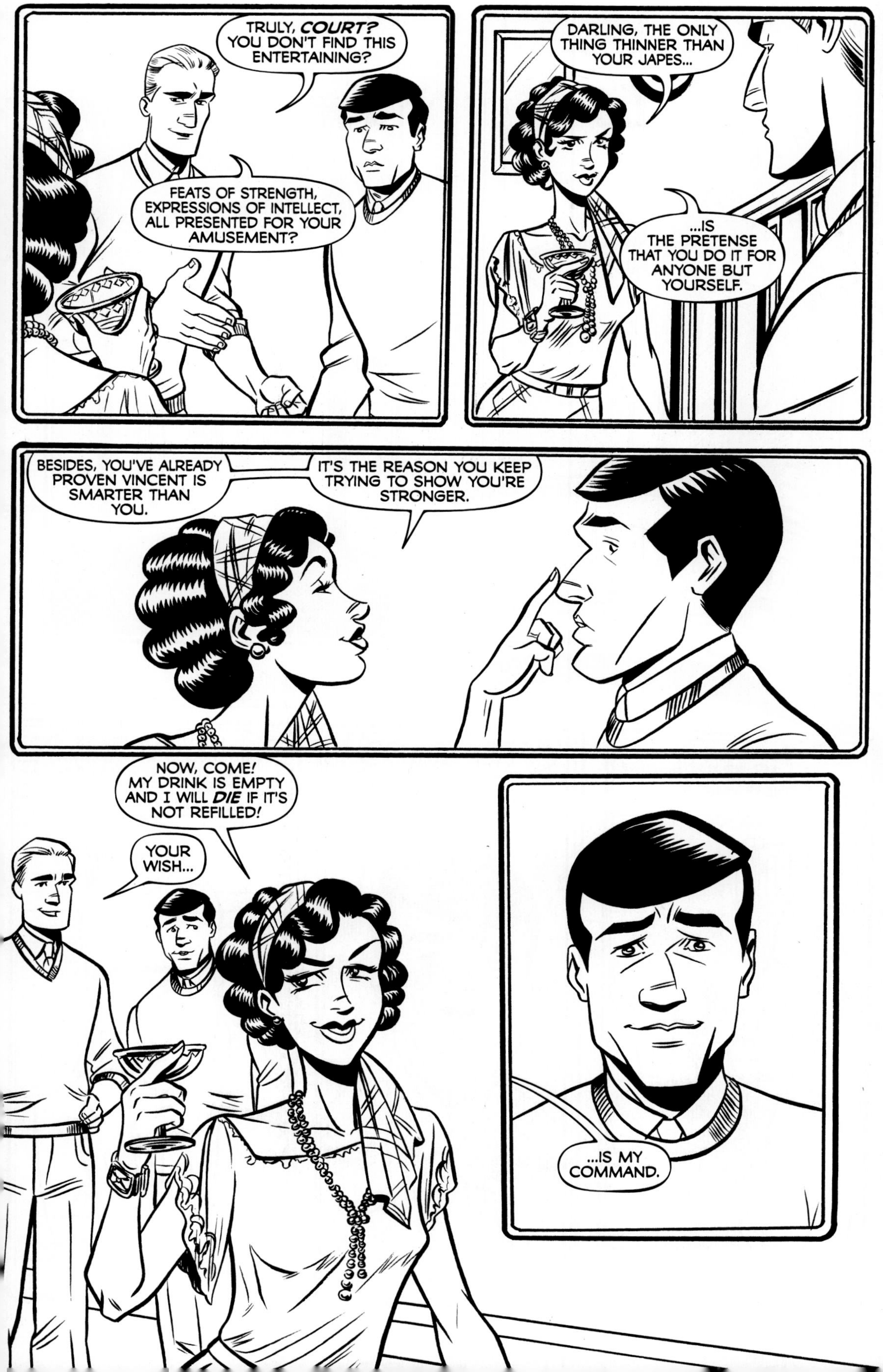

TRULY, *COURT?* YOU DON'T FIND THIS ENTERTAINING?
FEATS OF STRENGTH, EXPRESSIONS OF INTELLECT, ALL PRESENTED FOR YOUR AMUSEMENT?
DARLING, THE ONLY THING THINNER THAN YOUR JAPES...
...IS THE PRETENSE THAT YOU DO IT FOR ANYONE BUT YOURSELF.
BESIDES, YOU'VE ALREADY PROVEN VINCENT IS SMARTER THAN YOU.
IT'S THE REASON YOU KEEP TRYING TO SHOW YOU'RE STRONGER.
NOW, COME! MY DRINK IS EMPTY AND I WILL *DIE* IF IT'S NOT REFILLED!
YOUR WISH...
...IS MY COMMAND.

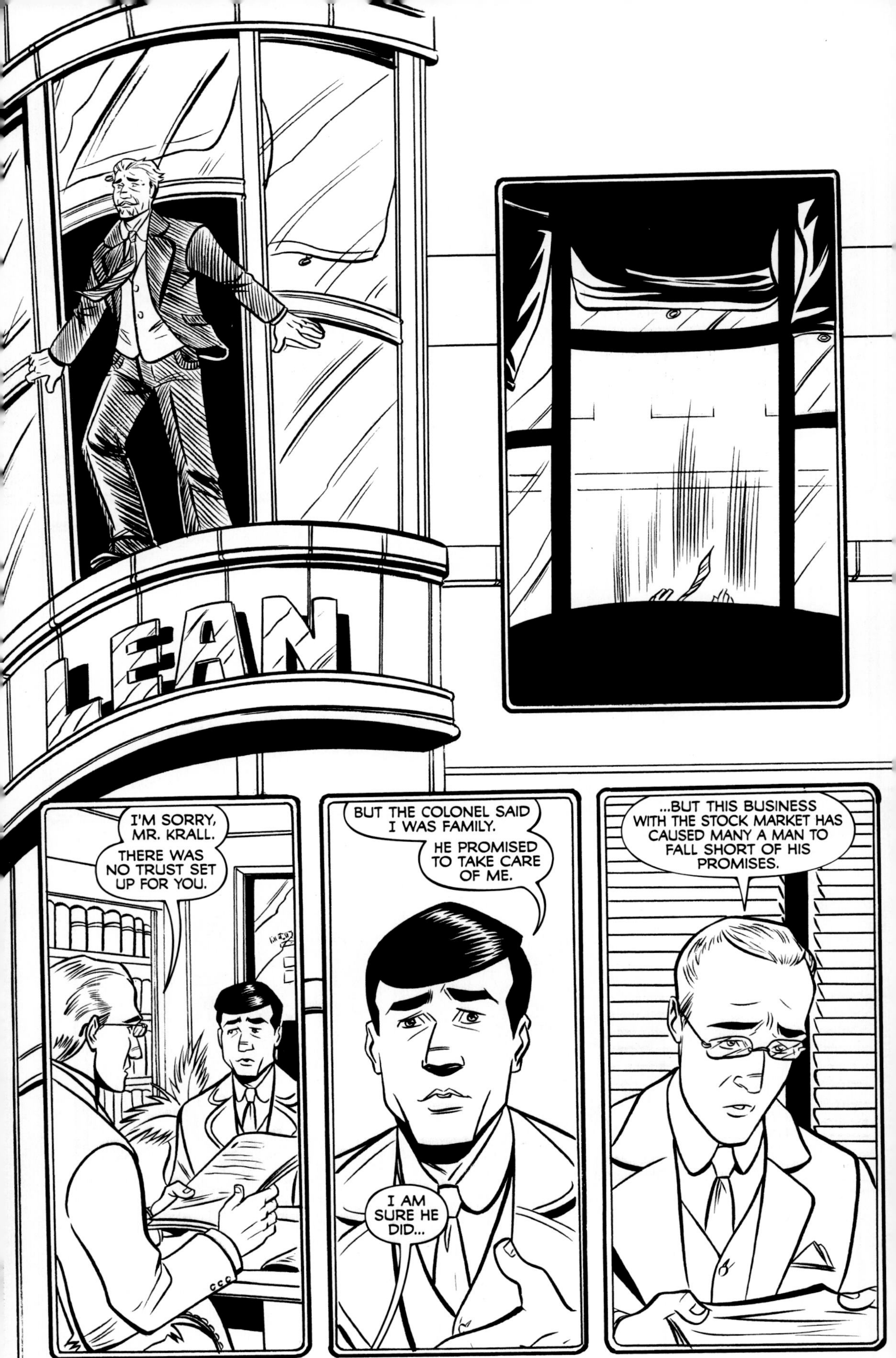
LEAN
I'M SORRY, MR. KRALL.
THERE WAS NO TRUST SET UP FOR YOU.
BUT THE COLONEL SAID I WAS FAMILY.
HE PROMISED TO TAKE CARE OF ME.
I AM SURE HE DID...
...BUT THIS BUSINESS WITH THE STOCK MARKET HAS CAUSED MANY A MAN TO FALL SHORT OF HIS PROMISES.

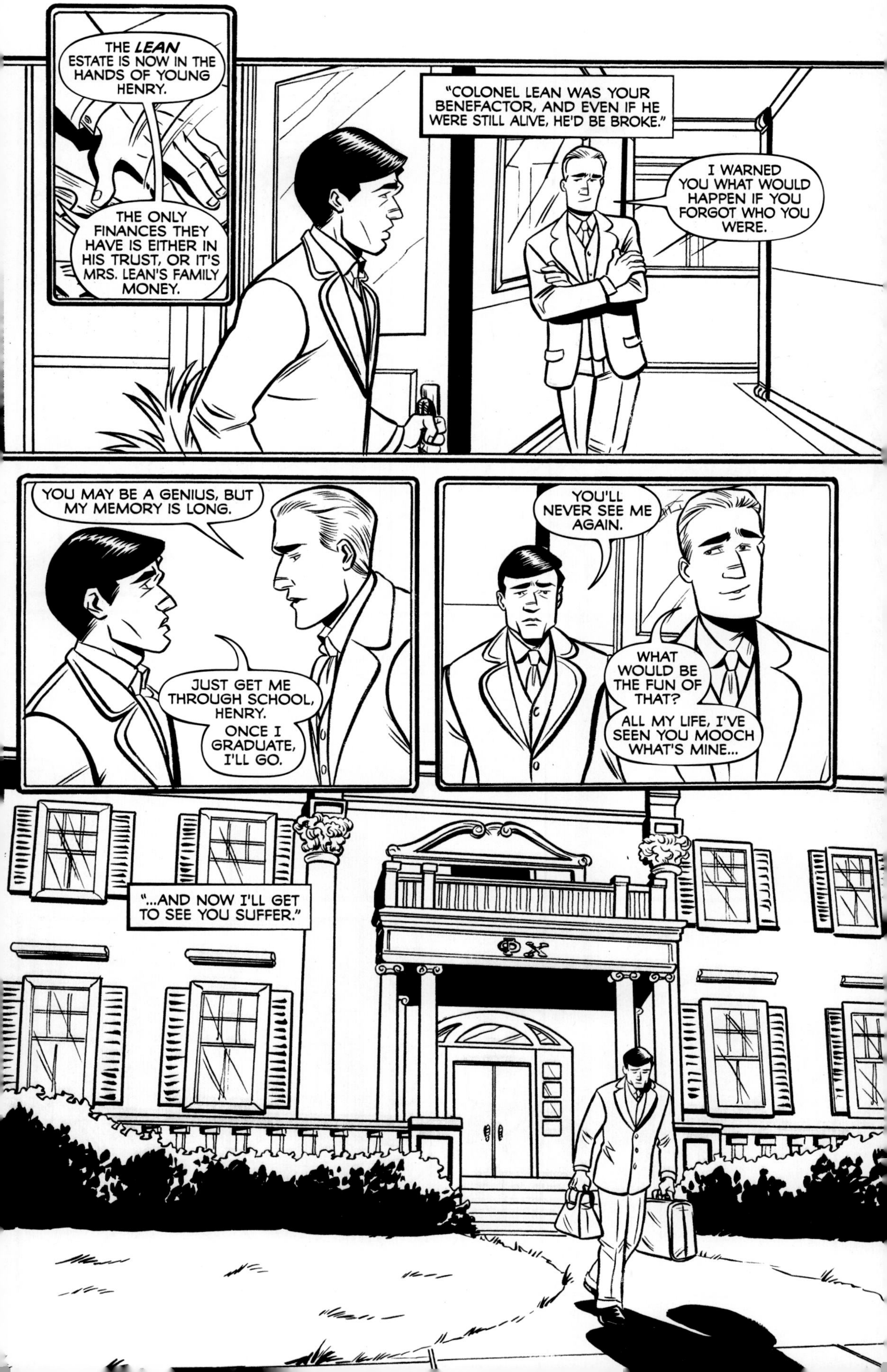
THE LEAN ESTATE IS NOW IN THE HANDS OF YOUNG HENRY.
THE ONLY FINANCES THEY HAVE IS EITHER IN HIS TRUST, OR IT'S MRS. LEAN'S FAMILY MONEY.
"COLONEL LEAN WAS YOUR BENEFACTOR, AND EVEN IF HE WERE STILL ALIVE, HE'D BE BROKE."
I WARNED YOU WHAT WOULD HAPPEN IF YOU FORGOT WHO YOU WERE.
YOU MAY BE A GENIUS, BUT MY MEMORY IS LONG.
JUST GET ME THROUGH SCHOOL, HENRY.
ONCE I GRADUATE, I'LL GO.
YOU'LL NEVER SEE ME AGAIN.
WHAT WOULD BE THE FUN OF THAT?
ALL MY LIFE, I'VE SEEN YOU MOOCH WHAT'S MINE...
"...AND NOW I'LL GET TO SEE YOU SUFFER."
ΦX

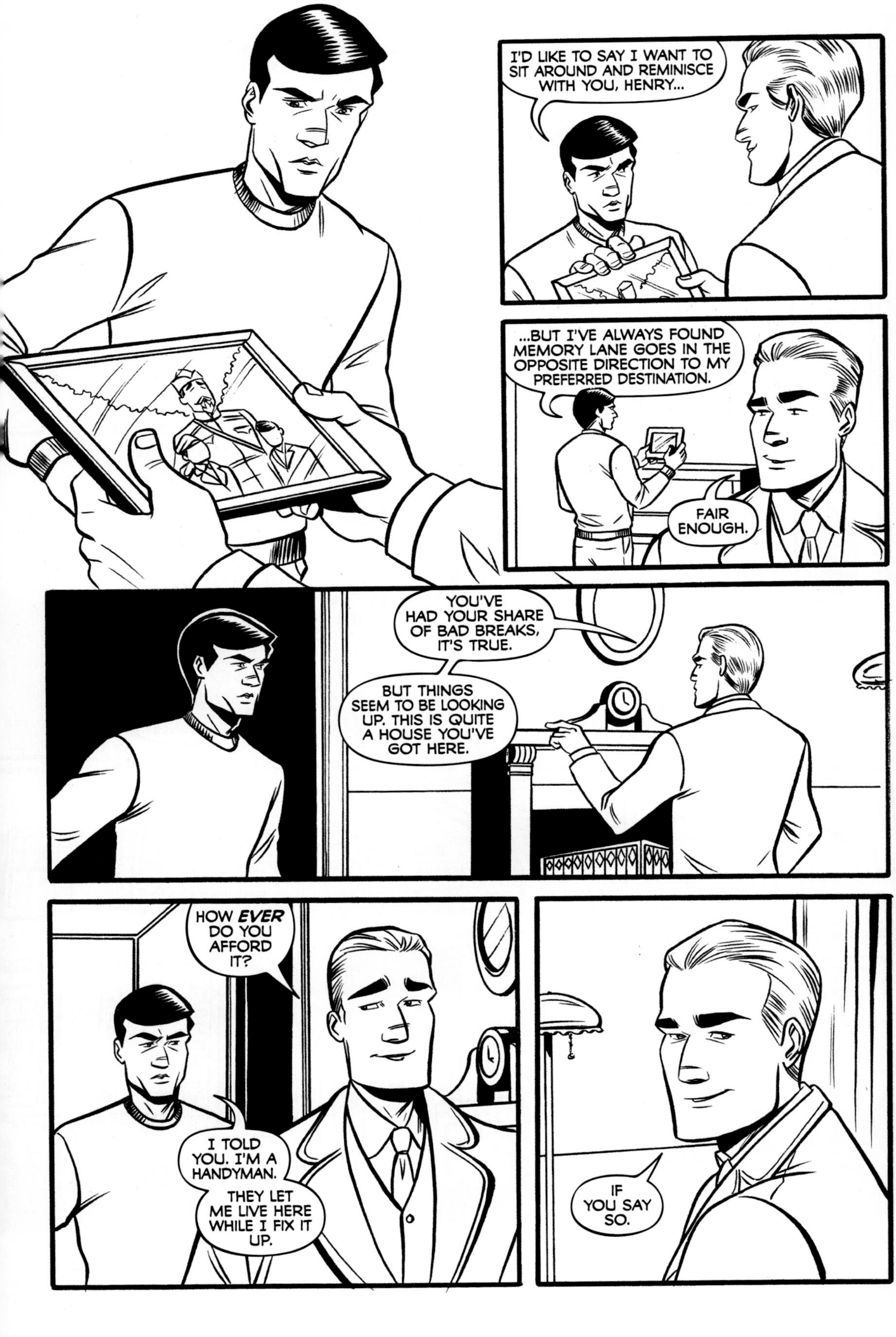
I'D LIKE TO SAY I WANT TO SIT AROUND AND REMINISCE WITH YOU, HENRY...
...BUT I'VE ALWAYS FOUND MEMORY LANE GOES IN THE OPPOSITE DIRECTION TO MY PREFERRED DESTINATION.
FAIR ENOUGH.
YOU'VE HAD YOUR SHARE OF BAD BREAKS, IT'S TRUE.
BUT THINGS SEEM TO BE LOOKING UP. THIS IS QUITE A HOUSE YOU'VE GOT HERE.
HOW *EVER* DO YOU AFFORD IT?
I TOLD YOU. I'M A HANDYMAN.
THEY LET ME LIVE HERE WHILE I FIX IT UP.
IF YOU SAY SO.

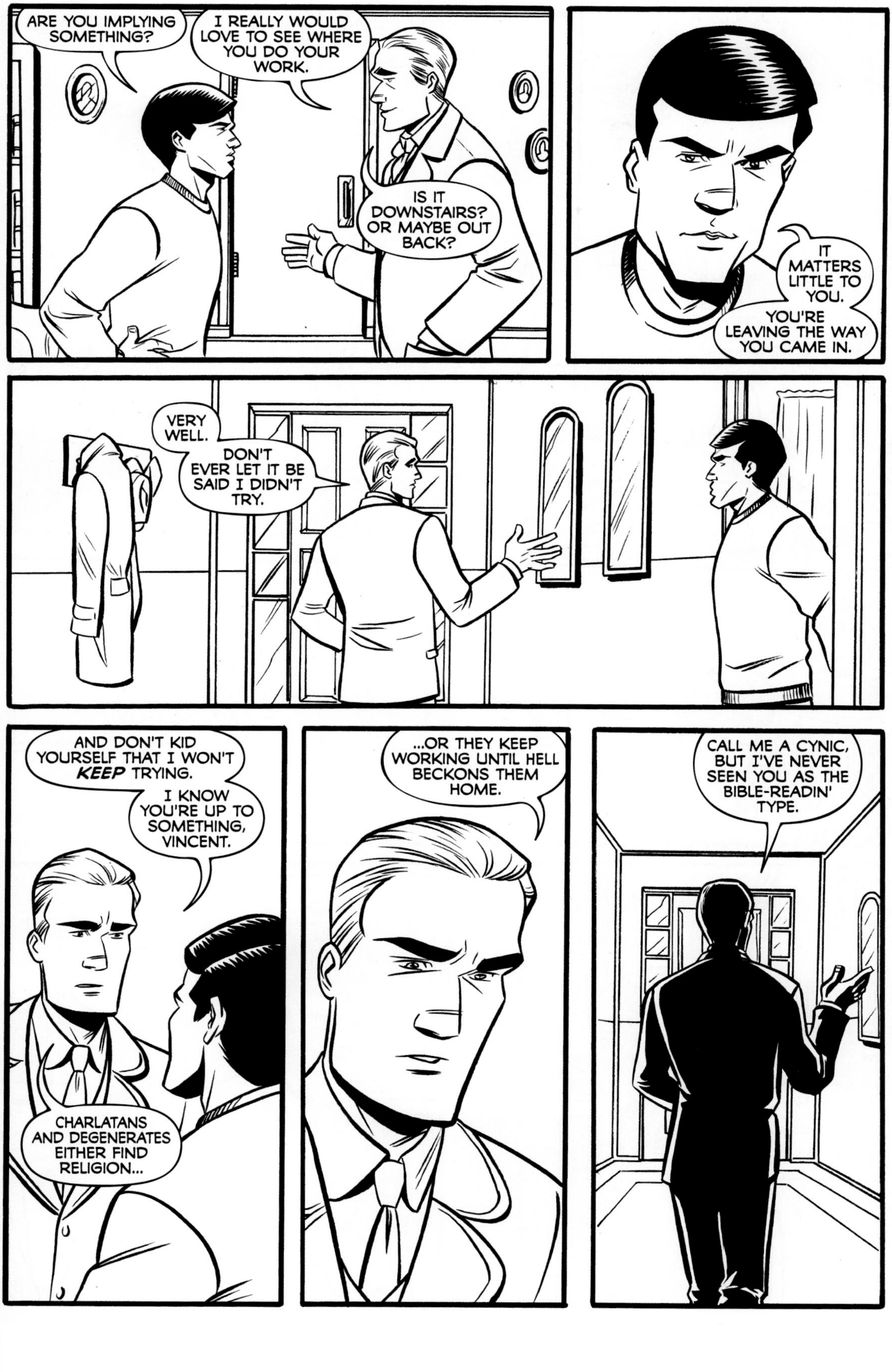
ARE YOU IMPLYING SOMETHING?
I REALLY WOULD LOVE TO SEE WHERE YOU DO YOUR WORK.
IS IT DOWNSTAIRS? OR MAYBE OUT BACK?
IT MATTERS LITTLE TO YOU.
YOU'RE LEAVING THE WAY YOU CAME IN.
VERY WELL.
DON'T EVER LET IT BE SAID I DIDN'T TRY.
AND DON'T KID YOURSELF THAT I WON'T *KEEP* TRYING.
I KNOW YOU'RE UP TO SOMETHING, VINCENT.
CHARLATANS AND DEGENERATES EITHER FIND RELIGION...
...OR THEY KEEP WORKING UNTIL HELL BECKONS THEM HOME.
CALL ME A CYNIC, BUT I'VE NEVER SEEN YOU AS THE BIBLE-READIN' TYPE.

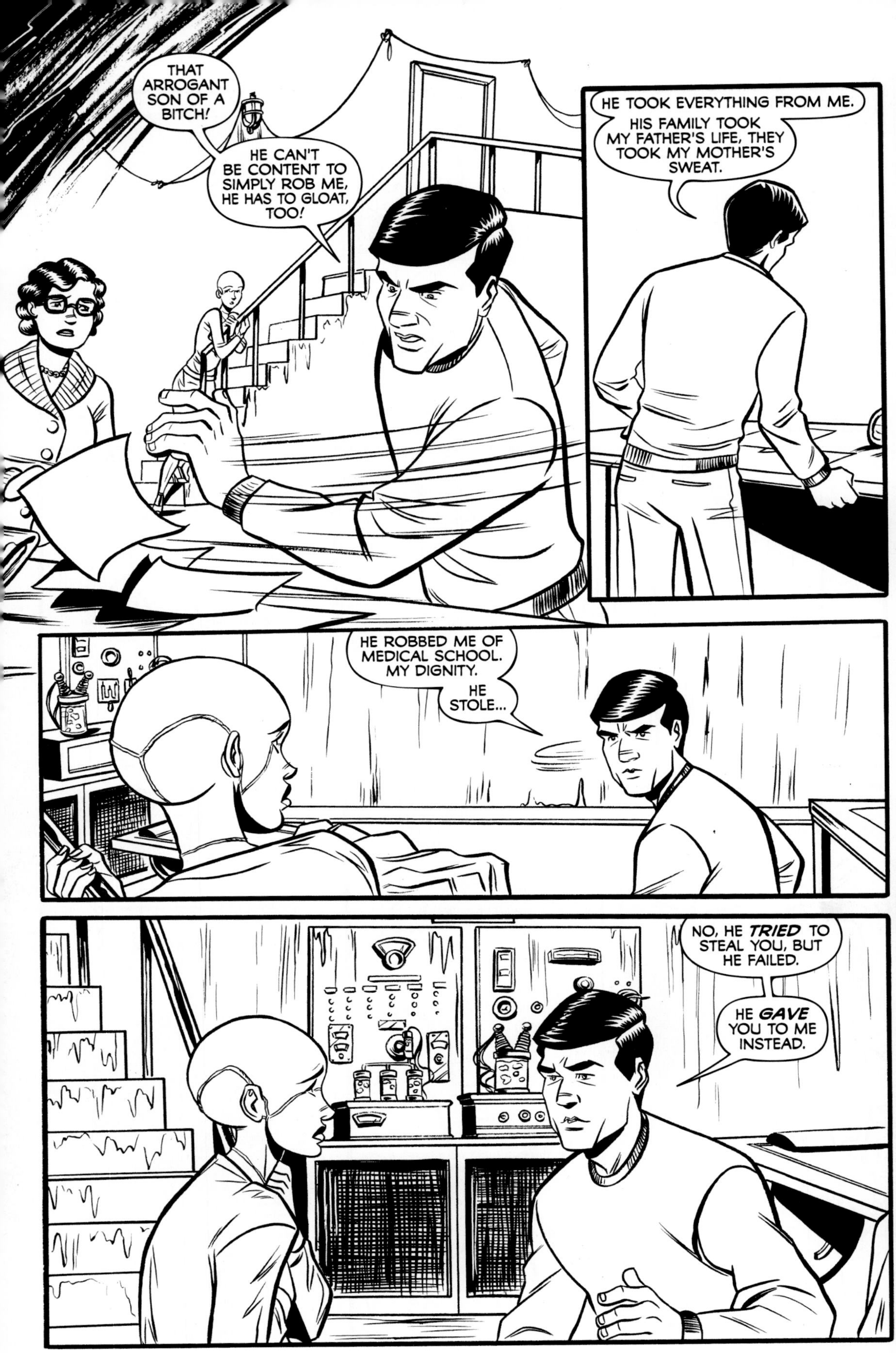
THAT ARROGANT SON OF A BITCH!
HE CAN'T BE CONTENT TO SIMPLY ROB ME, HE HAS TO GLOAT, TOO!
HE TOOK EVERYTHING FROM ME.
HIS FAMILY TOOK MY FATHER'S LIFE, THEY TOOK MY MOTHER'S SWEAT.
HE ROBBED ME OF MEDICAL SCHOOL. MY DIGNITY.
HE STOLE...
NO, HE TRIED TO STEAL YOU, BUT HE FAILED.
HE GAVE YOU TO ME INSTEAD.

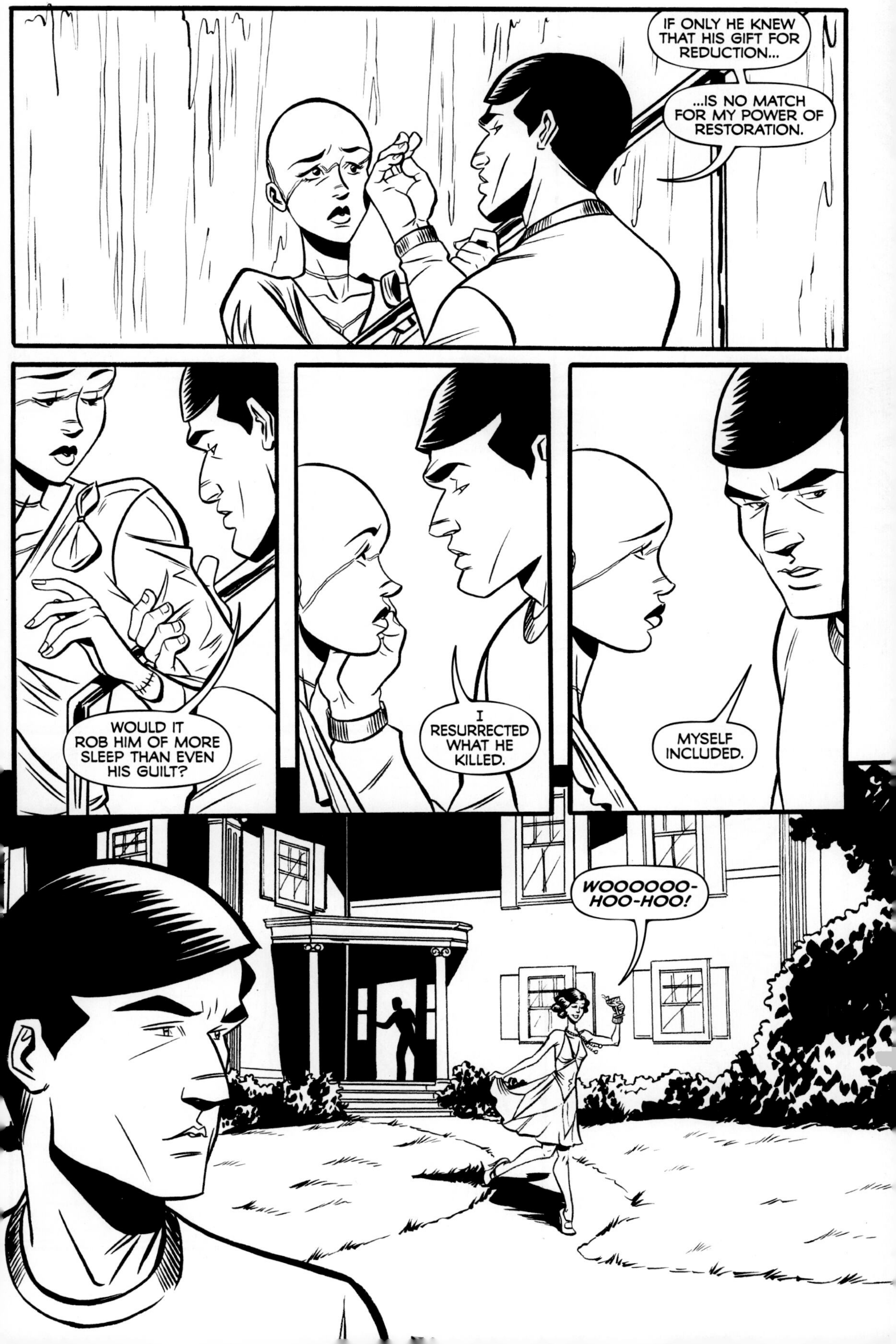
IF ONLY HE KNEW THAT HIS GIFT FOR REDUCTION...
...IS NO MATCH FOR MY POWER OF RESTORATION.
WOULD IT ROB HIM OF MORE SLEEP THAN EVEN HIS GUILT?
I RESURRECTED WHAT HE KILLED.
MYSELF INCLUDED.
WOOOOOO-HOO-HOO!

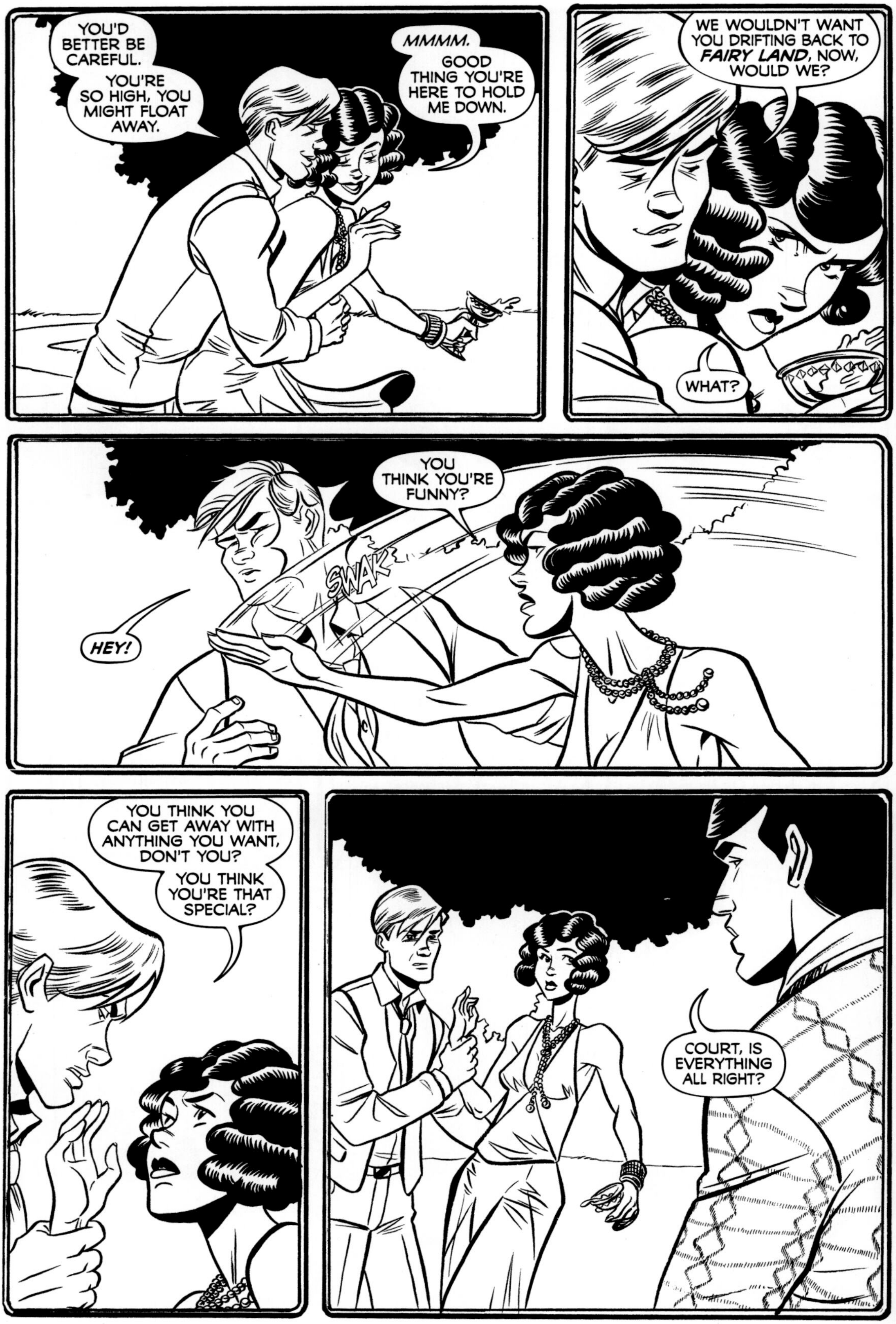
YOU'D BETTER BE CAREFUL.
YOU'RE SO HIGH, YOU MIGHT FLOAT AWAY.
MMMM.
GOOD THING YOU'RE HERE TO HOLD ME DOWN.
WE WOULDN'T WANT YOU DRIFTING BACK TO FAIRY LAND, NOW, WOULD WE?
WHAT?
YOU THINK YOU'RE FUNNY?
SWAK
HEY!
YOU THINK YOU CAN GET AWAY WITH ANYTHING YOU WANT, DON'T YOU?
YOU THINK YOU'RE THAT SPECIAL?
COURT, IS EVERYTHING ALL RIGHT?

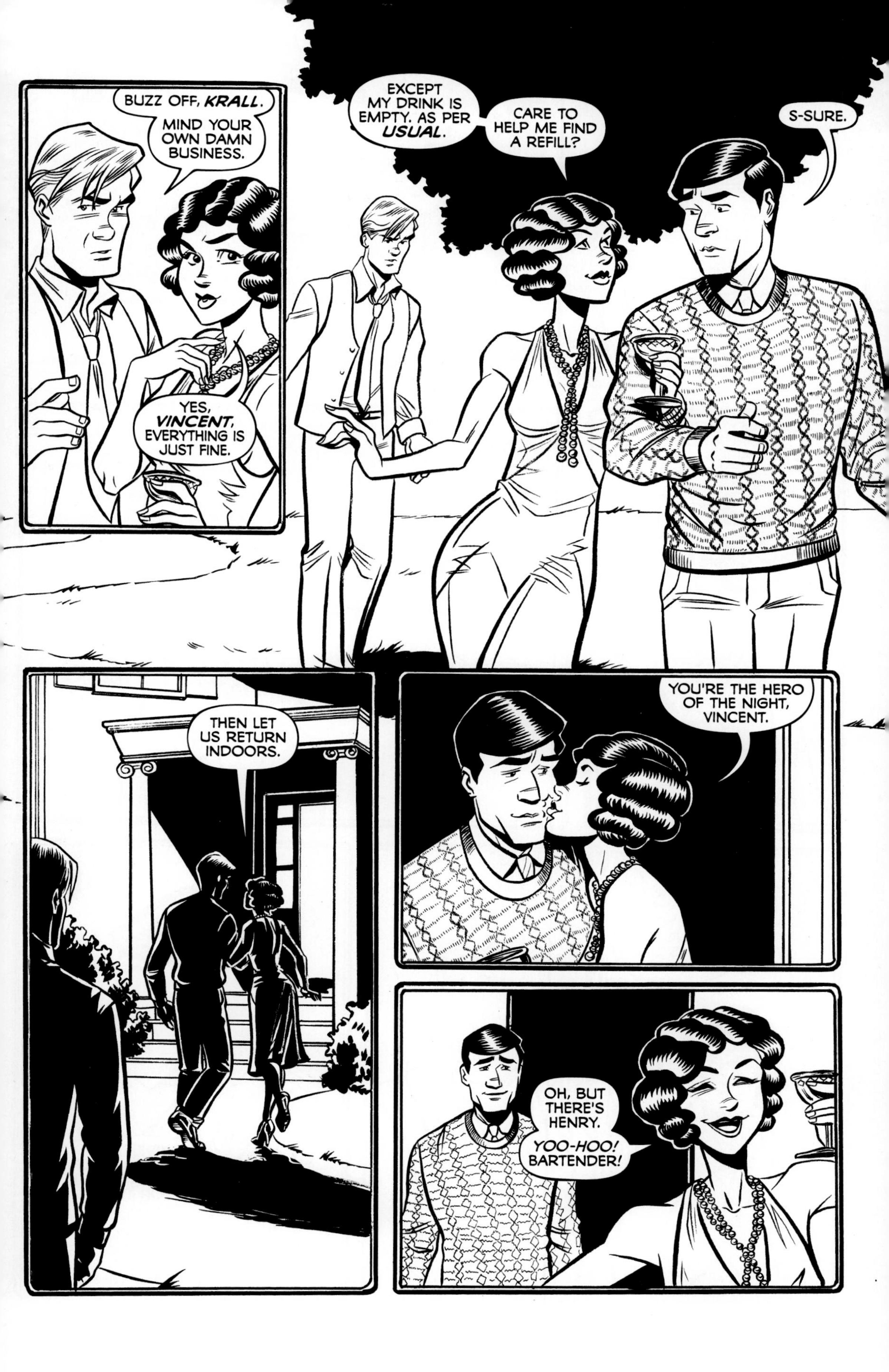
BUZZ OFF, KRALL.
MIND YOUR OWN DAMN BUSINESS.
YES, VINCENT, EVERYTHING IS JUST FINE.
EXCEPT MY DRINK IS EMPTY. AS PER USUAL.
CARE TO HELP ME FIND A REFILL?
S-SURE.
THEN LET US RETURN INDOORS.
YOU'RE THE HERO OF THE NIGHT, VINCENT.
OH, BUT THERE'S HENRY.
YOO-HOO! BARTENDER!

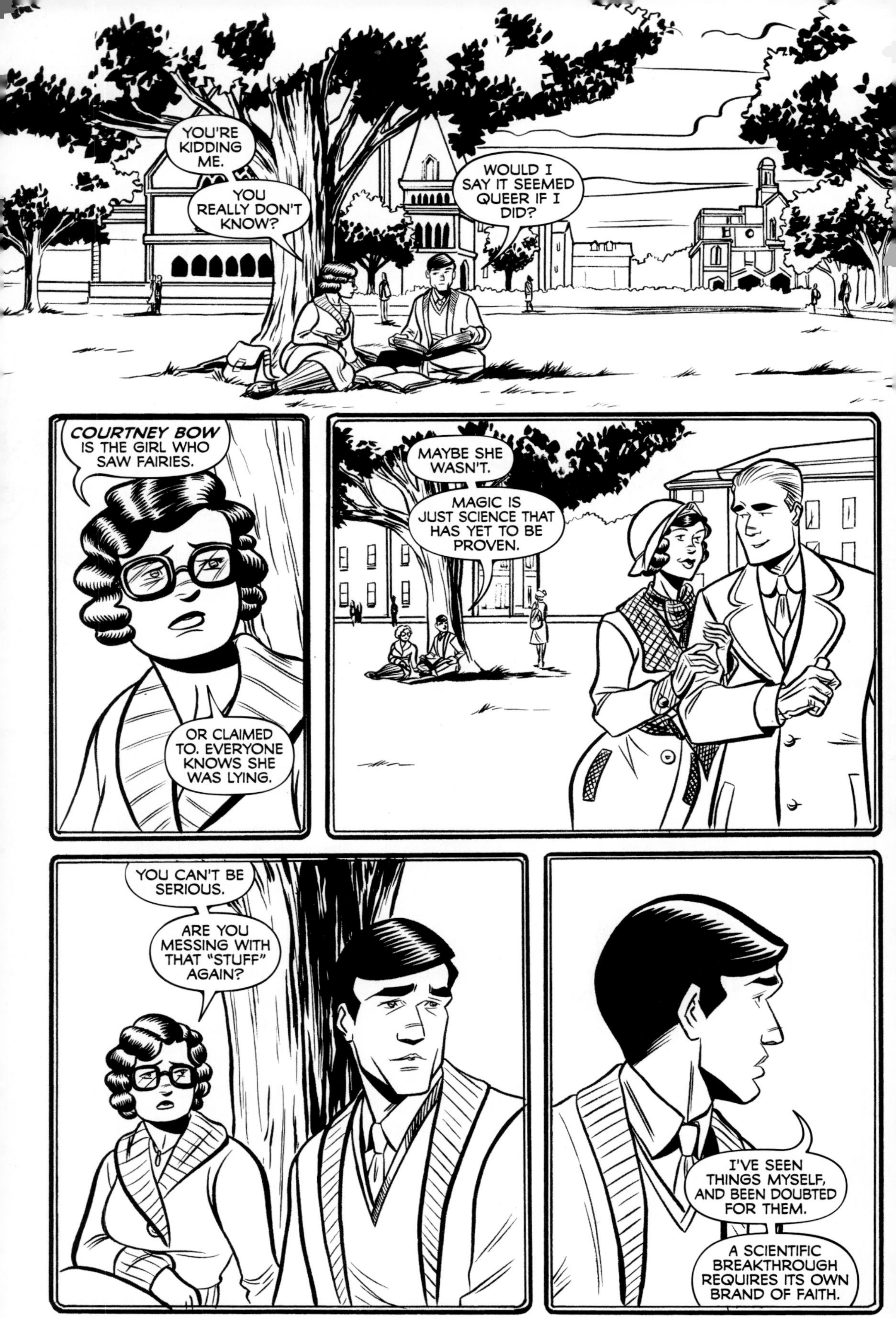
YOU'RE KIDDING ME.
YOU REALLY DON'T KNOW?
WOULD I SAY IT SEEMED QUEER IF I DID?
COURTNEY BOW IS THE GIRL WHO SAW FAIRIES.
OR CLAIMED TO. EVERYONE KNOWS SHE WAS LYING.
MAYBE SHE WASN'T.
MAGIC IS JUST SCIENCE THAT HAS YET TO BE PROVEN.
YOU CAN'T BE SERIOUS.
ARE YOU MESSING WITH THAT "STUFF" AGAIN?
I'VE SEEN THINGS MYSELF, AND BEEN DOUBTED FOR THEM.
A SCIENTIFIC BREAKTHROUGH REQUIRES ITS OWN BRAND OF FAITH.

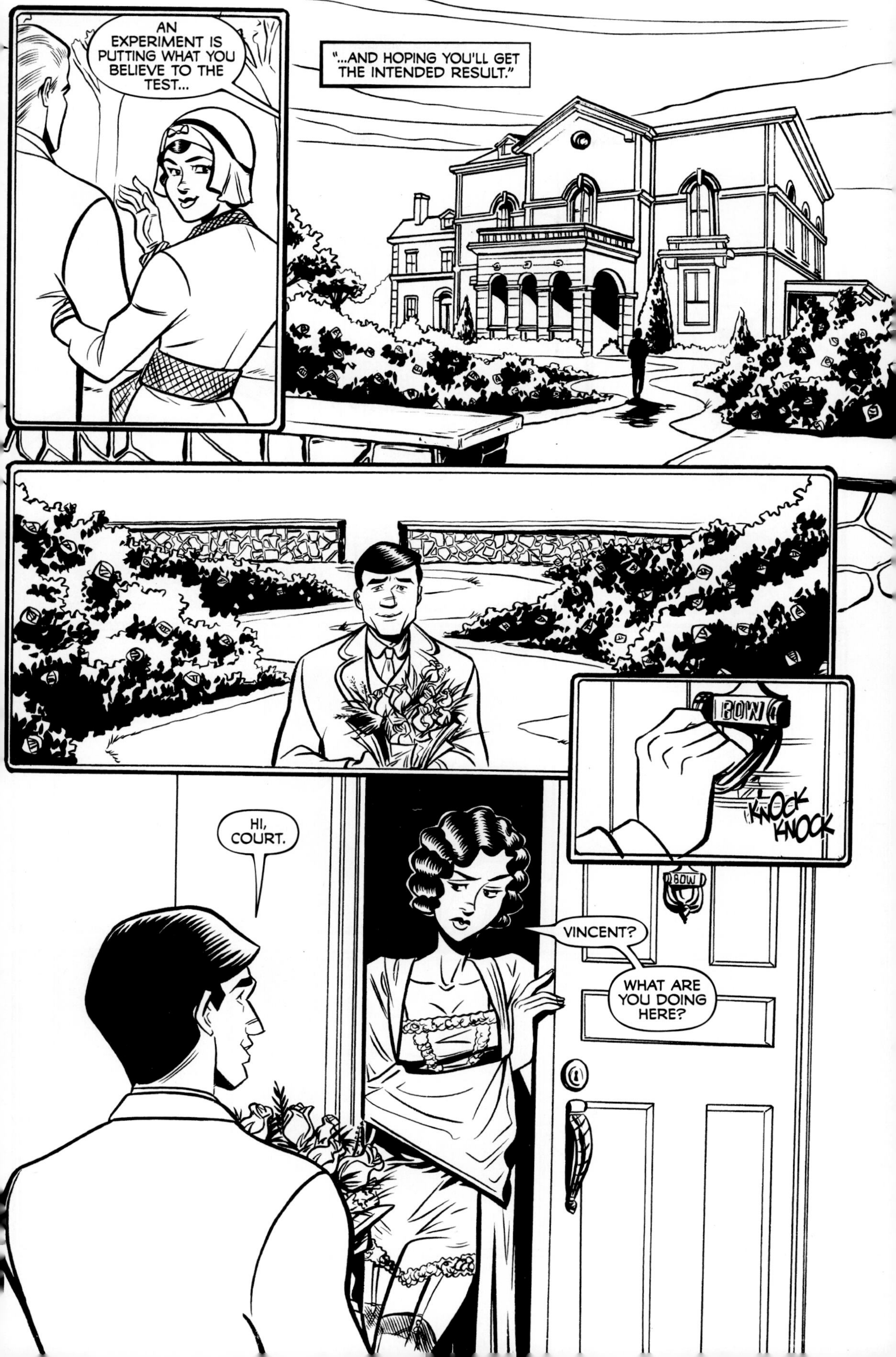
AN EXPERIMENT IS PUTTING WHAT YOU BELIEVE TO THE TEST...
"...AND HOPING YOU'LL GET THE INTENDED RESULT."
BOW
KNOCK KNOCK
HI, COURT.
BOW
VINCENT?
WHAT ARE YOU DOING HERE?

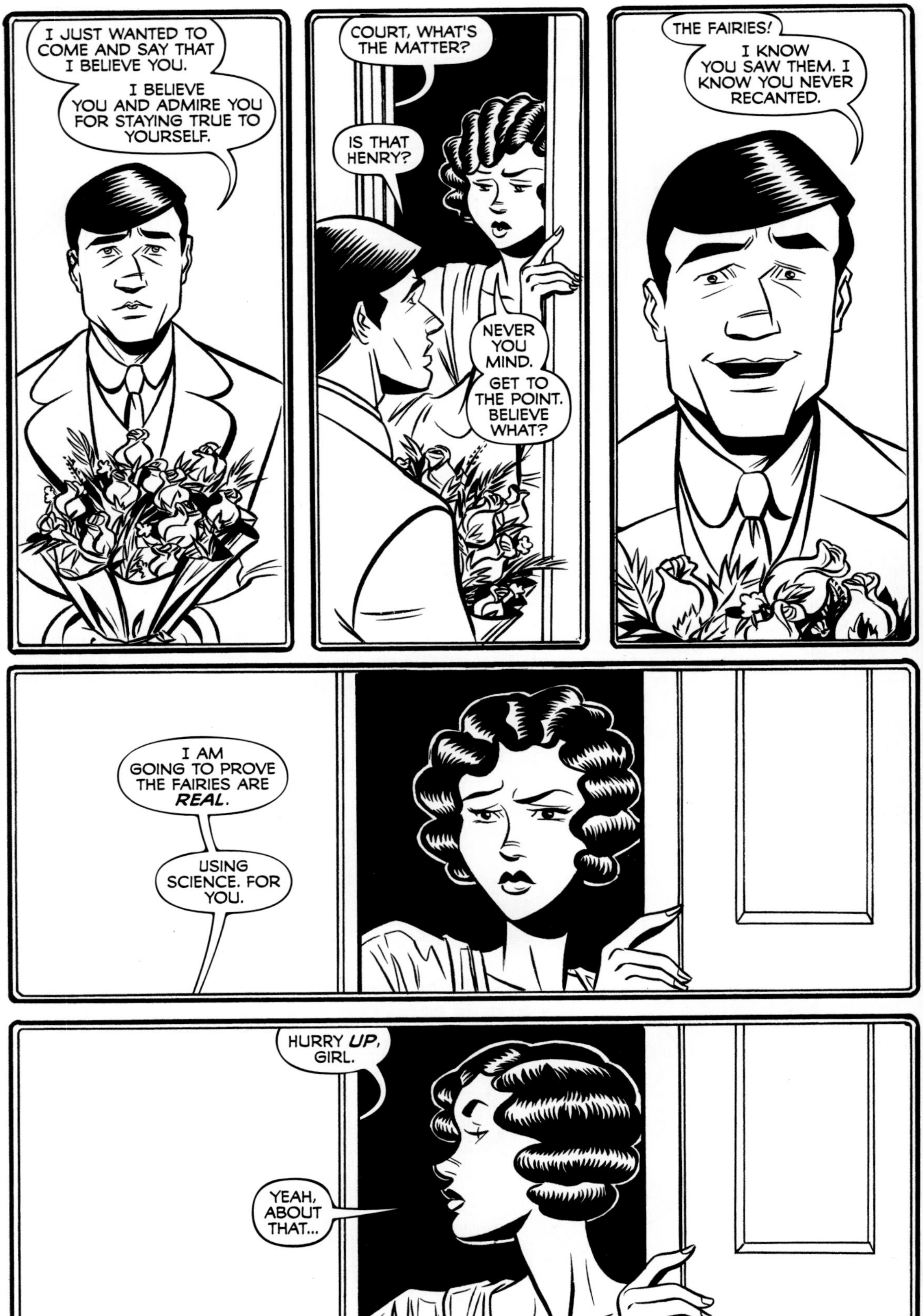
I JUST WANTED TO COME AND SAY THAT I BELIEVE YOU.
I BELIEVE YOU AND ADMIRE YOU FOR STAYING TRUE TO YOURSELF.
COURT, WHAT'S THE MATTER?
IS THAT HENRY?
NEVER YOU MIND.
GET TO THE POINT. BELIEVE WHAT?
THE FAIRIES!
I KNOW YOU SAW THEM. I KNOW YOU NEVER RECANTED.
I AM GOING TO PROVE THE FAIRIES ARE *REAL*.
USING SCIENCE. FOR YOU.
HURRY *UP*, GIRL.
YEAH, ABOUT THAT...

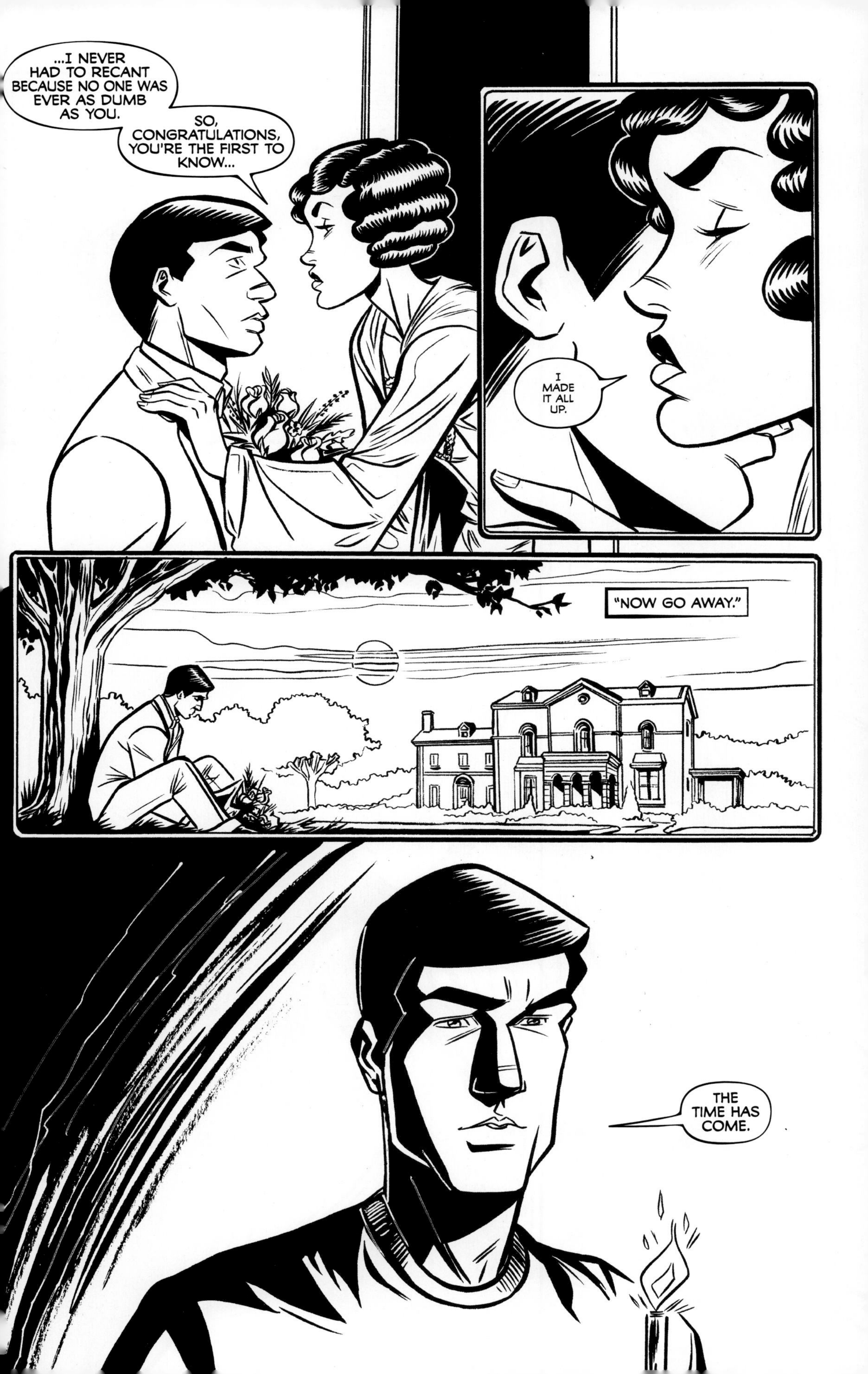

...I NEVER HAD TO RECANT BECAUSE NO ONE WAS EVER AS DUMB AS YOU.
SO, CONGRATULATIONS, YOU'RE THE FIRST TO KNOW...
I MADE IT ALL UP.
"NOW GO AWAY."
THE TIME HAS COME.

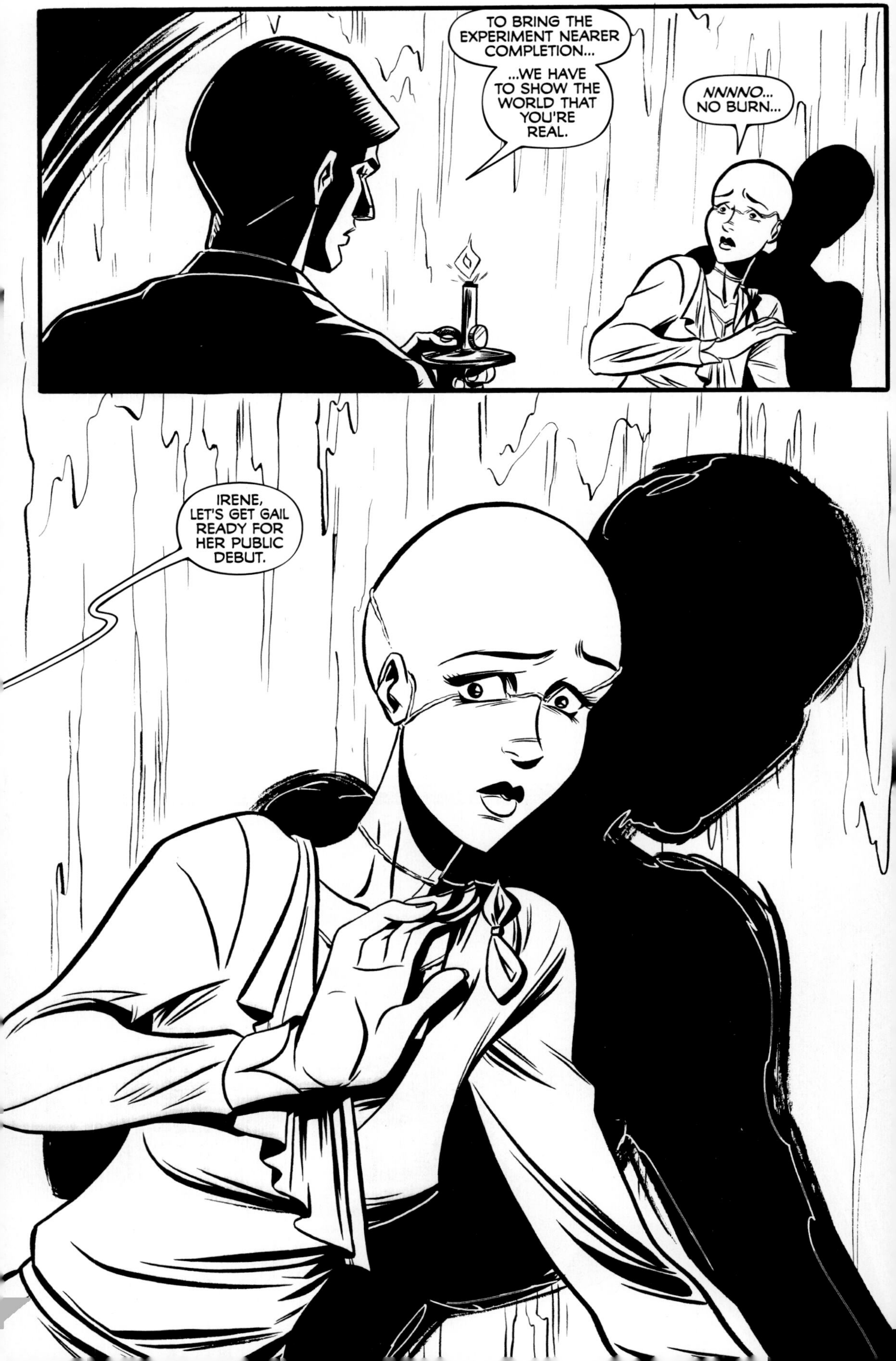

TO BRING THE EXPERIMENT NEARER COMPLETION...
...WE HAVE TO SHOW THE WORLD THAT YOU'RE REAL.
NNNNO... NO BURN...
IRENE, LET'S GET GAIL READY FOR HER PUBLIC DEBUT.

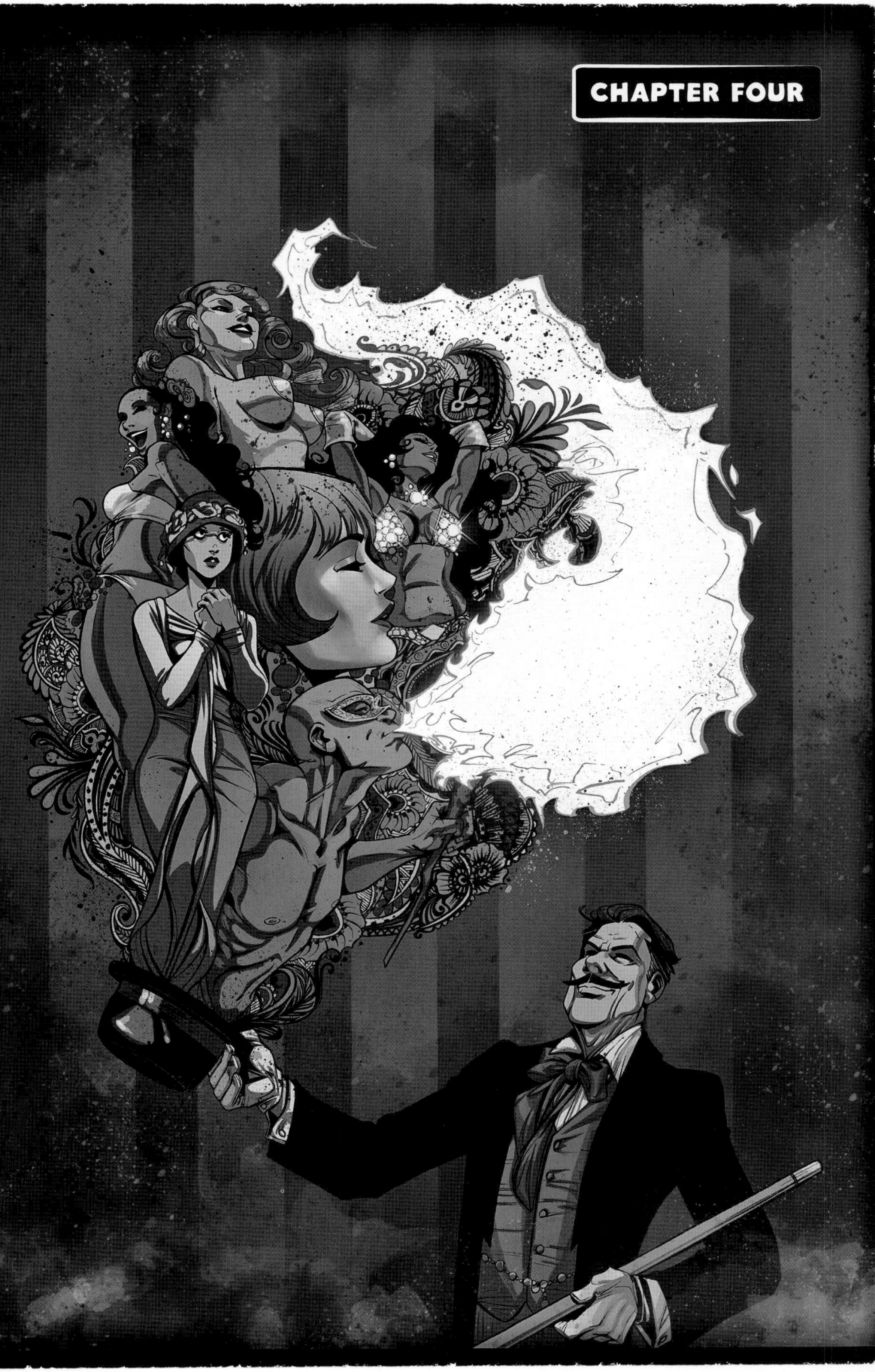
CHAPTER FOUR

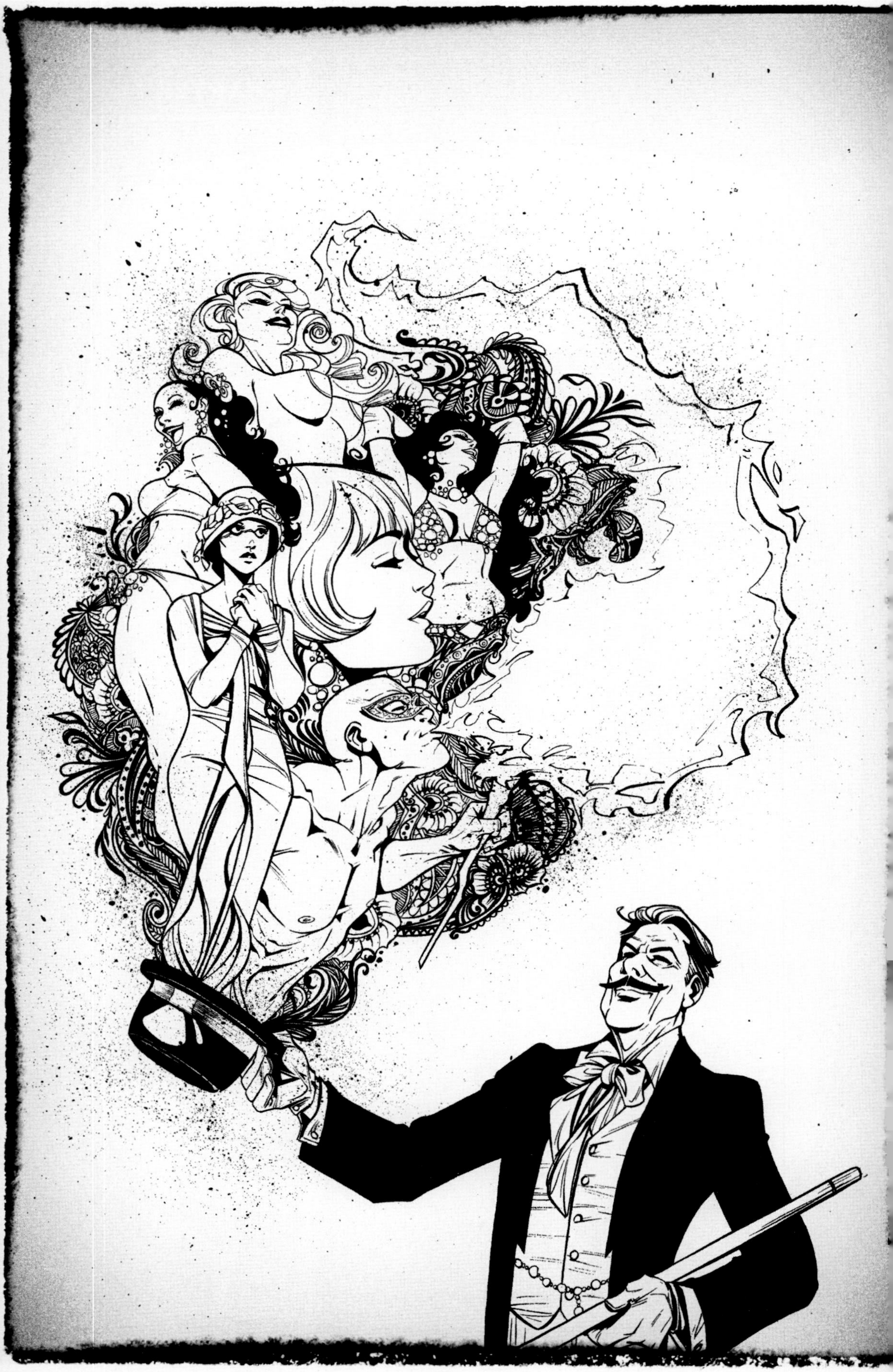

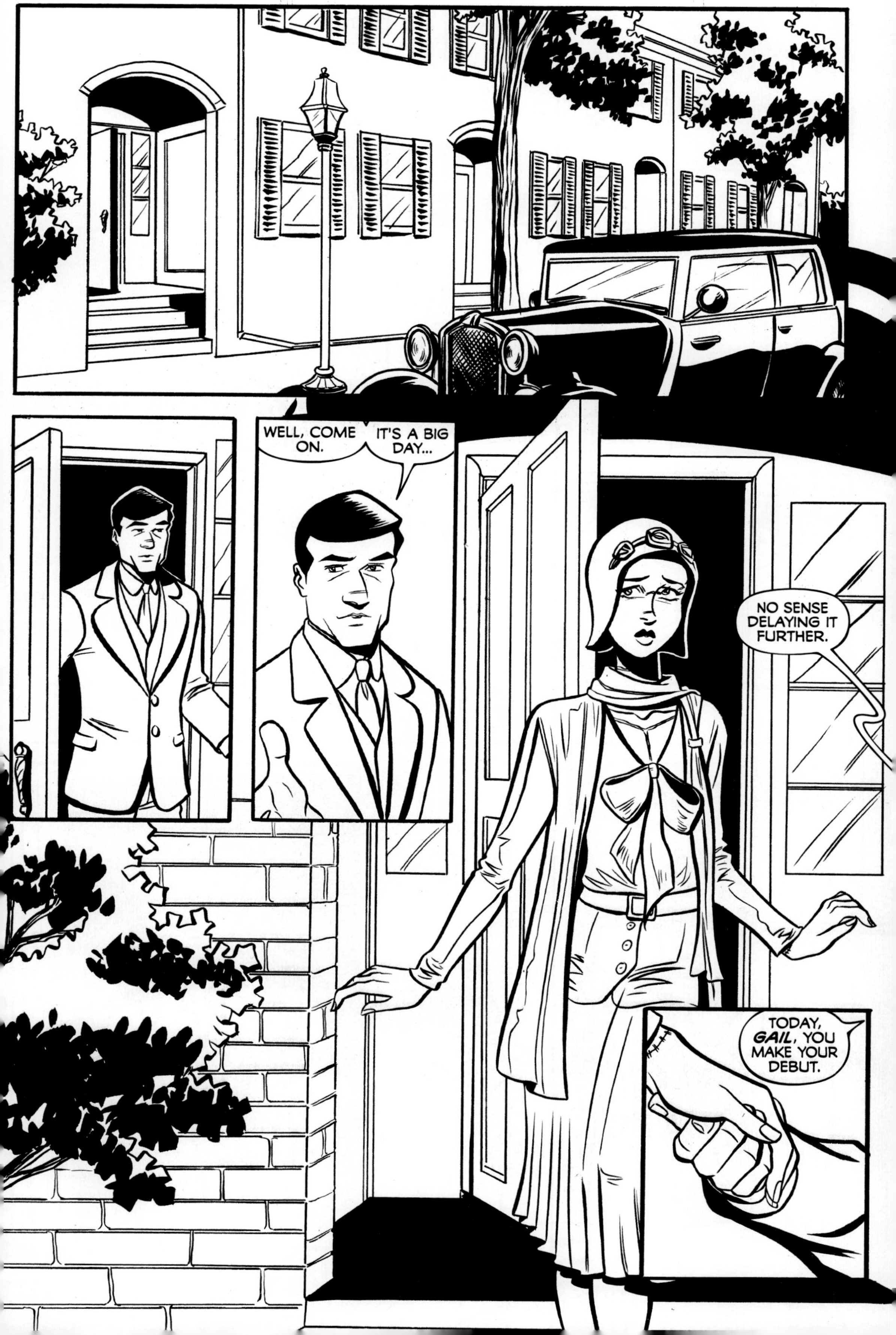

WELL, COME ON.
IT'S A BIG DAY...
NO SENSE DELAYING IT FURTHER.
TODAY, GAIL, YOU MAKE YOUR DEBUT.

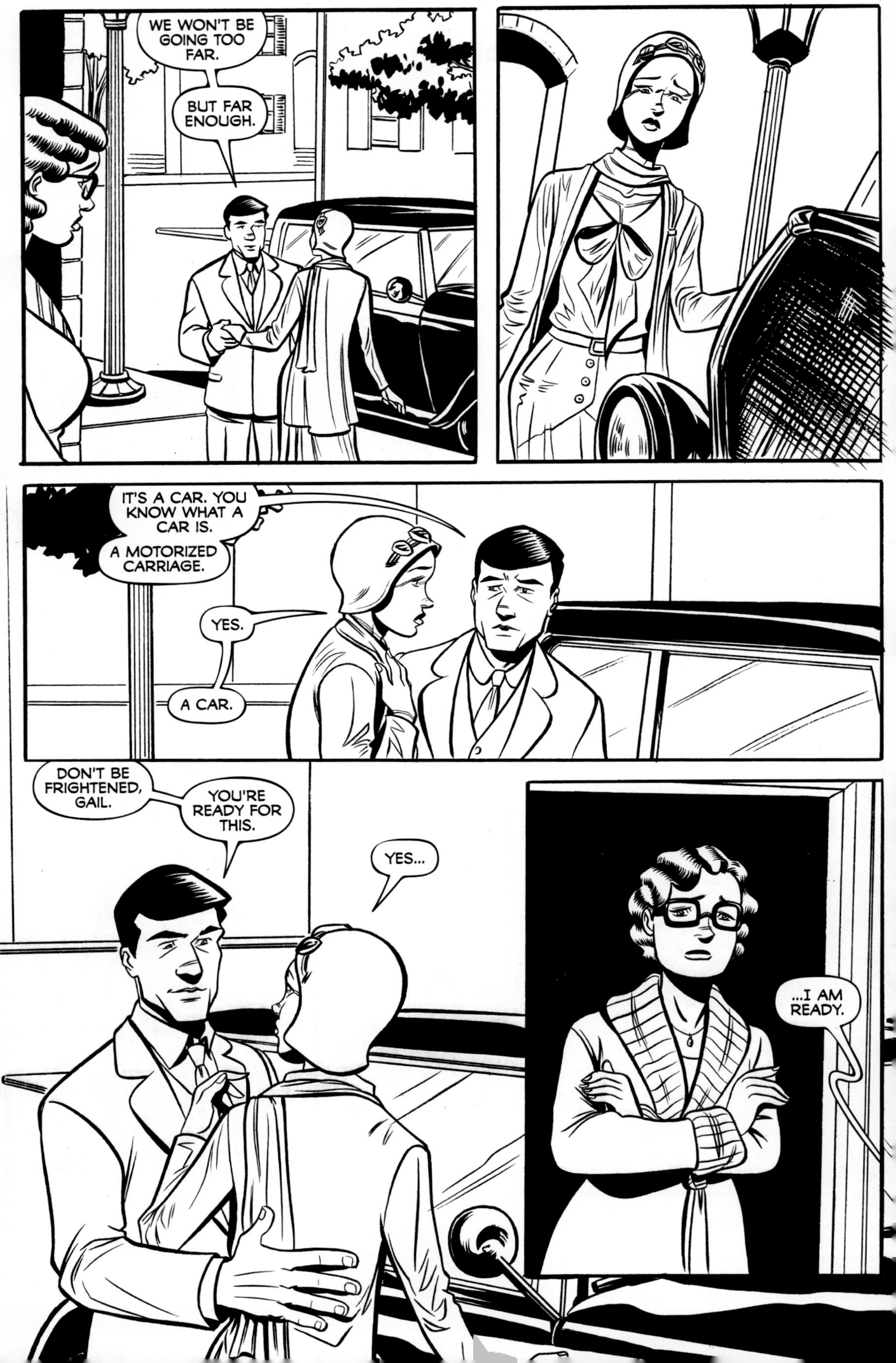
WE WON'T BE GOING TOO FAR.
BUT FAR ENOUGH.
IT'S A CAR. YOU KNOW WHAT A CAR IS.
A MOTORIZED CARRIAGE.
YES.
A CAR.
DON'T BE FRIGHTENED, GAIL.
YOU'RE READY FOR THIS.
YES...
...I AM READY.

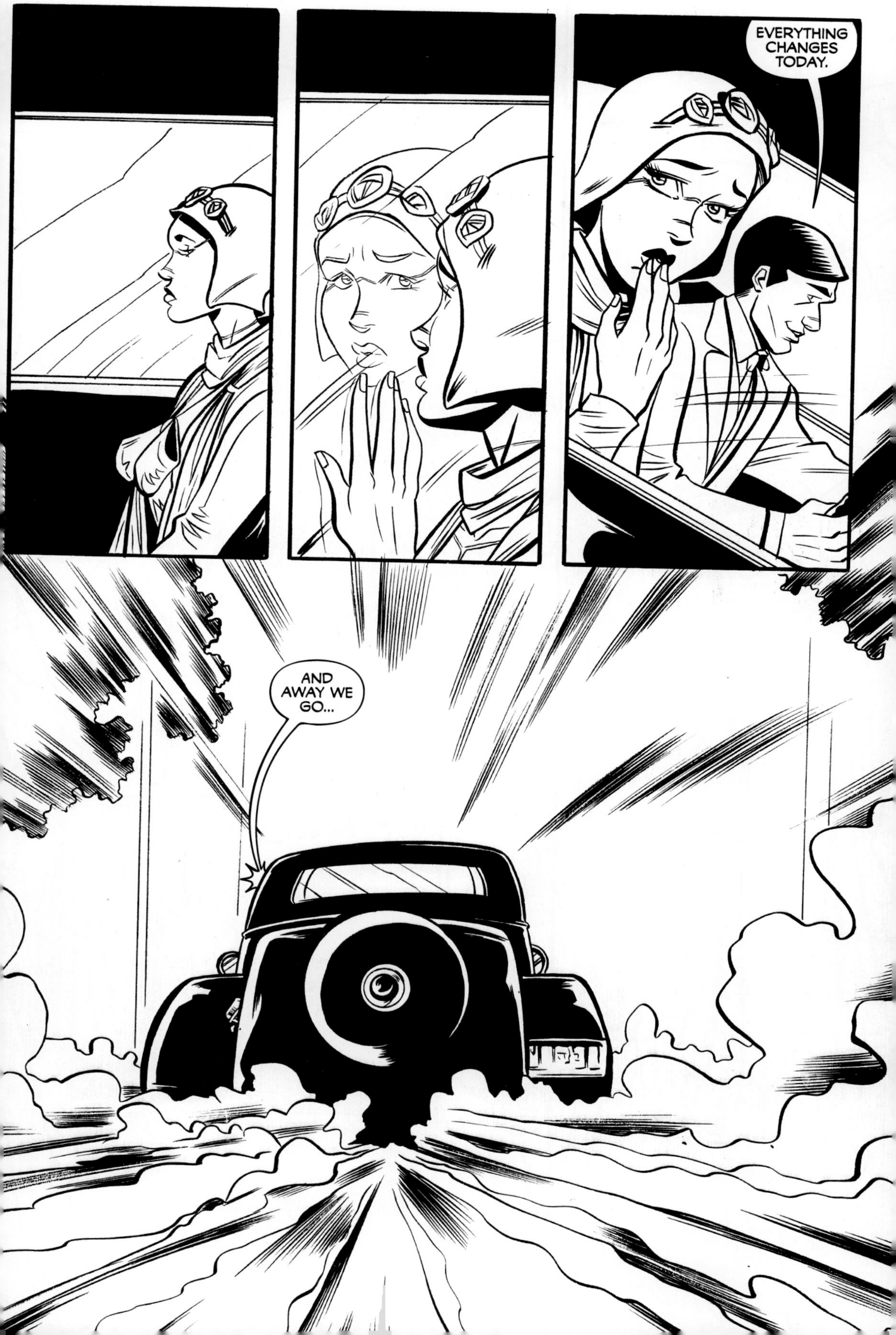
EVERYTHING CHANGES TODAY.
AND AWAY WE GO...

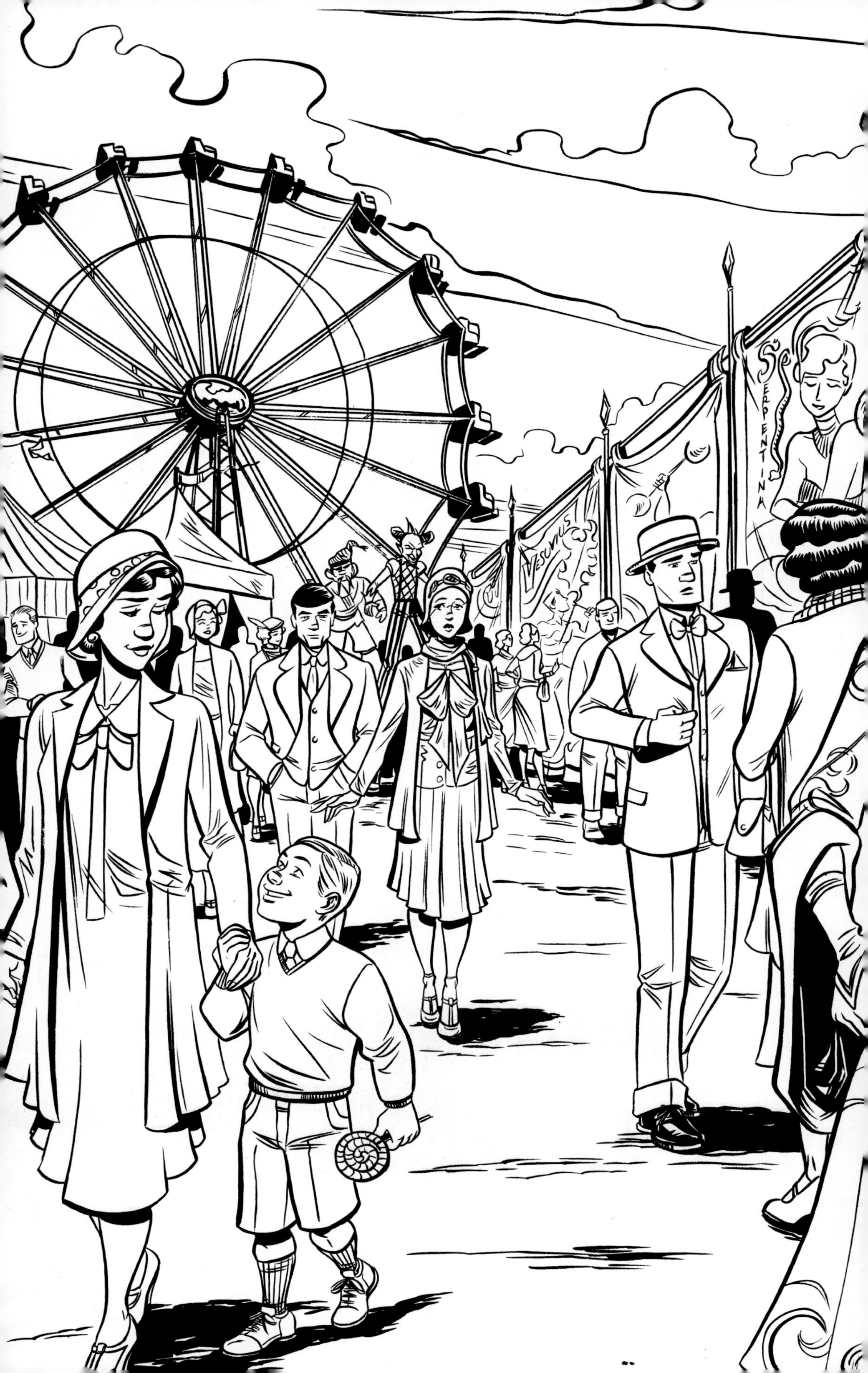
VESUVIUS
SERPENTINA

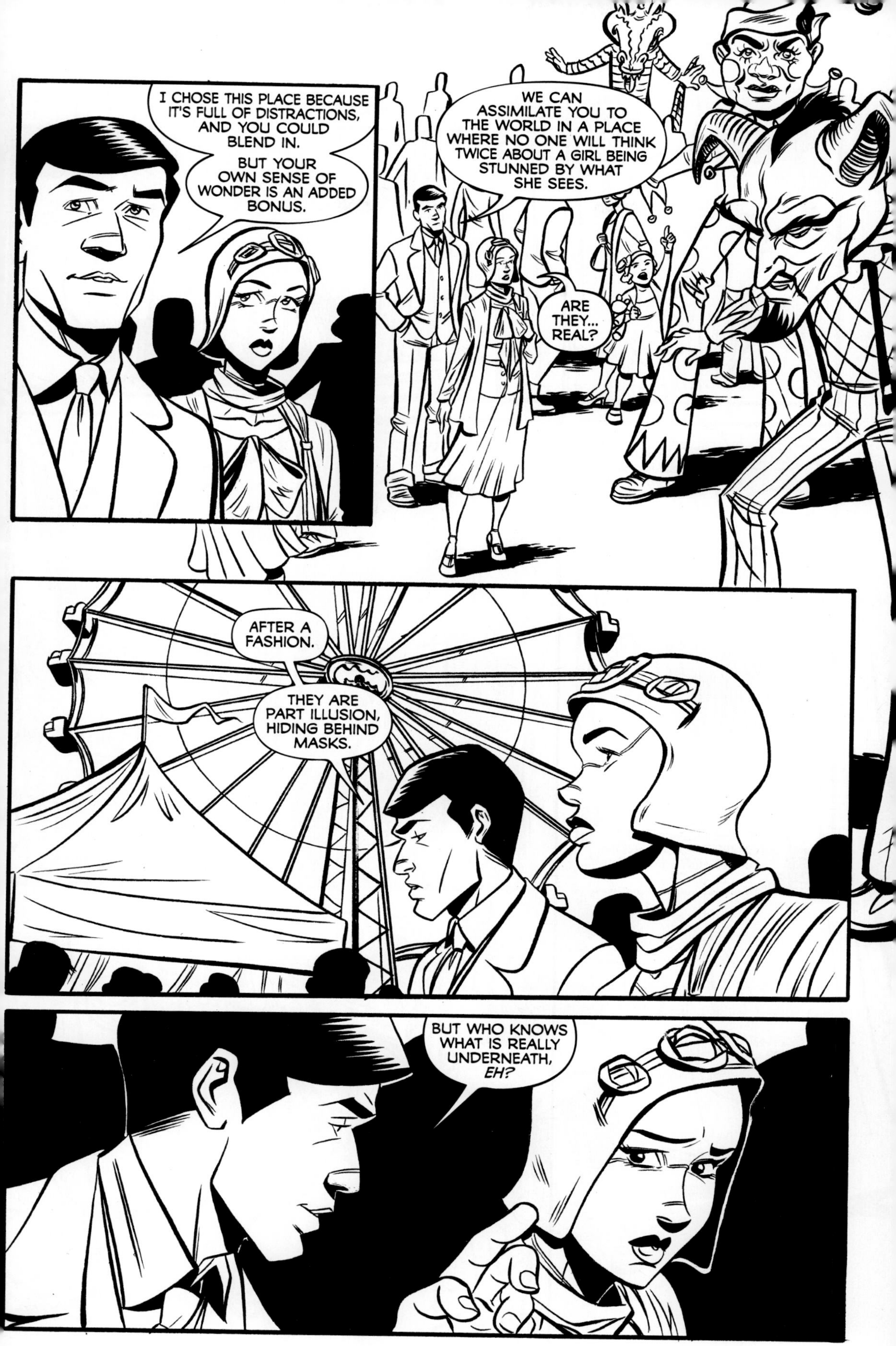
I CHOSE THIS PLACE BECAUSE IT'S FULL OF DISTRACTIONS, AND YOU COULD BLEND IN.
BUT YOUR OWN SENSE OF WONDER IS AN ADDED BONUS.
WE CAN ASSIMILATE YOU TO THE WORLD IN A PLACE WHERE NO ONE WILL THINK TWICE ABOUT A GIRL BEING STUNNED BY WHAT SHE SEES.
ARE THEY... REAL?
AFTER A FASHION.
THEY ARE PART ILLUSION, HIDING BEHIND MASKS.
BUT WHO KNOWS WHAT IS REALLY UNDERNEATH, *EH?*

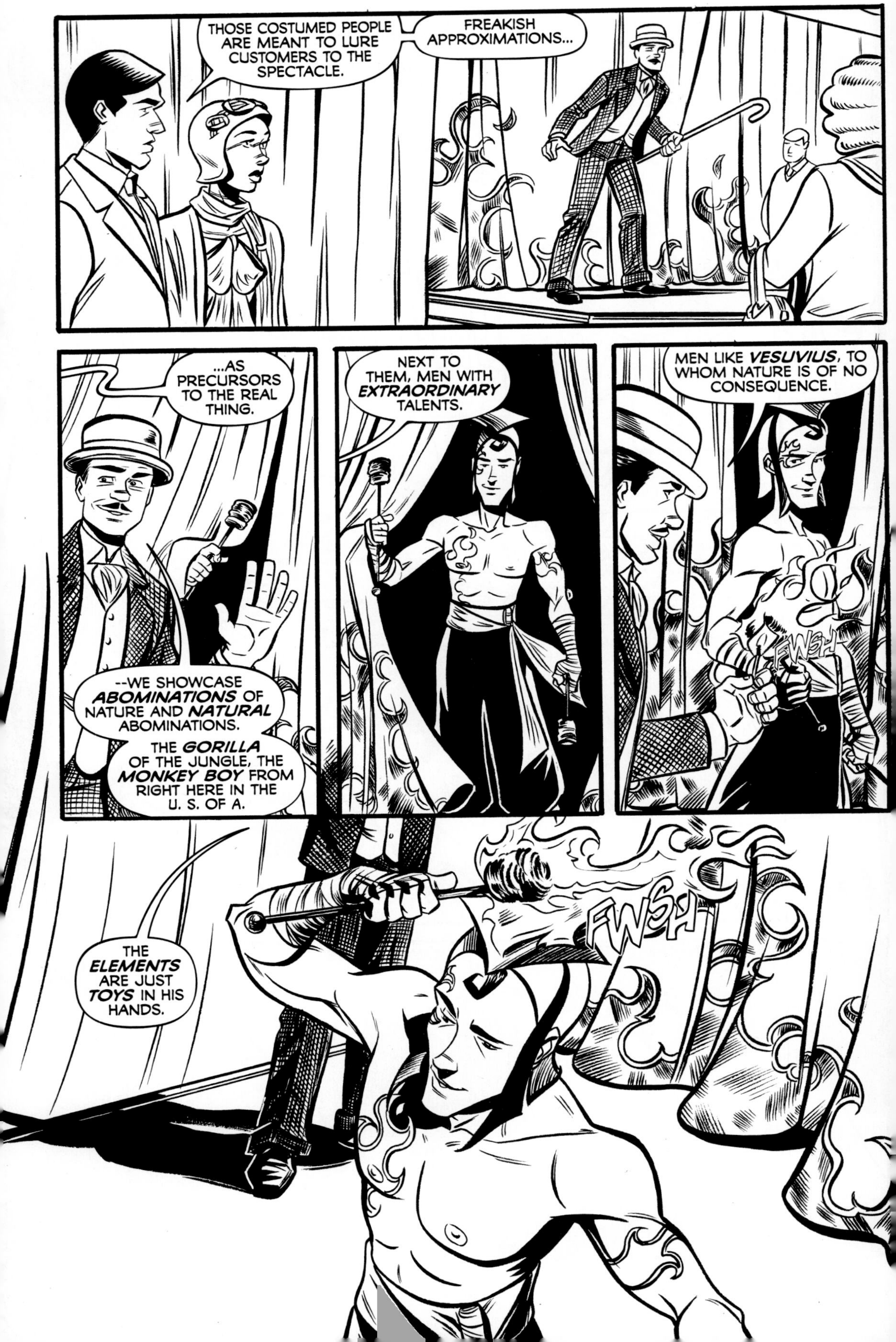
THOSE COSTUMED PEOPLE ARE MEANT TO LURE CUSTOMERS TO THE SPECTACLE.
FREAKISH APPROXIMATIONS...
...AS PRECURSORS TO THE REAL THING.
--WE SHOWCASE ABOMINATIONS OF NATURE AND NATURAL ABOMINATIONS.
THE GORILLA OF THE JUNGLE, THE MONKEY BOY FROM RIGHT HERE IN THE U. S. OF A.
NEXT TO THEM, MEN WITH EXTRAORDINARY TALENTS.
MEN LIKE VESUVIUS, TO WHOM NATURE IS OF NO CONSEQUENCE.
FWSH
THE ELEMENTS ARE JUST TOYS IN HIS HANDS.
FWSH

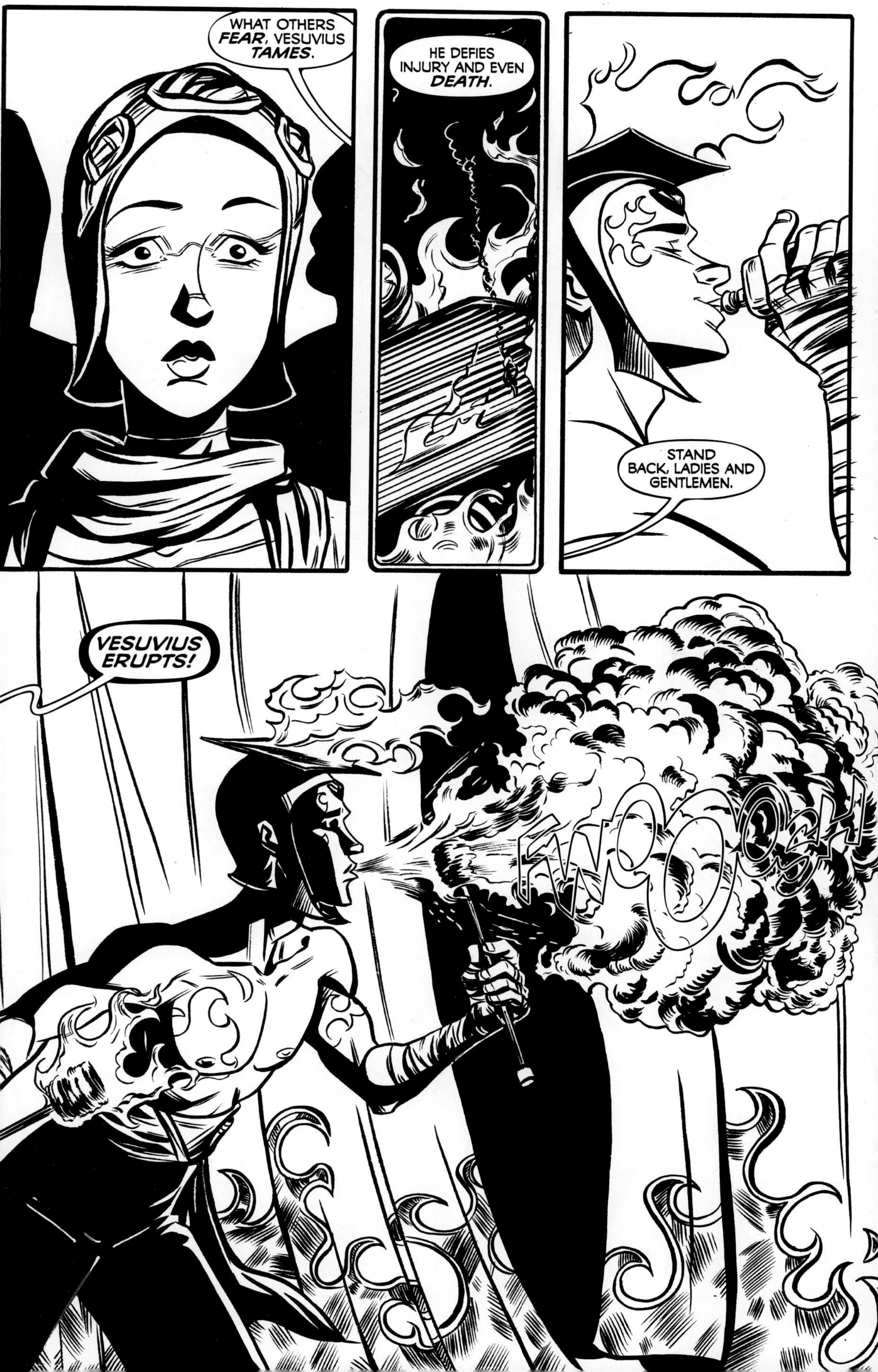
WHAT OTHERS FEAR, VESUVIUS TAMES.
HE DEFIES INJURY AND EVEN DEATH.
STAND BACK, LADIES AND GENTLEMEN.
VESUVIUS ERUPTS!
FWOOOOSH

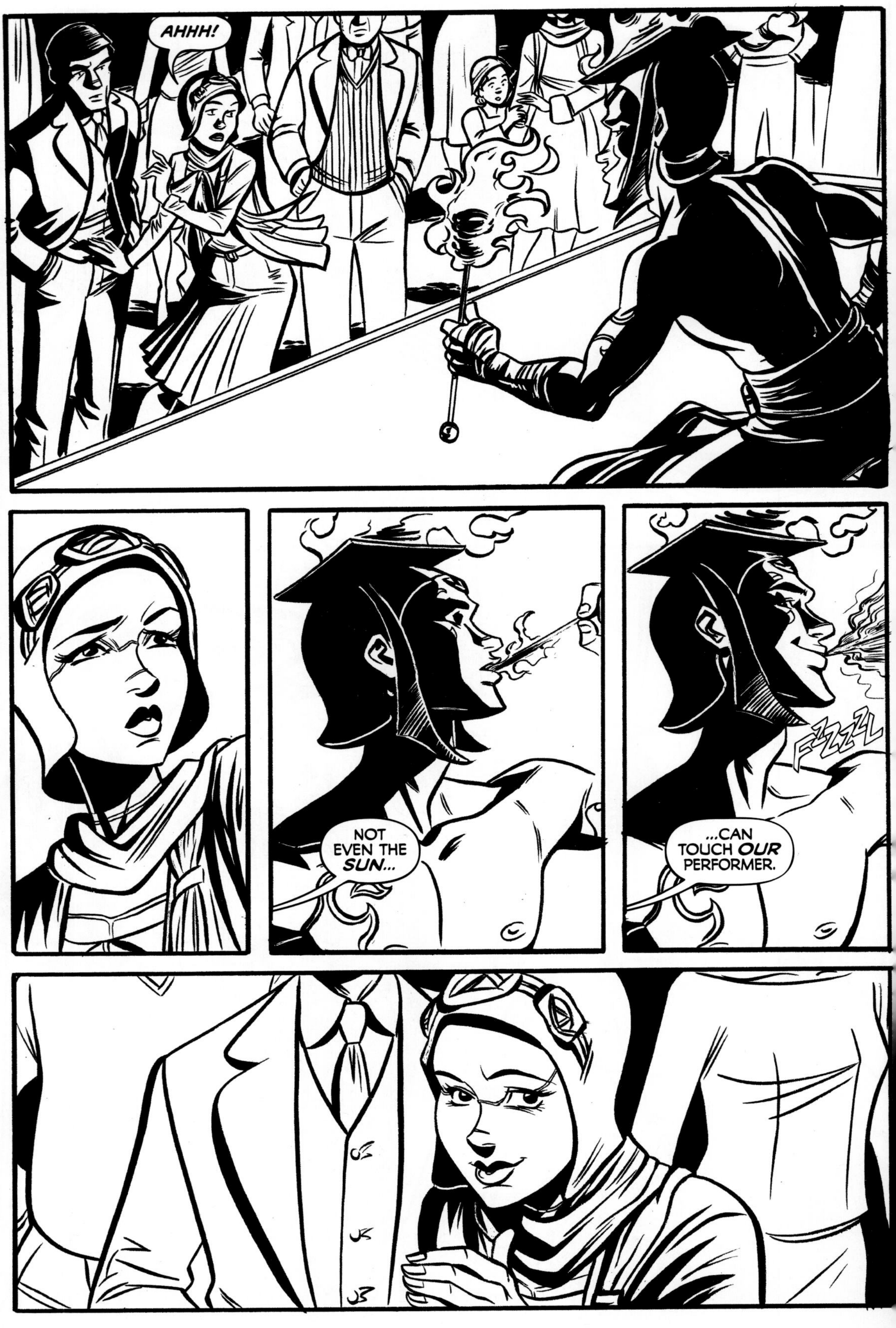
AHHH!
NOT EVEN THE SUN...
...CAN TOUCH OUR PERFORMER.
FZZZZ

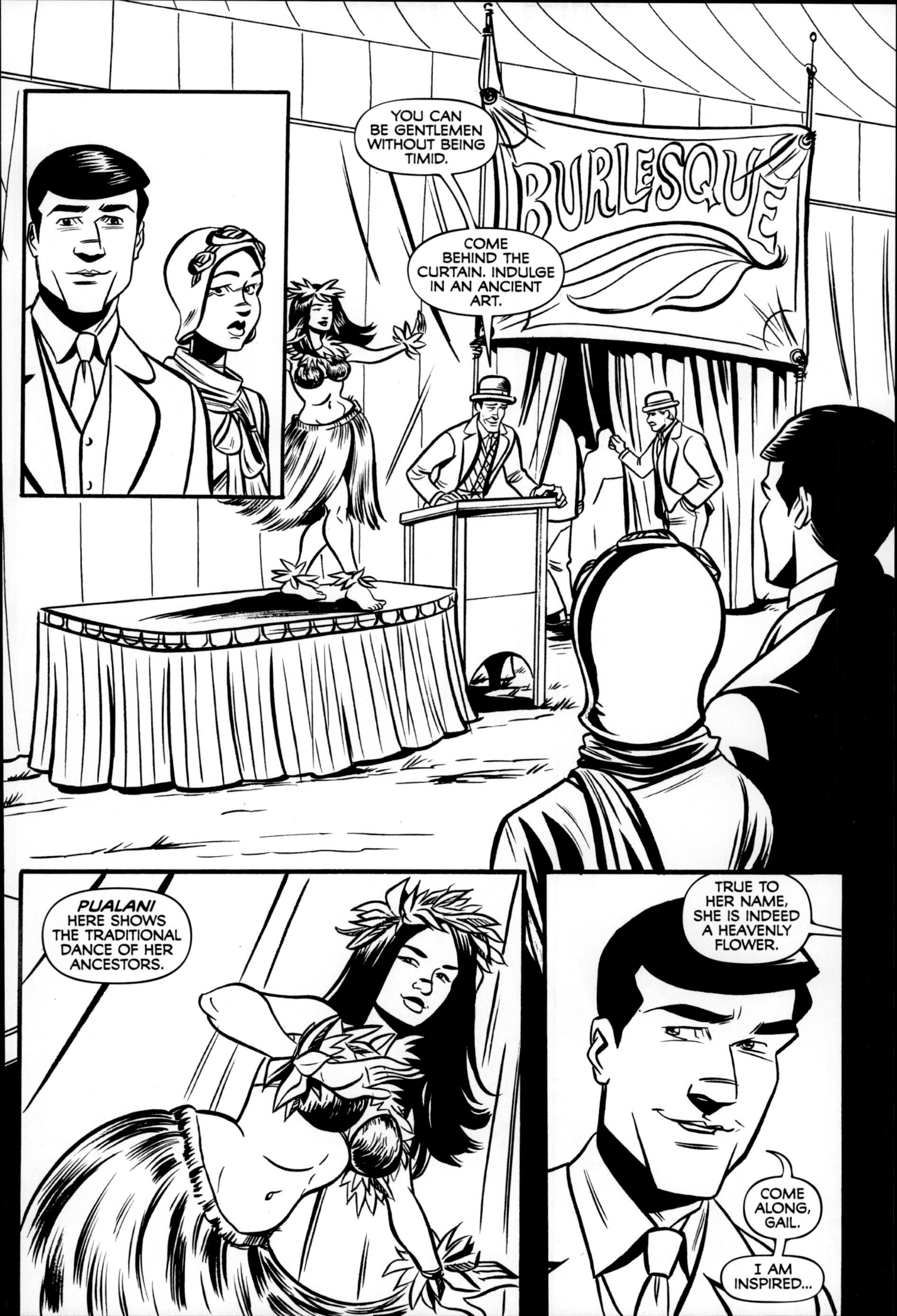
YOU CAN BE GENTLEMEN WITHOUT BEING TIMID.
BURLESQUE
COME BEHIND THE CURTAIN. INDULGE IN AN ANCIENT ART.
PUALANI HERE SHOWS THE TRADITIONAL DANCE OF HER ANCESTORS.
TRUE TO HER NAME, SHE IS INDEED A HEAVENLY FLOWER.
COME ALONG, GAIL.
I AM INSPIRED...

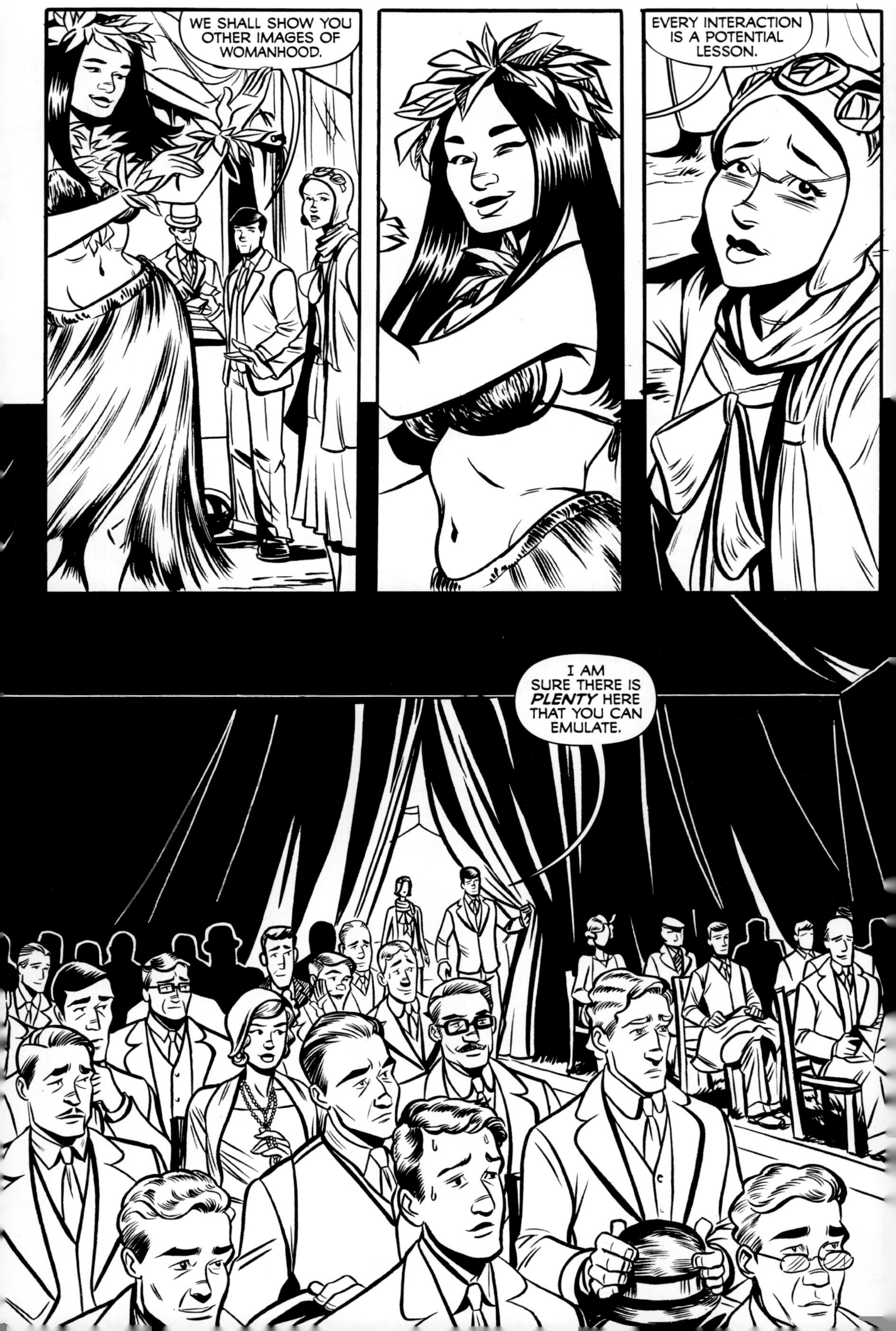
WE SHALL SHOW YOU OTHER IMAGES OF WOMANHOOD.
EVERY INTERACTION IS A POTENTIAL LESSON.
I AM SURE THERE IS *PLENTY* HERE THAT YOU CAN EMULATE.

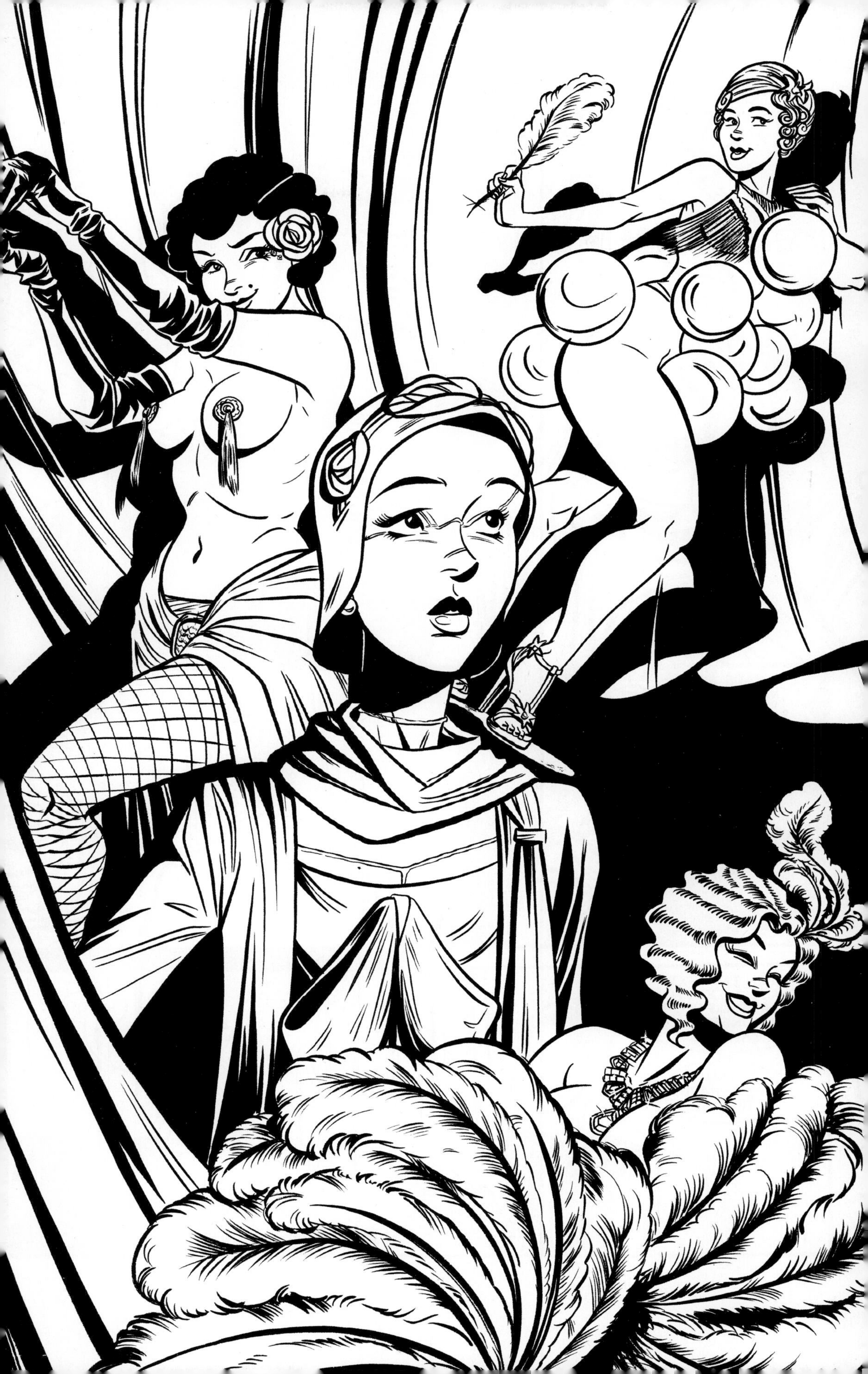

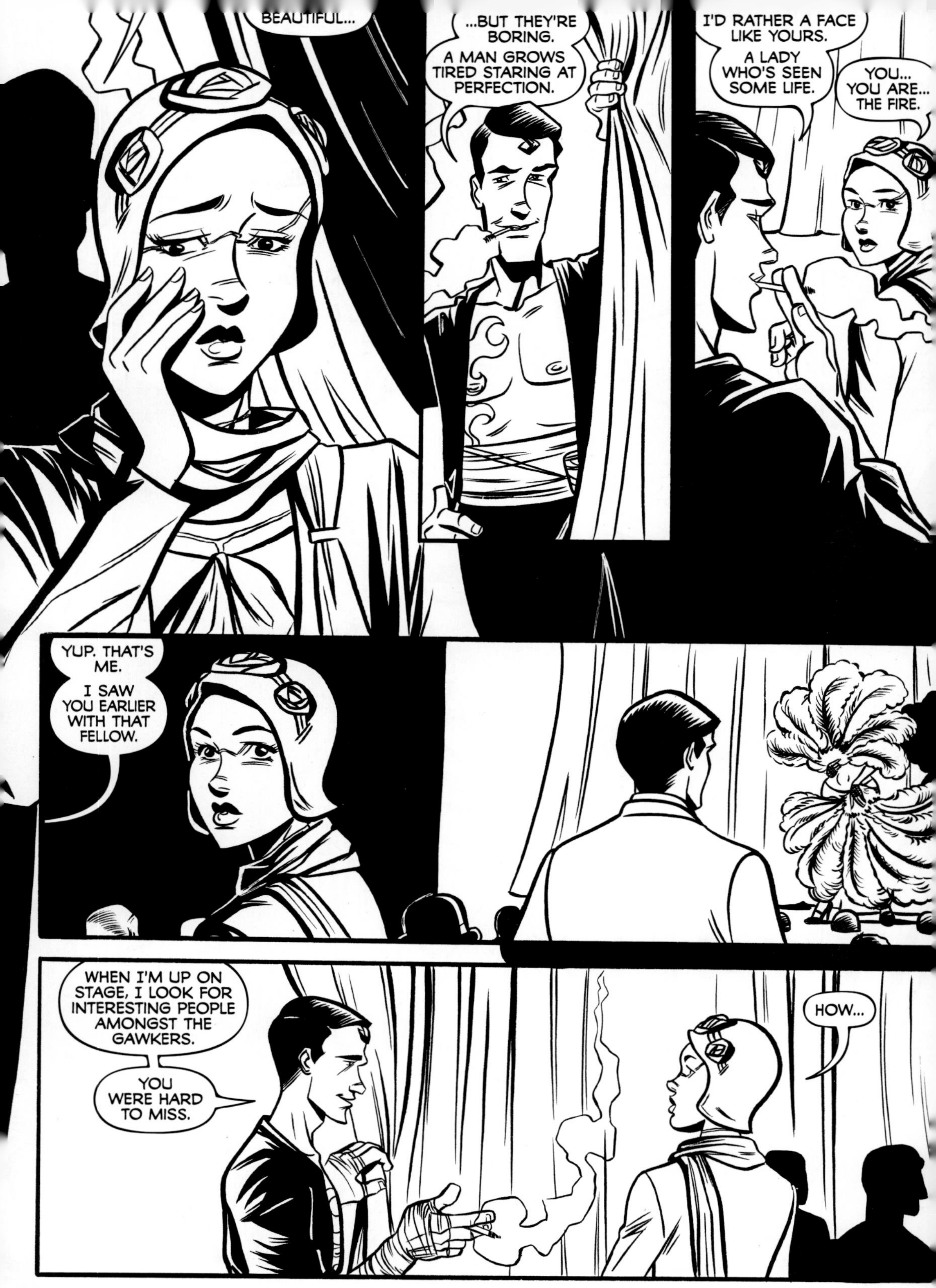
BEAUTIFUL...
...BUT THEY'RE BORING.
A MAN GROWS TIRED STARING AT PERFECTION.
I'D RATHER A FACE LIKE YOURS.
A LADY WHO'S SEEN SOME LIFE.
YOU... YOU ARE... THE FIRE.
YUP. THAT'S ME.
I SAW YOU EARLIER WITH THAT FELLOW.
WHEN I'M UP ON STAGE, I LOOK FOR INTERESTING PEOPLE AMONGST THE GAWKERS.
YOU WERE HARD TO MISS.
HOW...

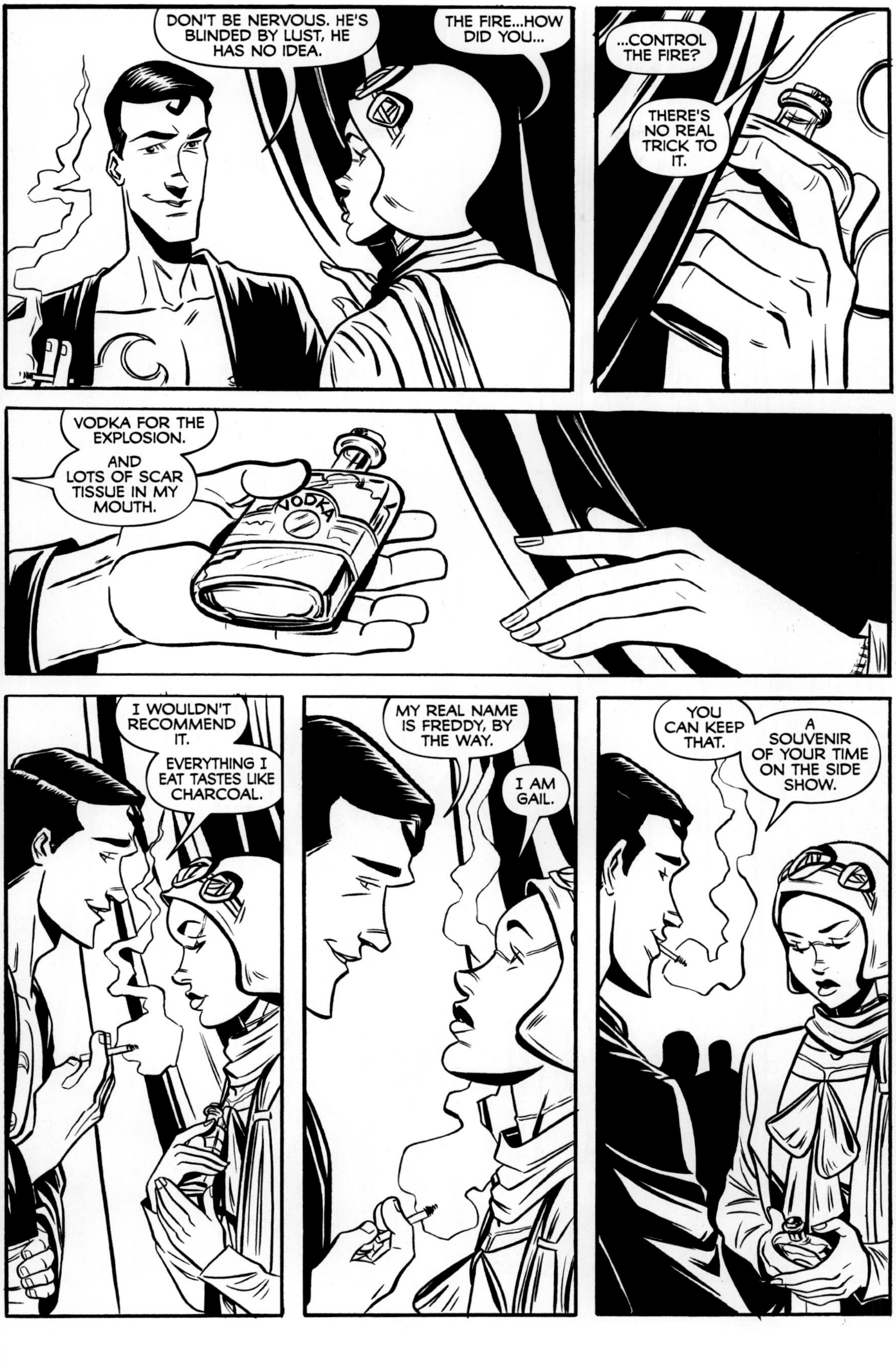
DON'T BE NERVOUS. HE'S BLINDED BY LUST, HE HAS NO IDEA.
THE FIRE...HOW DID YOU...
...CONTROL THE FIRE?
THERE'S NO REAL TRICK TO IT.
VODKA FOR THE EXPLOSION.
AND LOTS OF SCAR TISSUE IN MY MOUTH.
VODKA
I WOULDN'T RECOMMEND IT.
EVERYTHING I EAT TASTES LIKE CHARCOAL.
MY REAL NAME IS FREDDY, BY THE WAY.
I AM GAIL.
YOU CAN KEEP THAT.
A SOUVENIR OF YOUR TIME ON THE SIDE SHOW.

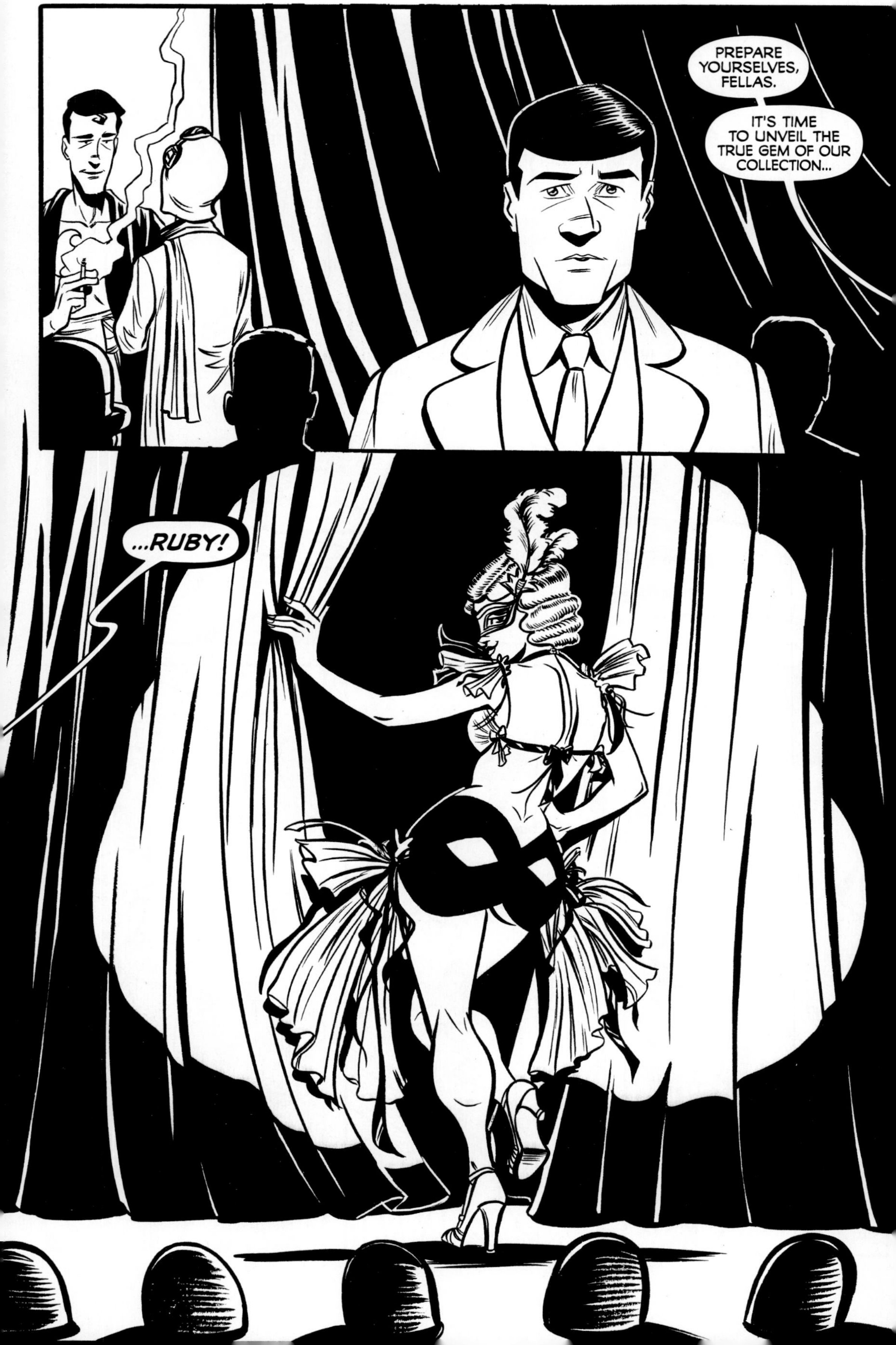
PREPARE YOURSELVES, FELLAS.
IT'S TIME TO UNVEIL THE TRUE GEM OF OUR COLLECTION...
...RUBY!

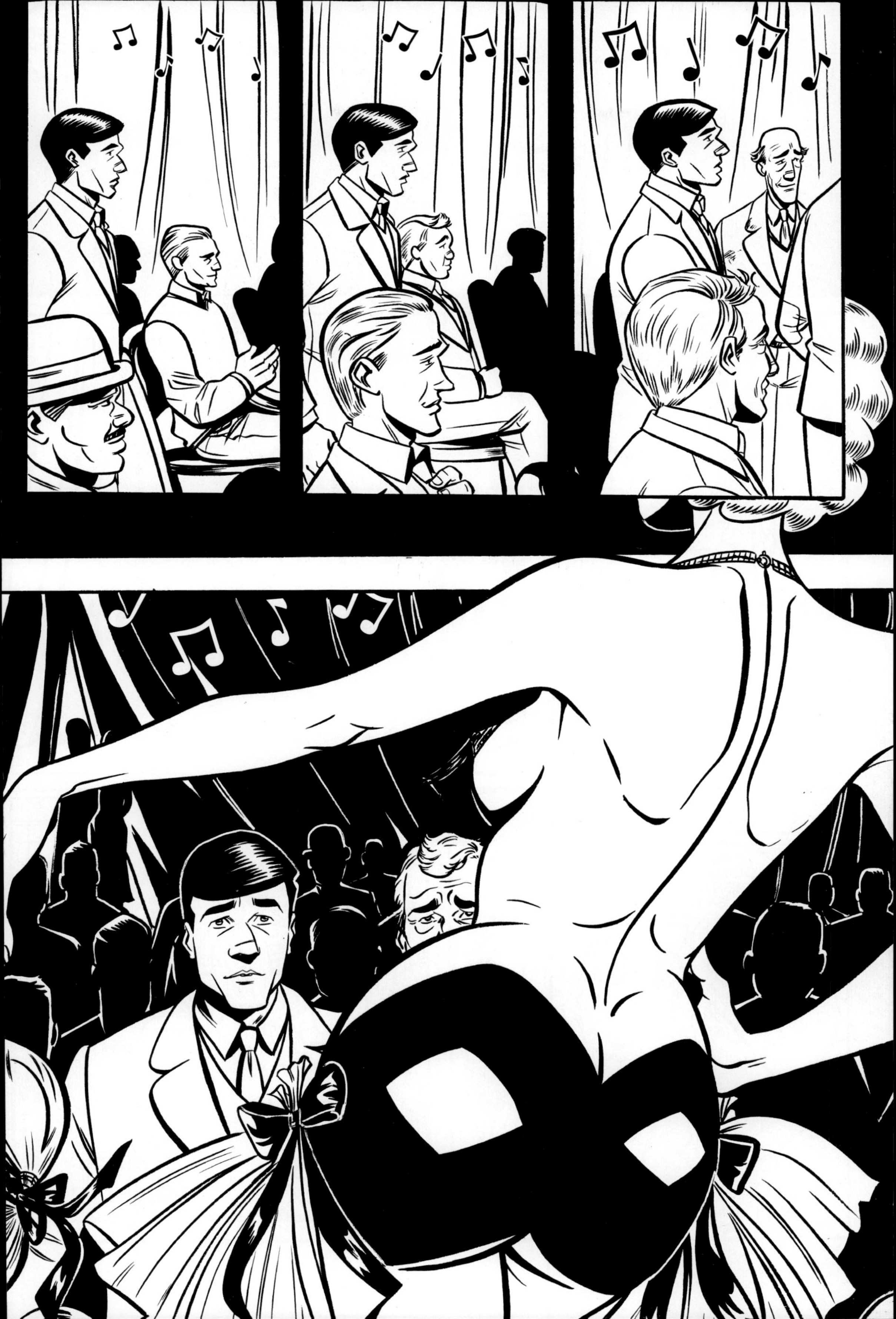

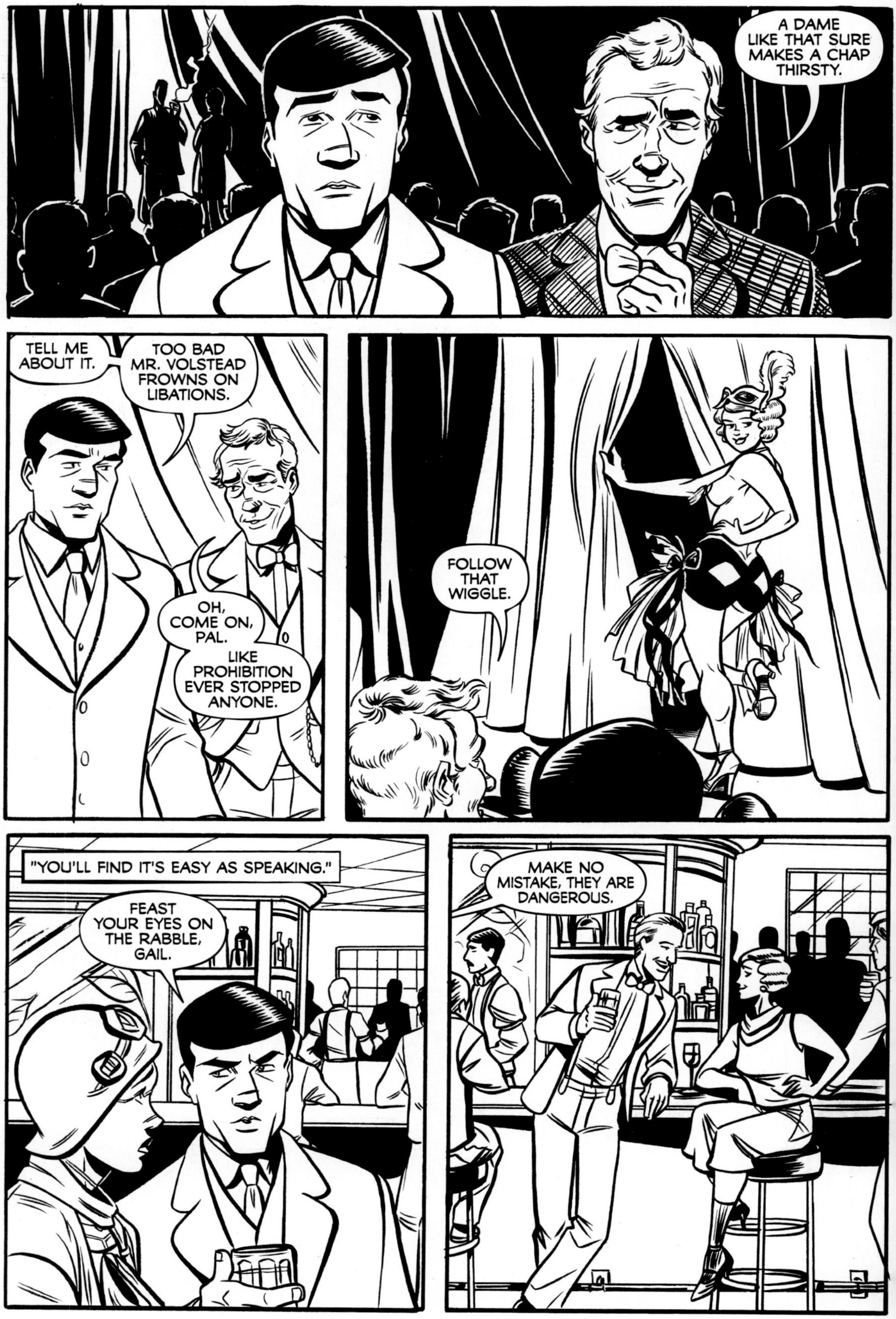
A DAME LIKE THAT SURE MAKES A CHAP THIRSTY.
TELL ME ABOUT IT.
TOO BAD MR. VOLSTEAD FROWNS ON LIBATIONS.
OH, COME ON, PAL.
LIKE PROHIBITION EVER STOPPED ANYONE.
FOLLOW THAT WIGGLE.
"YOU'LL FIND IT'S EASY AS SPEAKING."
FEAST YOUR EYES ON THE RABBLE, GAIL.
MAKE NO MISTAKE, THEY ARE DANGEROUS.

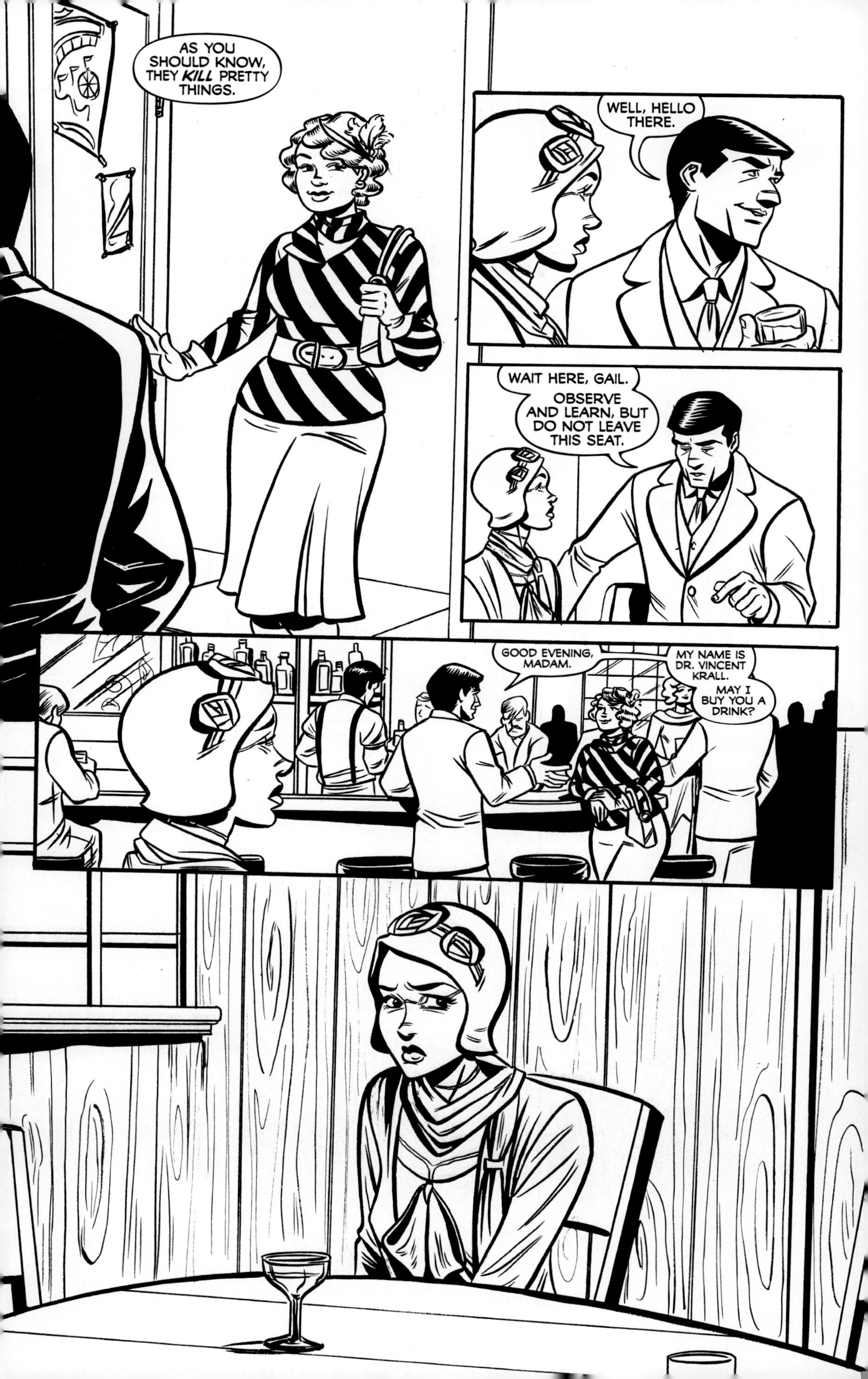
AS YOU SHOULD KNOW, THEY KILL PRETTY THINGS.
WELL, HELLO THERE.
WAIT HERE, GAIL.
OBSERVE AND LEARN, BUT DO NOT LEAVE THIS SEAT.
GOOD EVENING, MADAM.
MY NAME IS DR. VINCENT KRALL.
MAY I BUY YOU A DRINK?

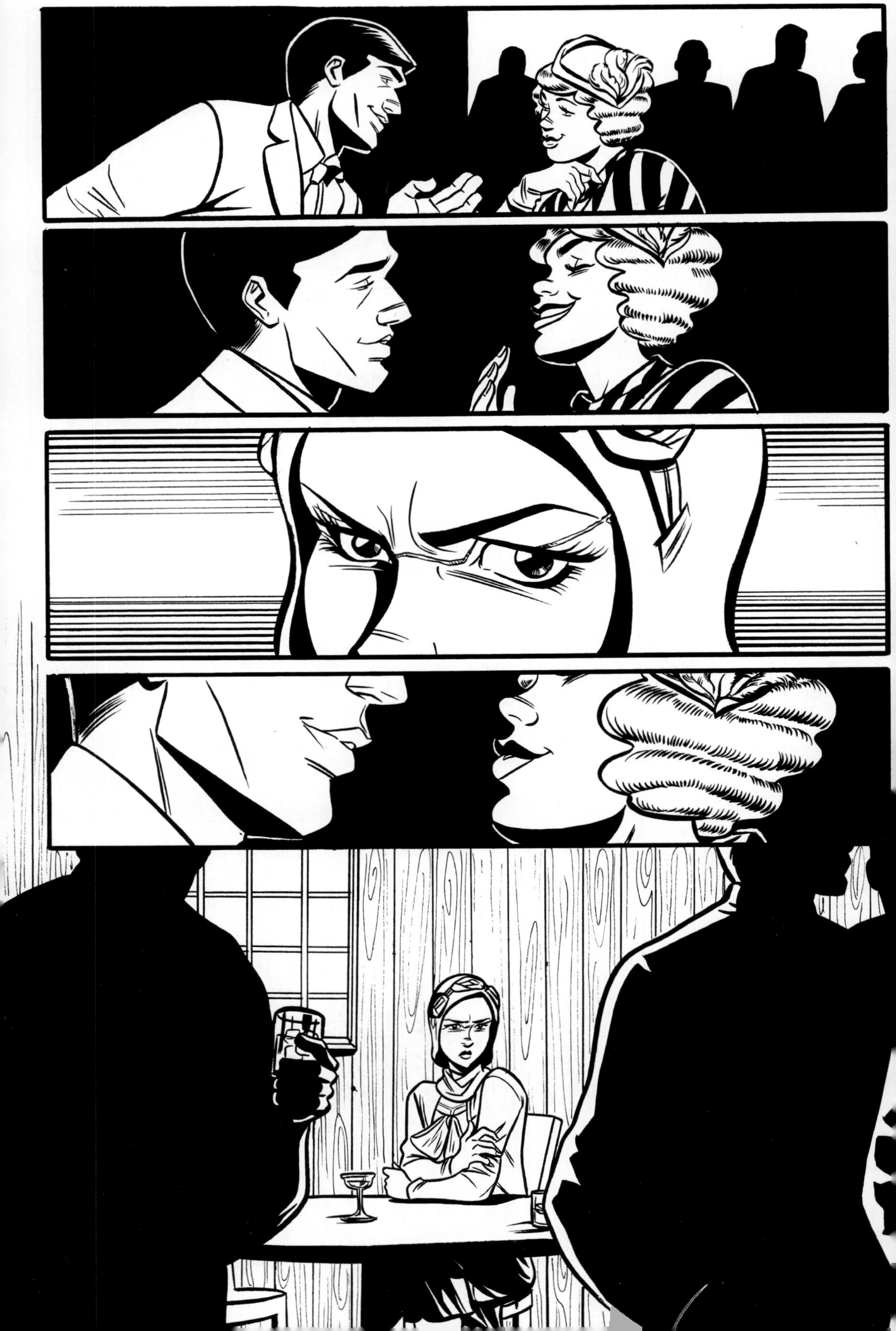

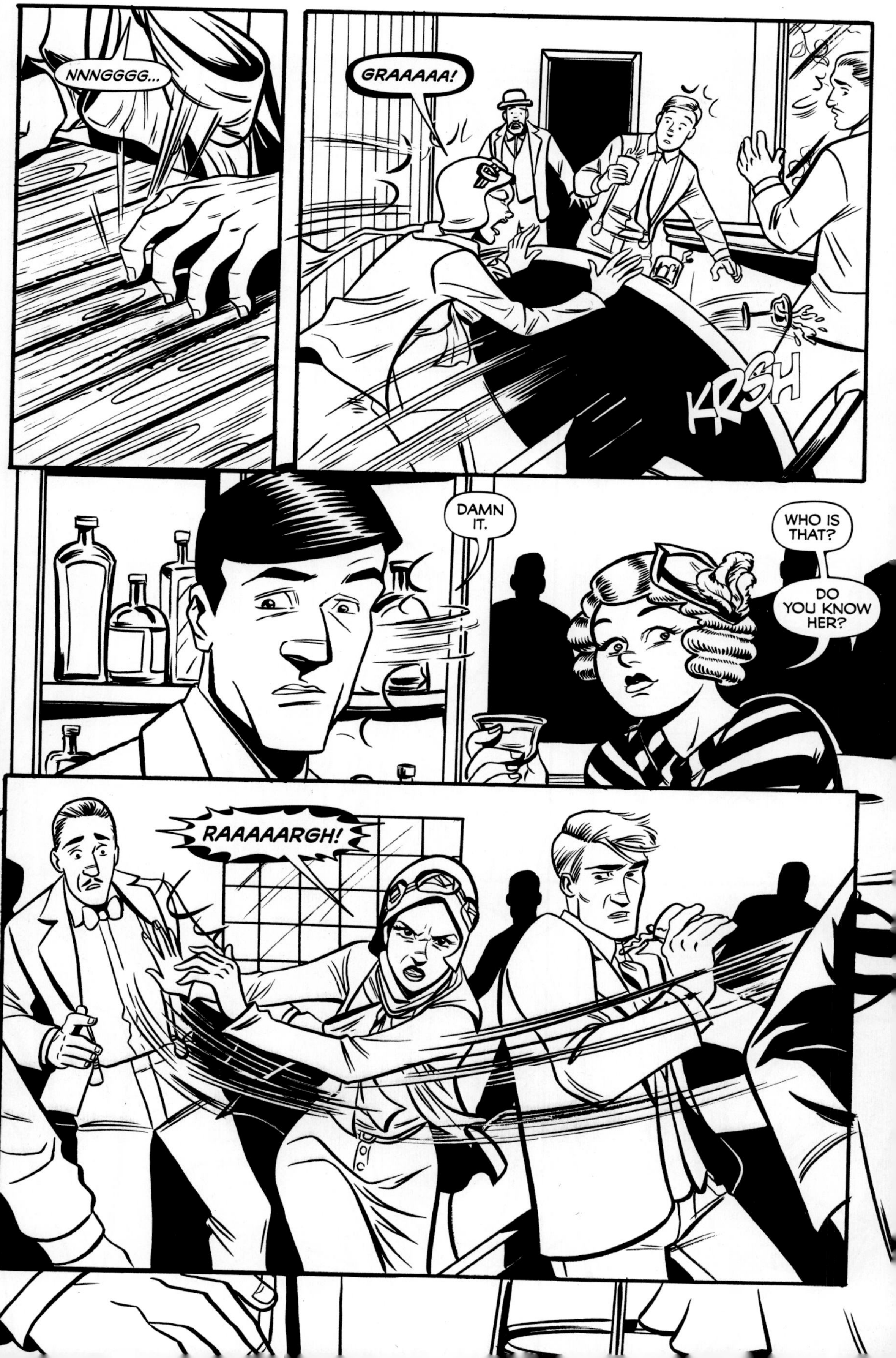
NNNGGGG...
GRAAAAA!
KRSH
DAMN IT.
WHO IS THAT?
DO YOU KNOW HER?
RAAAAARGH!

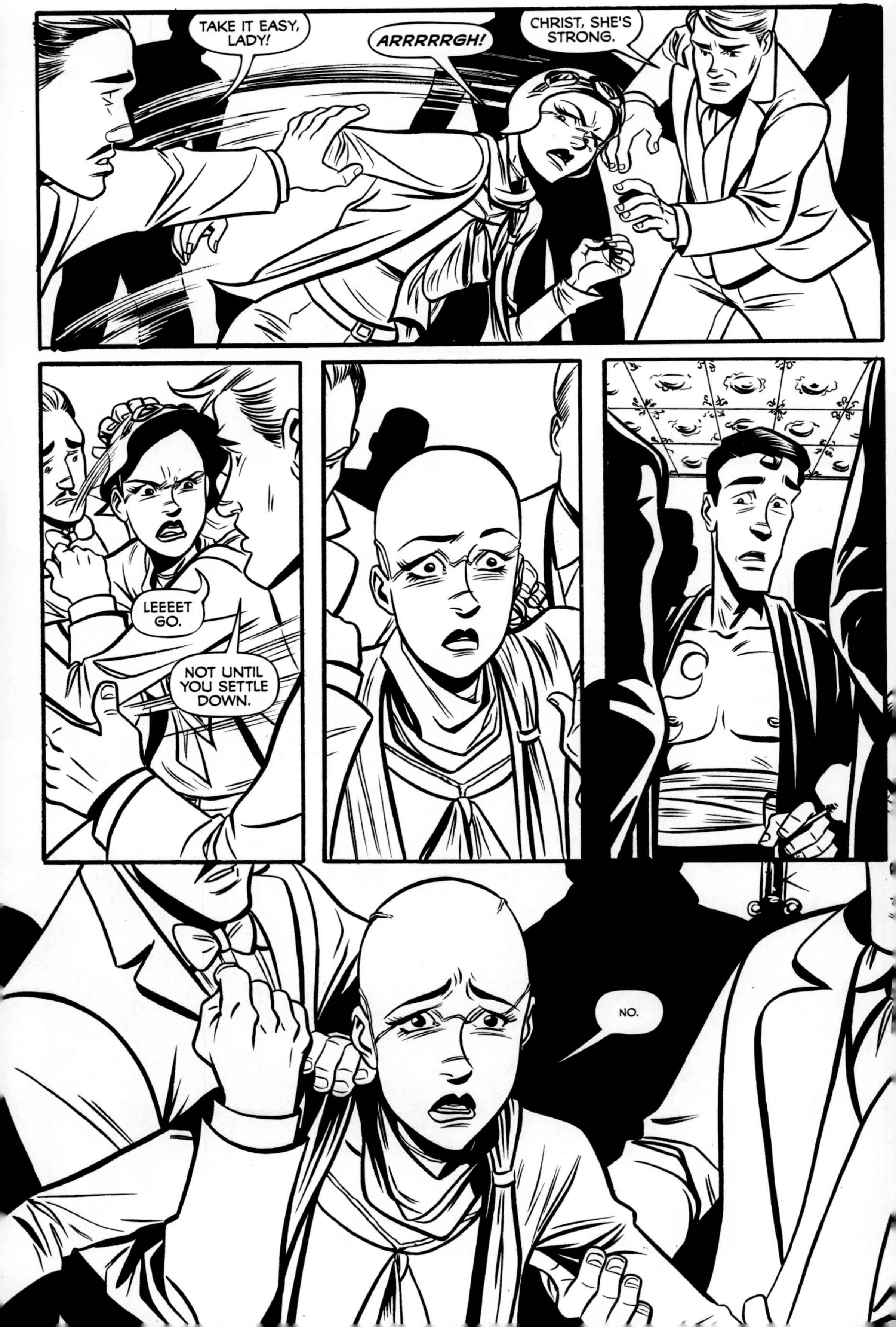
TAKE IT EASY, LADY!
ARRRRRGH!
CHRIST, SHE'S STRONG.
LEEEET GO.
NOT UNTIL YOU SETTLE DOWN.
NO.

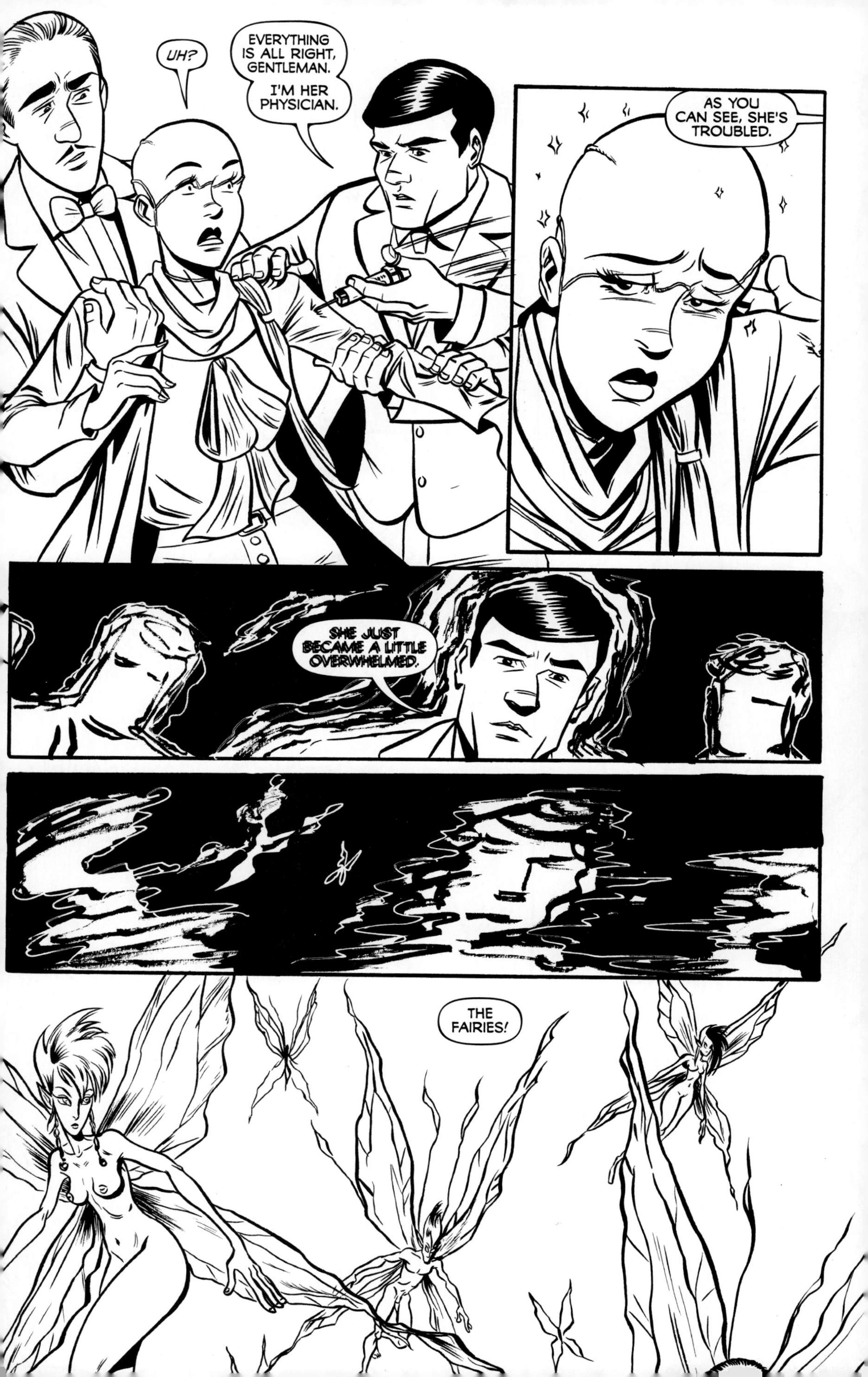
UH?
EVERYTHING IS ALL RIGHT, GENTLEMAN.
I'M HER PHYSICIAN.
AS YOU CAN SEE, SHE'S TROUBLED.
SHE JUST BECAME A LITTLE OVERWHELMED.
THE FAIRIES!

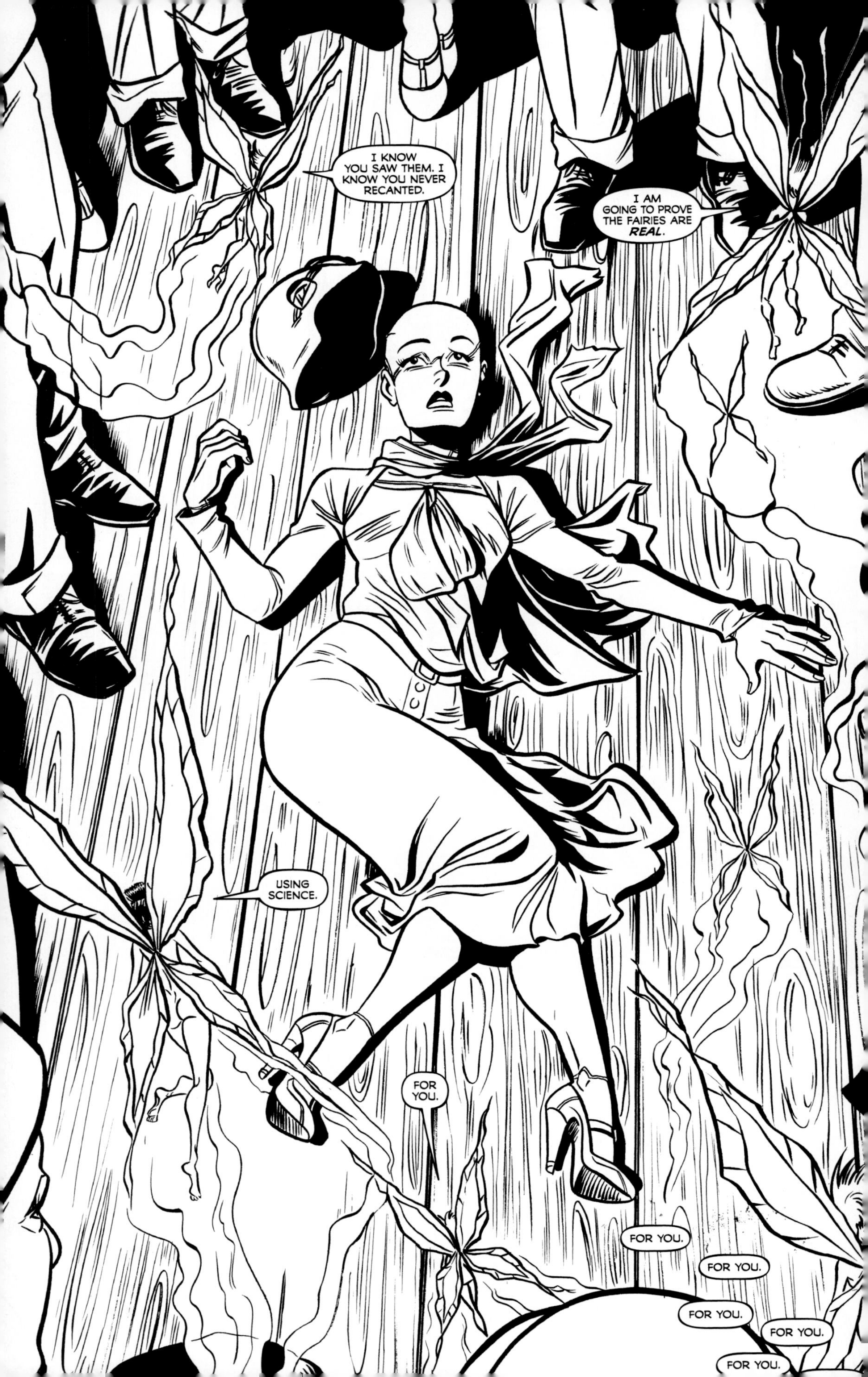

I KNOW YOU SAW THEM. I KNOW YOU NEVER RECANTED.
I AM GOING TO PROVE THE FAIRIES ARE *REAL*.
USING SCIENCE.
FOR YOU.
FOR YOU.
FOR YOU.
FOR YOU.
FOR YOU.
FOR YOU.

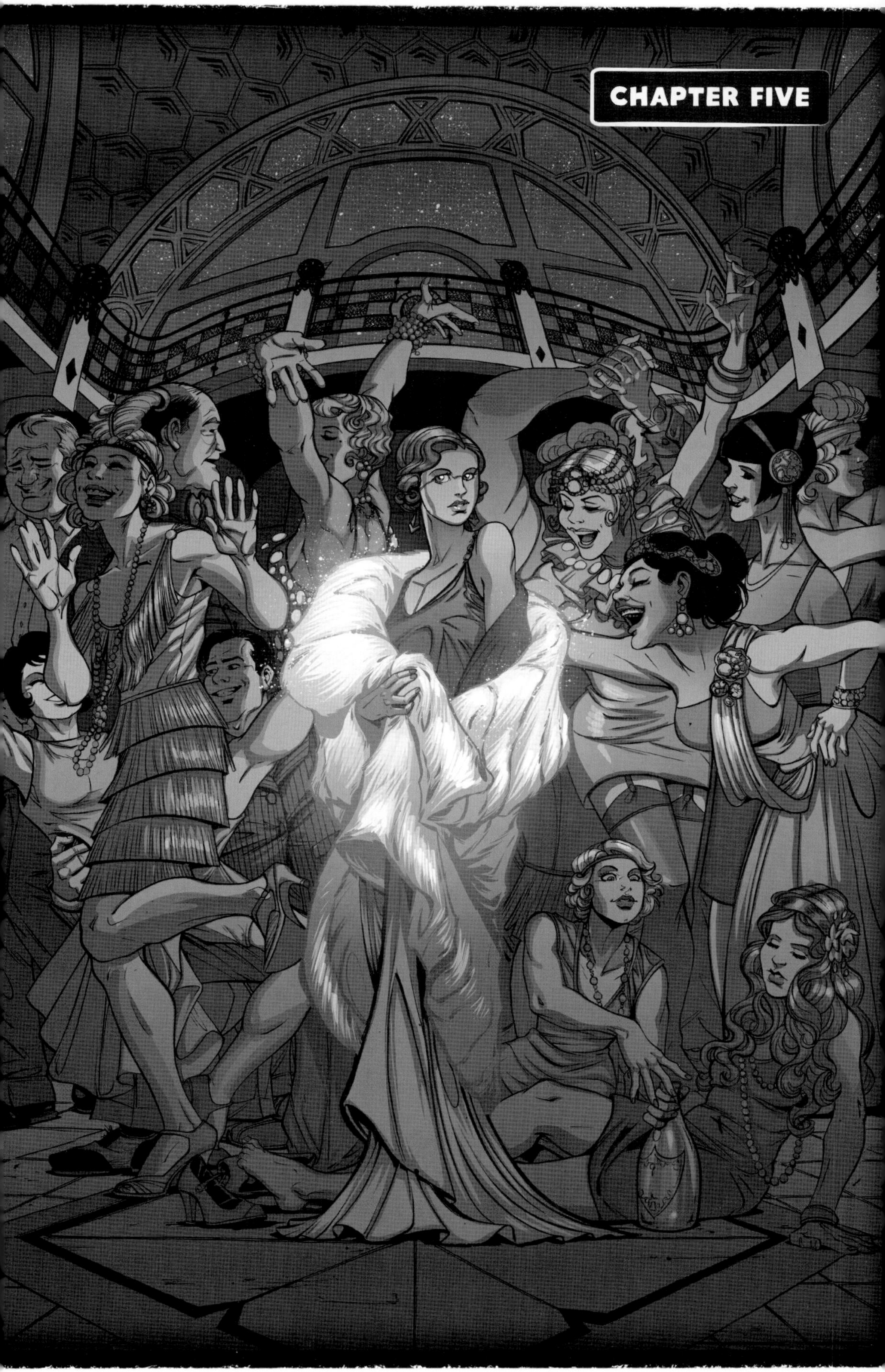
CHAPTER FIVE

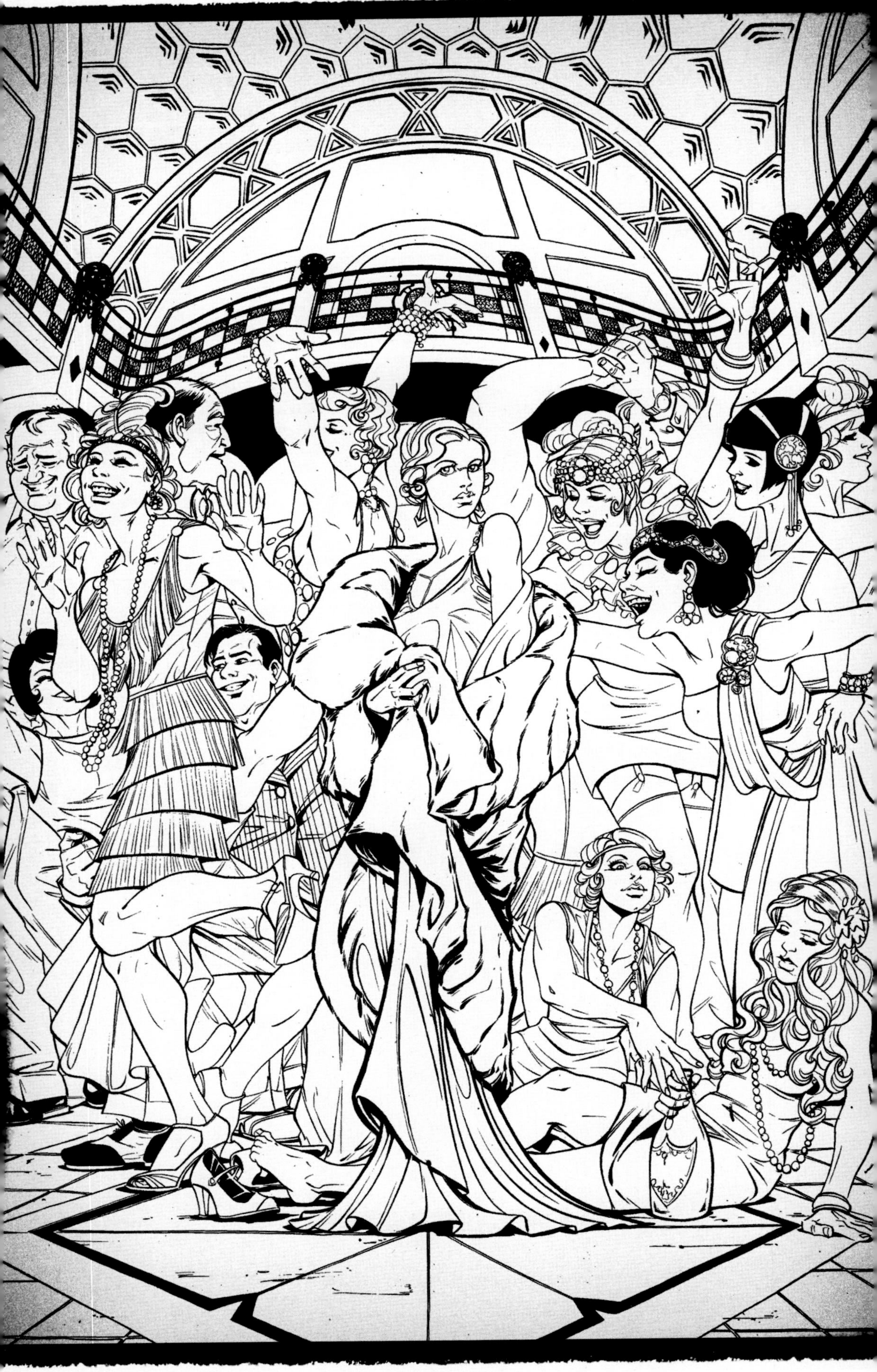

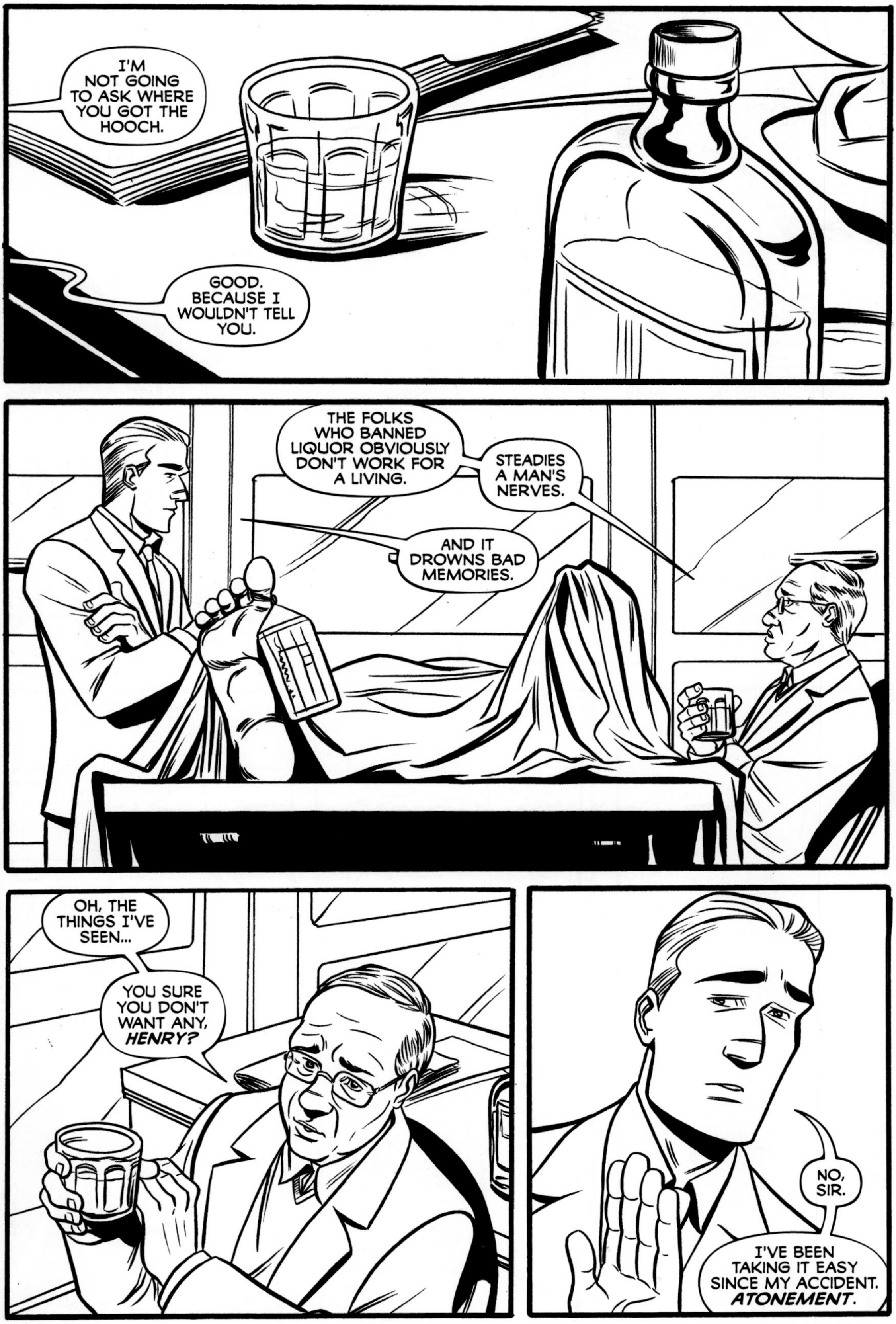
I'M NOT GOING TO ASK WHERE YOU GOT THE HOOCH.
GOOD. BECAUSE I WOULDN'T TELL YOU.
THE FOLKS WHO BANNED LIQUOR OBVIOUSLY DON'T WORK FOR A LIVING.
STEADIES A MAN'S NERVES.
AND IT DROWNS BAD MEMORIES.
OH, THE THINGS I'VE SEEN...
YOU SURE YOU DON'T WANT ANY, *HENRY?*
NO, SIR.
I'VE BEEN TAKING IT EASY SINCE MY ACCIDENT. *ATONEMENT*.

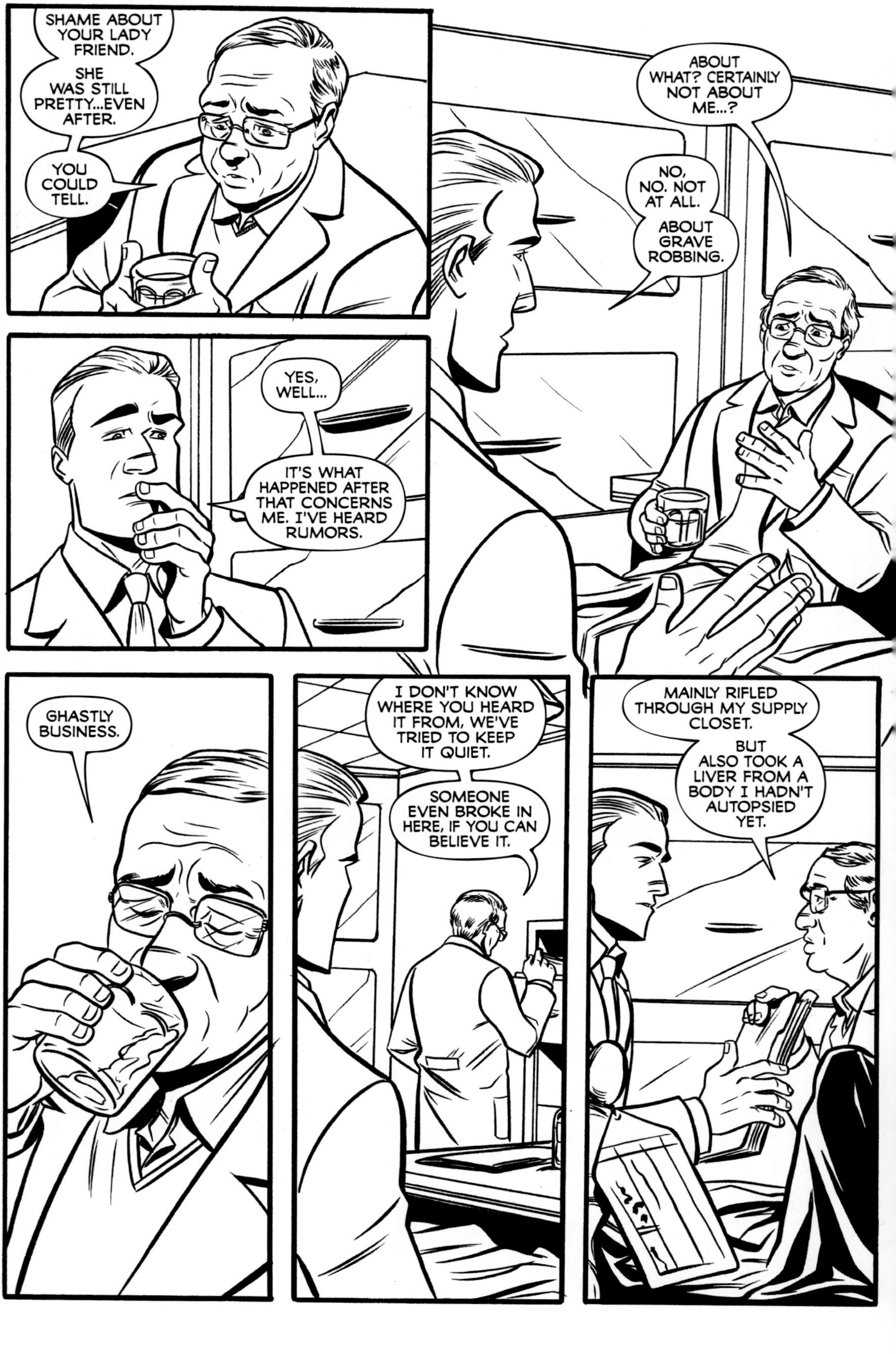
SHAME ABOUT YOUR LADY FRIEND.
SHE WAS STILL PRETTY...EVEN AFTER.
YOU COULD TELL.
YES, WELL...
IT'S WHAT HAPPENED AFTER THAT CONCERNS ME. I'VE HEARD RUMORS.
ABOUT WHAT? CERTAINLY NOT ABOUT ME...?
NO, NO. NOT AT ALL.
ABOUT GRAVE ROBBING.
GHASTLY BUSINESS.
I DON'T KNOW WHERE YOU HEARD IT FROM, WE'VE TRIED TO KEEP IT QUIET.
SOMEONE EVEN BROKE IN HERE, IF YOU CAN BELIEVE IT.
MAINLY RIFLED THROUGH MY SUPPLY CLOSET.
BUT ALSO TOOK A LIVER FROM A BODY I HADN'T AUTOPSIED YET.

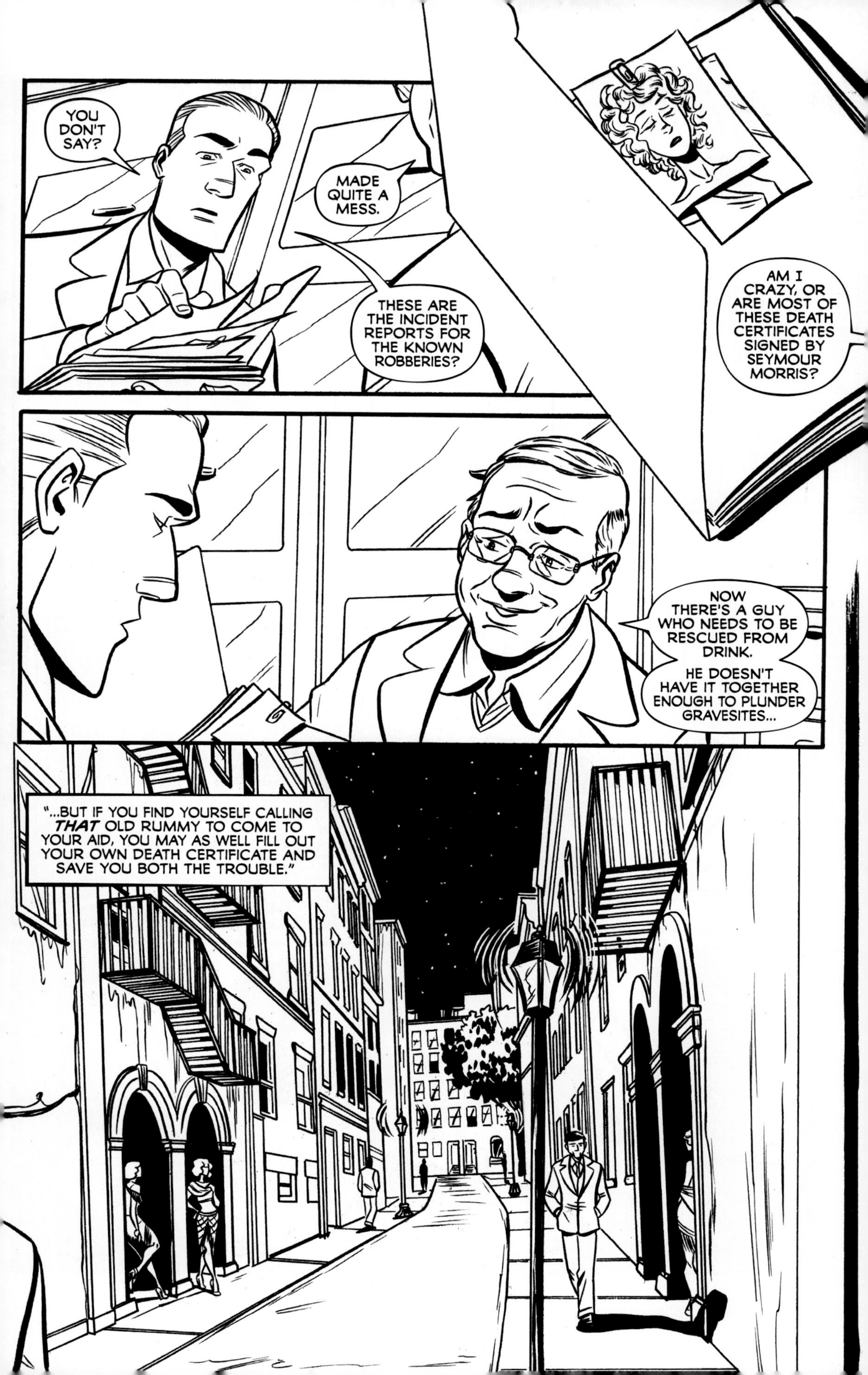
YOU DON'T SAY?
MADE QUITE A MESS.
THESE ARE THE INCIDENT REPORTS FOR THE KNOWN ROBBERIES?
AM I CRAZY, OR ARE MOST OF THESE DEATH CERTIFICATES SIGNED BY SEYMOUR MORRIS?
NOW THERE'S A GUY WHO NEEDS TO BE RESCUED FROM DRINK.
HE DOESN'T HAVE IT TOGETHER ENOUGH TO PLUNDER GRAVESITES...
"...BUT IF YOU FIND YOURSELF CALLING *THAT* OLD RUMMY TO COME TO YOUR AID, YOU MAY AS WELL FILL OUT YOUR OWN DEATH CERTIFICATE AND SAVE YOU BOTH THE TROUBLE."

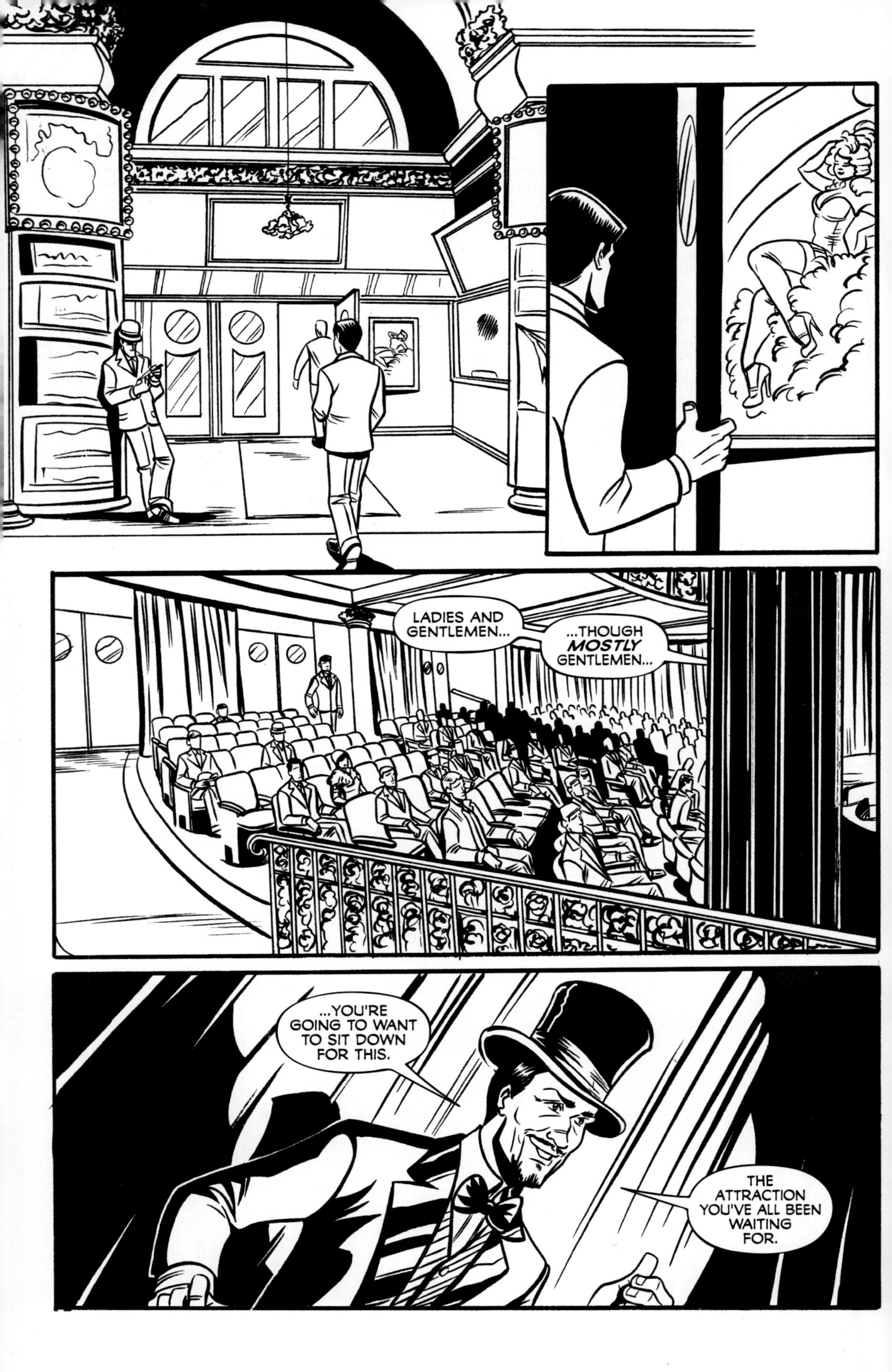
LADIES AND GENTLEMEN...
...THOUGH *MOSTLY* GENTLEMEN...
...YOU'RE GOING TO WANT TO SIT DOWN FOR THIS.
THE ATTRACTION YOU'VE ALL BEEN WAITING FOR.

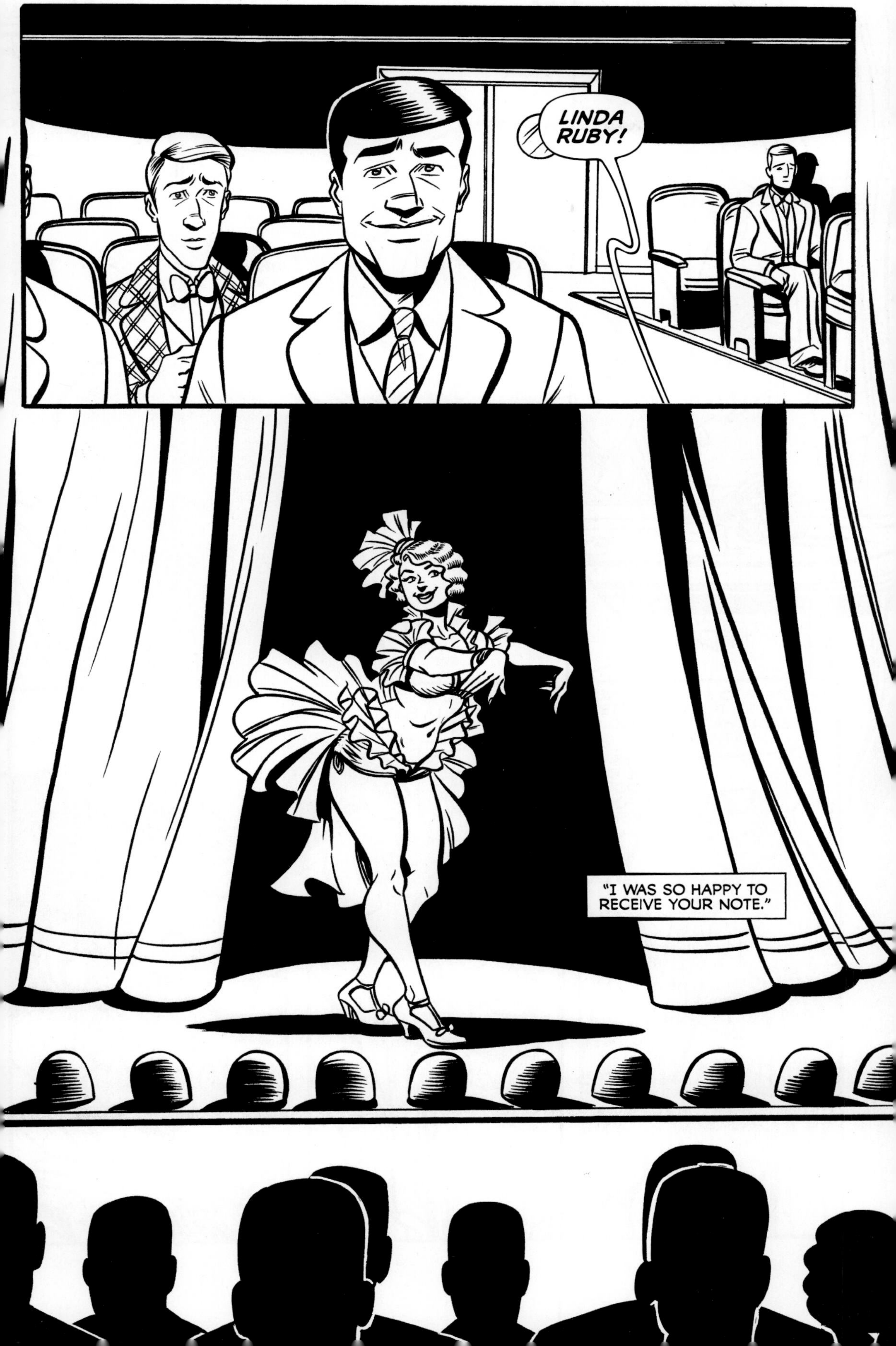
LINDA RUBY!
"I WAS SO HAPPY TO RECEIVE YOUR NOTE."

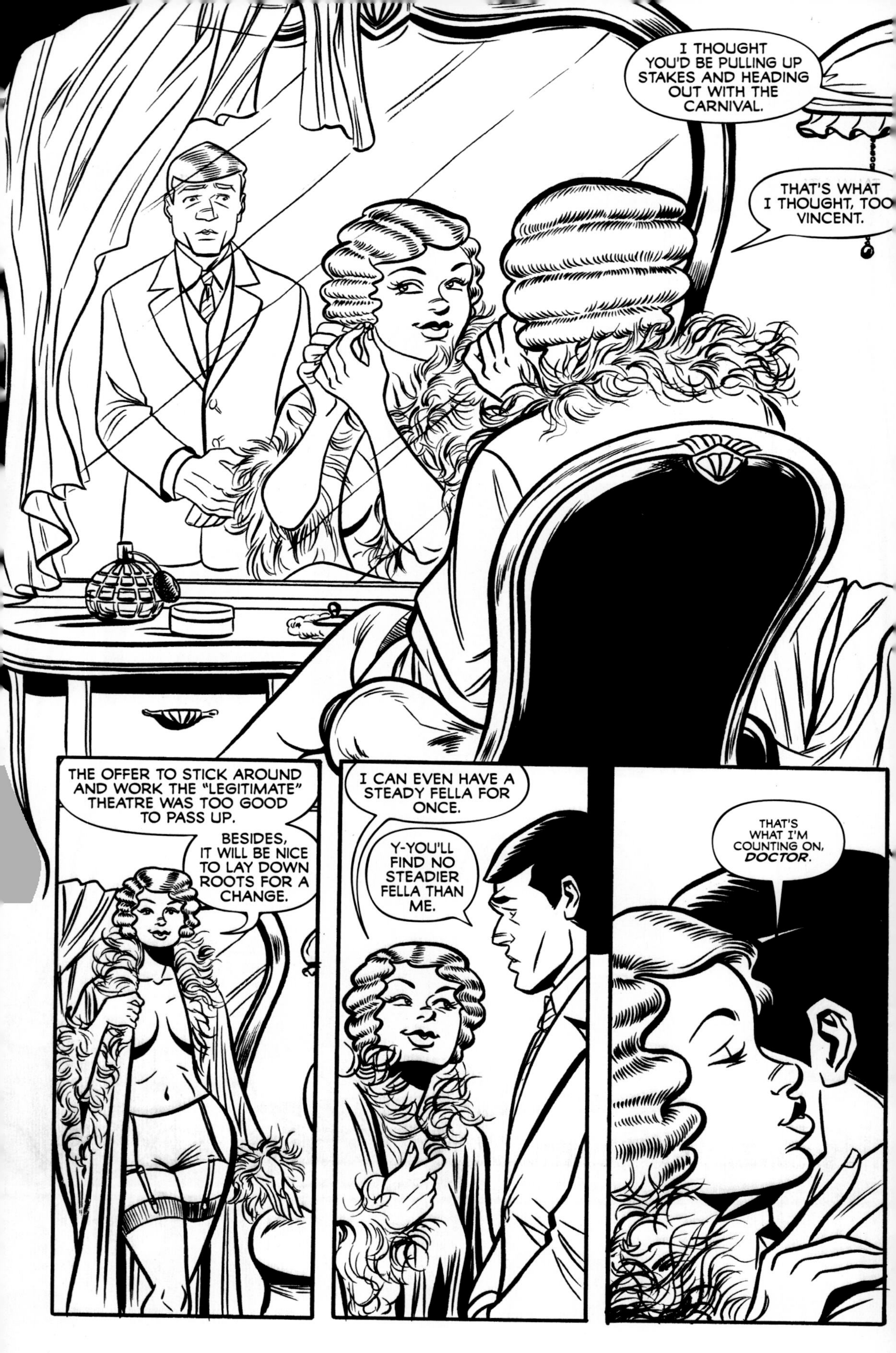

I THOUGHT YOU'D BE PULLING UP STAKES AND HEADING OUT WITH THE CARNIVAL.
THAT'S WHAT I THOUGHT, TOO VINCENT.
THE OFFER TO STICK AROUND AND WORK THE "LEGITIMATE" THEATRE WAS TOO GOOD TO PASS UP.
BESIDES, IT WILL BE NICE TO LAY DOWN ROOTS FOR A CHANGE.
I CAN EVEN HAVE A STEADY FELLA FOR ONCE.
Y-YOU'LL FIND NO STEADIER FELLA THAN ME.
THAT'S WHAT I'M COUNTING ON, ***DOCTOR***.

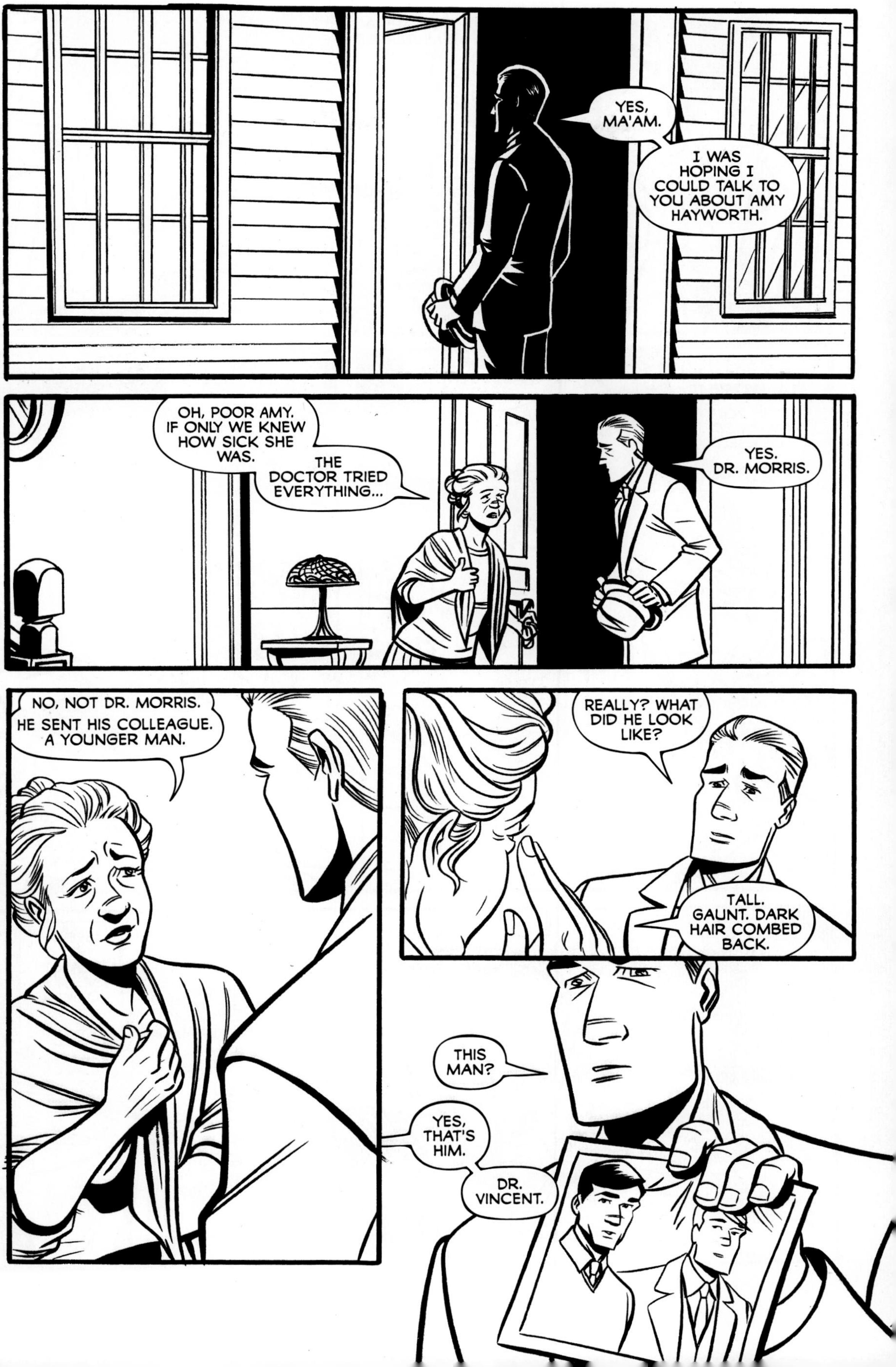
YES, MA'AM.
I WAS HOPING I COULD TALK TO YOU ABOUT AMY HAYWORTH.
OH, POOR AMY. IF ONLY WE KNEW HOW SICK SHE WAS.
THE DOCTOR TRIED EVERYTHING...
YES. DR. MORRIS.
NO, NOT DR. MORRIS.
HE SENT HIS COLLEAGUE. A YOUNGER MAN.
REALLY? WHAT DID HE LOOK LIKE?
TALL. GAUNT. DARK HAIR COMBED BACK.
THIS MAN?
YES, THAT'S HIM.
DR. VINCENT.

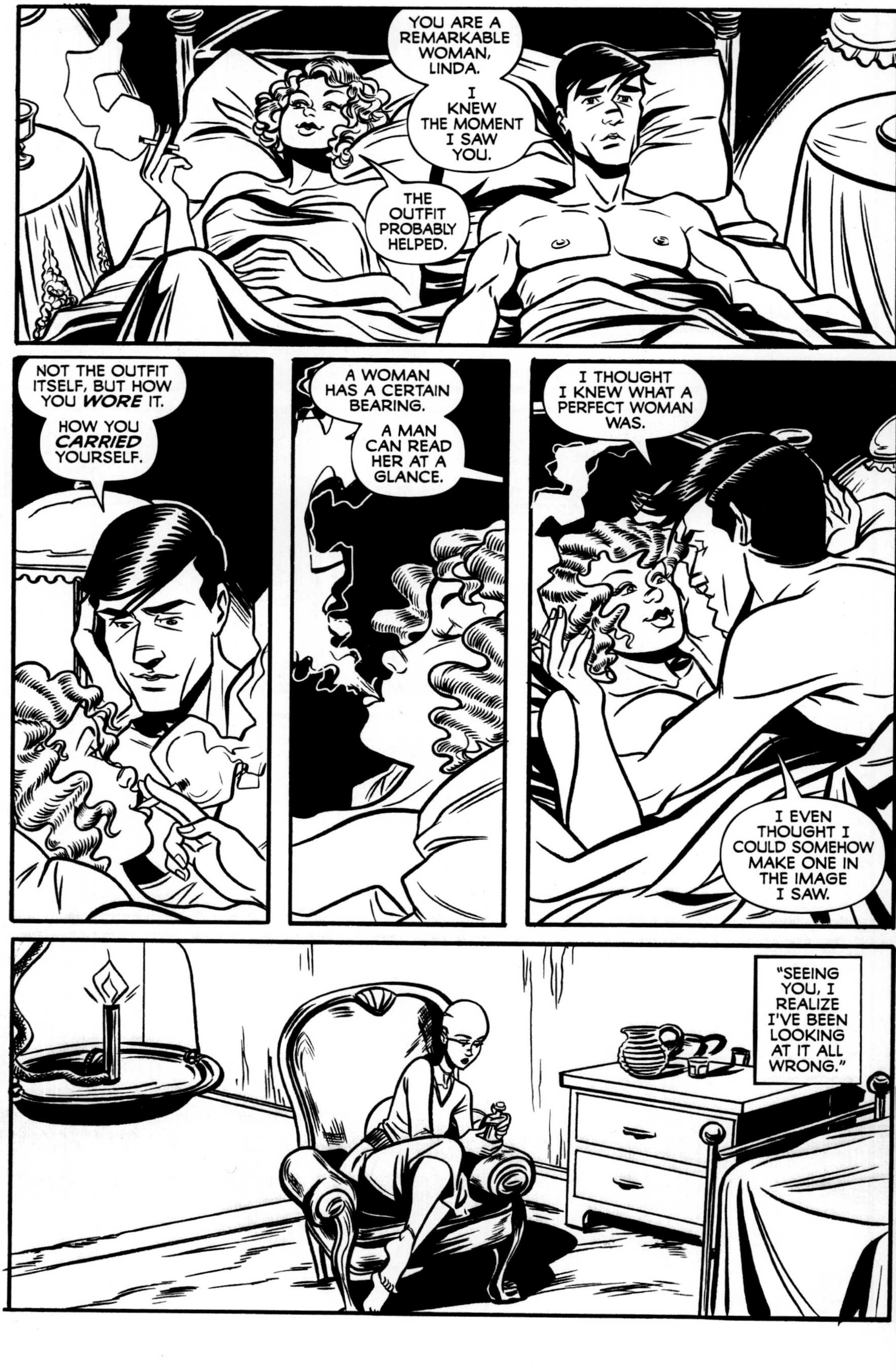
YOU ARE A REMARKABLE WOMAN, LINDA.
I KNEW THE MOMENT I SAW YOU.
THE OUTFIT PROBABLY HELPED.
NOT THE OUTFIT ITSELF, BUT HOW YOU WORE IT.
HOW YOU CARRIED YOURSELF.
A WOMAN HAS A CERTAIN BEARING.
A MAN CAN READ HER AT A GLANCE.
I THOUGHT I KNEW WHAT A PERFECT WOMAN WAS.
I EVEN THOUGHT I COULD SOMEHOW MAKE ONE IN THE IMAGE I SAW.
"SEEING YOU, I REALIZE I'VE BEEN LOOKING AT IT ALL WRONG."

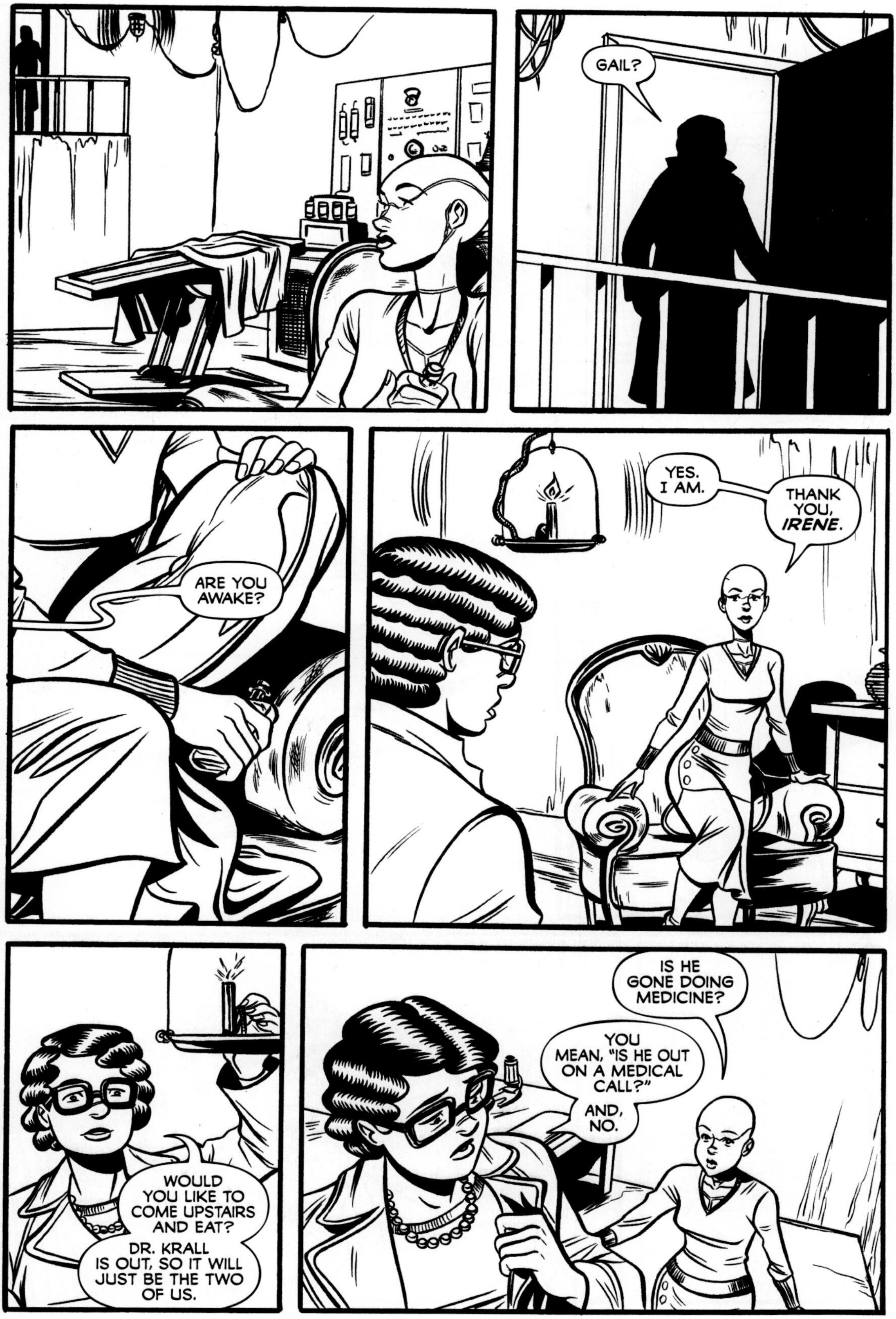
GAIL?
ARE YOU AWAKE?
YES. I AM.
THANK YOU, *IRENE*.
WOULD YOU LIKE TO COME UPSTAIRS AND EAT?
DR. KRALL IS OUT, SO IT WILL JUST BE THE TWO OF US.
IS HE GONE DOING MEDICINE?
YOU MEAN, "IS HE OUT ON A MEDICAL CALL?"
AND, NO.

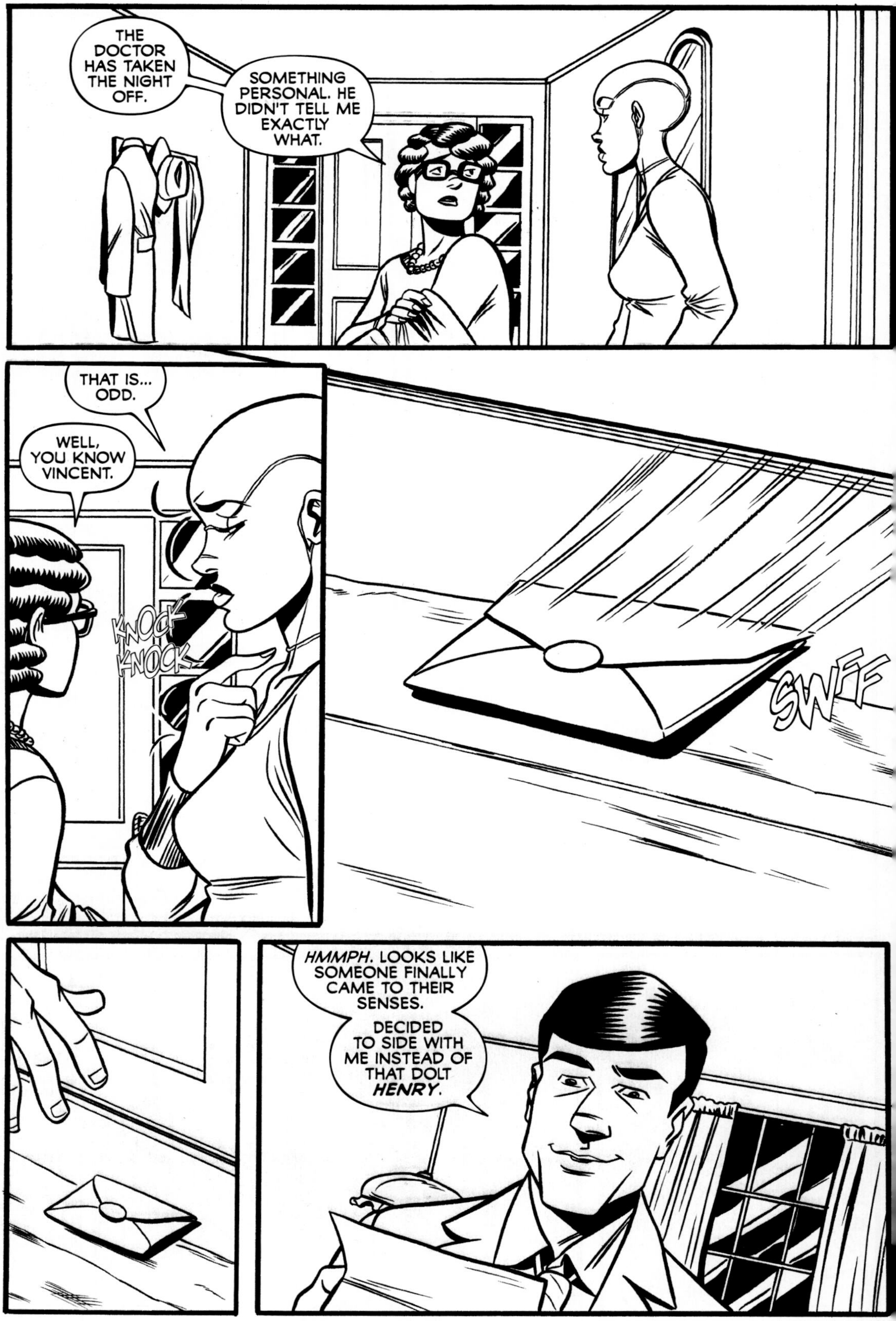
THE DOCTOR HAS TAKEN THE NIGHT OFF.
SOMETHING PERSONAL. HE DIDN'T TELL ME EXACTLY WHAT.
THAT IS... ODD.
WELL, YOU KNOW VINCENT.
KNOCK KNOCK
SWFF
HMMPH. LOOKS LIKE SOMEONE FINALLY CAME TO THEIR SENSES.
DECIDED TO SIDE WITH ME INSTEAD OF THAT DOLT ***HENRY***.

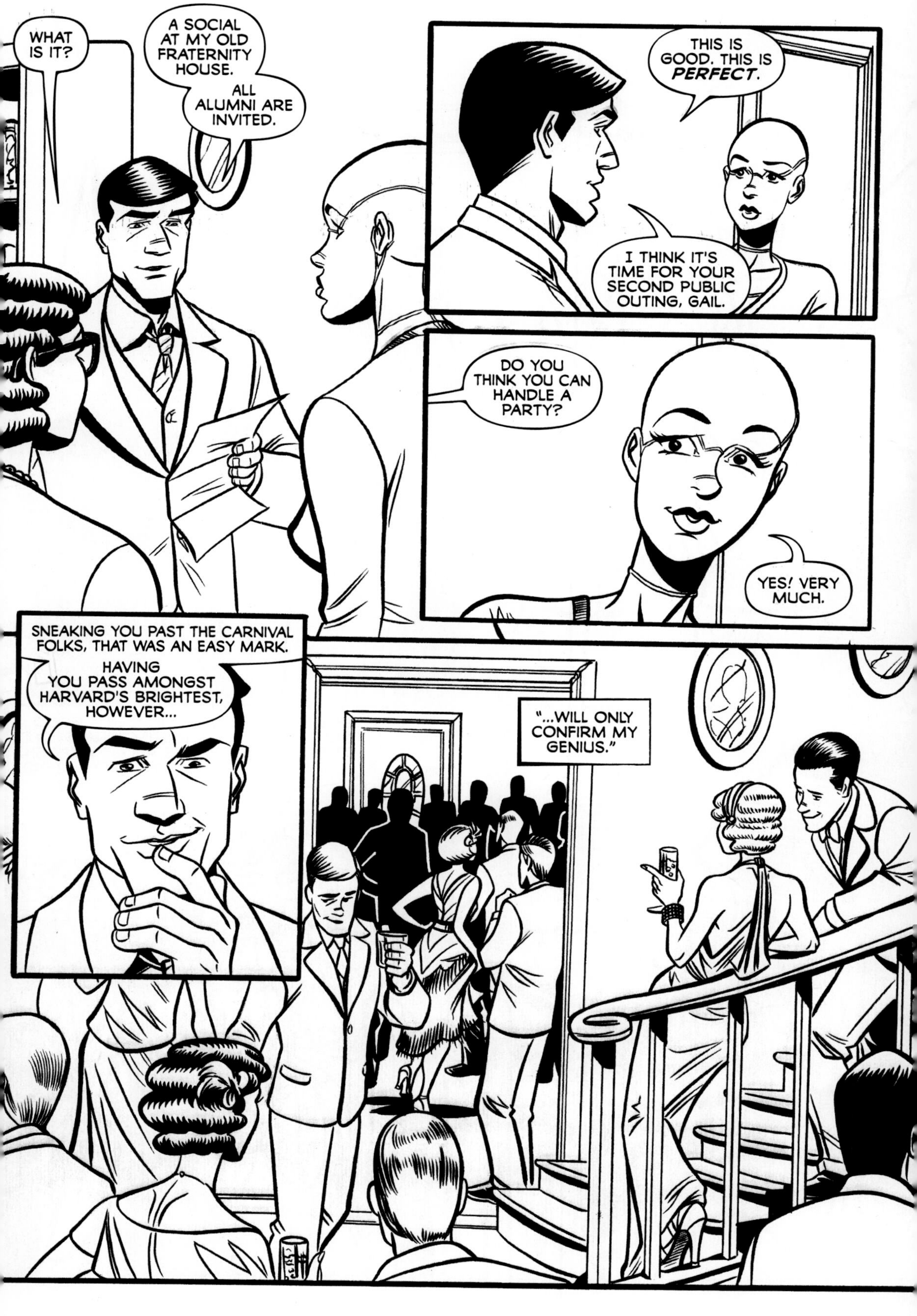

WHAT IS IT?
A SOCIAL AT MY OLD FRATERNITY HOUSE.
ALL ALUMNI ARE INVITED.
THIS IS GOOD. THIS IS PERFECT.
I THINK IT'S TIME FOR YOUR SECOND PUBLIC OUTING, GAIL.
DO YOU THINK YOU CAN HANDLE A PARTY?
YES! VERY MUCH.
SNEAKING YOU PAST THE CARNIVAL FOLKS, THAT WAS AN EASY MARK.
HAVING YOU PASS AMONGST HARVARD'S BRIGHTEST, HOWEVER...
"...WILL ONLY CONFIRM MY GENIUS."

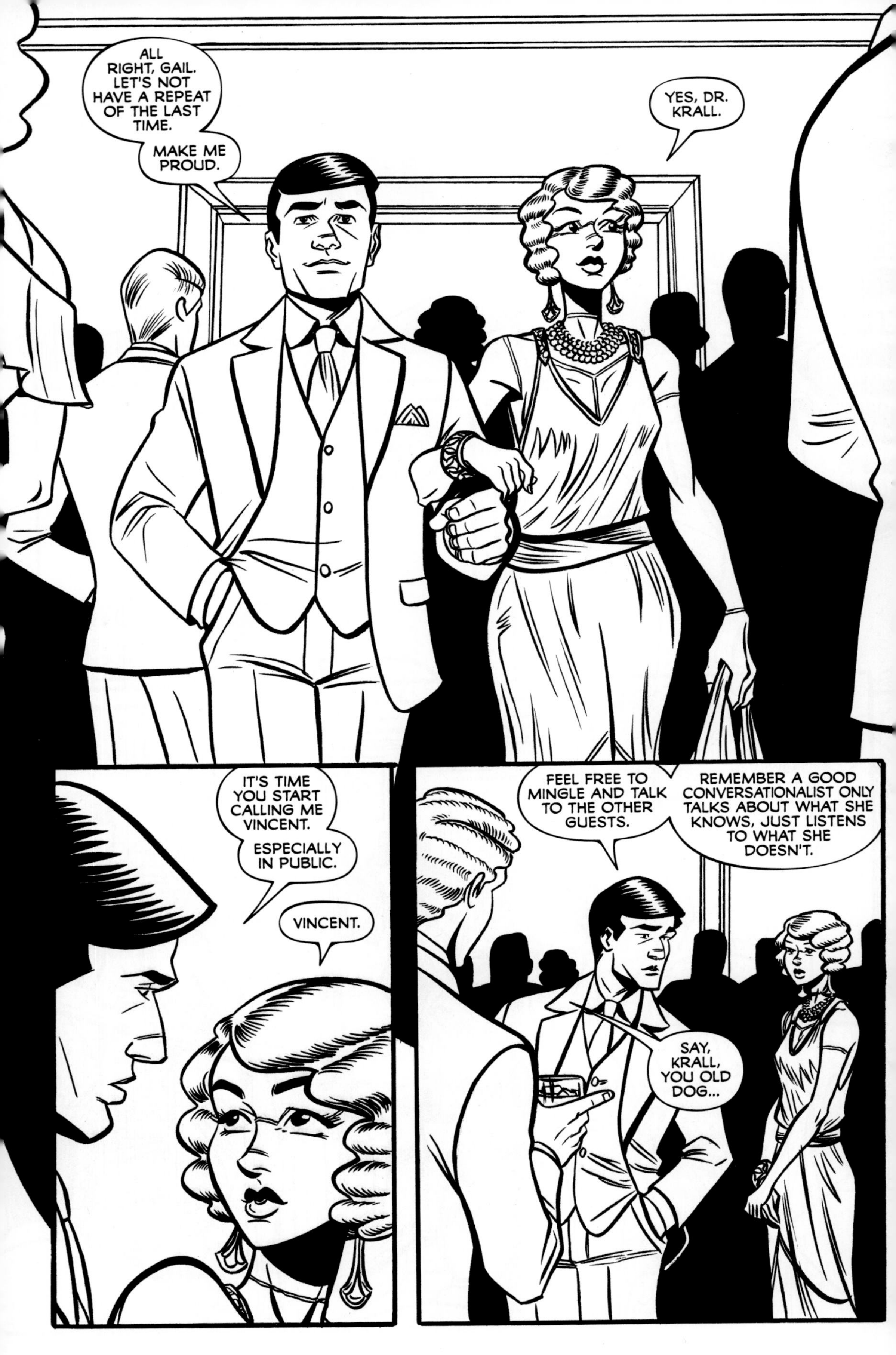
ALL RIGHT, GAIL. LET'S NOT HAVE A REPEAT OF THE LAST TIME.
MAKE ME PROUD.
YES, DR. KRALL.
IT'S TIME YOU START CALLING ME VINCENT.
ESPECIALLY IN PUBLIC.
VINCENT.
FEEL FREE TO MINGLE AND TALK TO THE OTHER GUESTS.
REMEMBER A GOOD CONVERSATIONALIST ONLY TALKS ABOUT WHAT SHE KNOWS, JUST LISTENS TO WHAT SHE DOESN'T.
SAY, KRALL, YOU OLD DOG...

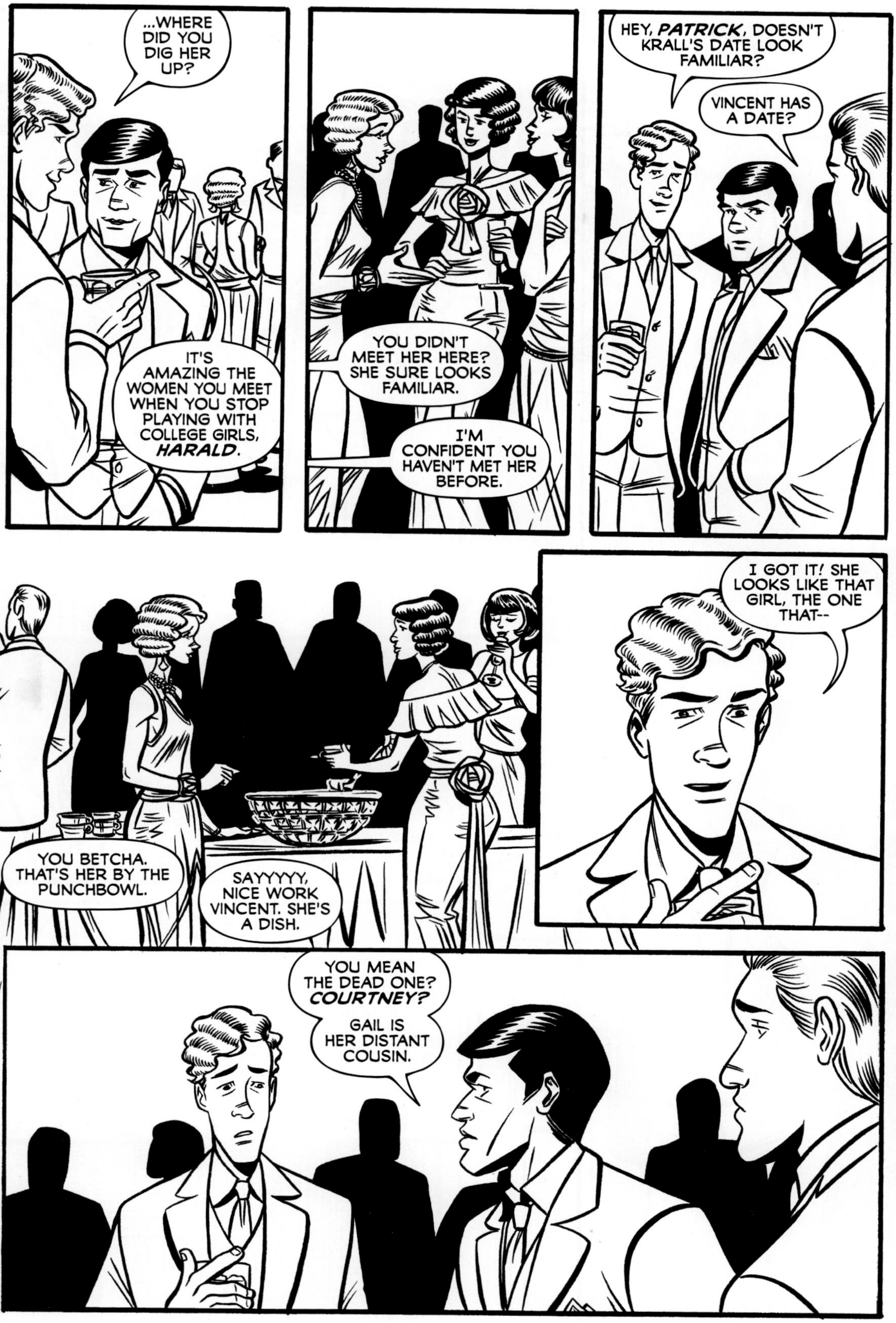
...WHERE DID YOU DIG HER UP?
IT'S AMAZING THE WOMEN YOU MEET WHEN YOU STOP PLAYING WITH COLLEGE GIRLS, ***HARALD***.
YOU DIDN'T MEET HER HERE? SHE SURE LOOKS FAMILIAR.
I'M CONFIDENT YOU HAVEN'T MET HER BEFORE.
HEY, ***PATRICK***, DOESN'T KRALL'S DATE LOOK FAMILIAR?
VINCENT HAS A DATE?
YOU BETCHA. THAT'S HER BY THE PUNCHBOWL.
SAYYYYY, NICE WORK VINCENT. SHE'S A DISH.
I GOT IT! SHE LOOKS LIKE THAT GIRL, THE ONE THAT--
YOU MEAN THE DEAD ONE? ***COURTNEY?***
GAIL IS HER DISTANT COUSIN.

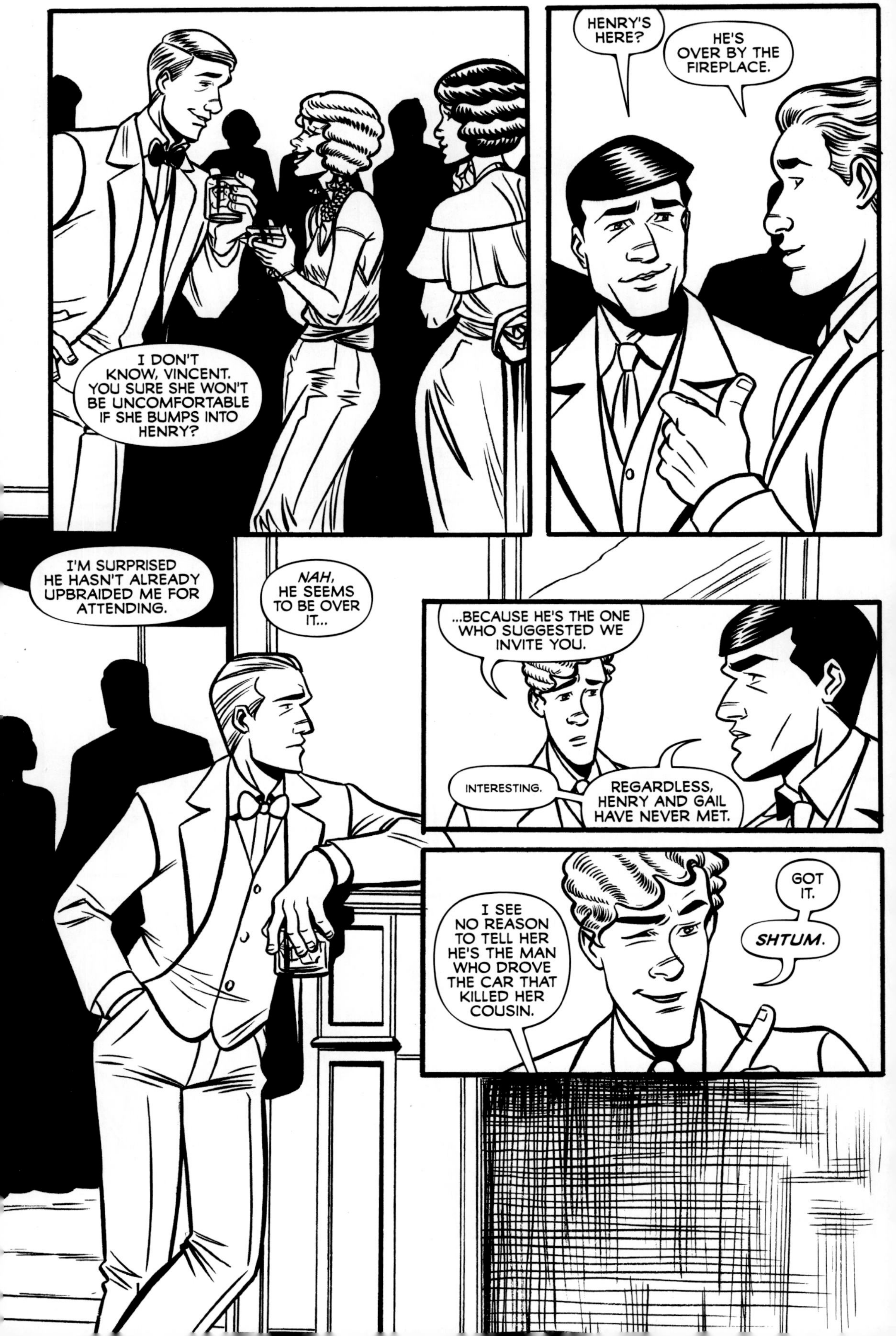
I DON'T KNOW, VINCENT. YOU SURE SHE WON'T BE UNCOMFORTABLE IF SHE BUMPS INTO HENRY?
HENRY'S HERE?
HE'S OVER BY THE FIREPLACE.
I'M SURPRISED HE HASN'T ALREADY UPBRAIDED ME FOR ATTENDING.
NAH, HE SEEMS TO BE OVER IT...
...BECAUSE HE'S THE ONE WHO SUGGESTED WE INVITE YOU.
INTERESTING.
REGARDLESS, HENRY AND GAIL HAVE NEVER MET.
I SEE NO REASON TO TELL HER HE'S THE MAN WHO DROVE THE CAR THAT KILLED HER COUSIN.
GOT IT.
SHTUM.

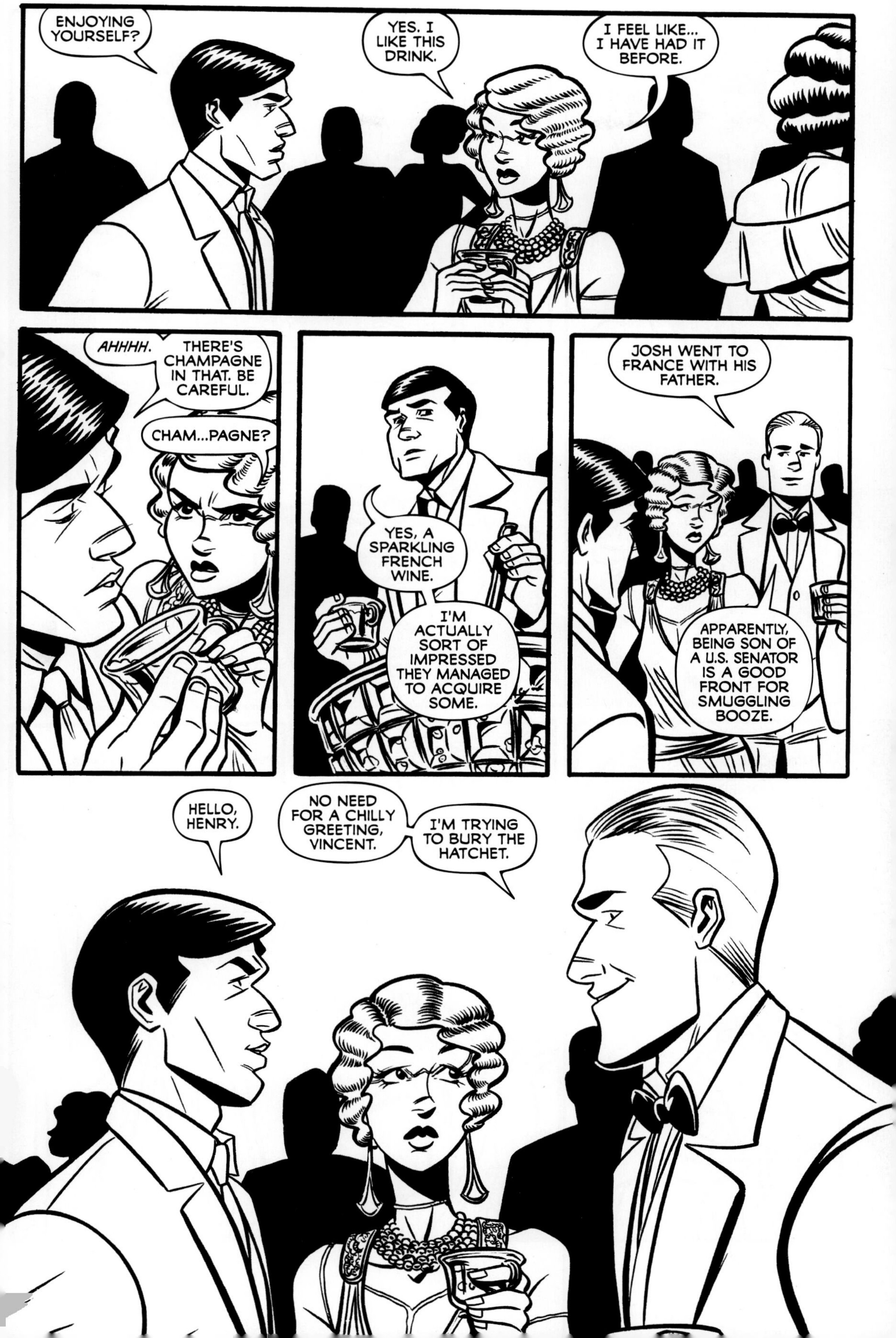
ENJOYING YOURSELF?
YES. I LIKE THIS DRINK.
I FEEL LIKE... I HAVE HAD IT BEFORE.
AHHHH.
THERE'S CHAMPAGNE IN THAT. BE CAREFUL.
CHAM...PAGNE?
YES, A SPARKLING FRENCH WINE.
I'M ACTUALLY SORT OF IMPRESSED THEY MANAGED TO ACQUIRE SOME.
JOSH WENT TO FRANCE WITH HIS FATHER.
APPARENTLY, BEING SON OF A U.S. SENATOR IS A GOOD FRONT FOR SMUGGLING BOOZE.
HELLO, HENRY.
NO NEED FOR A CHILLY GREETING, VINCENT.
I'M TRYING TO BURY THE HATCHET.

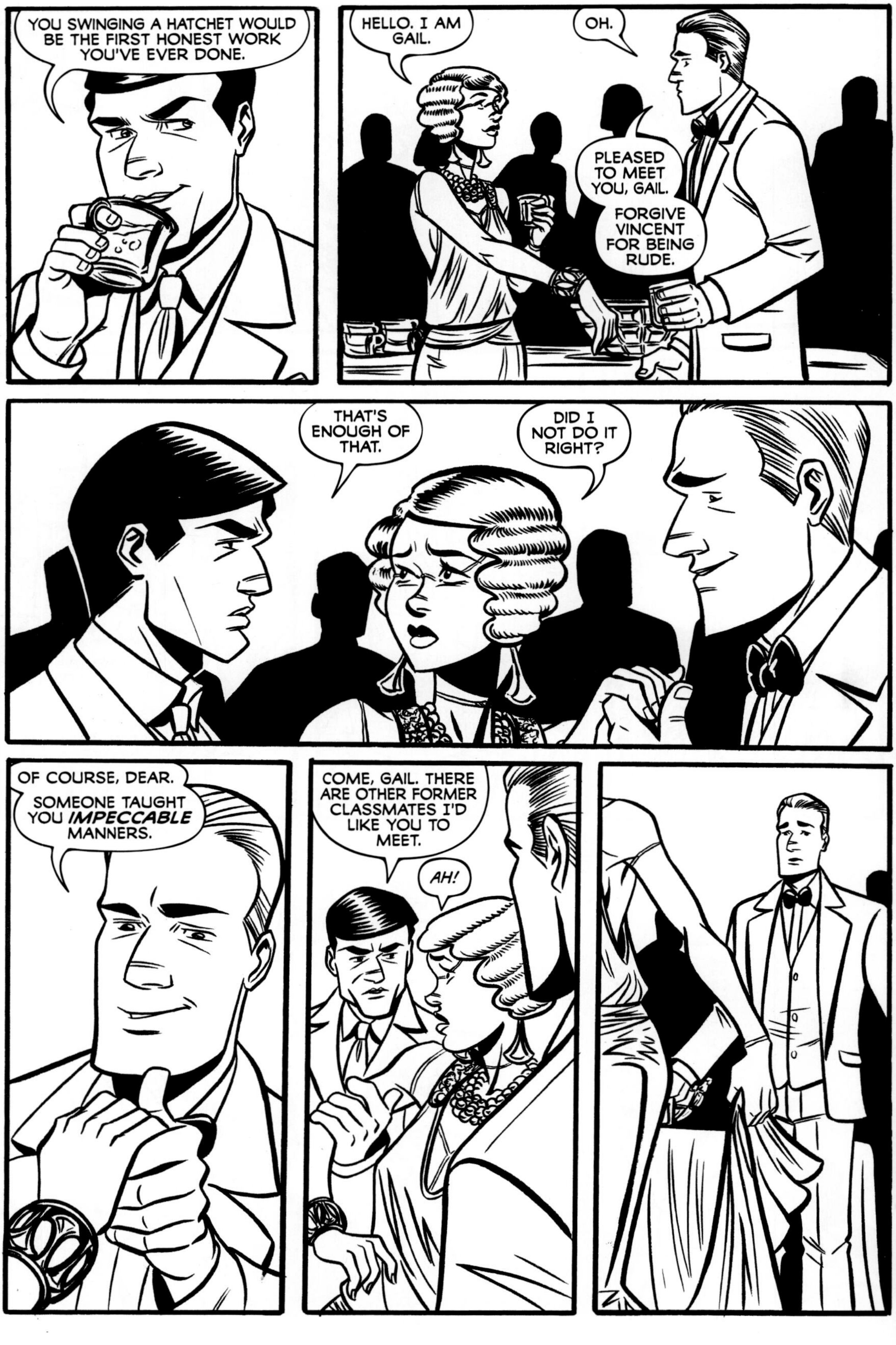
YOU SWINGING A HATCHET WOULD BE THE FIRST HONEST WORK YOU'VE EVER DONE.
HELLO. I AM GAIL.
OH.
PLEASED TO MEET YOU, GAIL.
FORGIVE VINCENT FOR BEING RUDE.
THAT'S ENOUGH OF THAT.
DID I NOT DO IT RIGHT?
OF COURSE, DEAR.
SOMEONE TAUGHT YOU *IMPECCABLE* MANNERS.
COME, GAIL. THERE ARE OTHER FORMER CLASSMATES I'D LIKE YOU TO MEET.
AH!

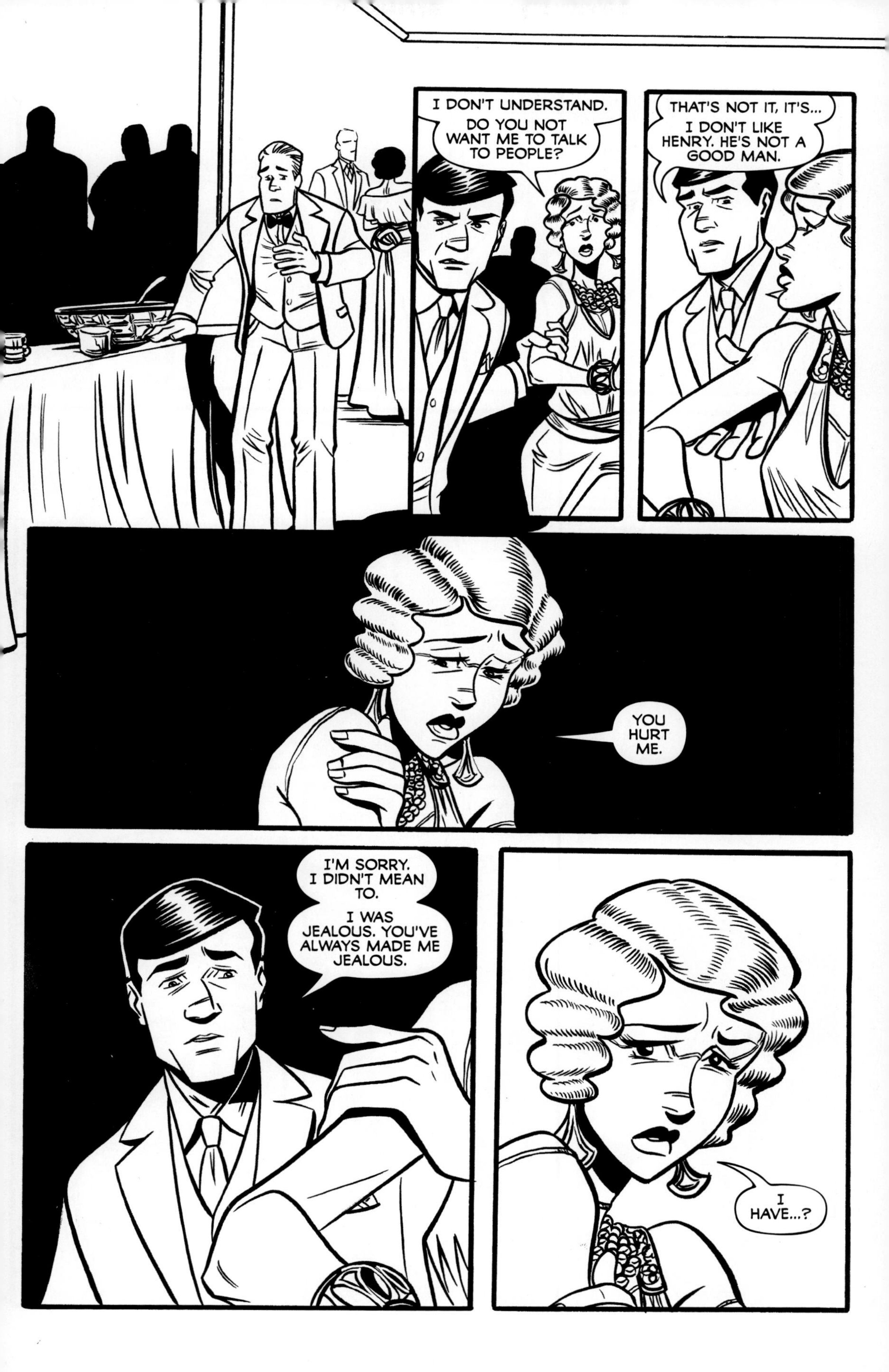
I DON'T UNDERSTAND.
DO YOU NOT WANT ME TO TALK TO PEOPLE?
THAT'S NOT IT, IT'S...
I DON'T LIKE HENRY. HE'S NOT A GOOD MAN.
YOU HURT ME.
I'M SORRY. I DIDN'T MEAN TO.
I WAS JEALOUS. YOU'VE ALWAYS MADE ME JEALOUS.
I HAVE...?

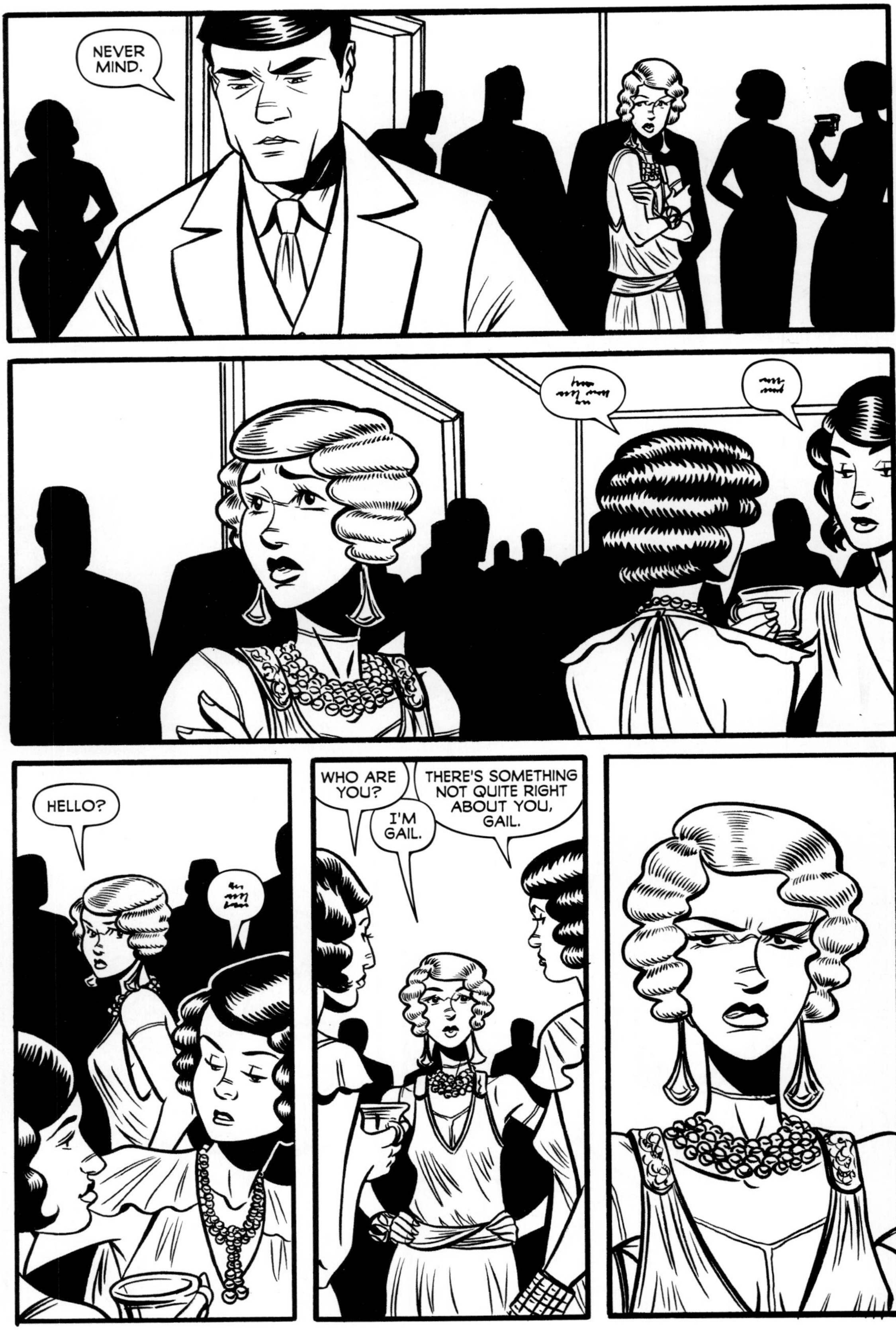
NEVER MIND.
HELLO?
WHO ARE YOU?
I'M GAIL.
THERE'S SOMETHING NOT QUITE RIGHT ABOUT YOU, GAIL.

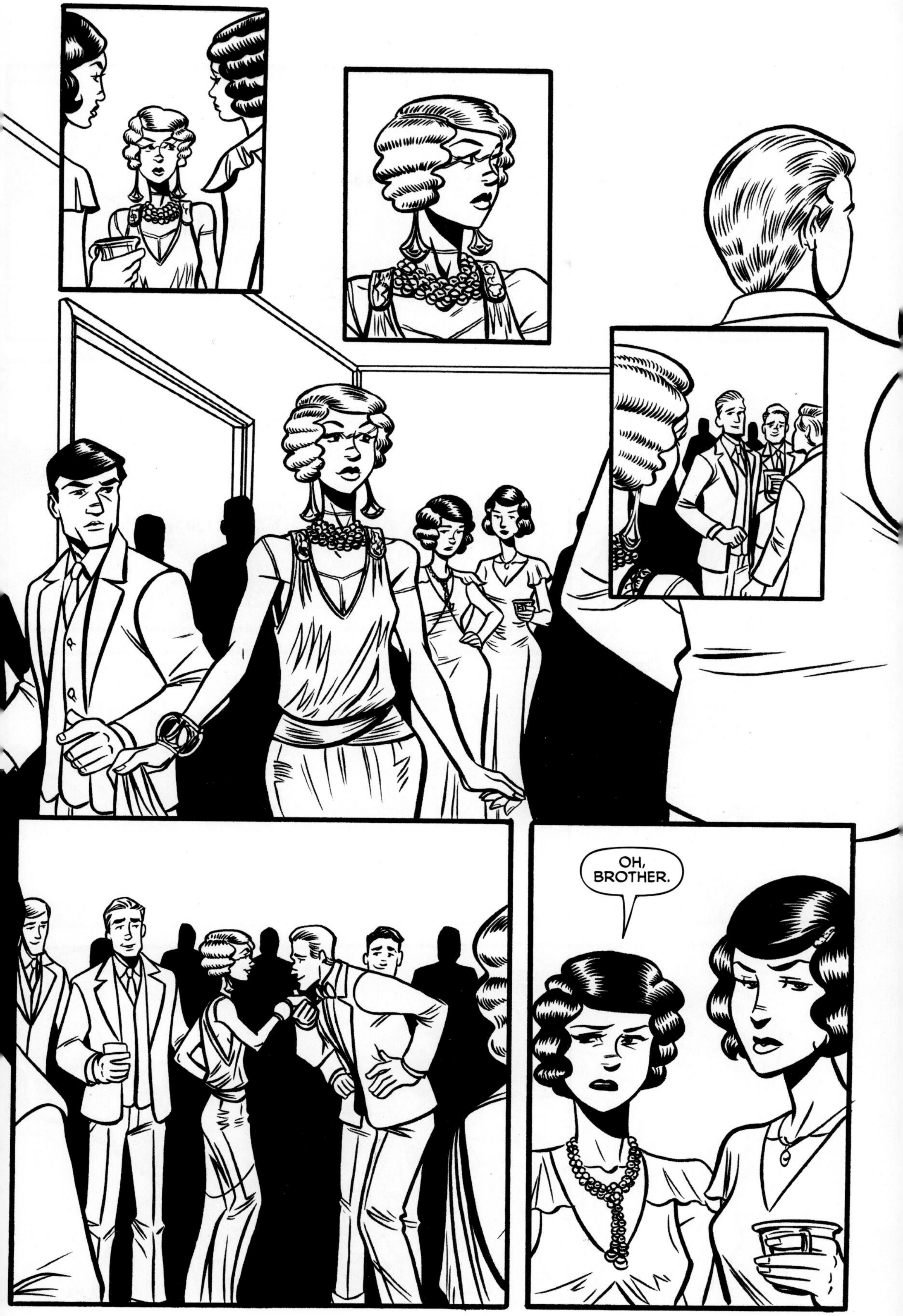
OH, BROTHER.

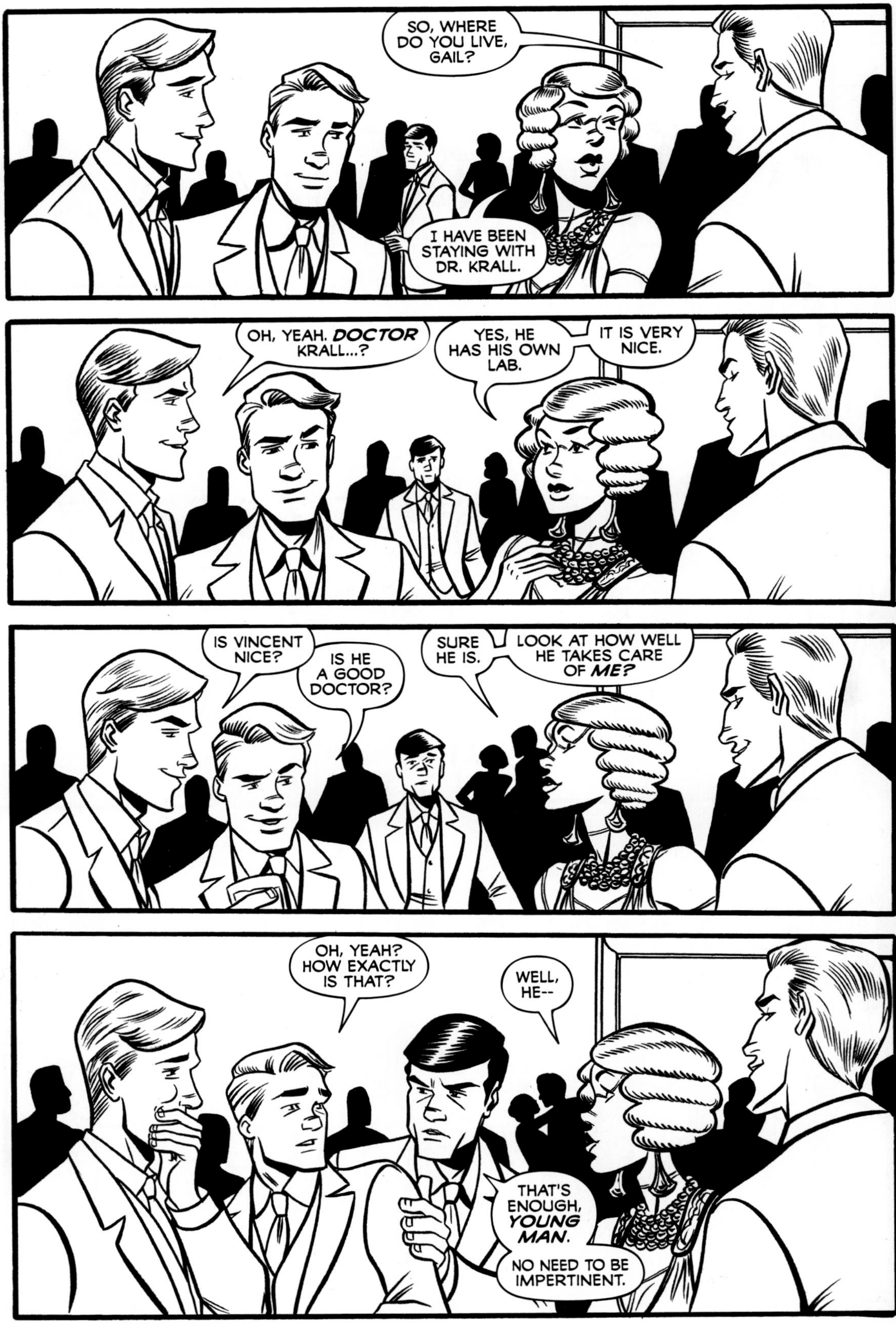
SO, WHERE DO YOU LIVE, GAIL?
I HAVE BEEN STAYING WITH DR. KRALL.
OH, YEAH. **DOCTOR** KRALL...?
YES, HE HAS HIS OWN LAB.
IT IS VERY NICE.
IS VINCENT NICE?
IS HE A GOOD DOCTOR?
SURE HE IS.
LOOK AT HOW WELL HE TAKES CARE OF **ME?**
OH, YEAH? HOW EXACTLY IS THAT?
WELL, HE--
THAT'S ENOUGH, **YOUNG MAN**.
NO NEED TO BE IMPERTINENT.

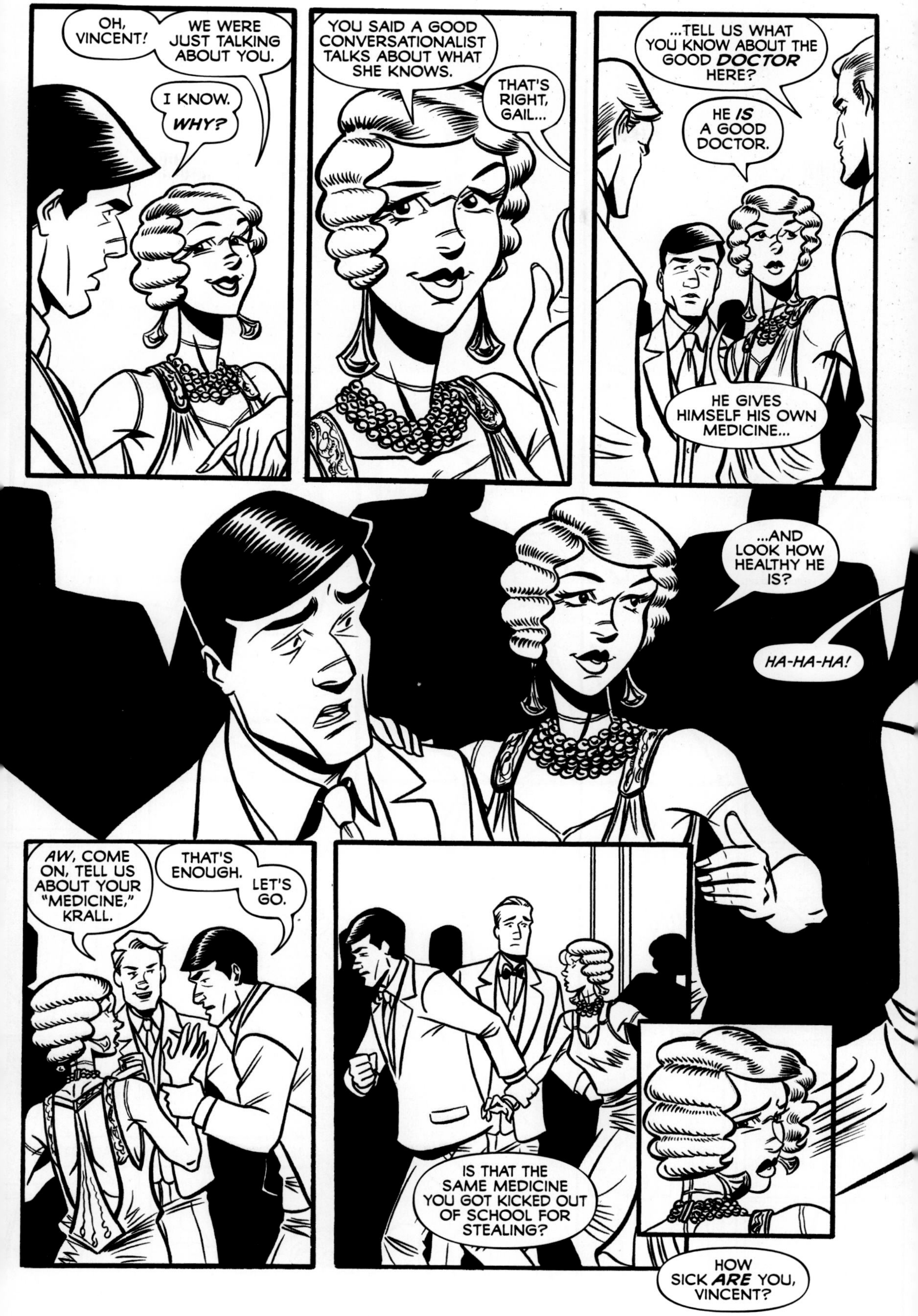
OH, VINCENT!
WE WERE JUST TALKING ABOUT YOU.
I KNOW. *WHY?*
YOU SAID A GOOD CONVERSATIONALIST TALKS ABOUT WHAT SHE KNOWS.
THAT'S RIGHT, GAIL...
...TELL US WHAT YOU KNOW ABOUT THE GOOD ***DOCTOR*** HERE?
HE *IS* A GOOD DOCTOR.
HE GIVES HIMSELF HIS OWN MEDICINE...
...AND LOOK HOW HEALTHY HE IS?
HA-HA-HA!
AW, COME ON, TELL US ABOUT YOUR "MEDICINE," KRALL.
THAT'S ENOUGH.
LET'S GO.
IS THAT THE SAME MEDICINE YOU GOT KICKED OUT OF SCHOOL FOR STEALING?
HOW SICK ***ARE*** YOU, VINCENT?

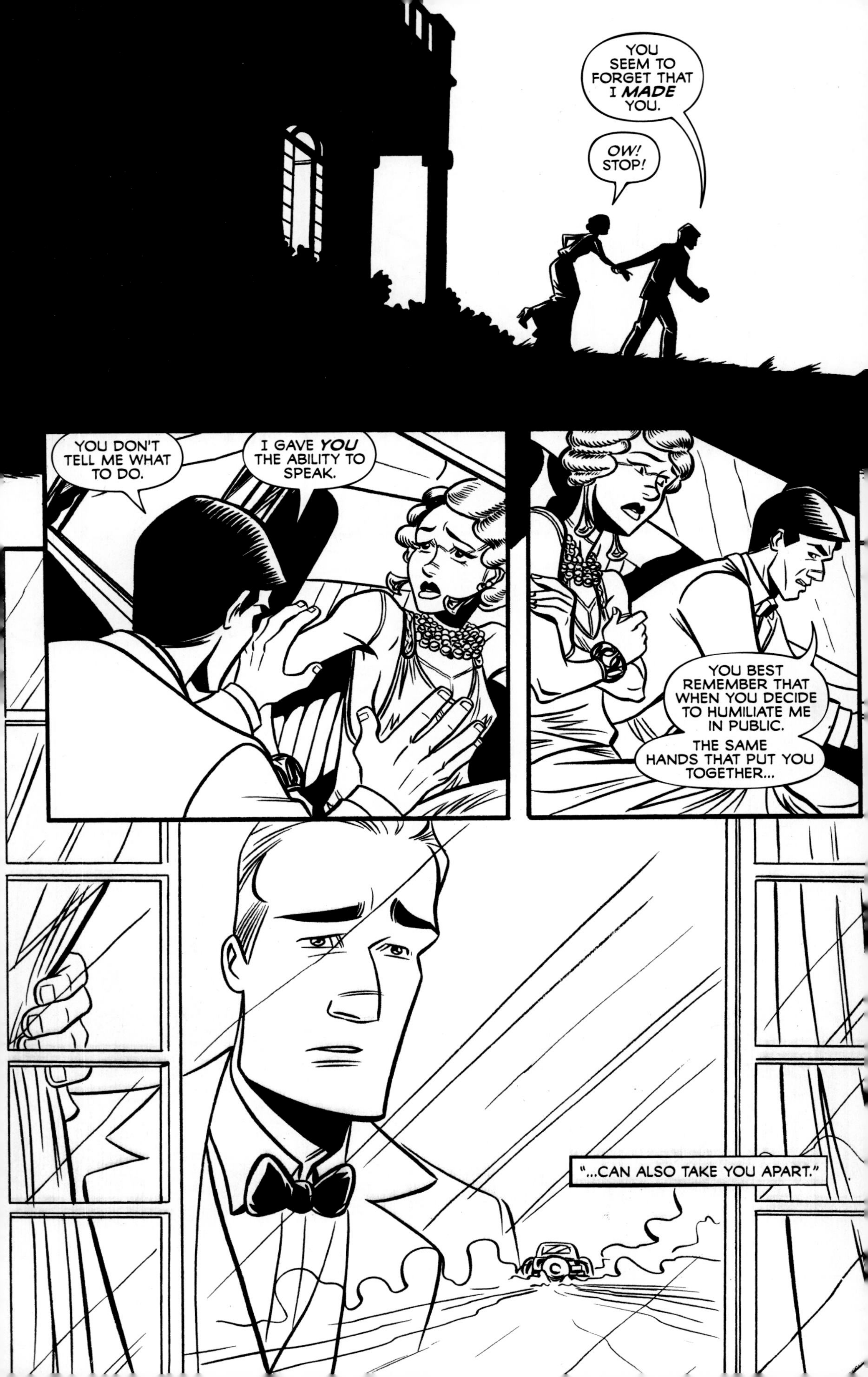
OW! STOP!
YOU SEEM TO FORGET THAT I *MADE* YOU.
YOU DON'T TELL ME WHAT TO DO.
I GAVE *YOU* THE ABILITY TO SPEAK.
YOU BEST REMEMBER THAT WHEN YOU DECIDE TO HUMILIATE ME IN PUBLIC.
THE SAME HANDS THAT PUT YOU TOGETHER...
"...CAN ALSO TAKE YOU APART."

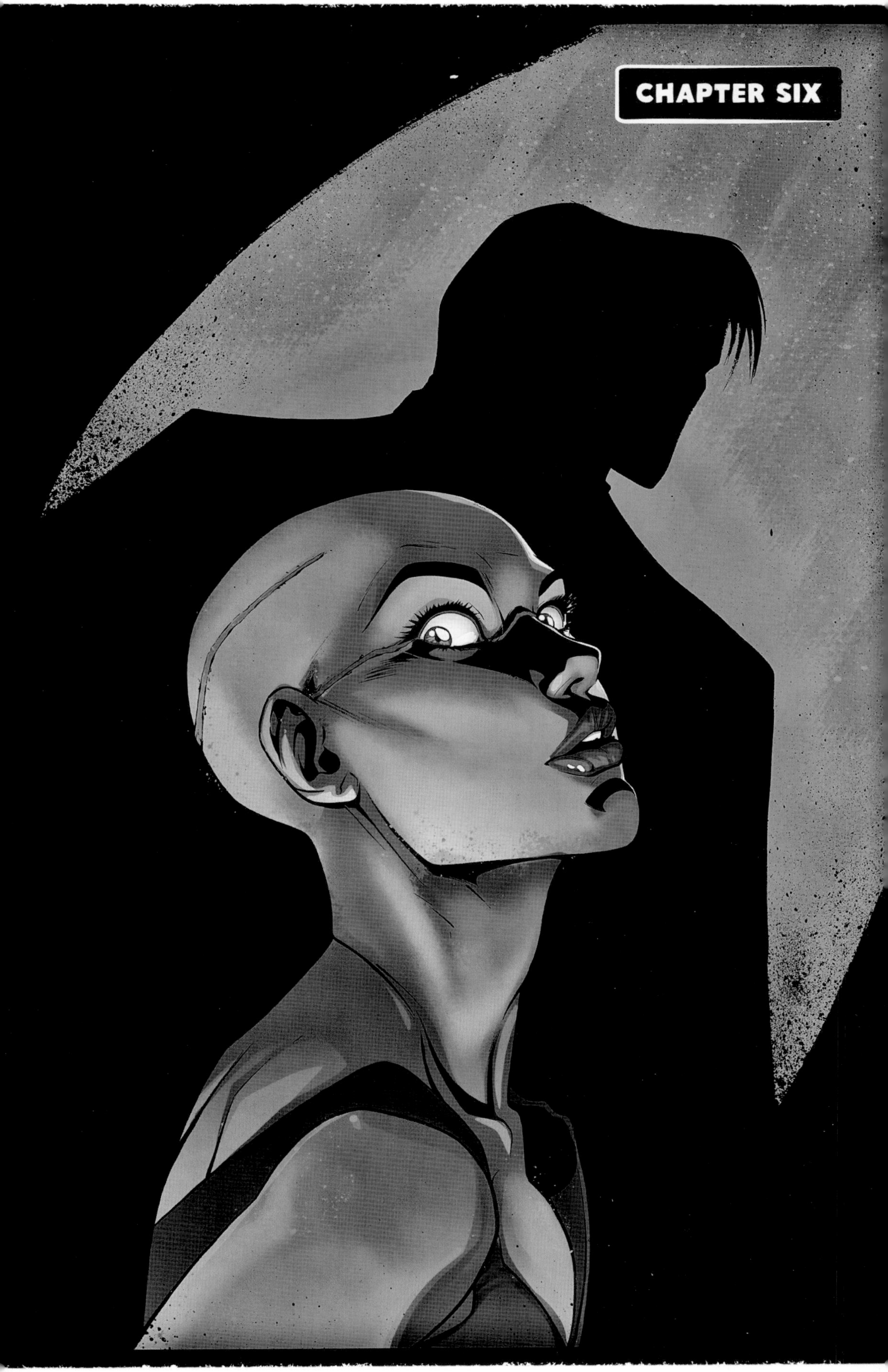
CHAPTER SIX

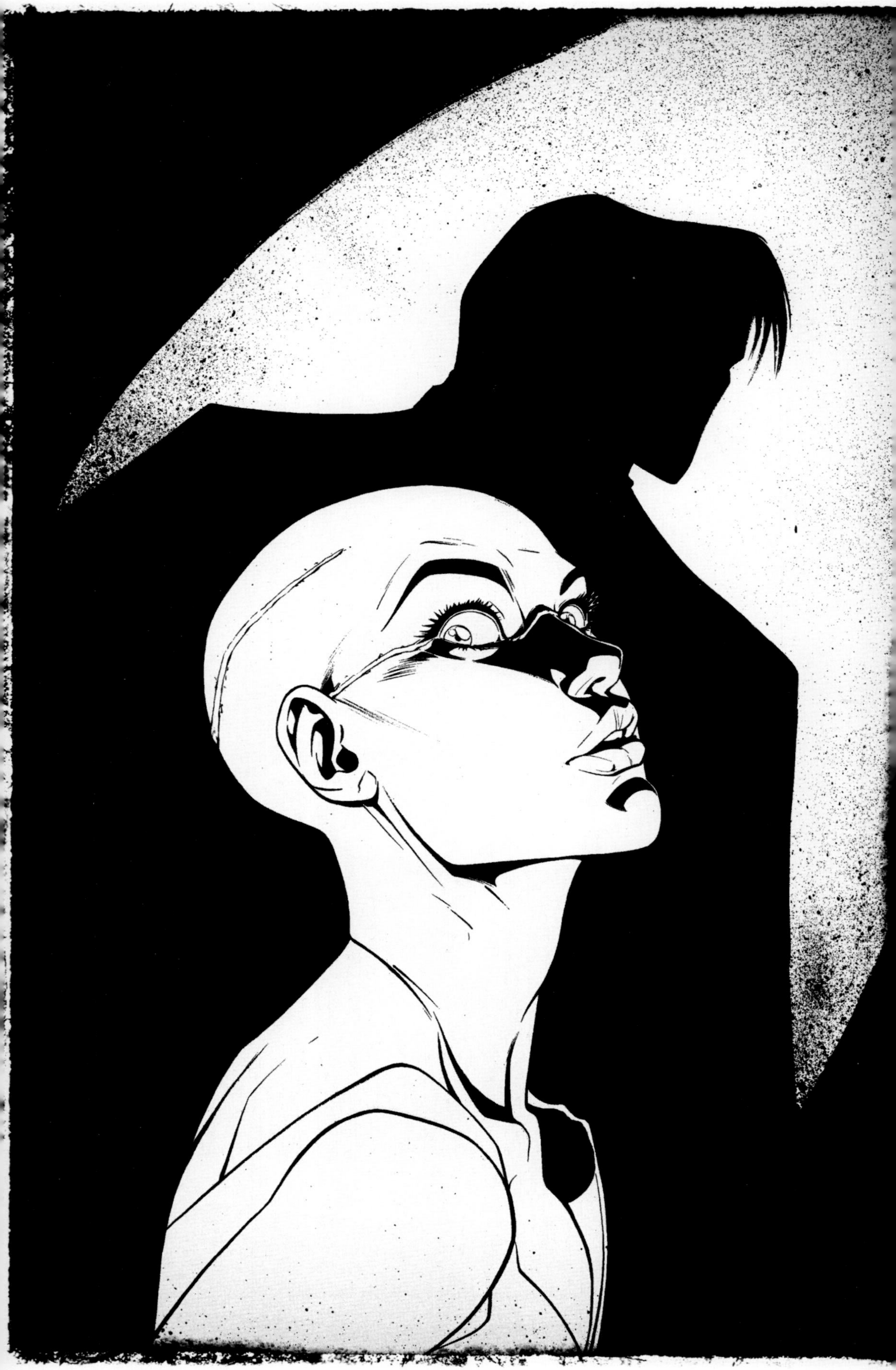

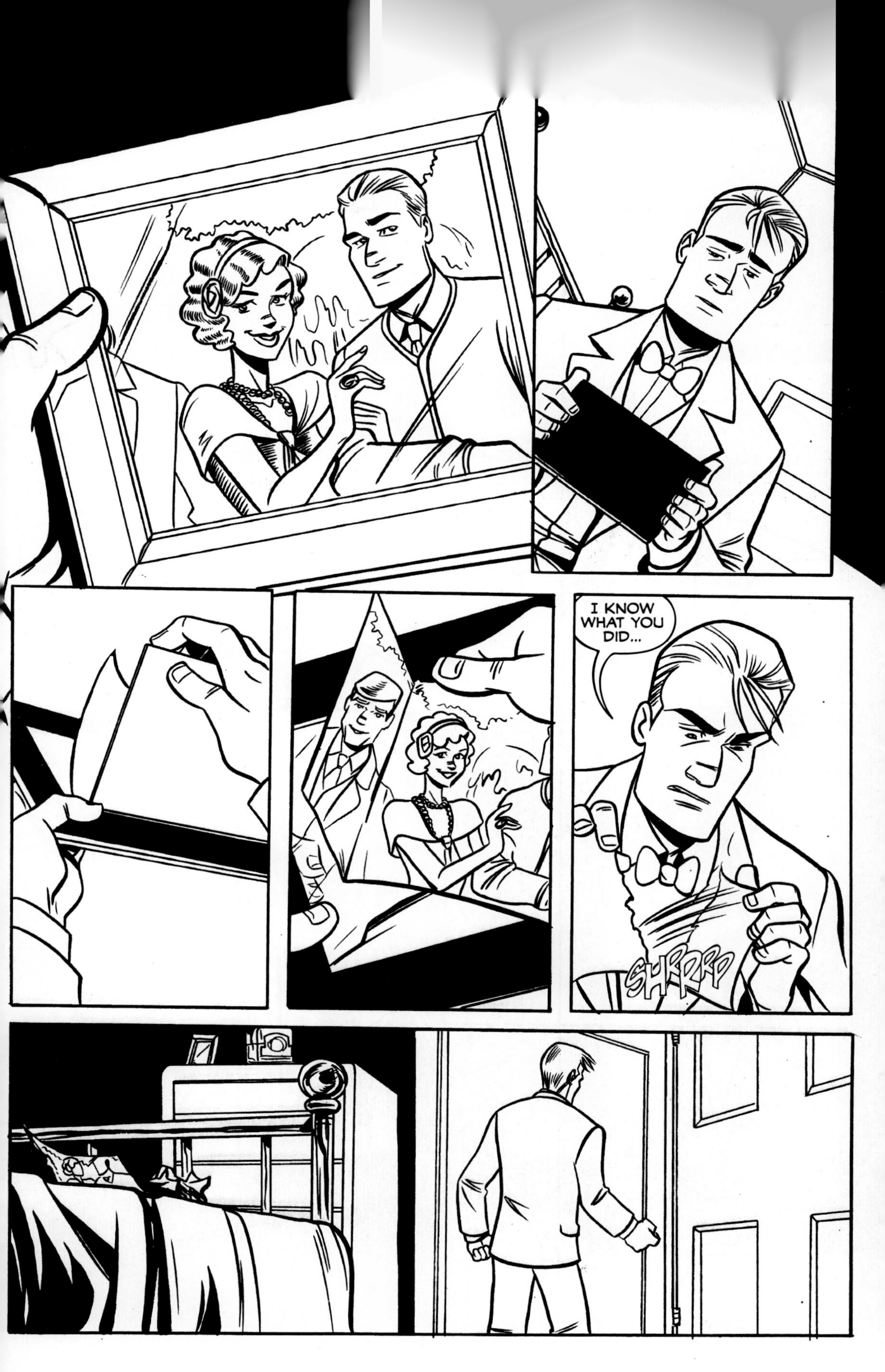
I KNOW WHAT YOU DID...
SHRRP

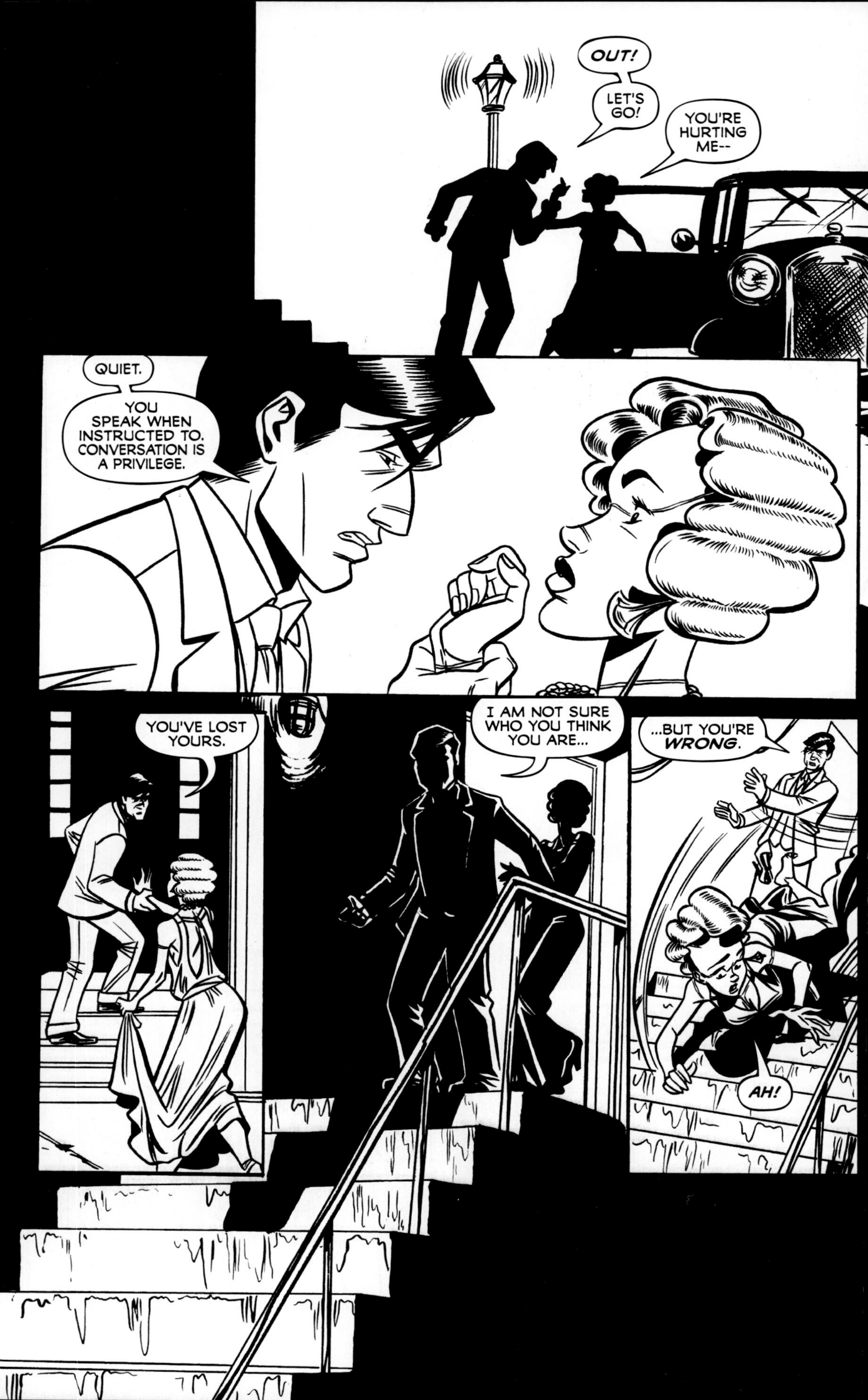
OUT!
LET'S GO!
YOU'RE HURTING ME--
QUIET.
YOU SPEAK WHEN INSTRUCTED TO. CONVERSATION IS A PRIVILEGE.
YOU'VE LOST YOURS.
I AM NOT SURE WHO YOU THINK YOU ARE...
...BUT YOU'RE *WRONG*.
AH!

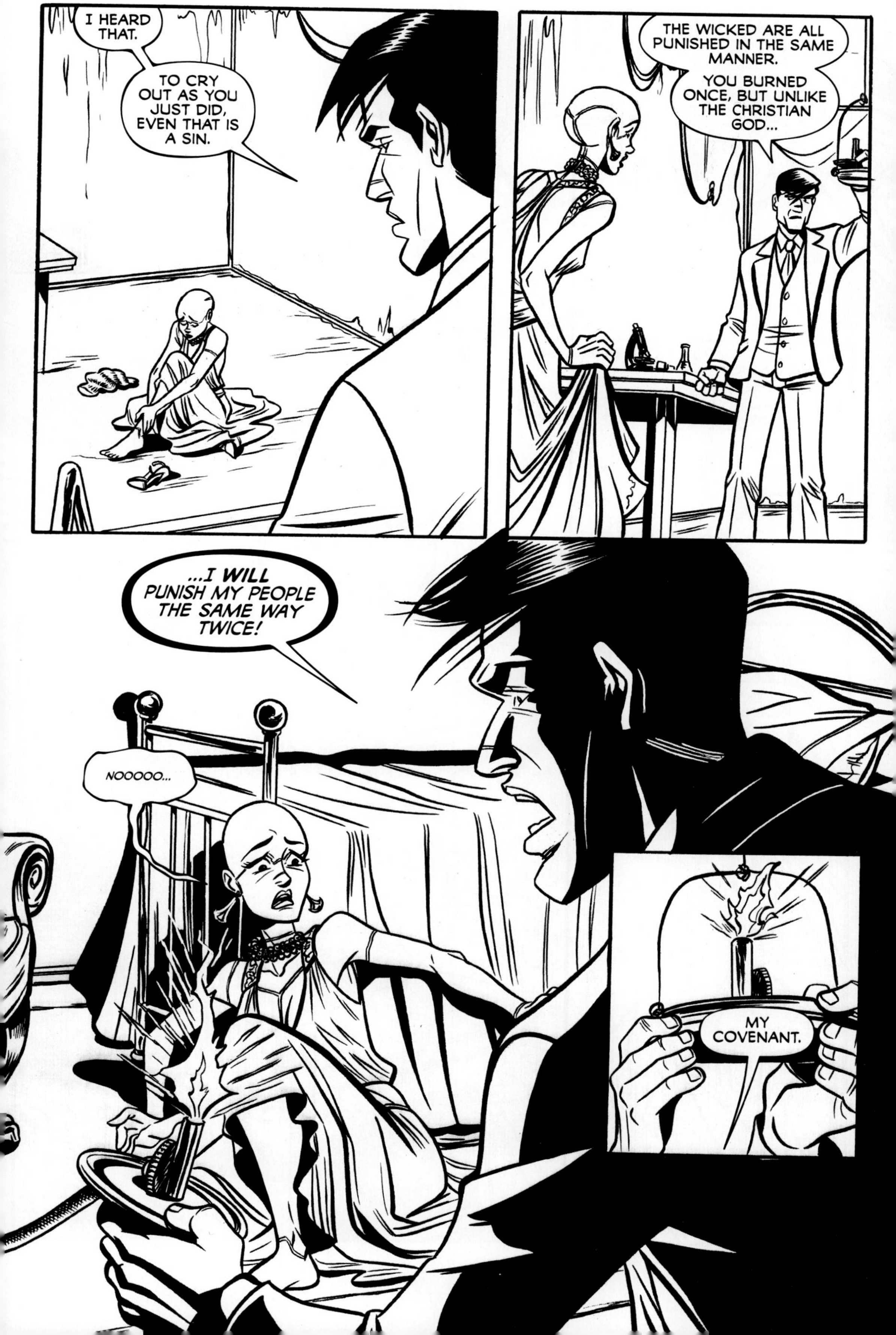
I HEARD THAT.
TO CRY OUT AS YOU JUST DID, EVEN THAT IS A SIN.
THE WICKED ARE ALL PUNISHED IN THE SAME MANNER.
YOU BURNED ONCE, BUT UNLIKE THE CHRISTIAN GOD...
...I WILL PUNISH MY PEOPLE THE SAME WAY TWICE!
NOOOOO...
MY COVENANT.

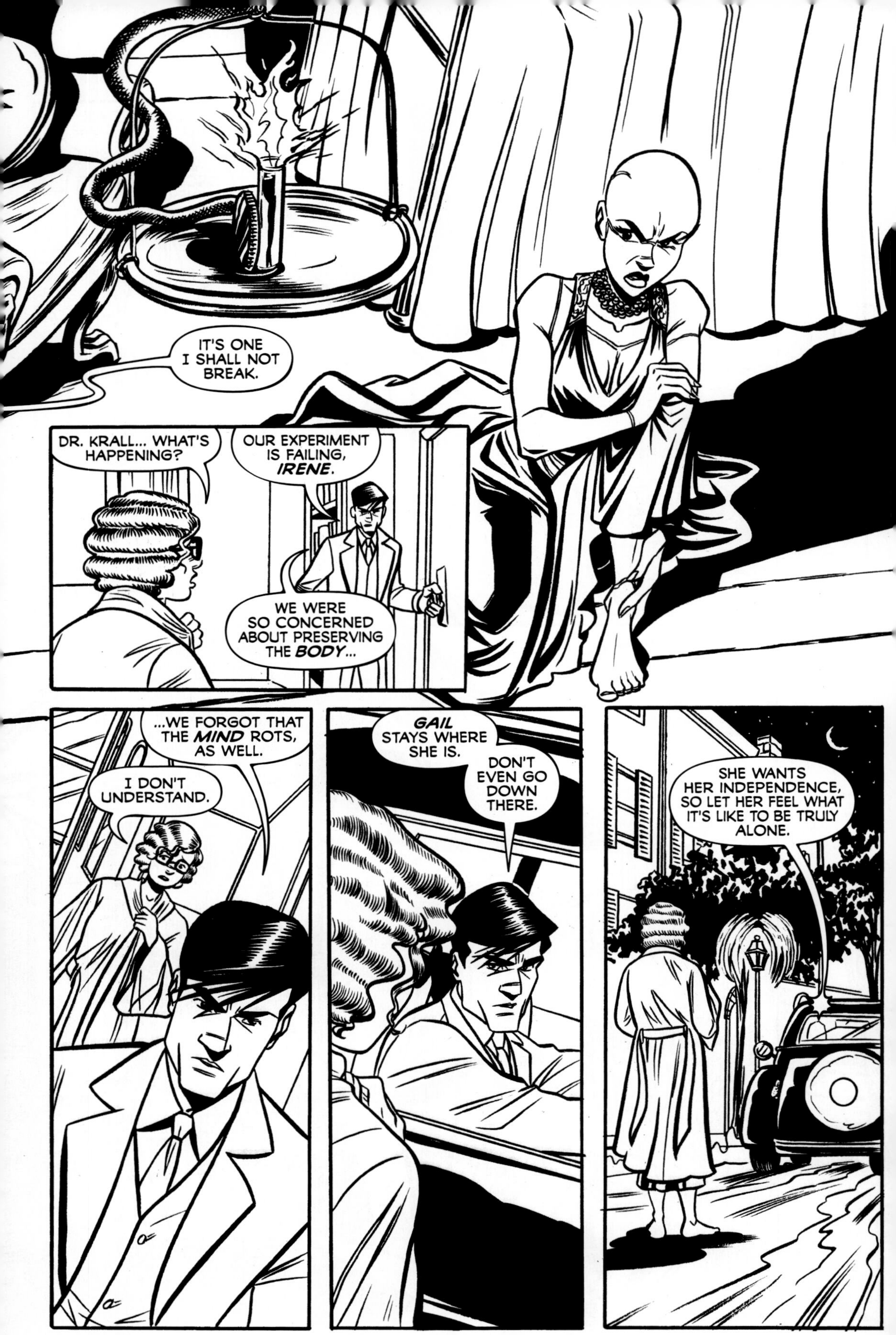
IT'S ONE I SHALL NOT BREAK.
DR. KRALL... WHAT'S HAPPENING?
OUR EXPERIMENT IS FAILING, *IRENE*.
WE WERE SO CONCERNED ABOUT PRESERVING THE *BODY*...
...WE FORGOT THAT THE *MIND* ROTS, AS WELL.
I DON'T UNDERSTAND.
GAIL STAYS WHERE SHE IS.
DON'T EVEN GO DOWN THERE.
SHE WANTS HER INDEPENDENCE, SO LET HER FEEL WHAT IT'S LIKE TO BE TRULY ALONE.

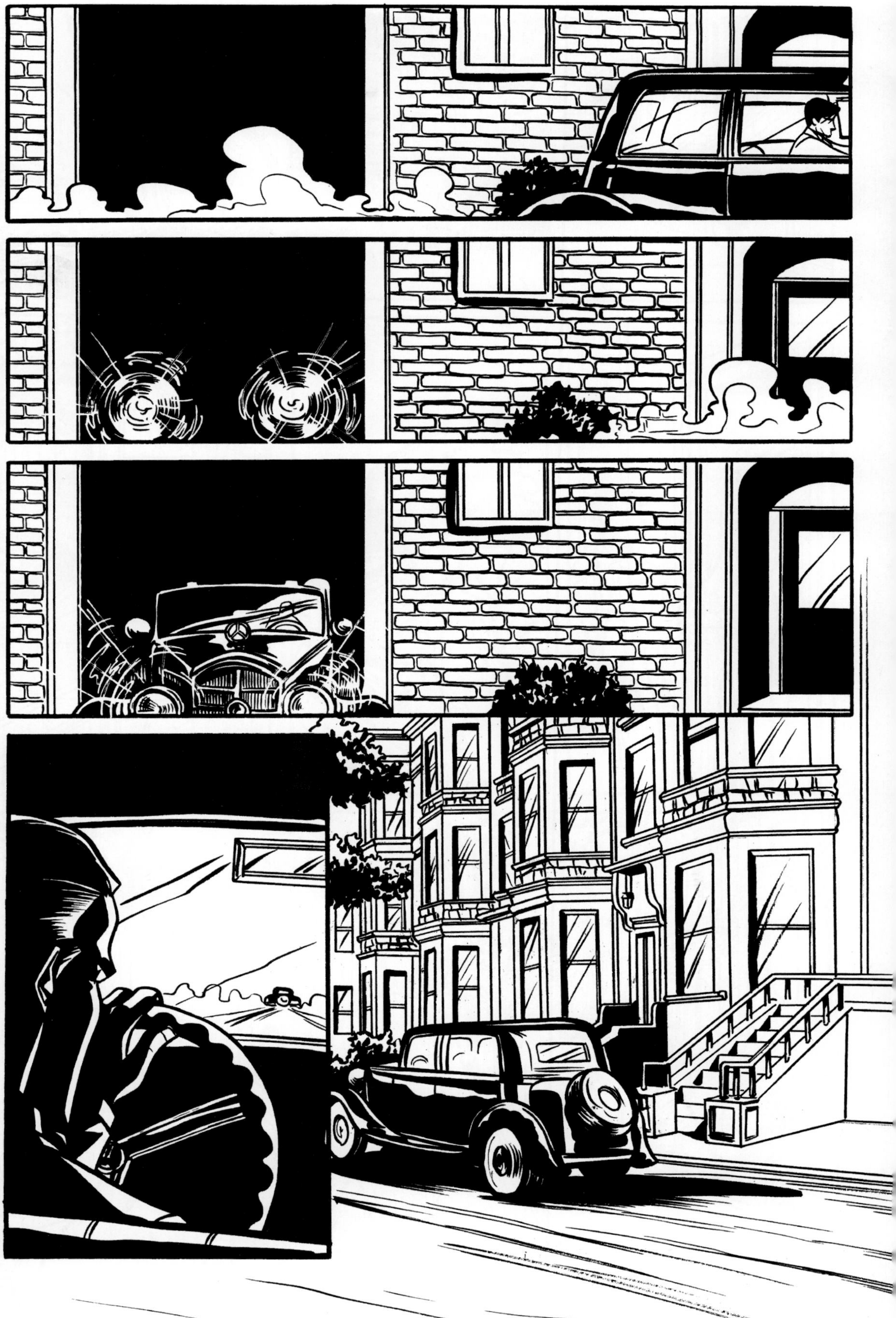

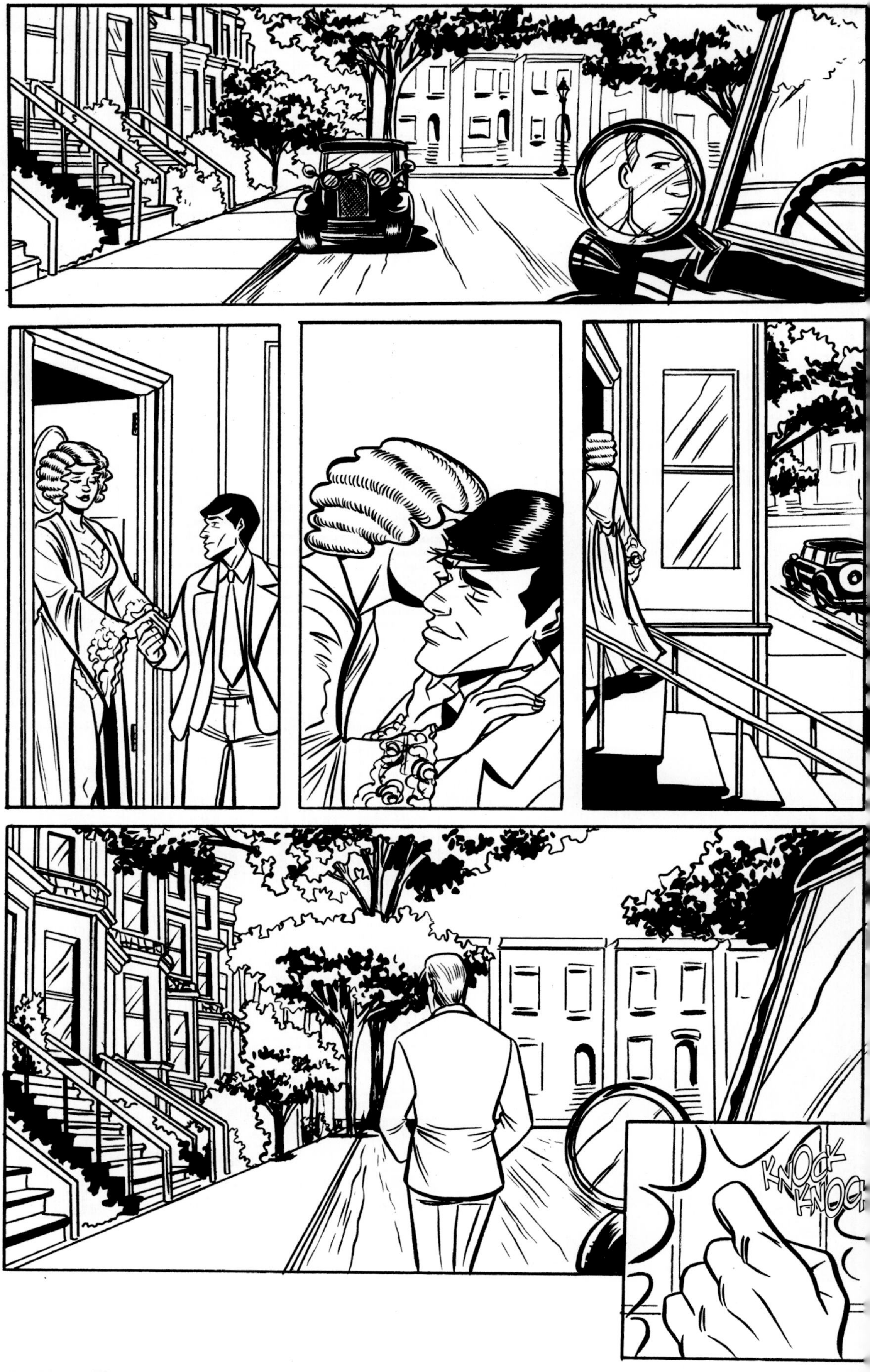
KNOCK
KNOCK

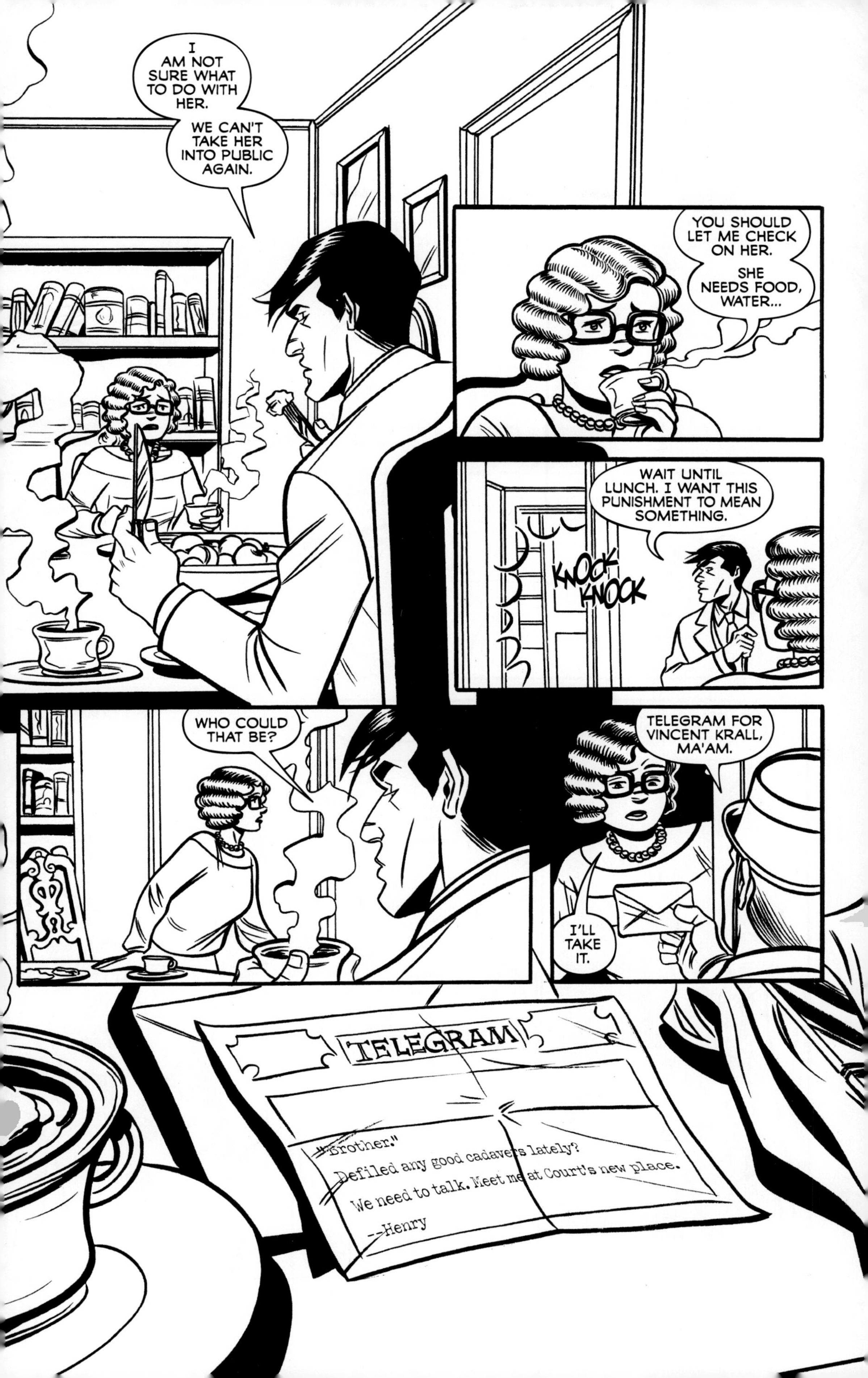
I AM NOT SURE WHAT TO DO WITH HER.
WE CAN'T TAKE HER INTO PUBLIC AGAIN.
YOU SHOULD LET ME CHECK ON HER.
SHE NEEDS FOOD, WATER...
WAIT UNTIL LUNCH. I WANT THIS PUNISHMENT TO MEAN SOMETHING.
KNOCK KNOCK
WHO COULD THAT BE?
TELEGRAM FOR VINCENT KRALL, MA'AM.
I'LL TAKE IT.
TELEGRAM
"Brother."
Defiled any good cadavers lately?
We need to talk. Meet me at Court's new place.
--Henry

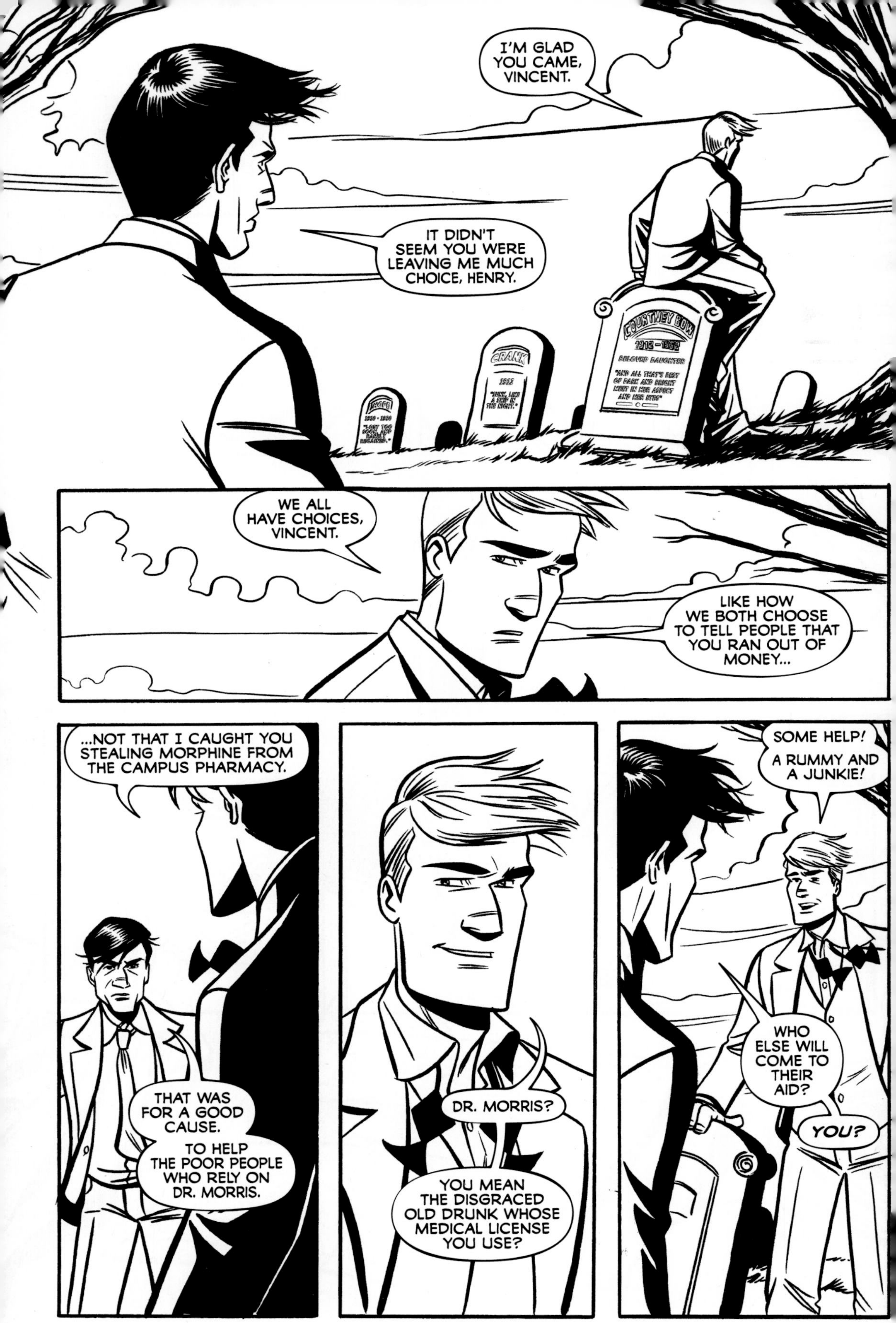
I'M GLAD YOU CAME, VINCENT.
IT DIDN'T SEEM YOU WERE LEAVING ME MUCH CHOICE, HENRY.
HOPE
"LOST TOO SOON, AND BARELY REGAINED."
CRANK
"SUNK, LIKE A SHIP IN THE NIGHT."
COURTNEY BOW
BELOVED DAUGHTER
"AND ALL THAT'S BEST OF DARK AND BRIGHT MEET IN HER ASPECT AND HER EYES"
WE ALL HAVE CHOICES, VINCENT.
LIKE HOW WE BOTH CHOOSE TO TELL PEOPLE THAT YOU RAN OUT OF MONEY...
...NOT THAT I CAUGHT YOU STEALING MORPHINE FROM THE CAMPUS PHARMACY.
THAT WAS FOR A GOOD CAUSE.
TO HELP THE POOR PEOPLE WHO RELY ON DR. MORRIS.
DR. MORRIS?
YOU MEAN THE DISGRACED OLD DRUNK WHOSE MEDICAL LICENSE YOU USE?
SOME HELP!
A RUMMY AND A JUNKIE!
WHO ELSE WILL COME TO THEIR AID?
YOU?

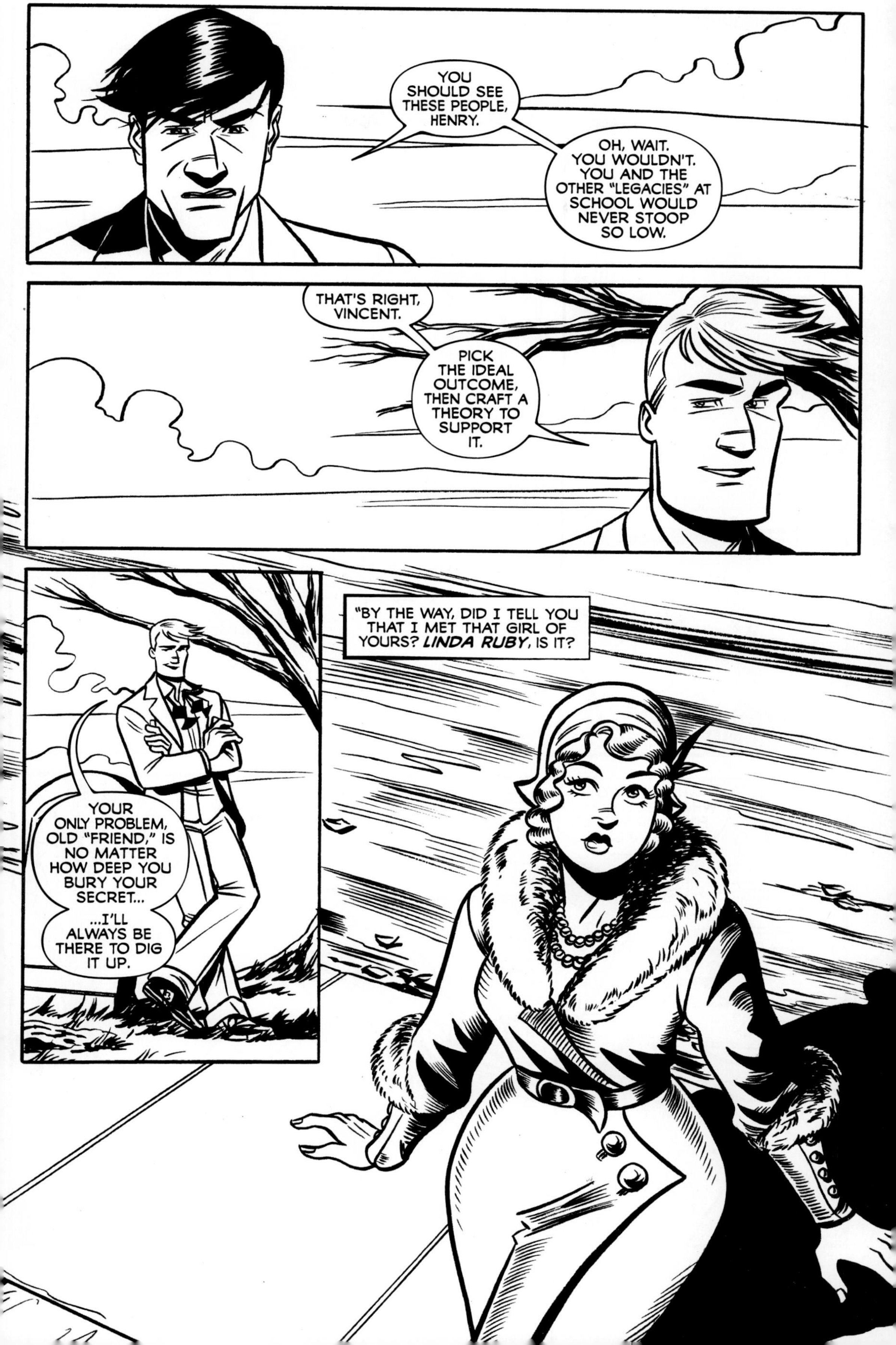
YOU SHOULD SEE THESE PEOPLE, HENRY.
OH, WAIT. YOU WOULDN'T. YOU AND THE OTHER "LEGACIES" AT SCHOOL WOULD NEVER STOOP SO LOW.
THAT'S RIGHT, VINCENT.
PICK THE IDEAL OUTCOME, THEN CRAFT A THEORY TO SUPPORT IT.
YOUR ONLY PROBLEM, OLD "FRIEND," IS NO MATTER HOW DEEP YOU BURY YOUR SECRET...
...I'LL ALWAYS BE THERE TO DIG IT UP.
"BY THE WAY, DID I TELL YOU THAT I MET THAT GIRL OF YOURS? LINDA RUBY, IS IT?

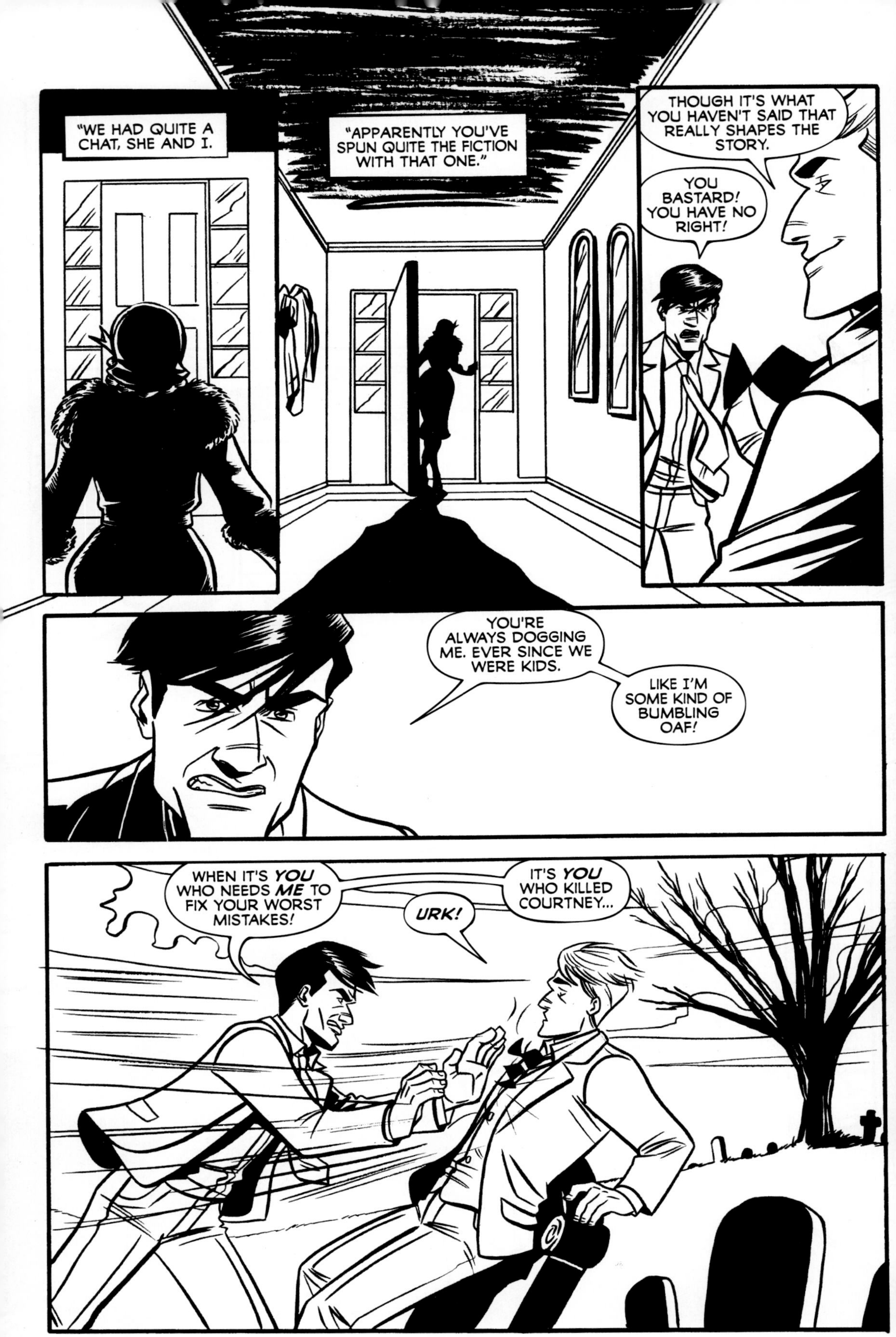
"WE HAD QUITE A CHAT, SHE AND I.
"APPARENTLY YOU'VE SPUN QUITE THE FICTION WITH THAT ONE."
THOUGH IT'S WHAT YOU HAVEN'T SAID THAT REALLY SHAPES THE STORY.
YOU BASTARD! YOU HAVE NO RIGHT!
YOU'RE ALWAYS DOGGING ME. EVER SINCE WE WERE KIDS.
LIKE I'M SOME KIND OF BUMBLING OAF!
WHEN IT'S YOU WHO NEEDS ME TO FIX YOUR WORST MISTAKES!
URK!
IT'S YOU WHO KILLED COURTNEY...

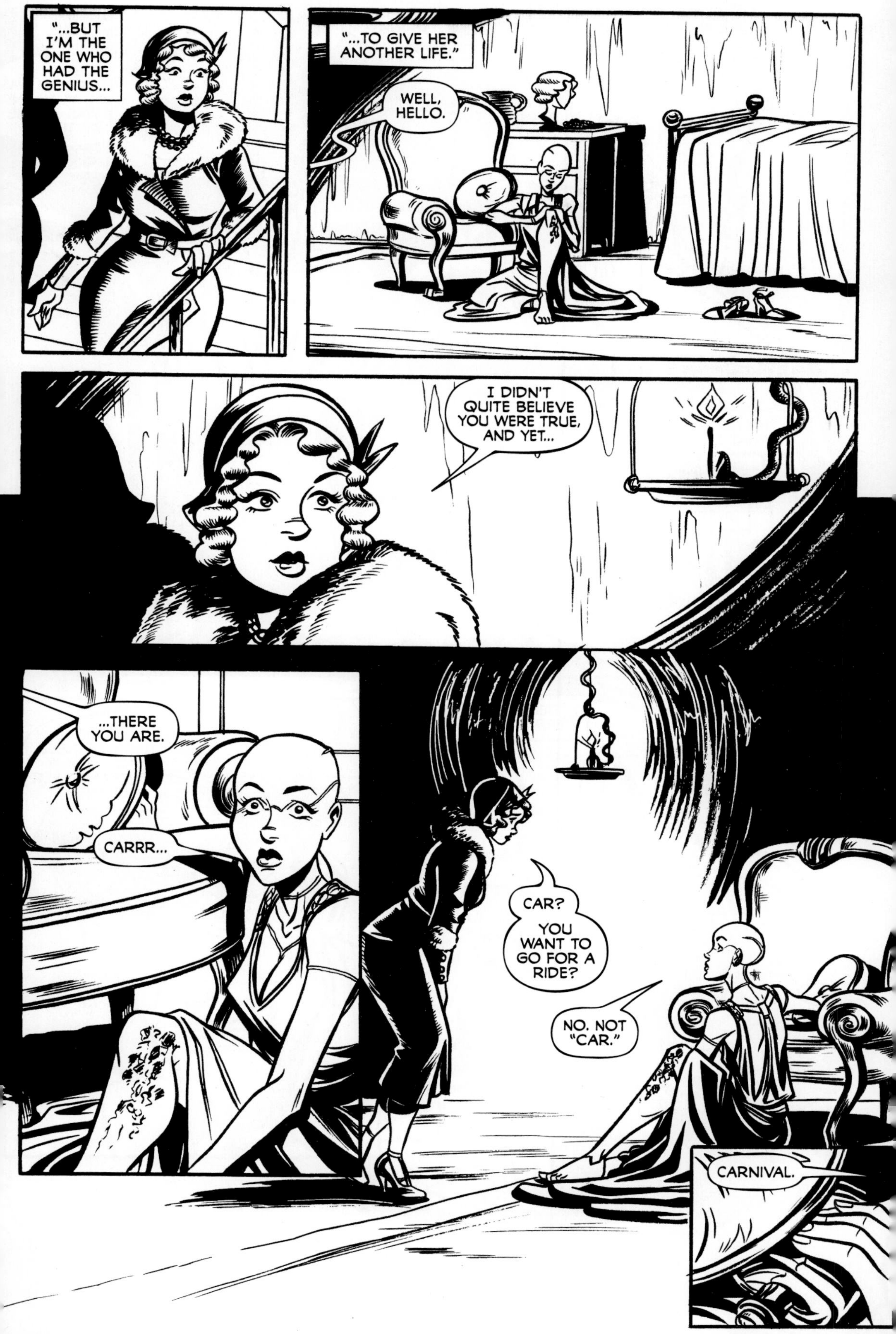
"...BUT I'M THE ONE WHO HAD THE GENIUS...
"...TO GIVE HER ANOTHER LIFE."
WELL, HELLO.
I DIDN'T QUITE BELIEVE YOU WERE TRUE, AND YET...
...THERE YOU ARE.
CARRR...
CAR?
YOU WANT TO GO FOR A RIDE?
NO. NOT "CAR."
CARNIVAL.

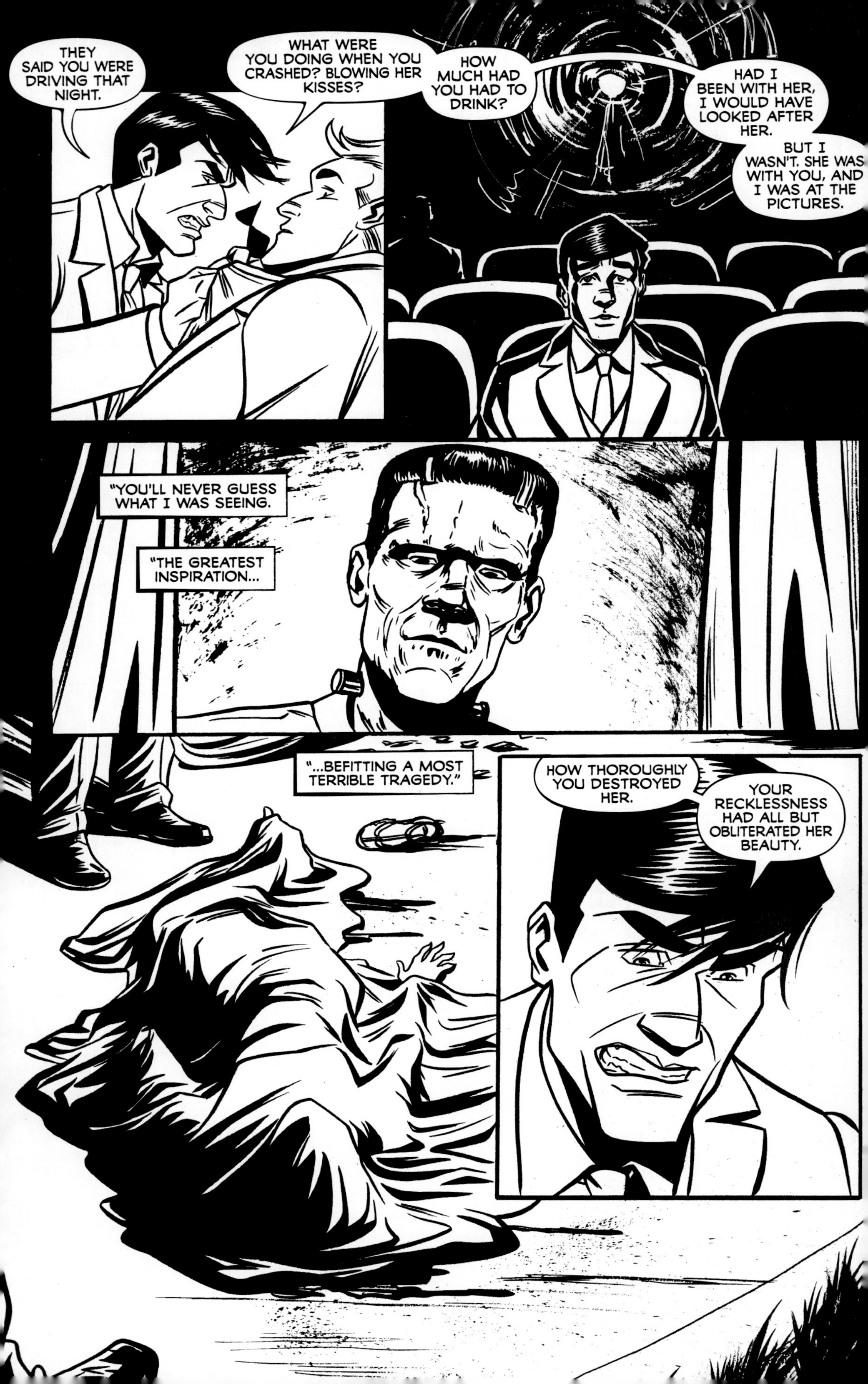
THEY SAID YOU WERE DRIVING THAT NIGHT.
WHAT WERE YOU DOING WHEN YOU CRASHED? BLOWING HER KISSES?
HOW MUCH HAD YOU HAD TO DRINK?
HAD I BEEN WITH HER, I WOULD HAVE LOOKED AFTER HER.
BUT I WASN'T. SHE WAS WITH YOU, AND I WAS AT THE PICTURES.
"YOU'LL NEVER GUESS WHAT I WAS SEEING.
"THE GREATEST INSPIRATION...
"...BEFITTING A MOST TERRIBLE TRAGEDY."
HOW THOROUGHLY YOU DESTROYED HER.
YOUR RECKLESSNESS HAD ALL BUT OBLITERATED HER BEAUTY.

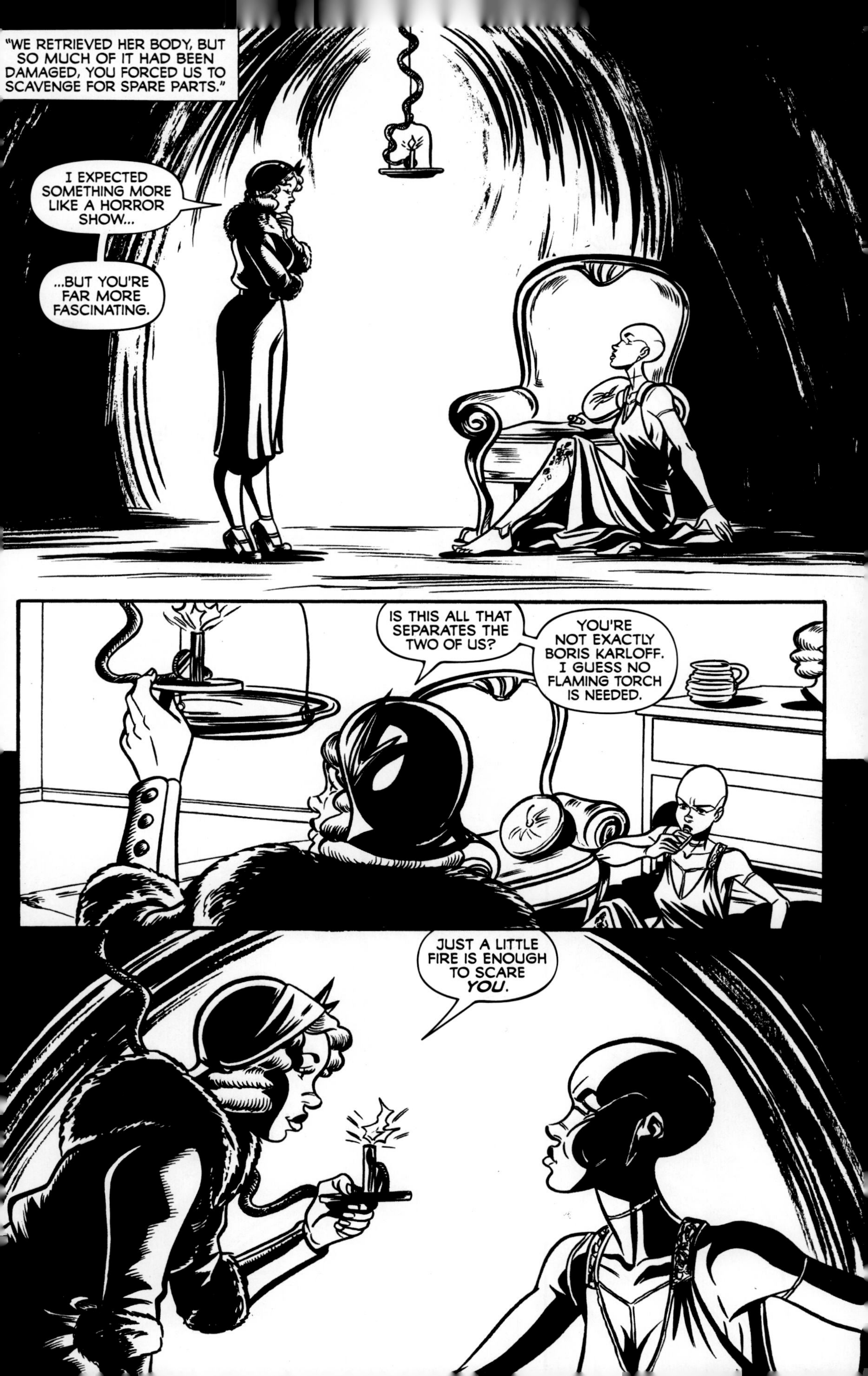

"WE RETRIEVED HER BODY, BUT SO MUCH OF IT HAD BEEN DAMAGED, YOU FORCED US TO SCAVENGE FOR SPARE PARTS."
I EXPECTED SOMETHING MORE LIKE A HORROR SHOW...
...BUT YOU'RE FAR MORE FASCINATING.
IS THIS ALL THAT SEPARATES THE TWO OF US?
YOU'RE NOT EXACTLY BORIS KARLOFF. I GUESS NO FLAMING TORCH IS NEEDED.
JUST A LITTLE FIRE IS ENOUGH TO SCARE *YOU*.

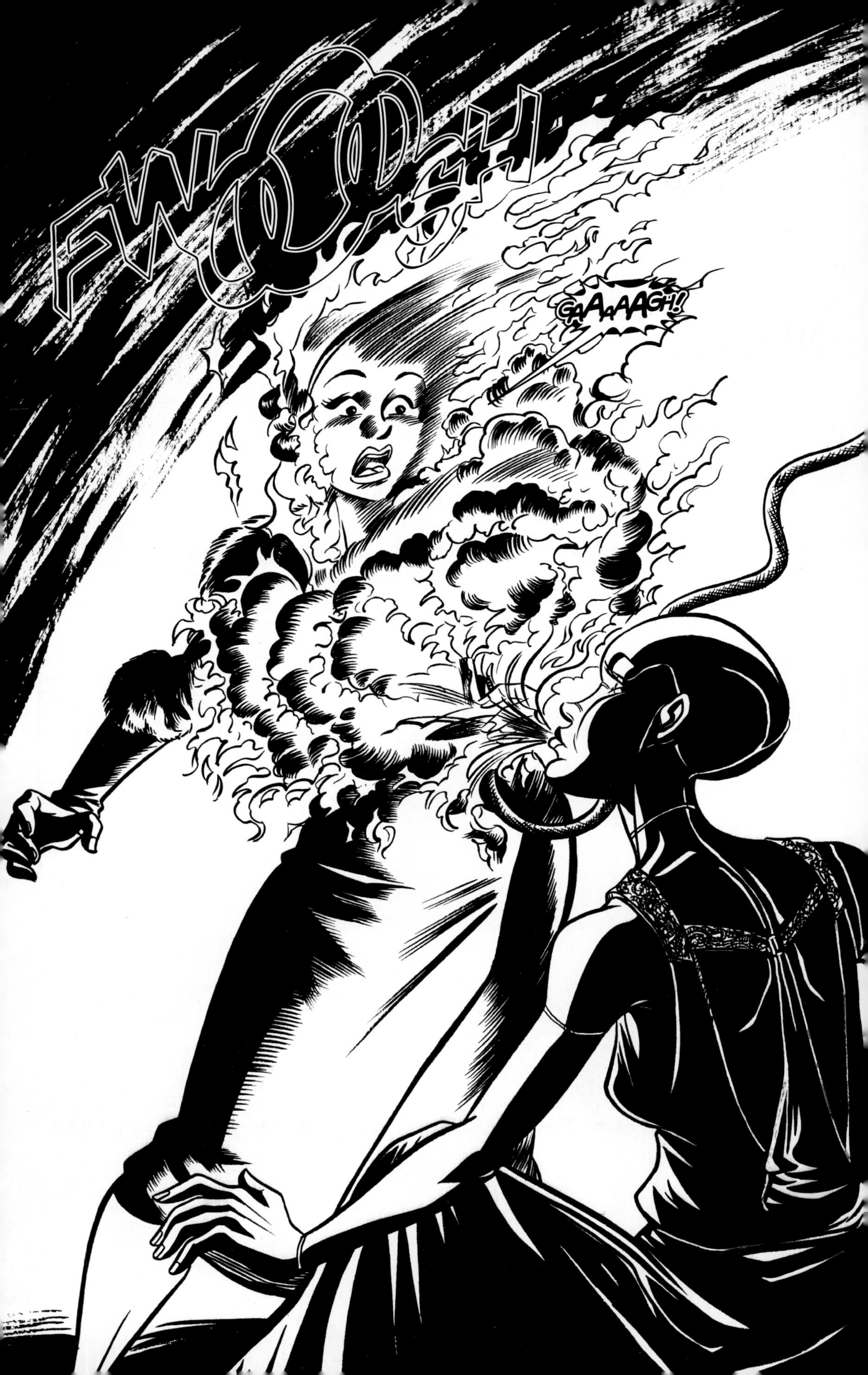
FWOOSH
GAAAAAGH!!

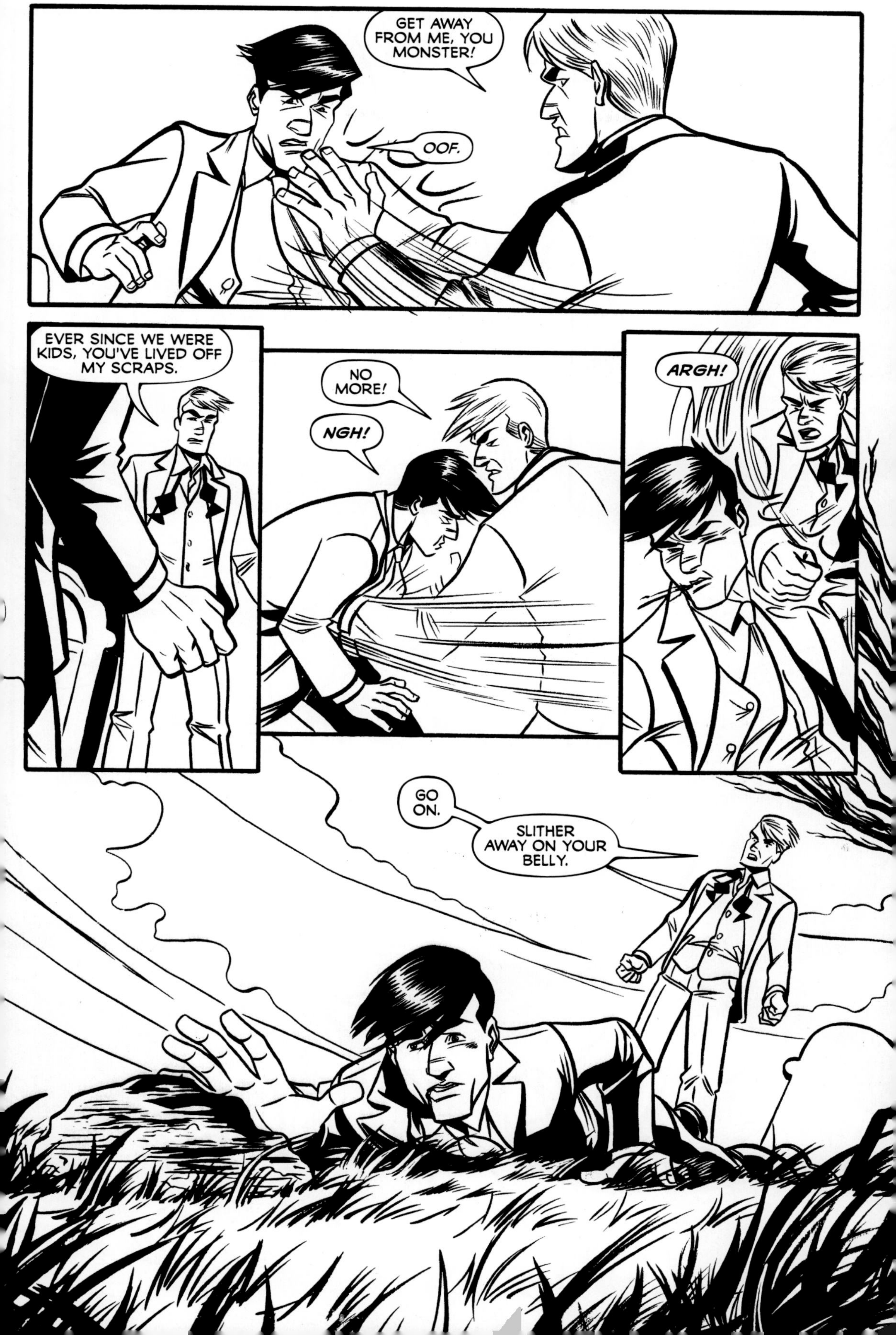
GET AWAY FROM ME, YOU MONSTER!
OOF.
EVER SINCE WE WERE KIDS, YOU'VE LIVED OFF MY SCRAPS.
NO MORE!
NGH!
ARGH!
GO ON.
SLITHER AWAY ON YOUR BELLY.

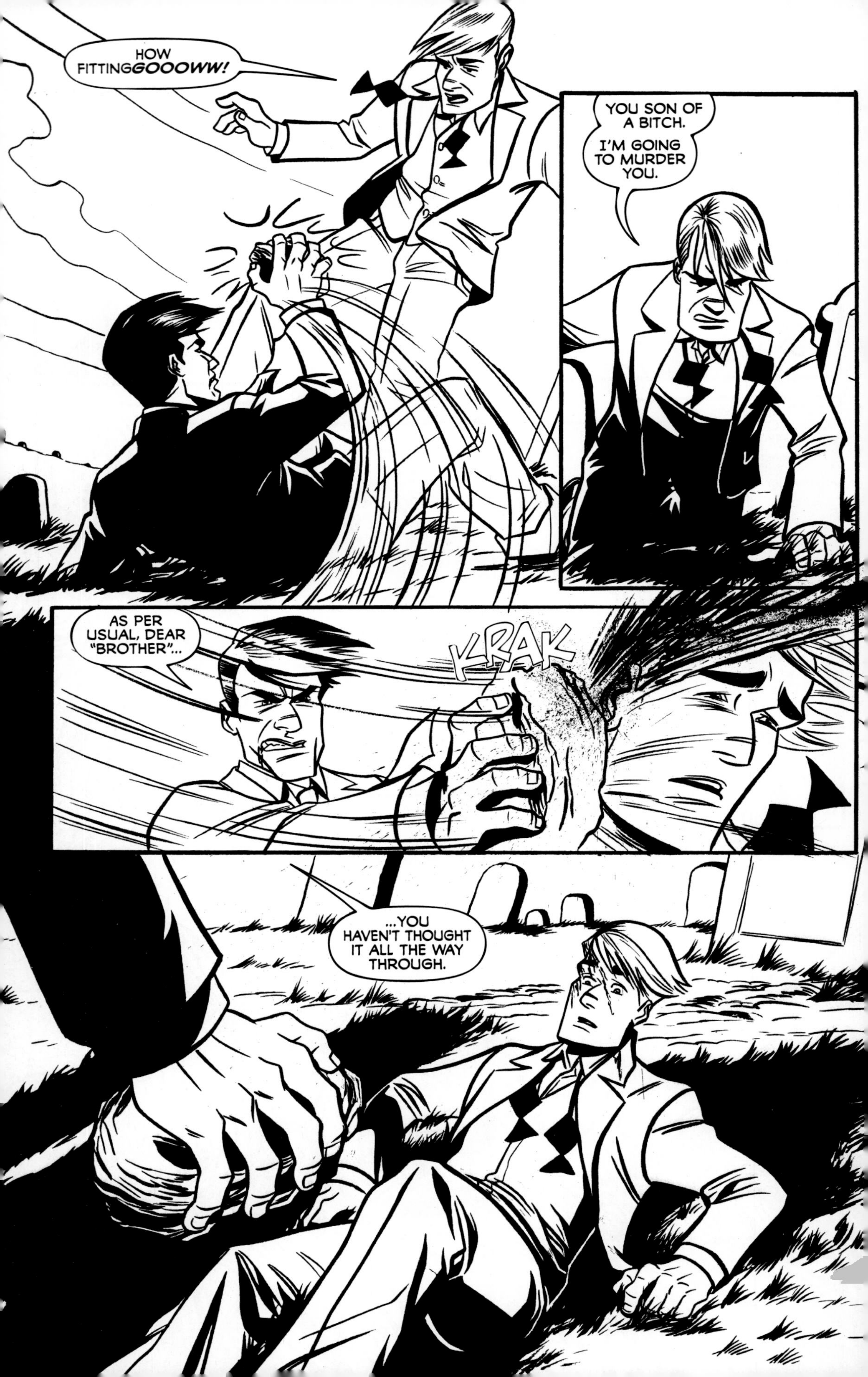
HOW FITTINGGOOOWW!
YOU SON OF A BITCH.
I'M GOING TO MURDER YOU.
AS PER USUAL, DEAR "BROTHER"...
KRAK
...YOU HAVEN'T THOUGHT IT ALL THE WAY THROUGH.

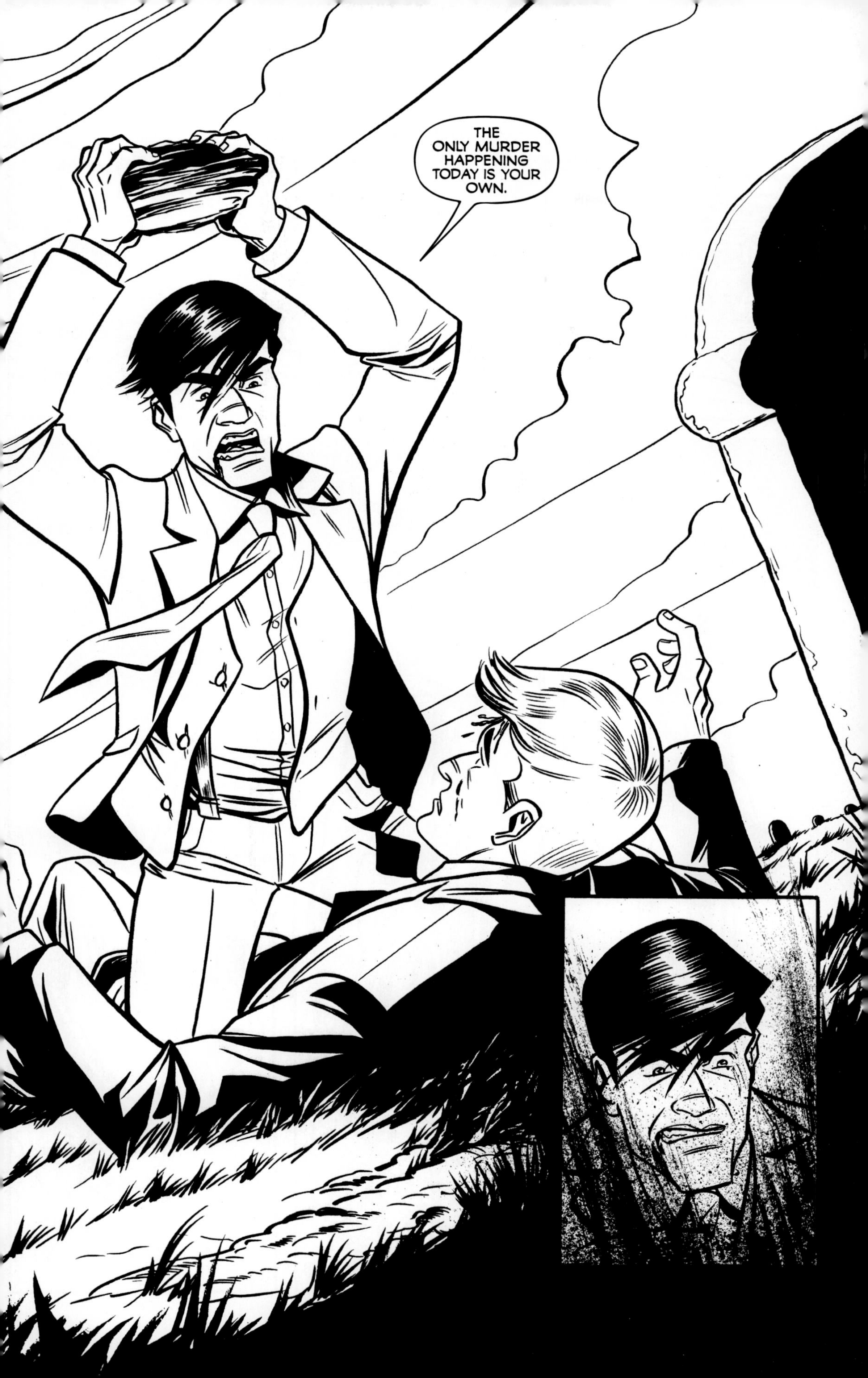
THE ONLY MURDER HAPPENING TODAY IS YOUR OWN.

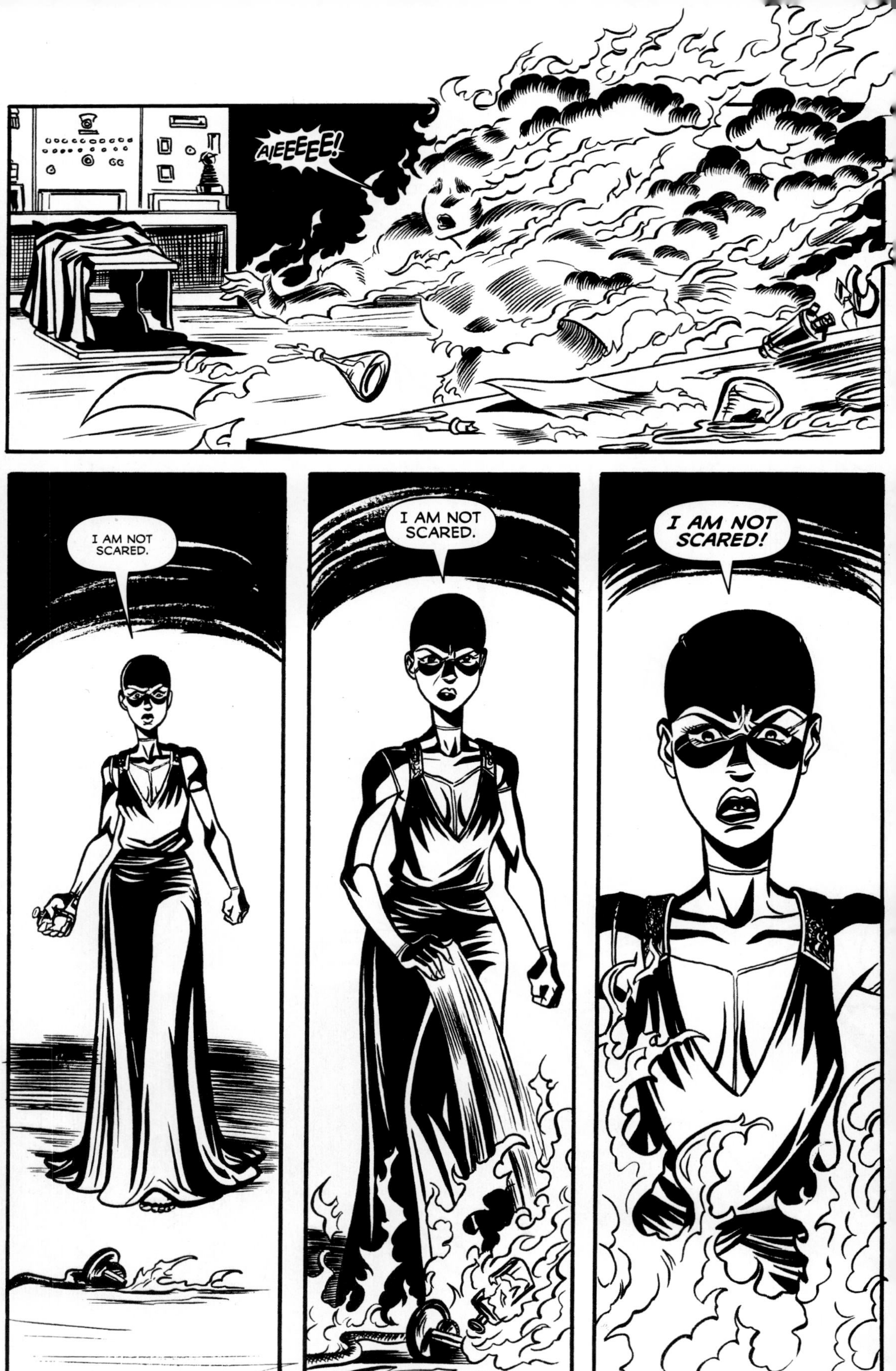
AIEEEEE!
I AM NOT SCARED.
I AM NOT SCARED.
I AM NOT SCARED!

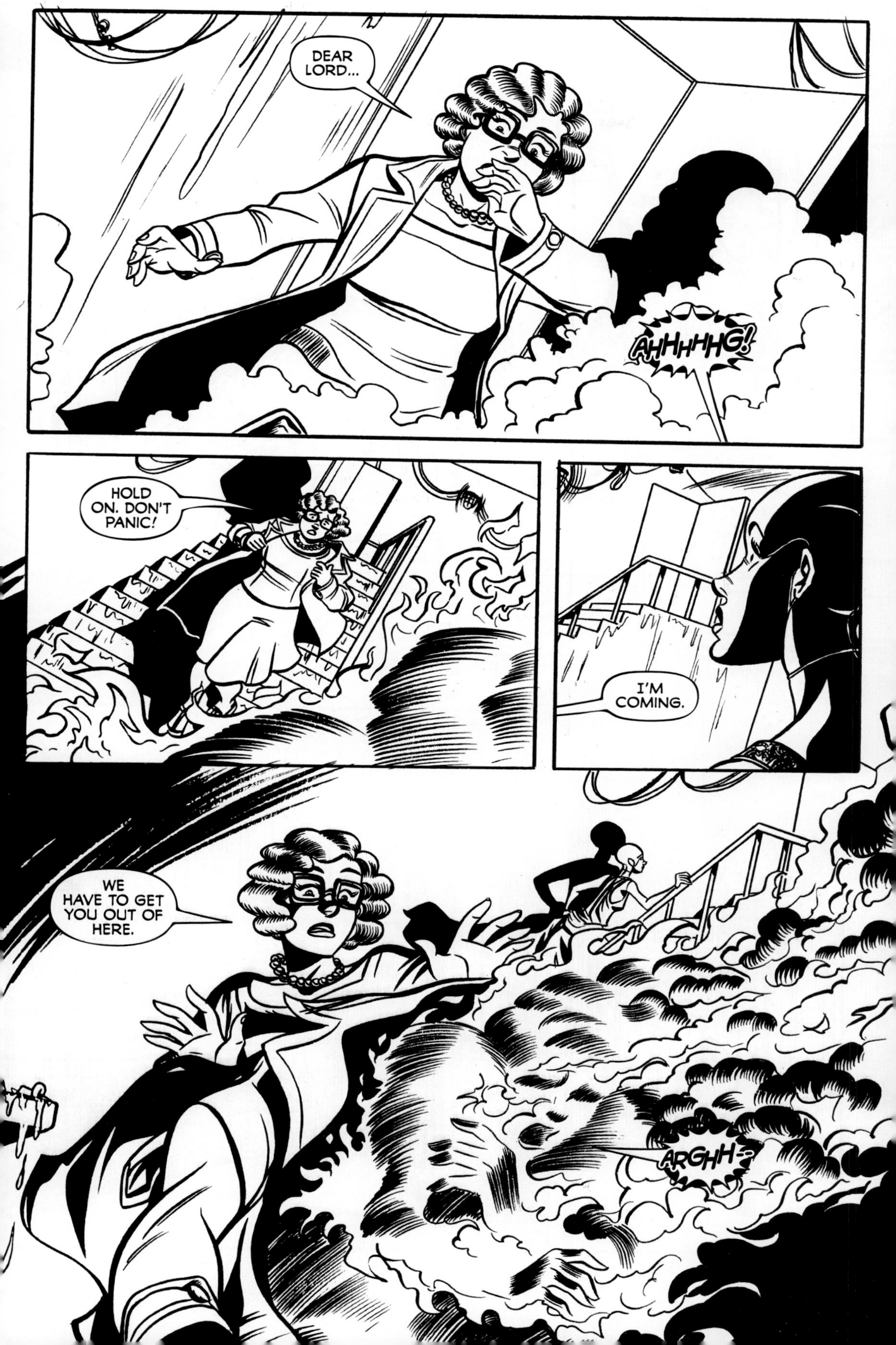
DEAR LORD...
AHHHHHG!
HOLD ON. DON'T PANIC!
I'M COMING.
WE HAVE TO GET YOU OUT OF HERE.
ARGHH

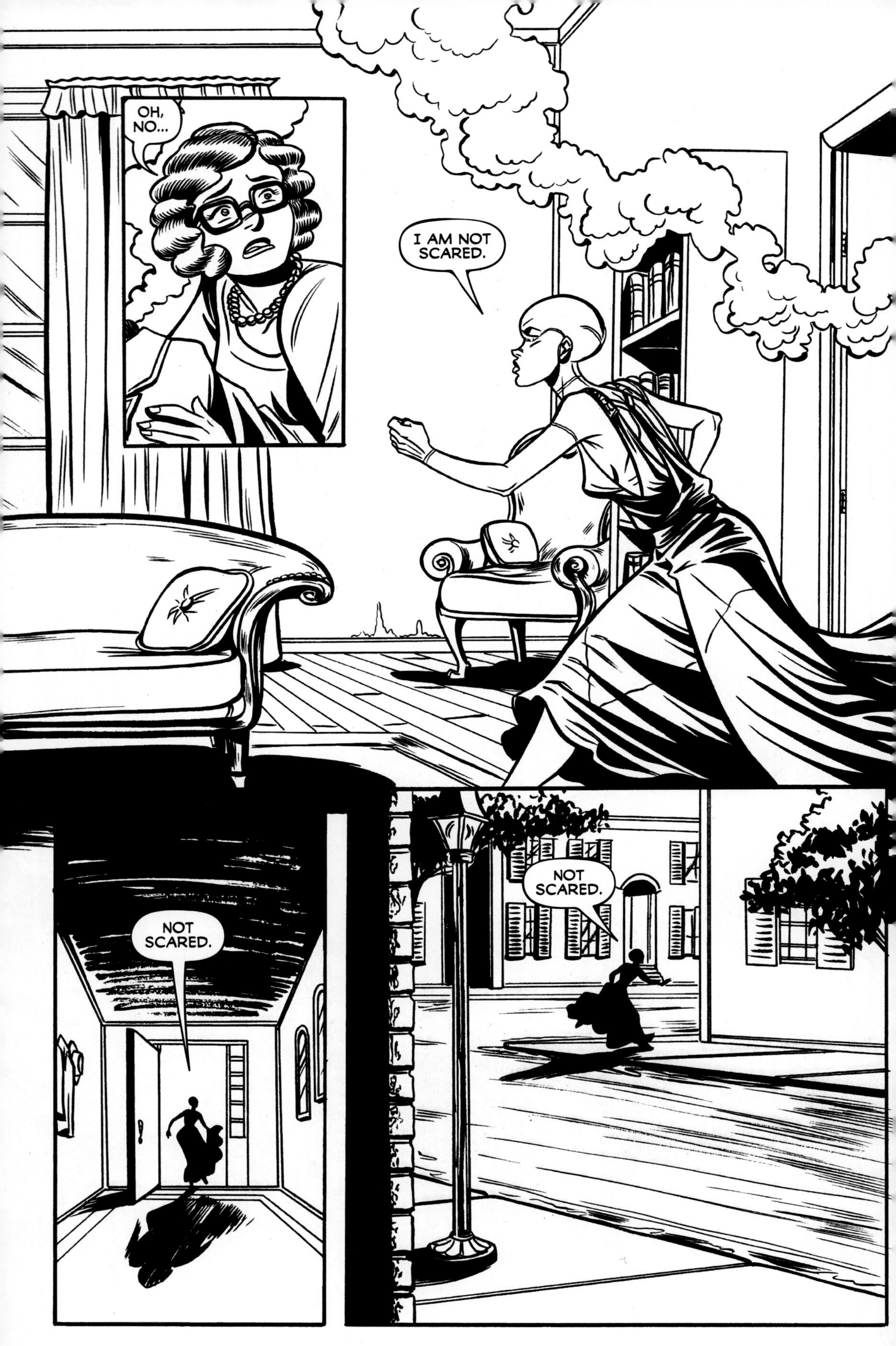
OH, NO...
I AM NOT SCARED.
NOT SCARED.
NOT SCARED.

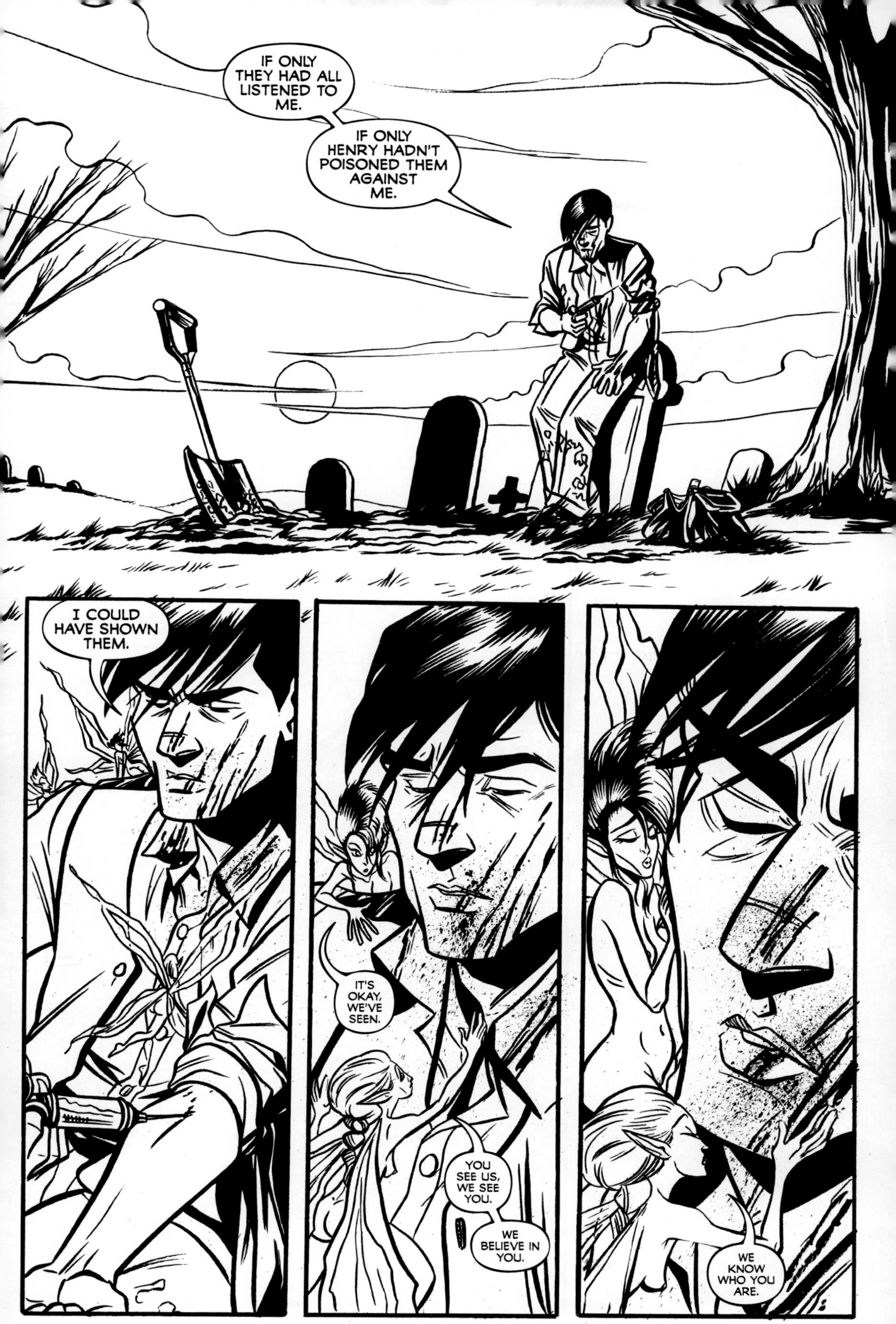
IF ONLY THEY HAD ALL LISTENED TO ME.
IF ONLY HENRY HADN'T POISONED THEM AGAINST ME.
I COULD HAVE SHOWN THEM.
IT'S OKAY, WE'VE SEEN.
YOU SEE US, WE SEE YOU.
WE BELIEVE IN YOU.
WE KNOW WHO YOU ARE.

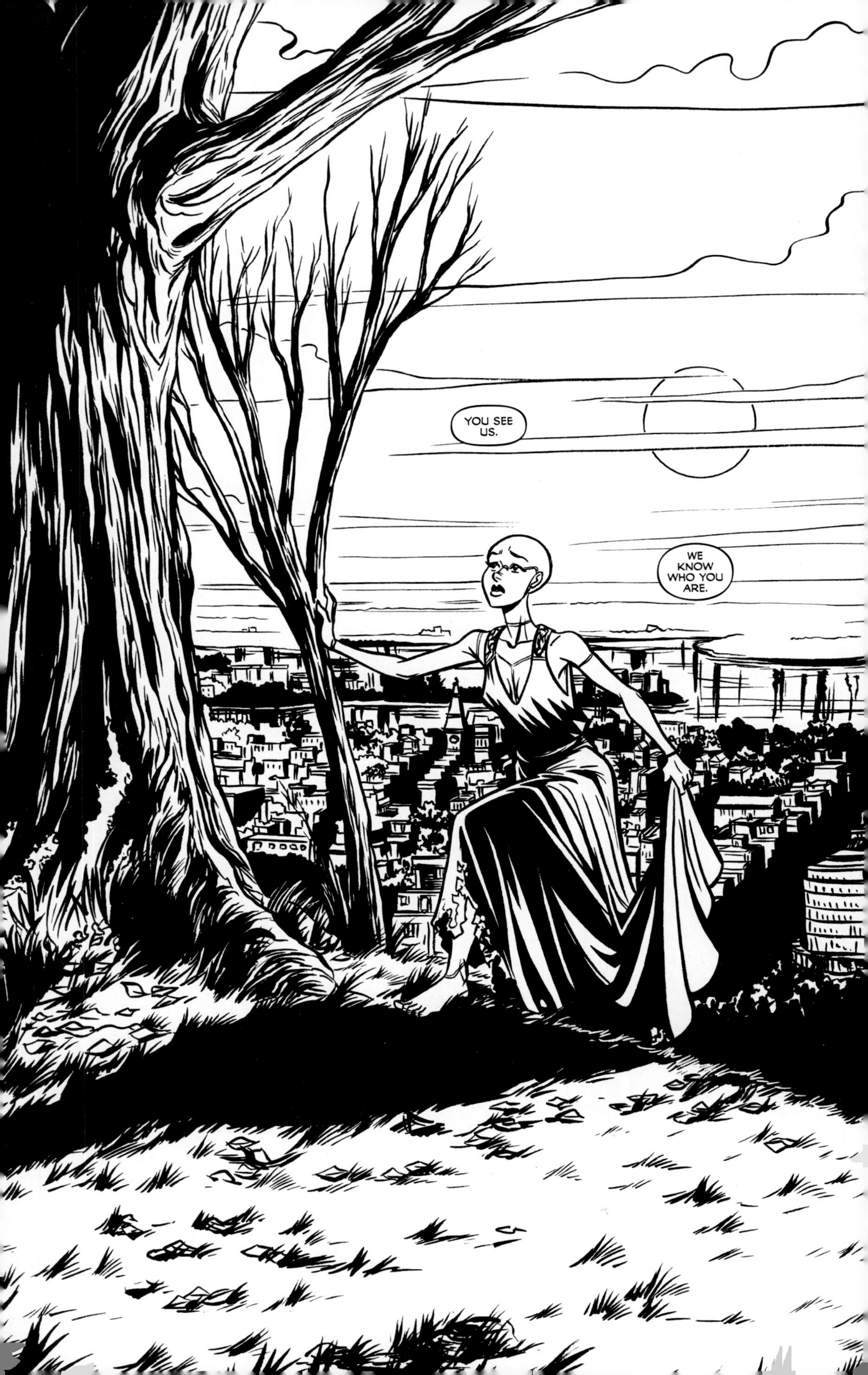
YOU SEE US.
WE KNOW WHO YOU ARE.

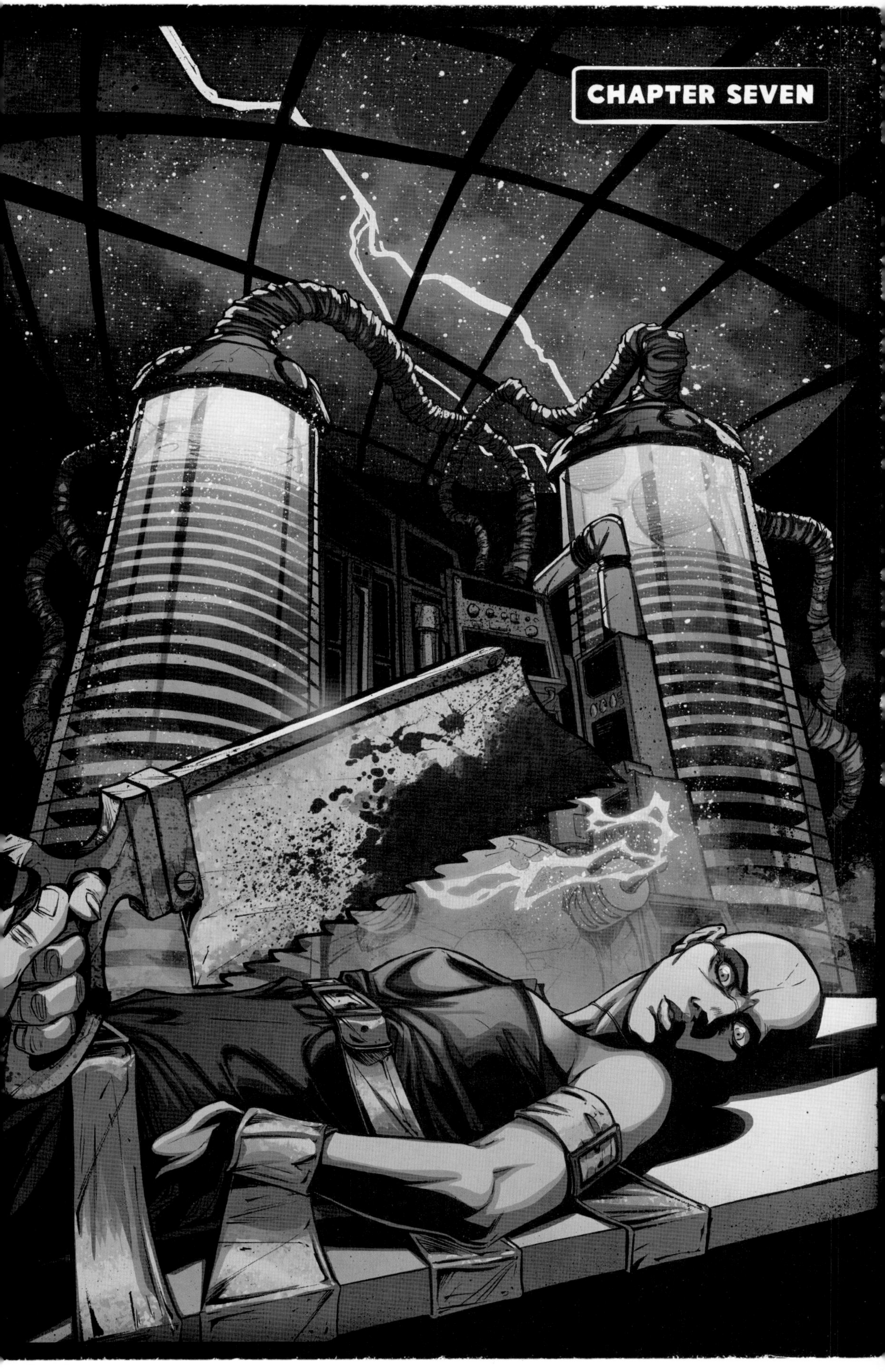
CHAPTER SEVEN

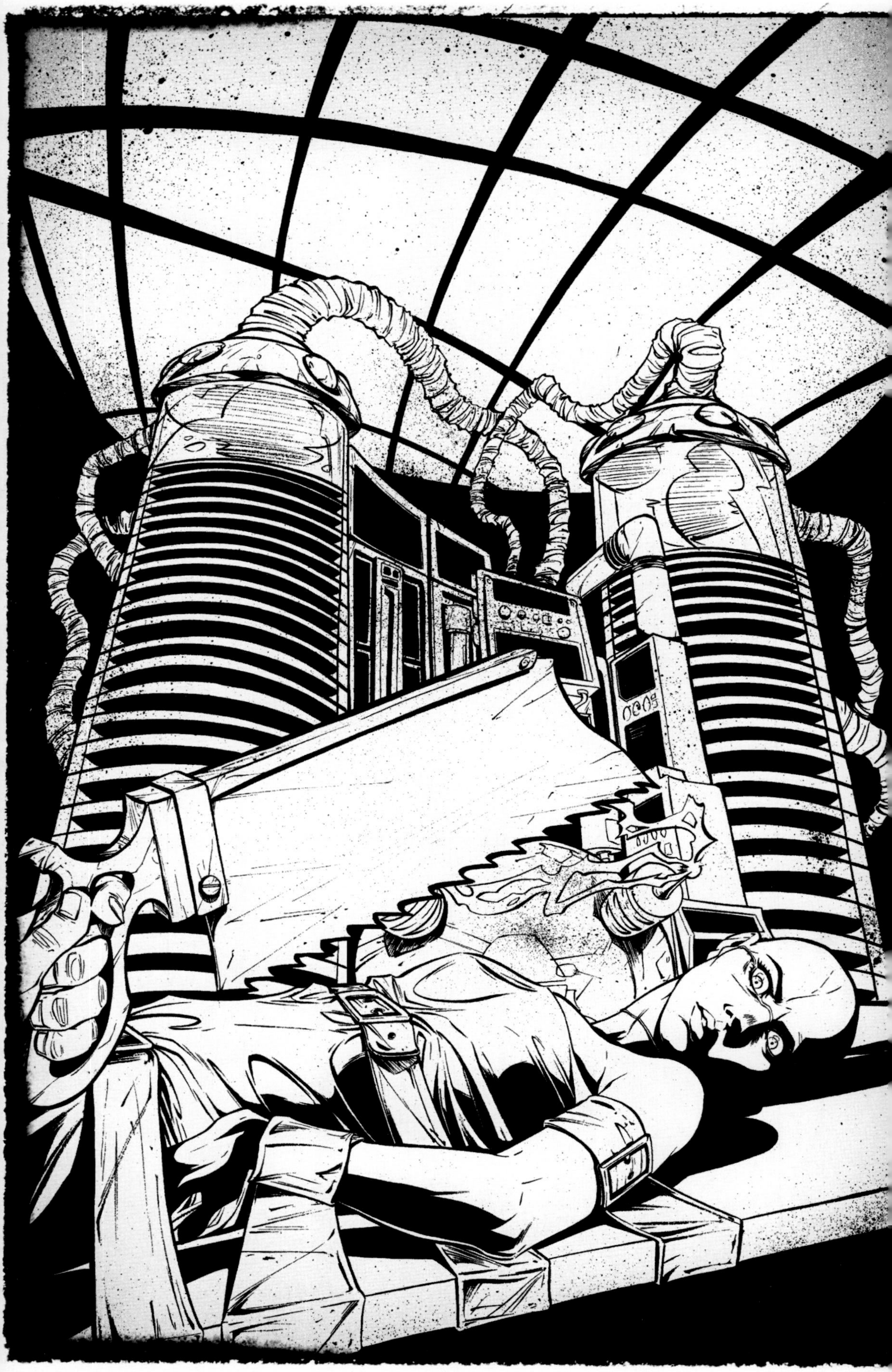

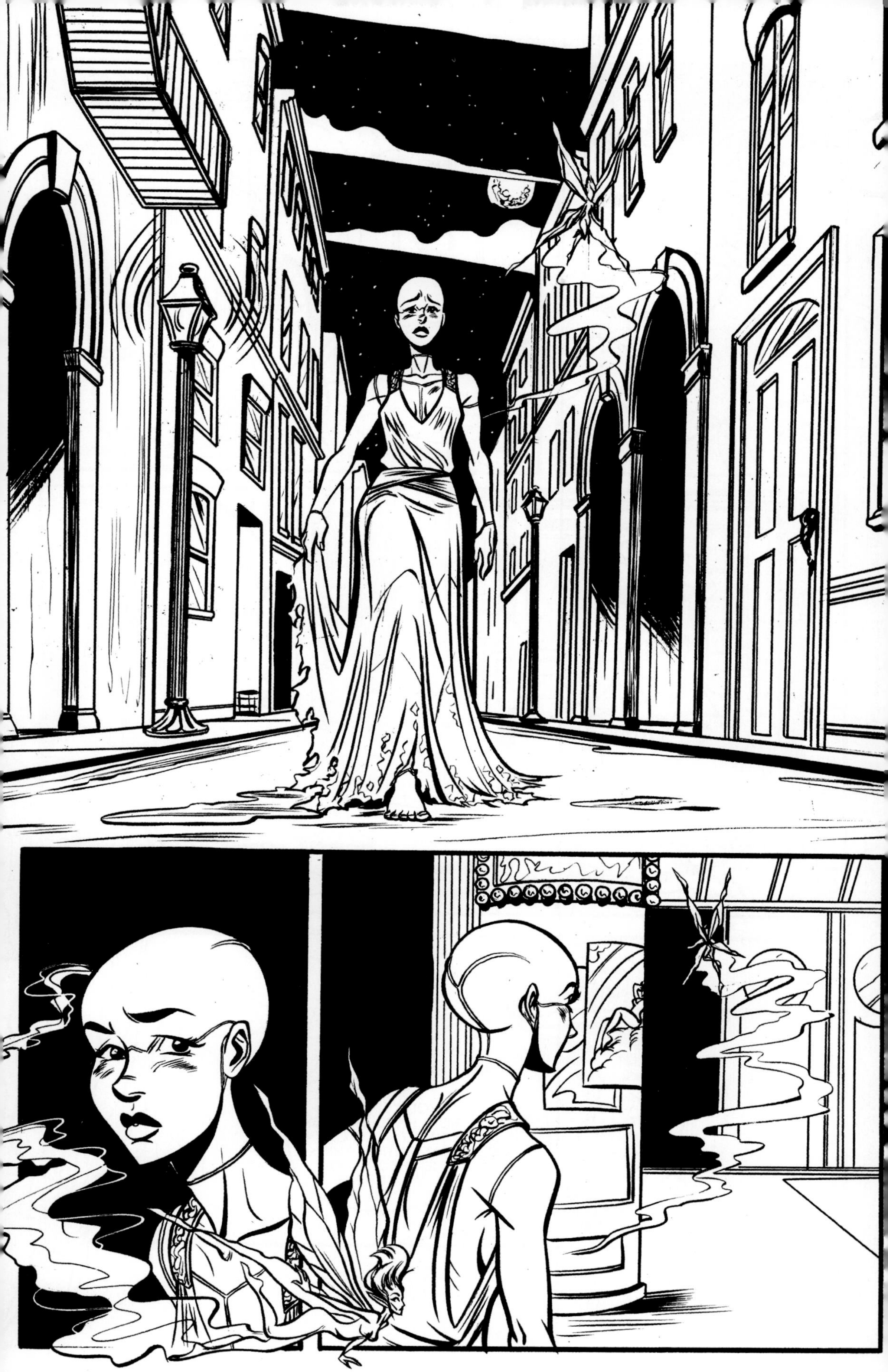

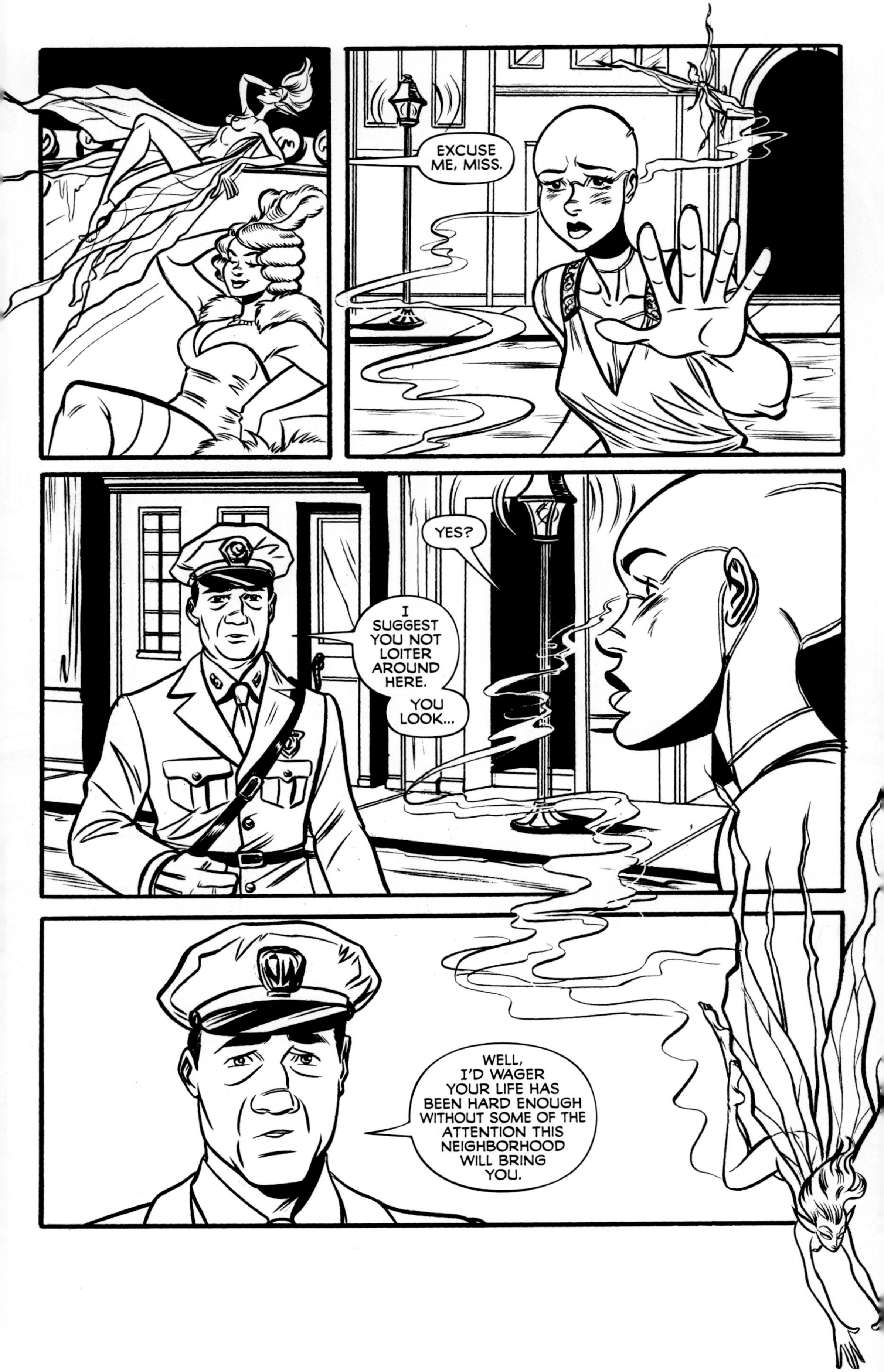
EXCUSE ME, MISS.
YES?
I SUGGEST YOU NOT LOITER AROUND HERE.
YOU LOOK...
WELL, I'D WAGER YOUR LIFE HAS BEEN HARD ENOUGH WITHOUT SOME OF THE ATTENTION THIS NEIGHBORHOOD WILL BRING YOU.

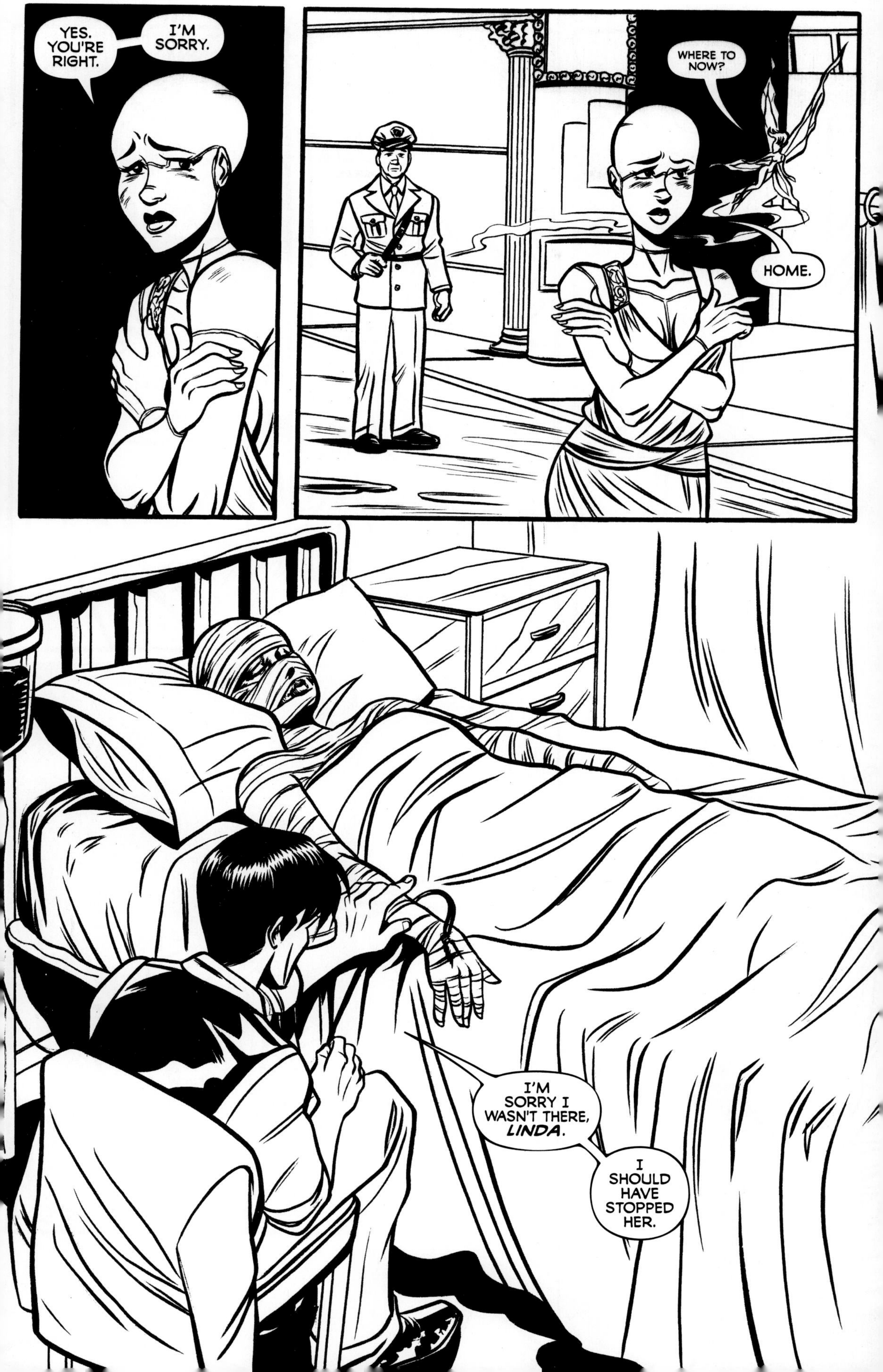

YES. YOU'RE RIGHT.
I'M SORRY.
WHERE TO NOW?
HOME.
I'M SORRY I WASN'T THERE, *LINDA*.
I SHOULD HAVE STOPPED HER.

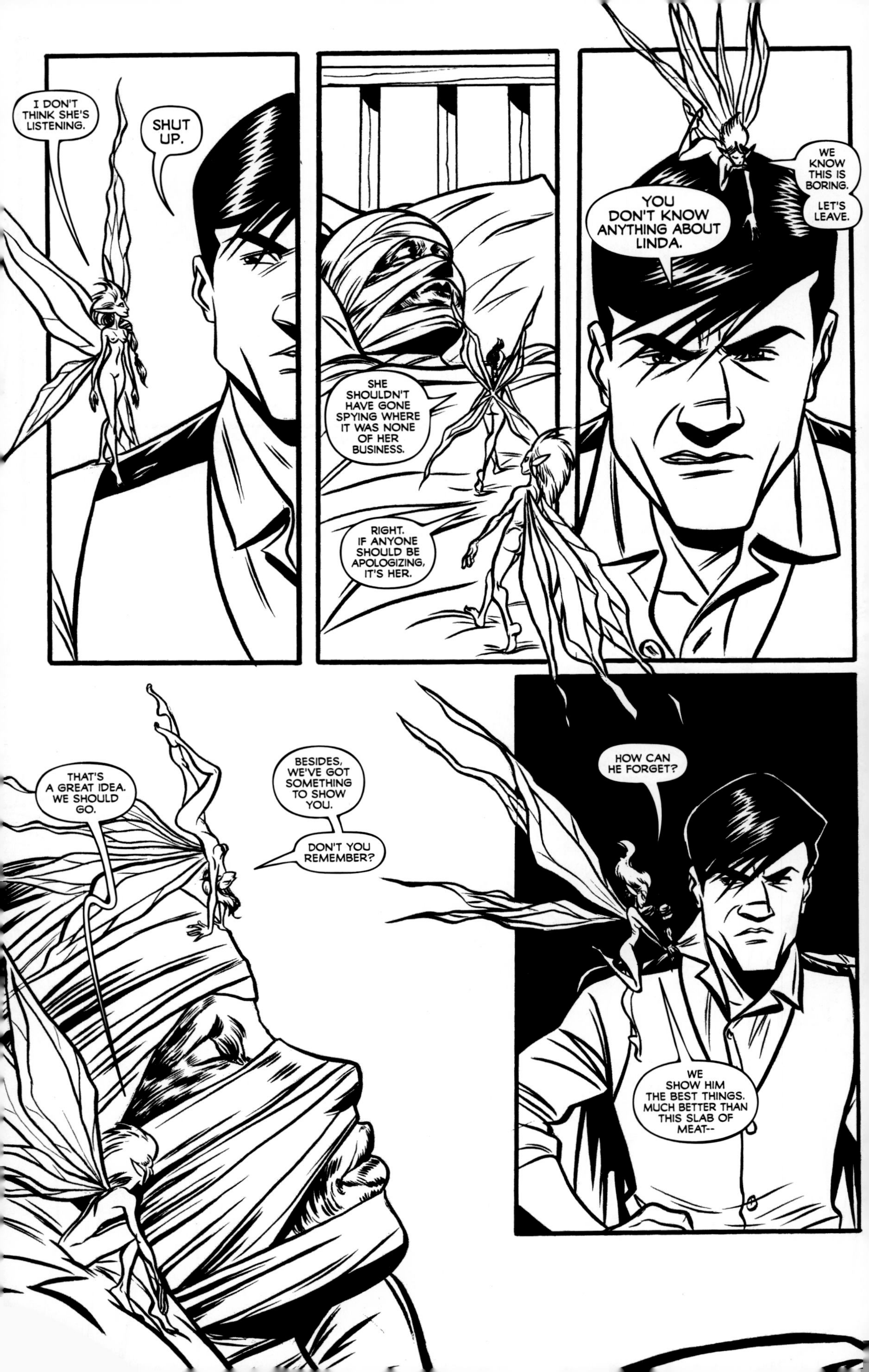
I DON'T THINK SHE'S LISTENING.
SHUT UP.
SHE SHOULDN'T HAVE GONE SPYING WHERE IT WAS NONE OF HER BUSINESS.
RIGHT. IF ANYONE SHOULD BE APOLOGIZING, IT'S HER.
YOU DON'T KNOW ANYTHING ABOUT LINDA.
WE KNOW THIS IS BORING.
LET'S LEAVE.
THAT'S A GREAT IDEA. WE SHOULD GO.
BESIDES, WE'VE GOT SOMETHING TO SHOW YOU.
DON'T YOU REMEMBER?
HOW CAN HE FORGET?
WE SHOW HIM THE BEST THINGS. MUCH BETTER THAN THIS SLAB OF MEAT--

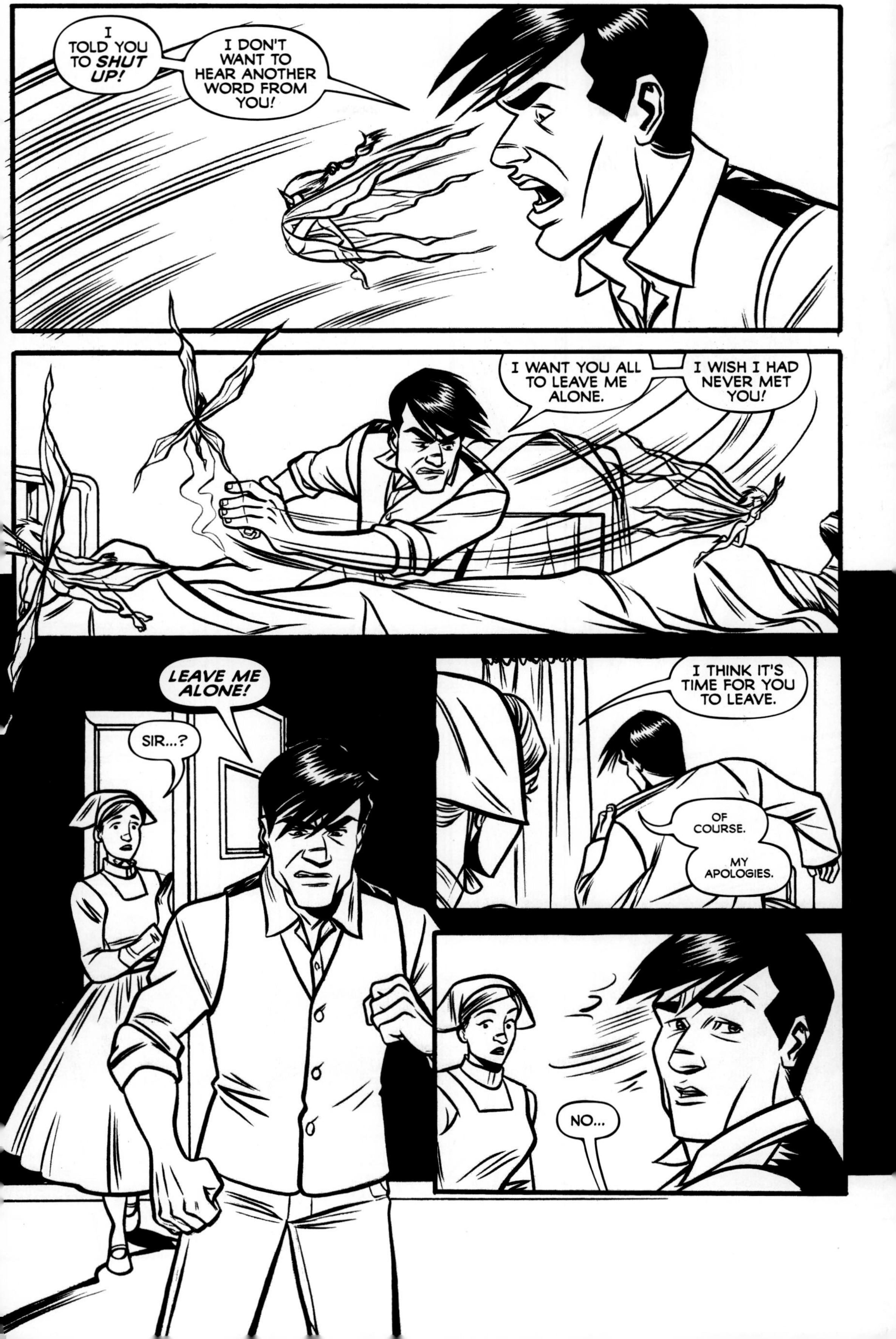
I TOLD YOU TO *SHUT UP!*
I DON'T WANT TO HEAR ANOTHER WORD FROM YOU!
I WANT YOU ALL TO LEAVE ME ALONE.
I WISH I HAD NEVER MET YOU!
LEAVE ME ALONE!
SIR...?
I THINK IT'S TIME FOR YOU TO LEAVE.
OF COURSE.
MY APOLOGIES.
NO...

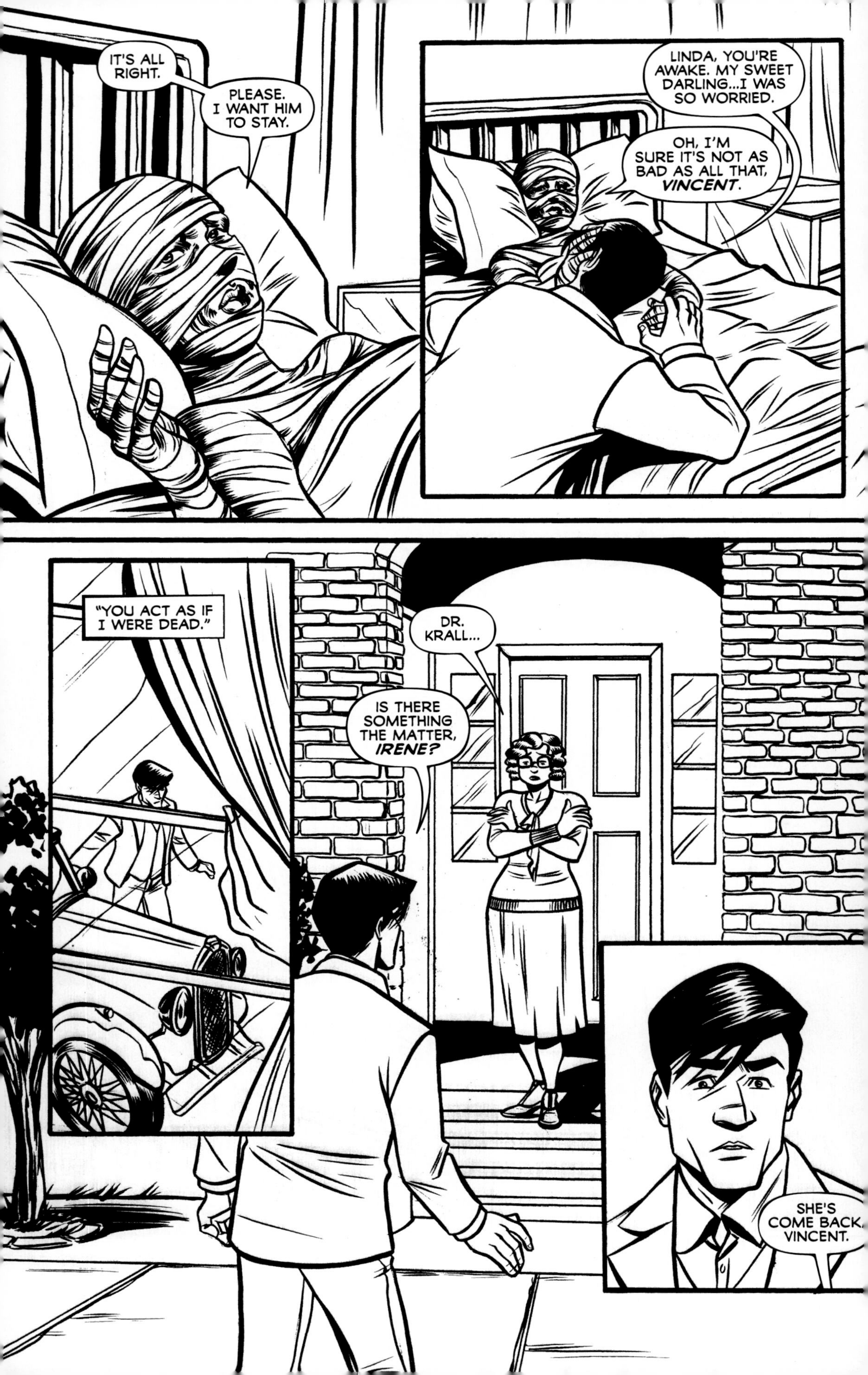

IT'S ALL RIGHT.
PLEASE. I WANT HIM TO STAY.
LINDA, YOU'RE AWAKE. MY SWEET DARLING...I WAS SO WORRIED.
OH, I'M SURE IT'S NOT AS BAD AS ALL THAT, VINCENT.
"YOU ACT AS IF I WERE DEAD."
DR. KRALL...
IS THERE SOMETHING THE MATTER, IRENE?
SHE'S COME BACK, VINCENT.

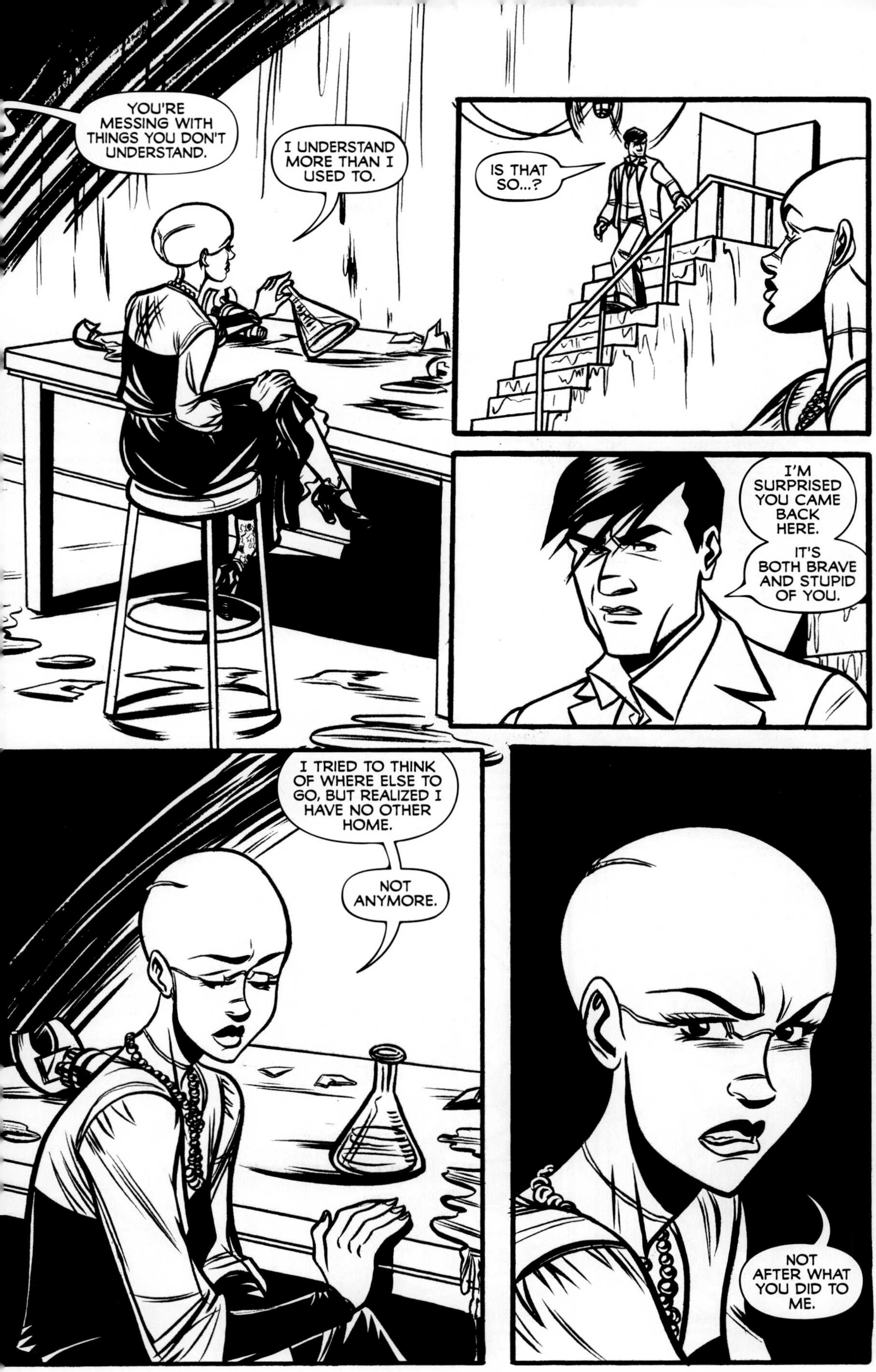
YOU'RE MESSING WITH THINGS YOU DON'T UNDERSTAND.
I UNDERSTAND MORE THAN I USED TO.
IS THAT SO...?
I'M SURPRISED YOU CAME BACK HERE.
IT'S BOTH BRAVE AND STUPID OF YOU.
I TRIED TO THINK OF WHERE ELSE TO GO, BUT REALIZED I HAVE NO OTHER HOME.
NOT ANYMORE.
NOT AFTER WHAT YOU DID TO ME.

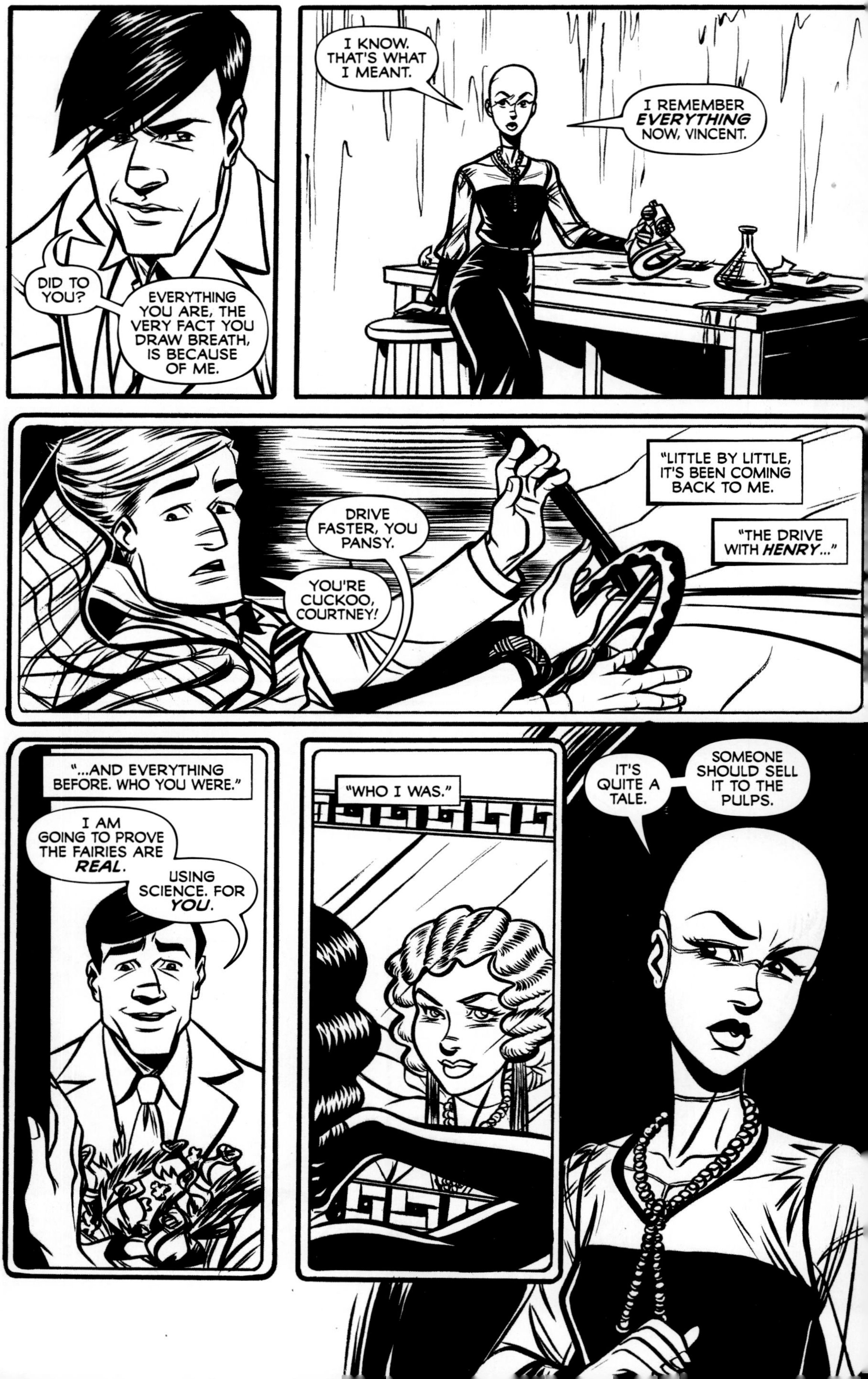
DID TO YOU?
EVERYTHING YOU ARE, THE VERY FACT YOU DRAW BREATH, IS BECAUSE OF ME.
I KNOW. THAT'S WHAT I MEANT.
I REMEMBER *EVERYTHING* NOW, VINCENT.
"LITTLE BY LITTLE, IT'S BEEN COMING BACK TO ME.
"THE DRIVE WITH *HENRY*..."
DRIVE FASTER, YOU PANSY.
YOU'RE CUCKOO, COURTNEY!
"...AND EVERYTHING BEFORE. WHO YOU WERE."
I AM GOING TO PROVE THE FAIRIES ARE *REAL*.
USING SCIENCE. FOR *YOU*.
"WHO I WAS."
IT'S QUITE A TALE.
SOMEONE SHOULD SELL IT TO THE PULPS.

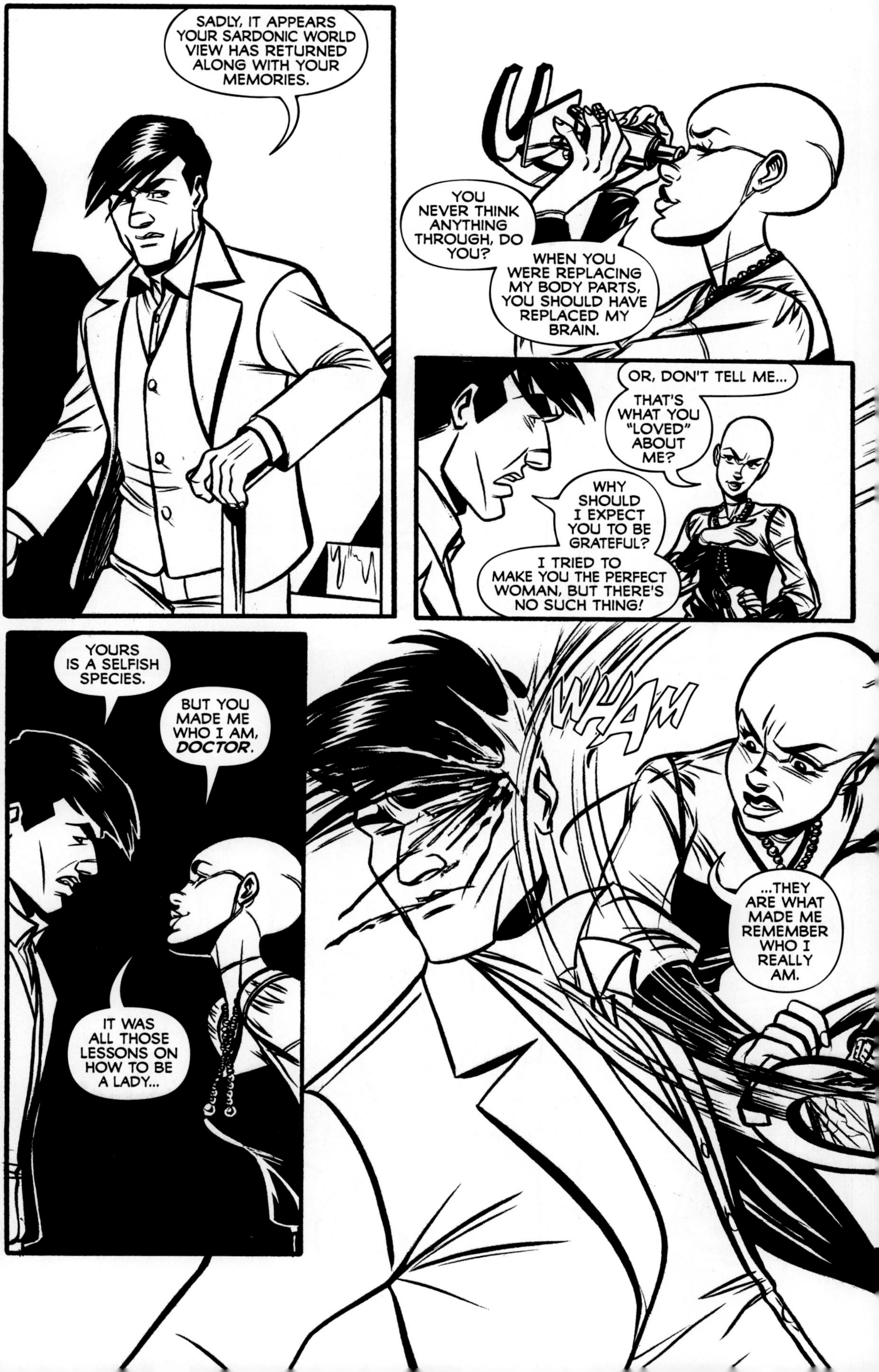
SADLY, IT APPEARS YOUR SARDONIC WORLD VIEW HAS RETURNED ALONG WITH YOUR MEMORIES.
YOU NEVER THINK ANYTHING THROUGH, DO YOU?
WHEN YOU WERE REPLACING MY BODY PARTS, YOU SHOULD HAVE REPLACED MY BRAIN.
OR, DON'T TELL ME...
THAT'S WHAT YOU "LOVED" ABOUT ME?
WHY SHOULD I EXPECT YOU TO BE GRATEFUL?
I TRIED TO MAKE YOU THE PERFECT WOMAN, BUT THERE'S NO SUCH THING!
YOURS IS A SELFISH SPECIES.
BUT YOU MADE ME WHO I AM, *DOCTOR*.
IT WAS ALL THOSE LESSONS ON HOW TO BE A LADY...
WHAM
...THEY ARE WHAT MADE ME REMEMBER WHO I REALLY AM.

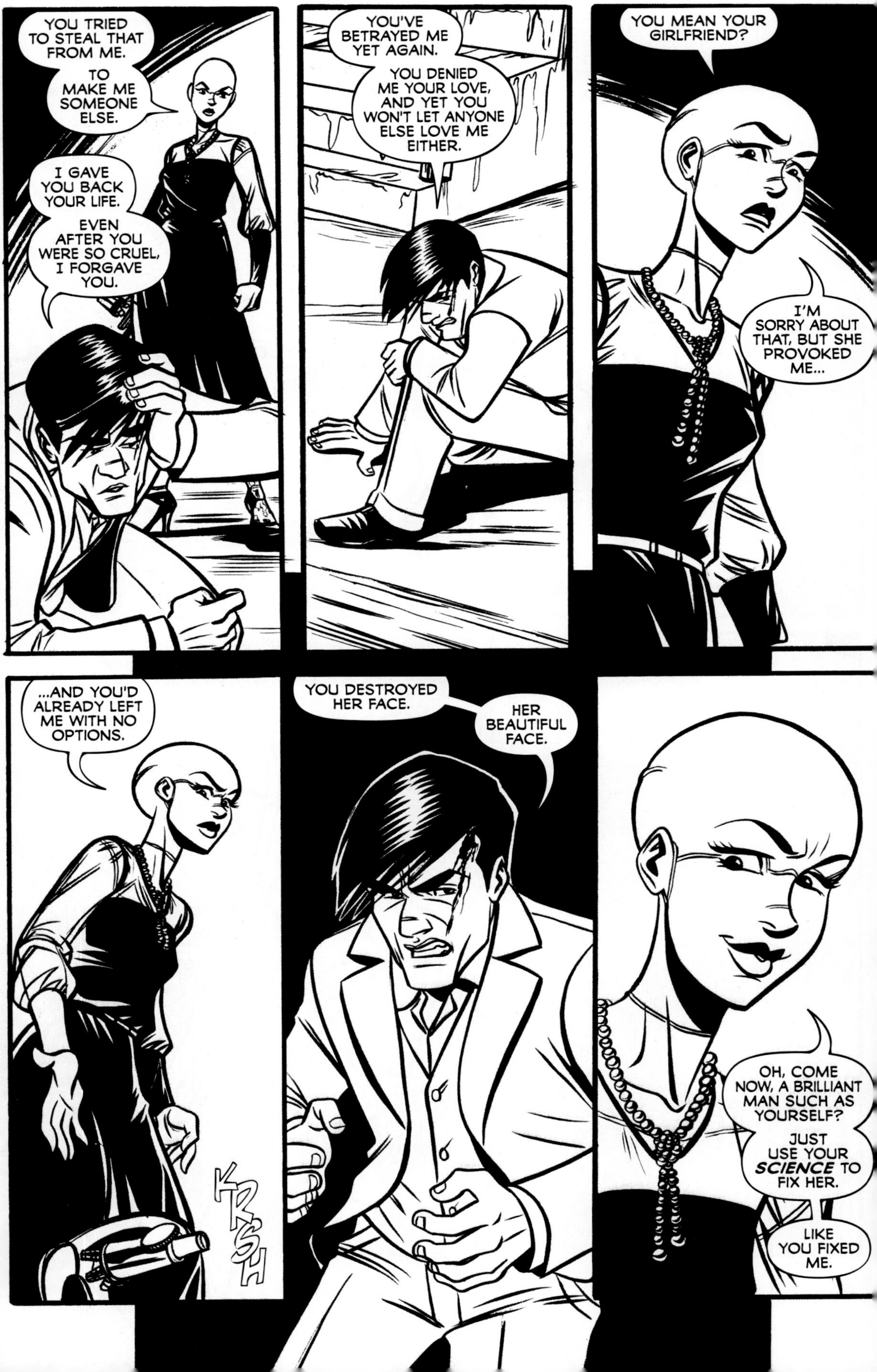
YOU TRIED TO STEAL THAT FROM ME.
TO MAKE ME SOMEONE ELSE.
I GAVE YOU BACK YOUR LIFE.
EVEN AFTER YOU WERE SO CRUEL, I FORGAVE YOU.
YOU'VE BETRAYED ME YET AGAIN.
YOU DENIED ME YOUR LOVE, AND YET YOU WON'T LET ANYONE ELSE LOVE ME EITHER.
YOU MEAN YOUR GIRLFRIEND?
I'M SORRY ABOUT THAT, BUT SHE PROVOKED ME...
...AND YOU'D ALREADY LEFT ME WITH NO OPTIONS.
KRSH
YOU DESTROYED HER FACE.
HER BEAUTIFUL FACE.
OH, COME NOW, A BRILLIANT MAN SUCH AS YOURSELF?
JUST USE YOUR *SCIENCE* TO FIX HER.
LIKE YOU FIXED ME.

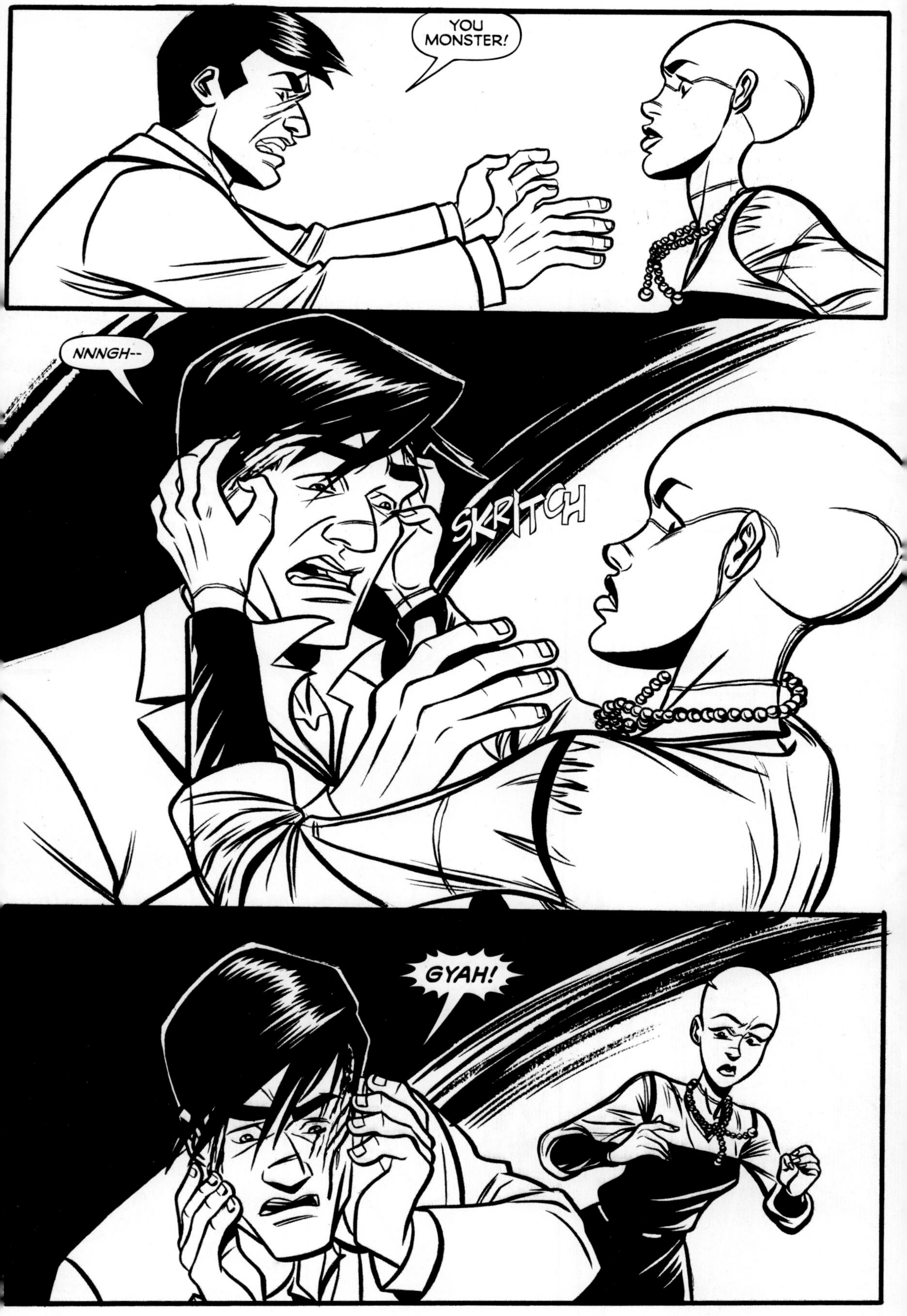
YOU MONSTER!
NNNGH--
SKRITCH
GYAH!

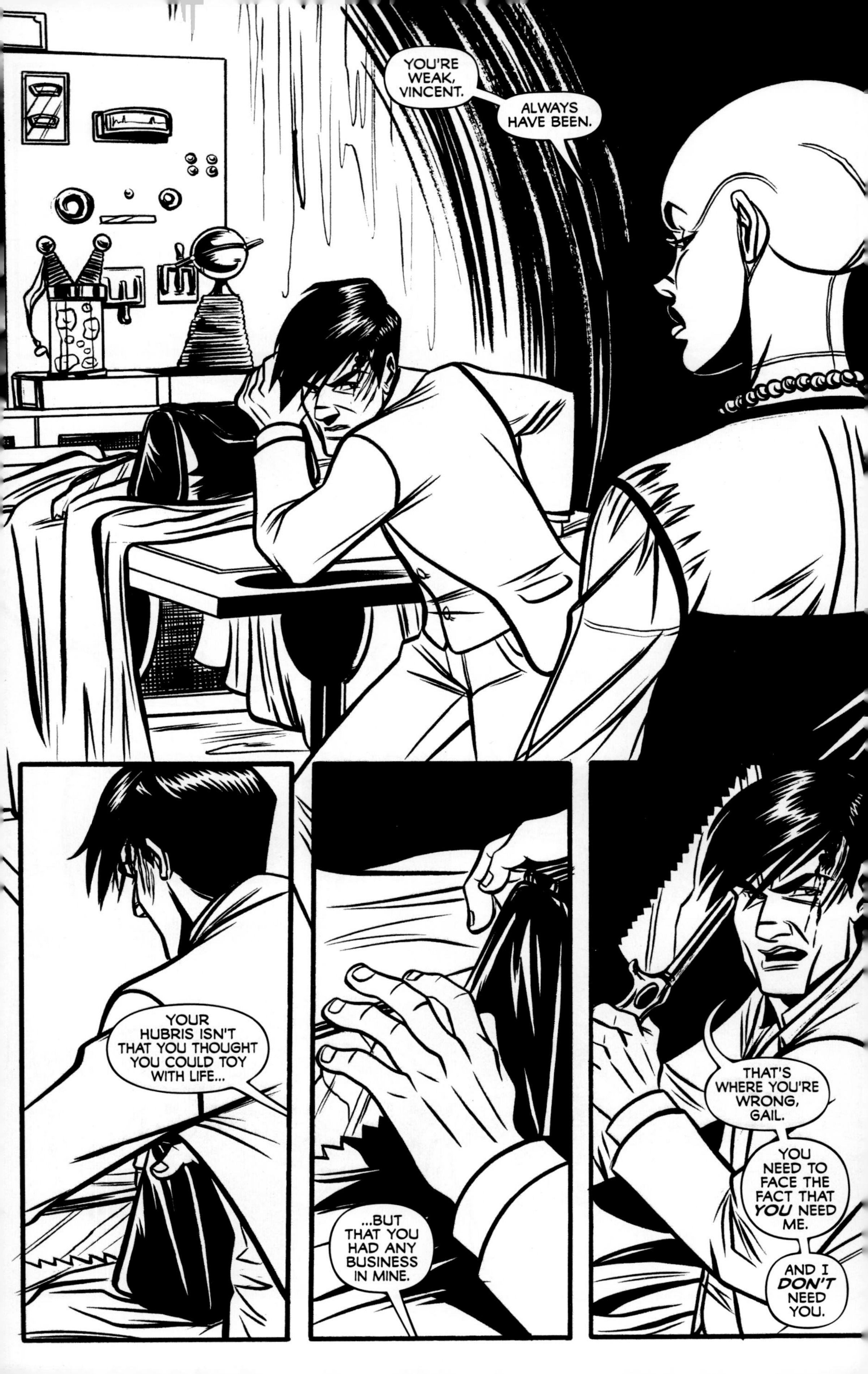
YOU'RE WEAK, VINCENT.
ALWAYS HAVE BEEN.
YOUR HUBRIS ISN'T THAT YOU THOUGHT YOU COULD TOY WITH LIFE...
...BUT THAT YOU HAD ANY BUSINESS IN MINE.
THAT'S WHERE YOU'RE WRONG, GAIL.
YOU NEED TO FACE THE FACT THAT *YOU* NEED ME.
AND I *DON'T* NEED YOU.

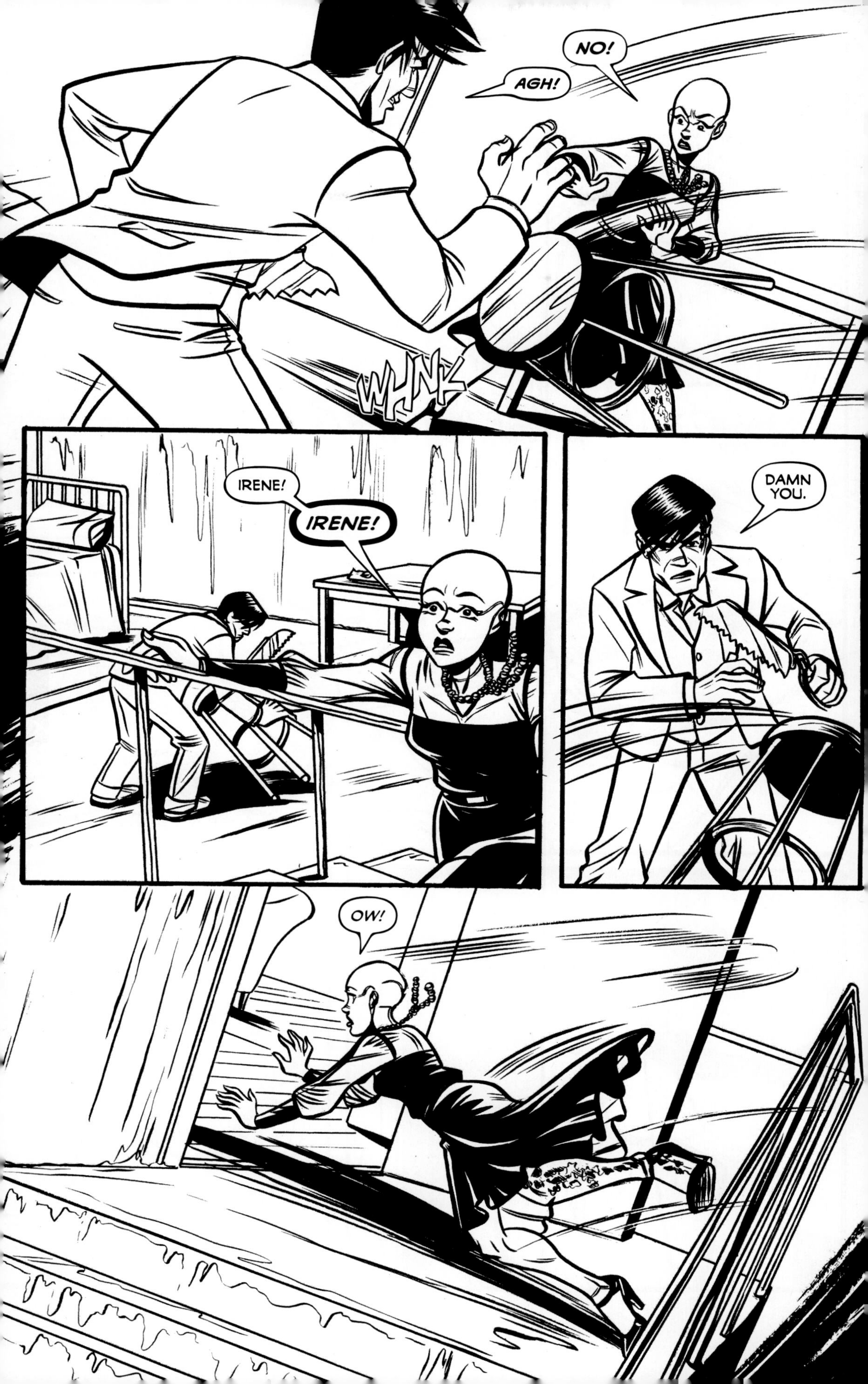
NO!
AGH!
WHNK
IRENE!
IRENE!
DAMN YOU.
OW!

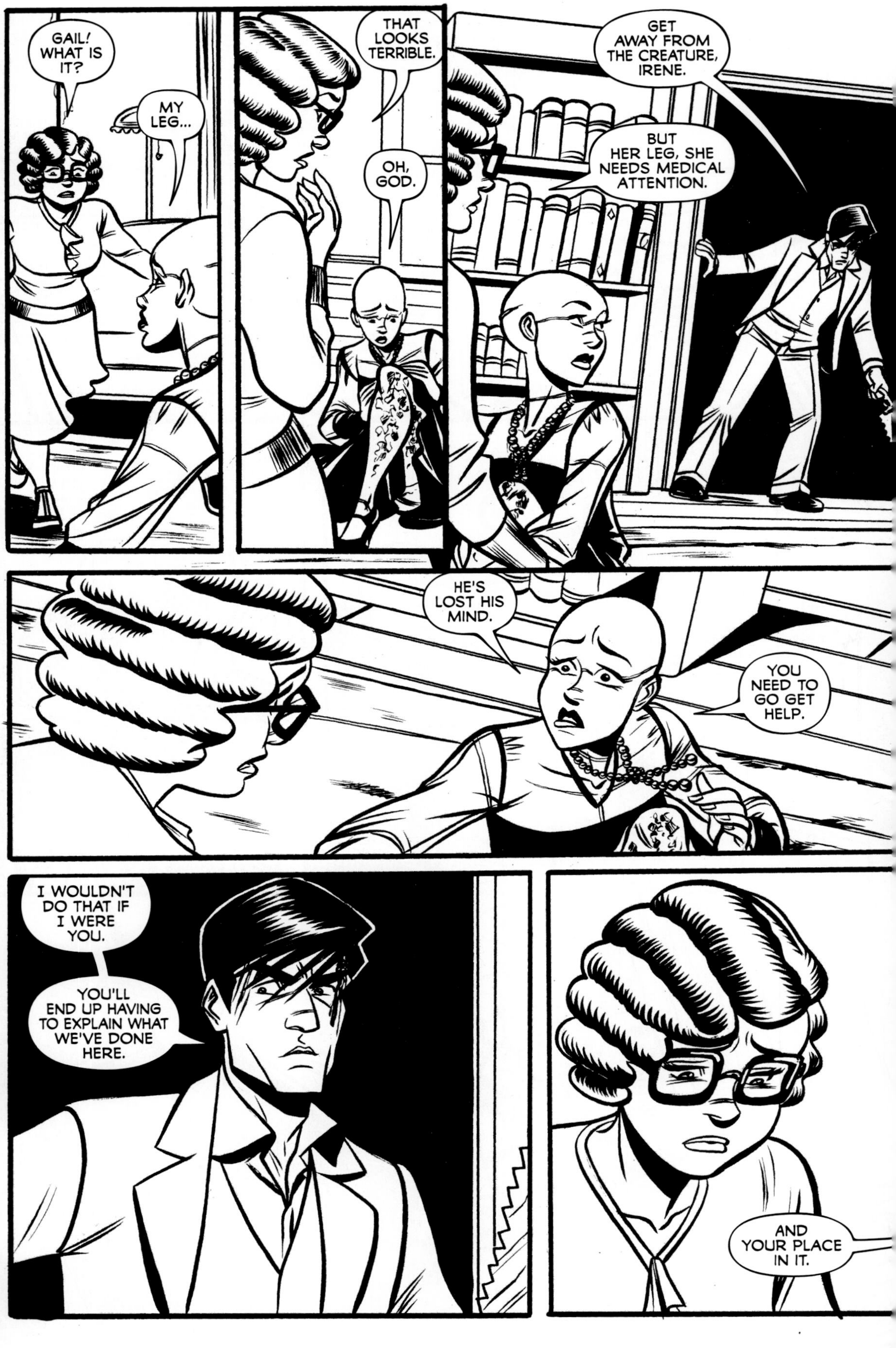
GAIL! WHAT IS IT?
MY LEG...
THAT LOOKS TERRIBLE.
OH, GOD.
GET AWAY FROM THE CREATURE, IRENE.
BUT HER LEG, SHE NEEDS MEDICAL ATTENTION.
HE'S LOST HIS MIND.
YOU NEED TO GO GET HELP.
I WOULDN'T DO THAT IF I WERE YOU.
YOU'LL END UP HAVING TO EXPLAIN WHAT WE'VE DONE HERE.
AND YOUR PLACE IN IT.

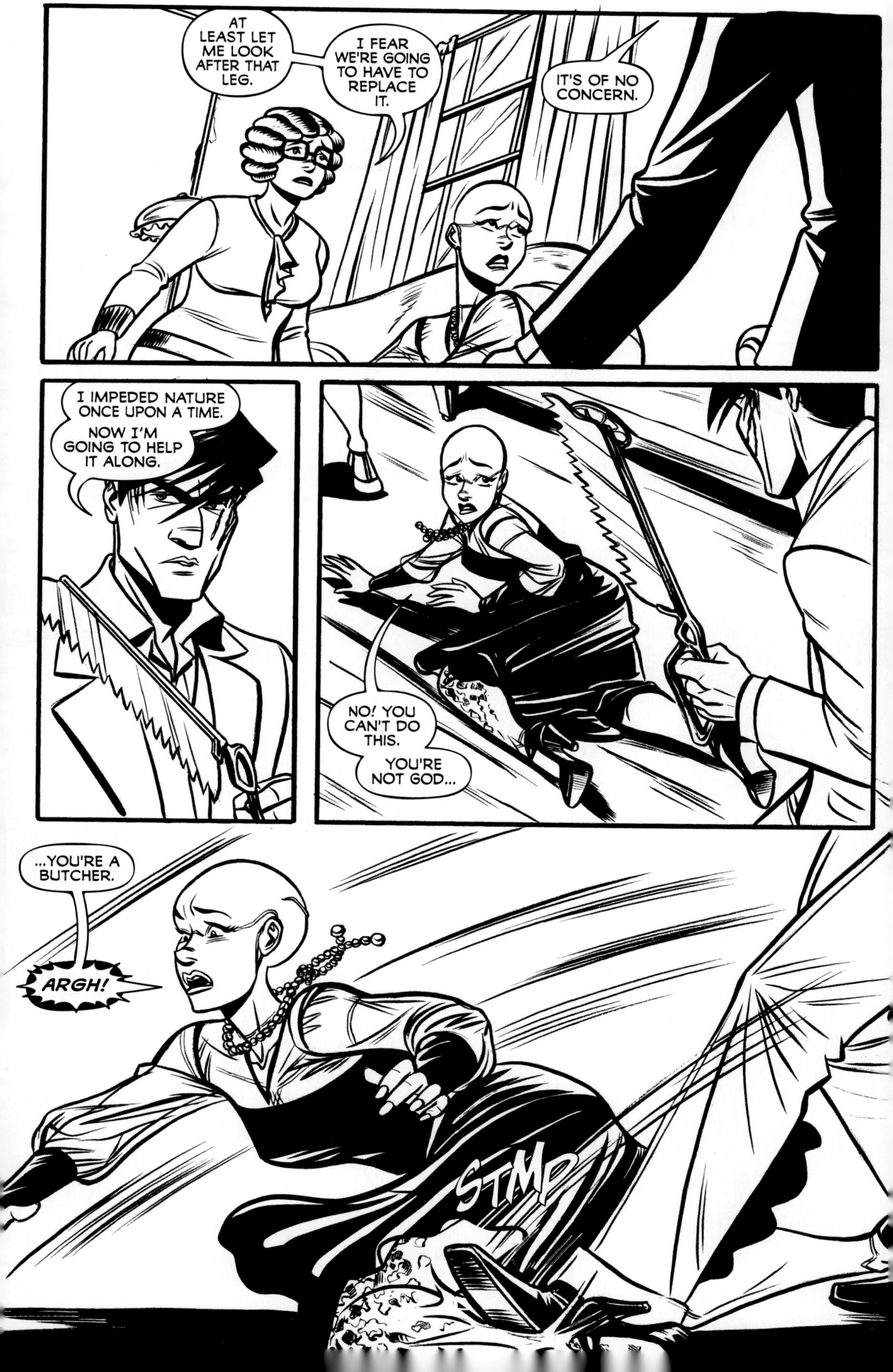

AT LEAST LET ME LOOK AFTER THAT LEG.
I FEAR WE'RE GOING TO HAVE TO REPLACE IT.
IT'S OF NO CONCERN.
I IMPEDED NATURE ONCE UPON A TIME.
NOW I'M GOING TO HELP IT ALONG.
NO! YOU CAN'T DO THIS.
YOU'RE NOT GOD...
...YOU'RE A BUTCHER.
ARGH!
STMP

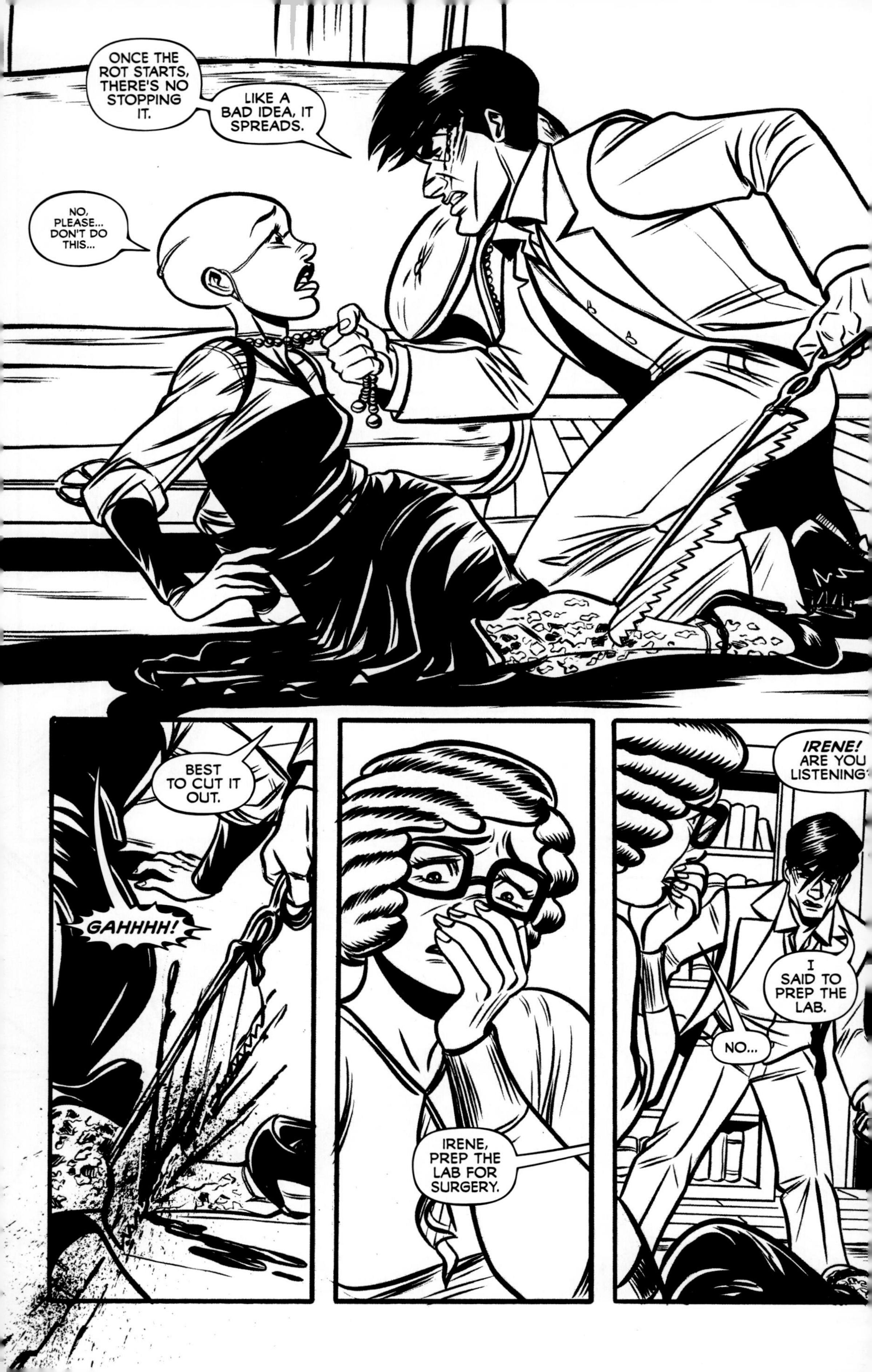

ONCE THE ROT STARTS, THERE'S NO STOPPING IT.
LIKE A BAD IDEA, IT SPREADS.
NO, PLEASE... DON'T DO THIS...
BEST TO CUT IT OUT.
GAHHHH!
IRENE, PREP THE LAB FOR SURGERY.
IRENE! ARE YOU LISTENING?
I SAID TO PREP THE LAB.
NO...

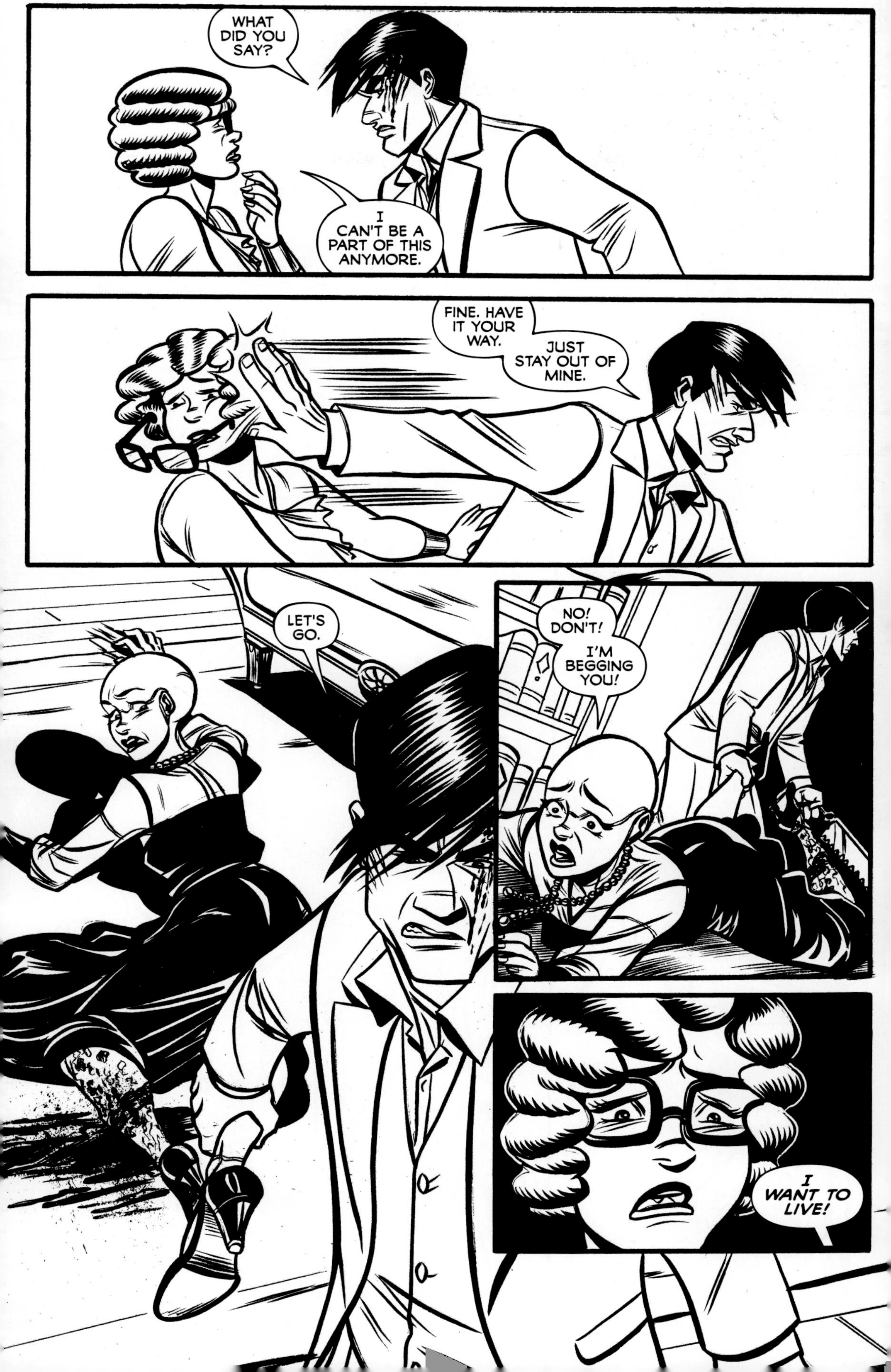
WHAT DID YOU SAY?
I CAN'T BE A PART OF THIS ANYMORE.
FINE. HAVE IT YOUR WAY.
JUST STAY OUT OF MINE.
LET'S GO.
NO! DON'T!
I'M BEGGING YOU!
I WANT TO LIVE!

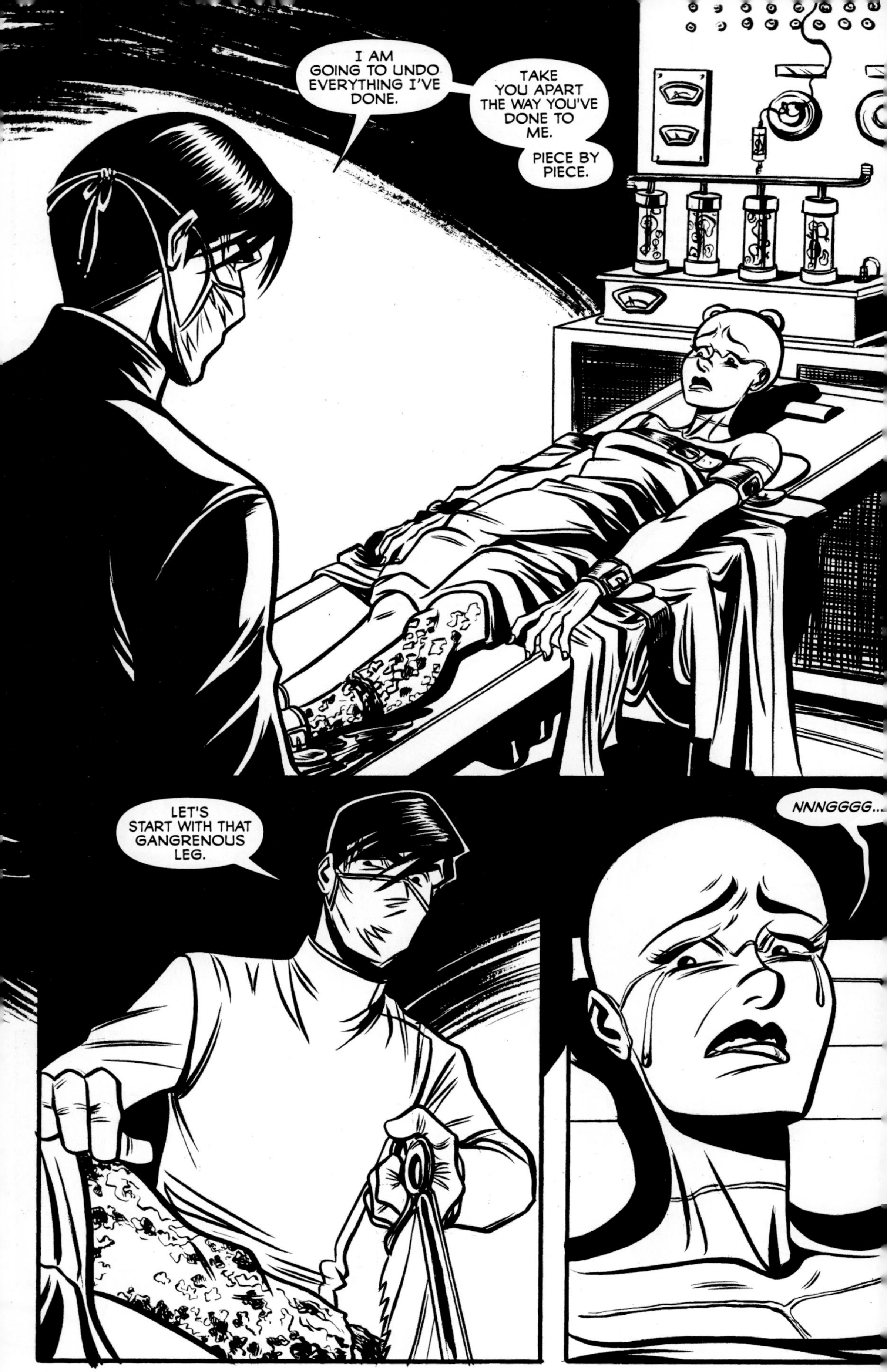
I AM GOING TO UNDO EVERYTHING I'VE DONE.
TAKE YOU APART THE WAY YOU'VE DONE TO ME.
PIECE BY PIECE.
LET'S START WITH THAT GANGRENOUS LEG.
NNNGGGG...

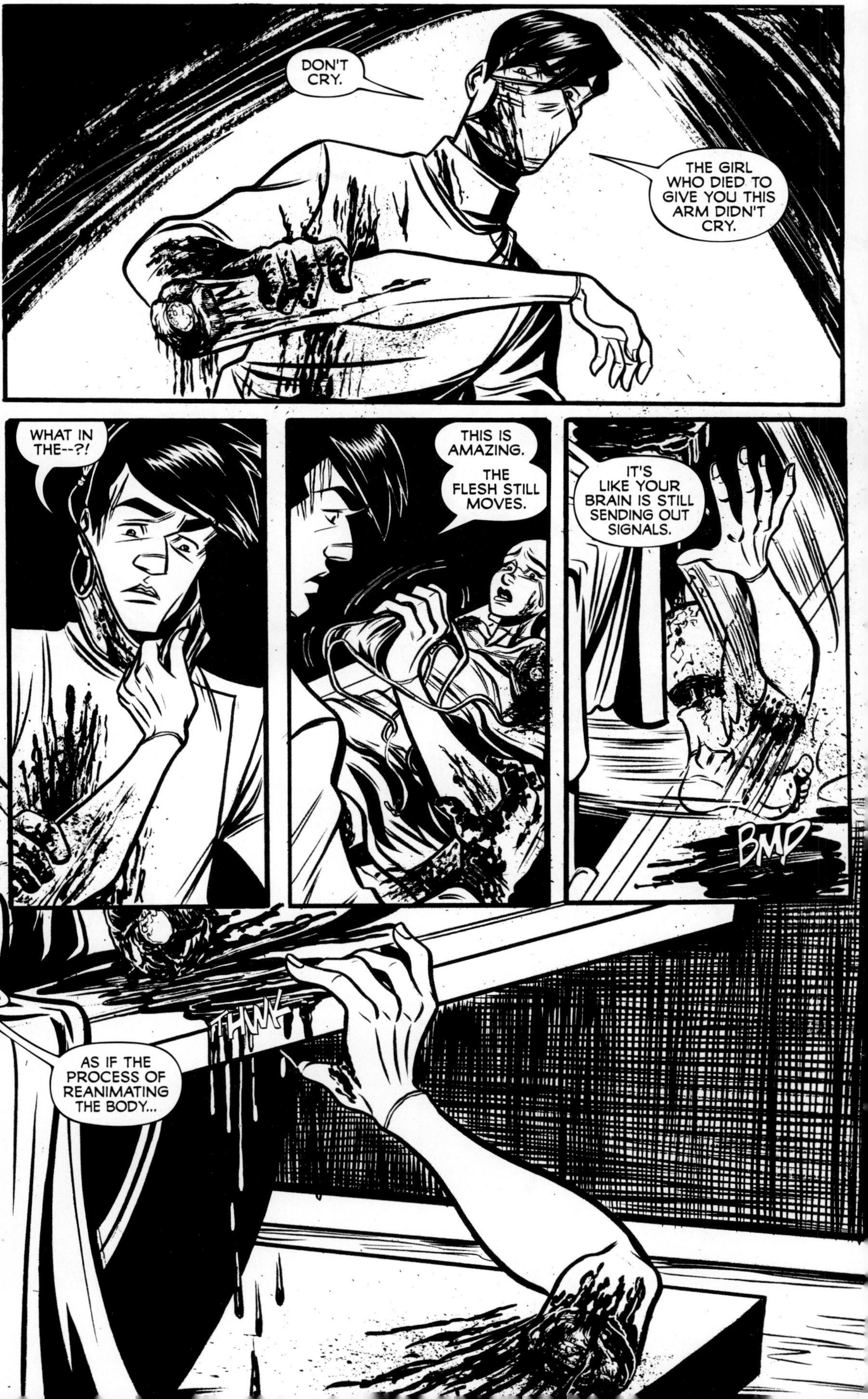
DON'T CRY.
THE GIRL WHO DIED TO GIVE YOU THIS ARM DIDN'T CRY.
WHAT IN THE--?!
THIS IS AMAZING.
THE FLESH STILL MOVES.
IT'S LIKE YOUR BRAIN IS STILL SENDING OUT SIGNALS.
BMP
THWK
AS IF THE PROCESS OF REANIMATING THE BODY...

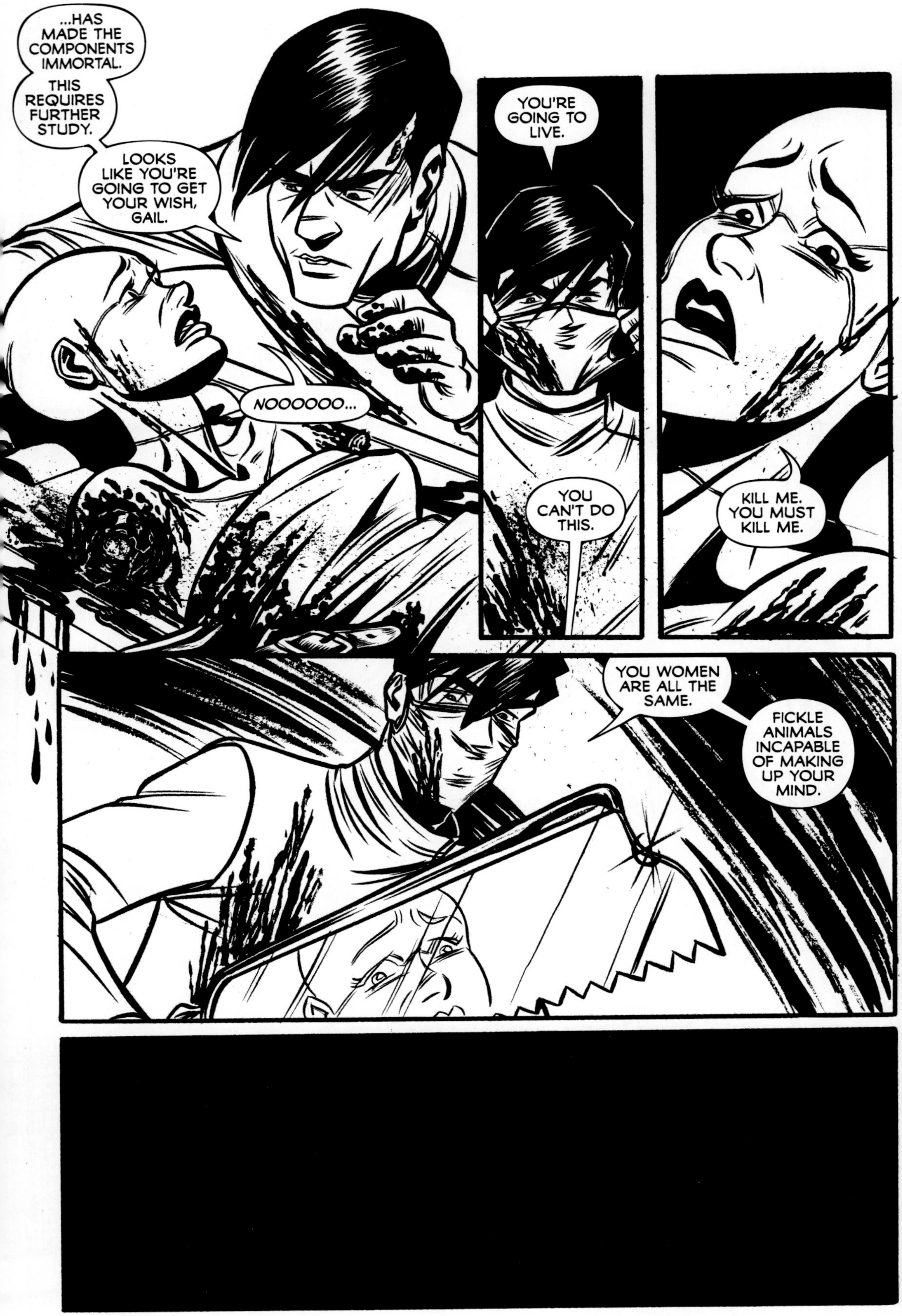
...HAS MADE THE COMPONENTS IMMORTAL.
THIS REQUIRES FURTHER STUDY.
LOOKS LIKE YOU'RE GOING TO GET YOUR WISH, GAIL.
NOOOOOO...
YOU'RE GOING TO LIVE.
YOU CAN'T DO THIS.
KILL ME. YOU MUST KILL ME.
YOU WOMEN ARE ALL THE SAME.
FICKLE ANIMALS INCAPABLE OF MAKING UP YOUR MIND.

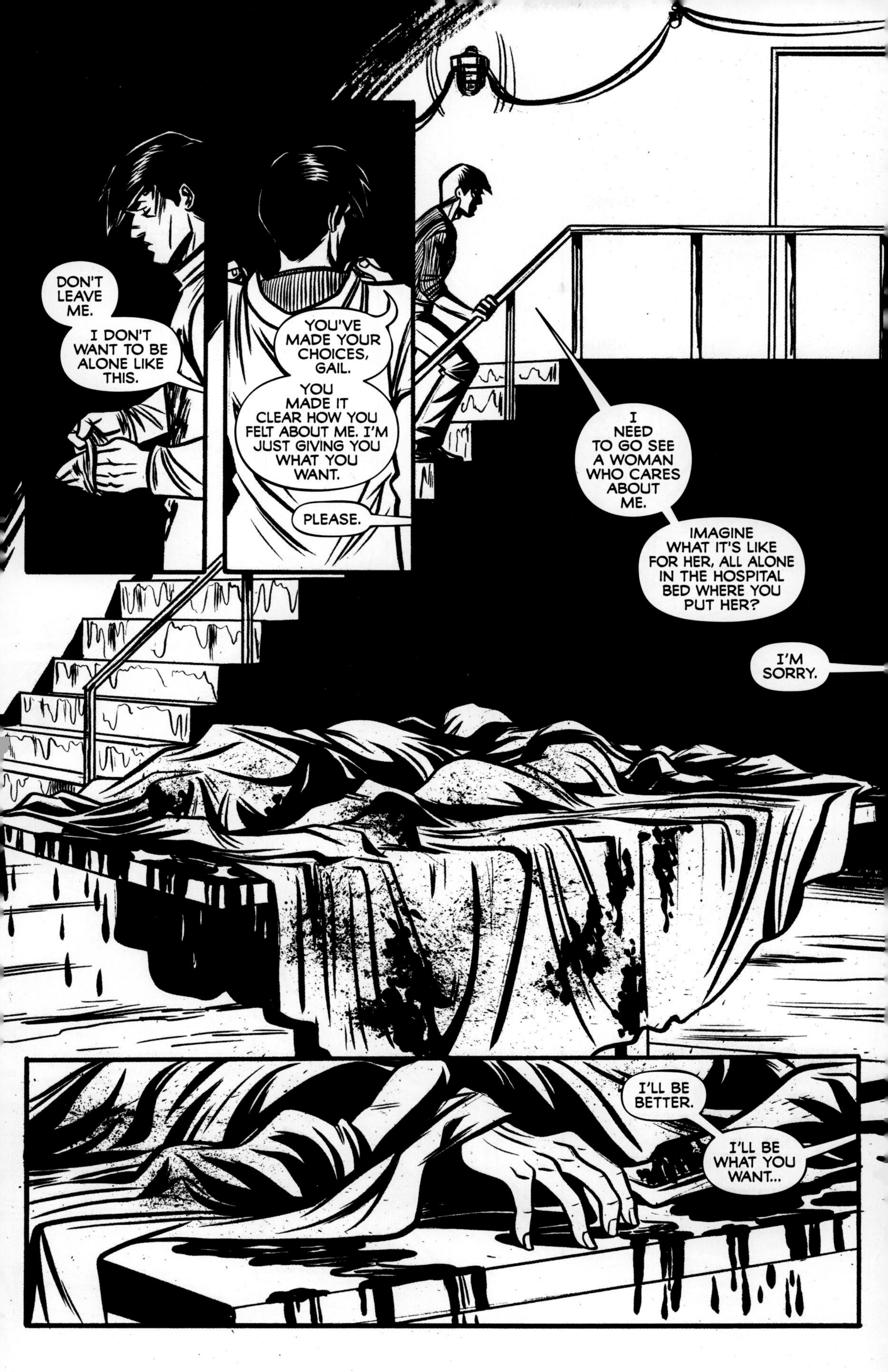

DON'T LEAVE ME.
I DON'T WANT TO BE ALONE LIKE THIS.
YOU'VE MADE YOUR CHOICES, GAIL.
YOU MADE IT CLEAR HOW YOU FELT ABOUT ME. I'M JUST GIVING YOU WHAT YOU WANT.
PLEASE.
I NEED TO GO SEE A WOMAN WHO CARES ABOUT ME.
IMAGINE WHAT IT'S LIKE FOR HER, ALL ALONE IN THE HOSPITAL BED WHERE YOU PUT HER?
I'M SORRY.
I'LL BE BETTER.
I'LL BE WHAT YOU WANT...

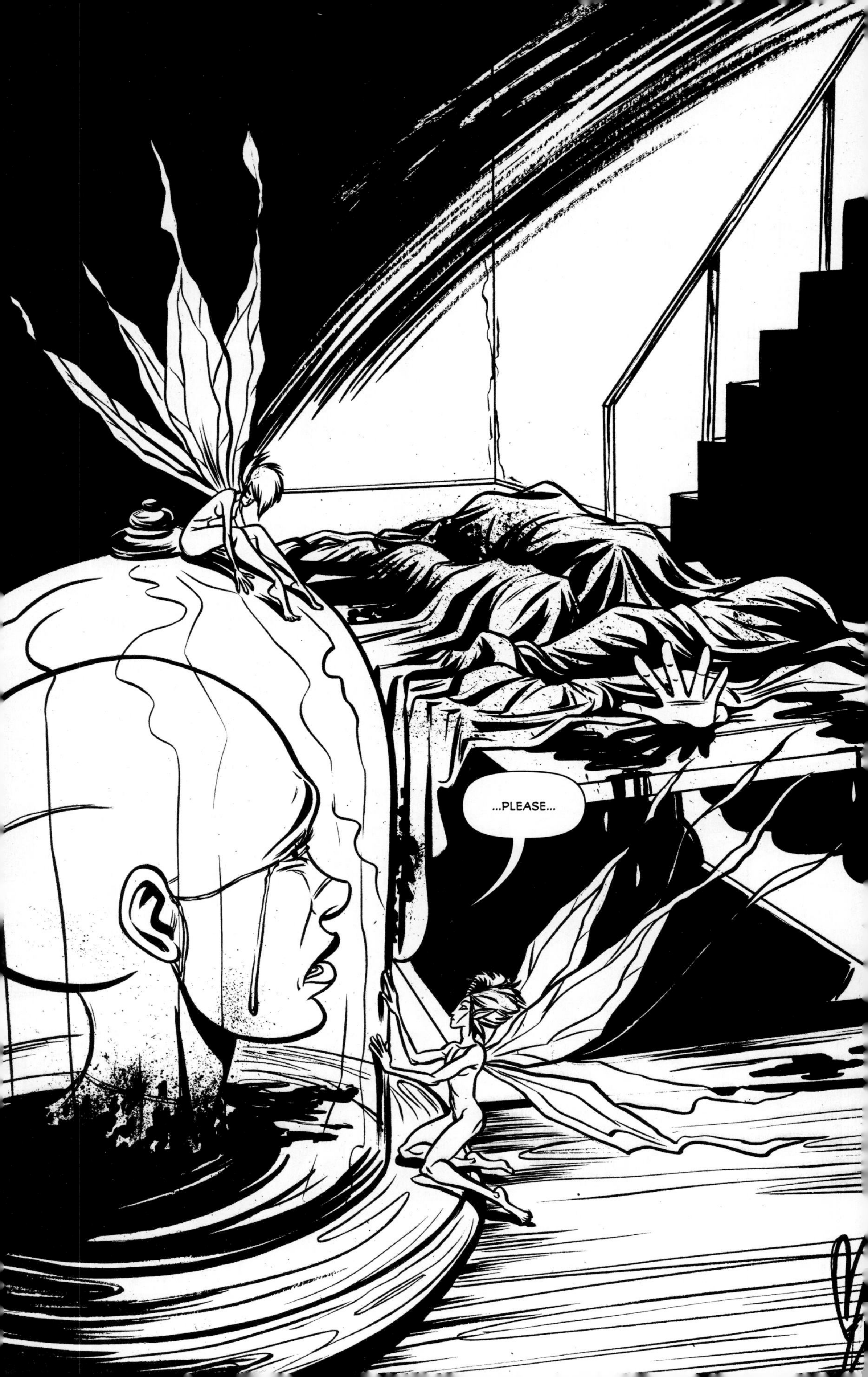
...PLEASE...

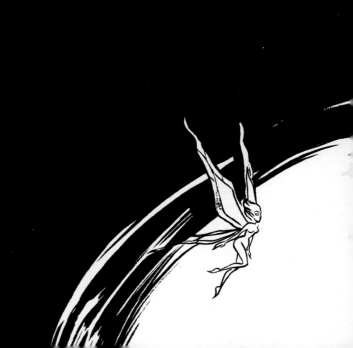

SKETCH GALLERY

In preparing *Madame Frankenstein*, Megan did
a variety of proof-of-concept sketches to work
out the look and feel of the series.

Many of these were ultimately included in the
pitch document that was sent to Image Comics.

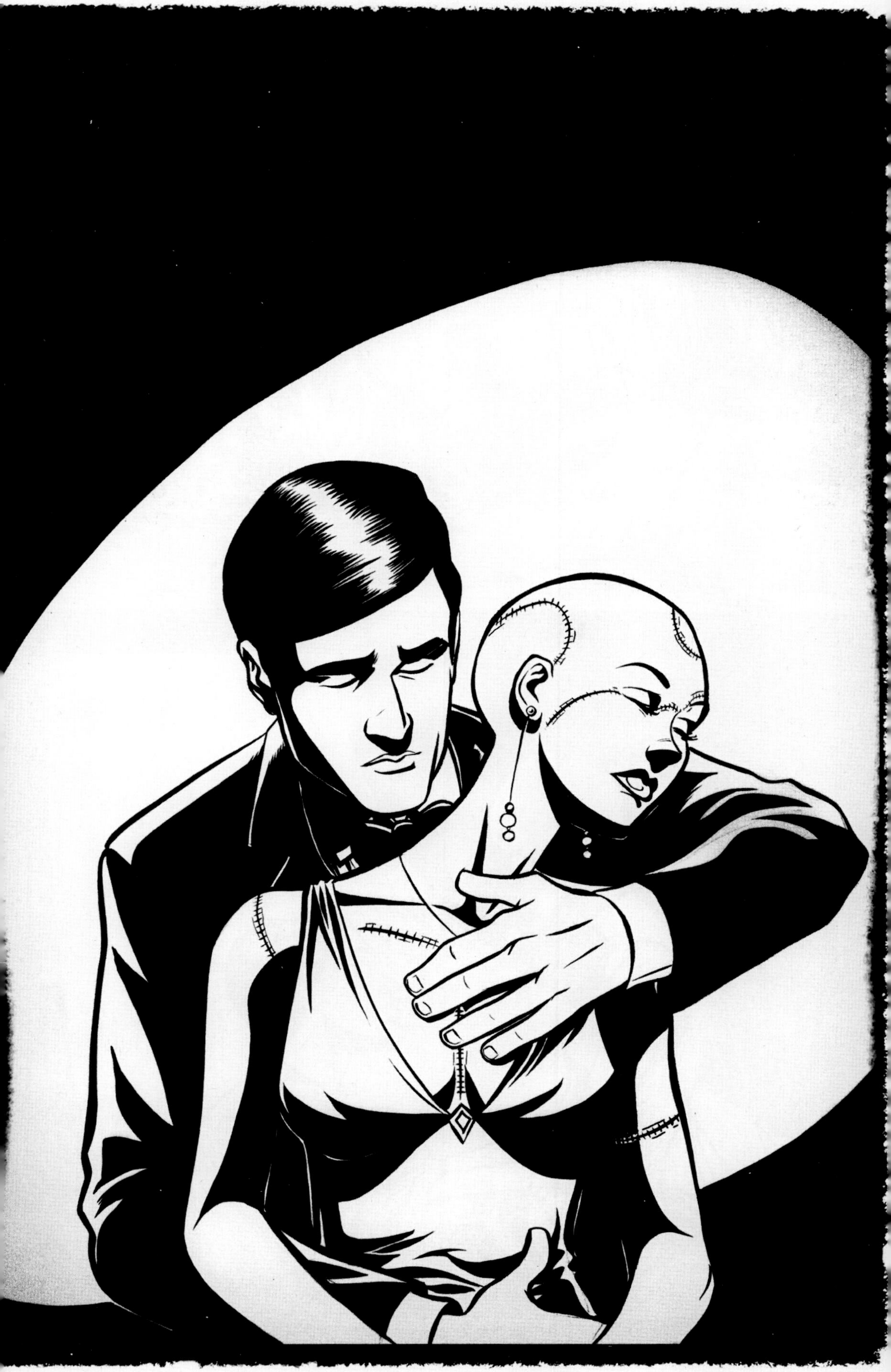

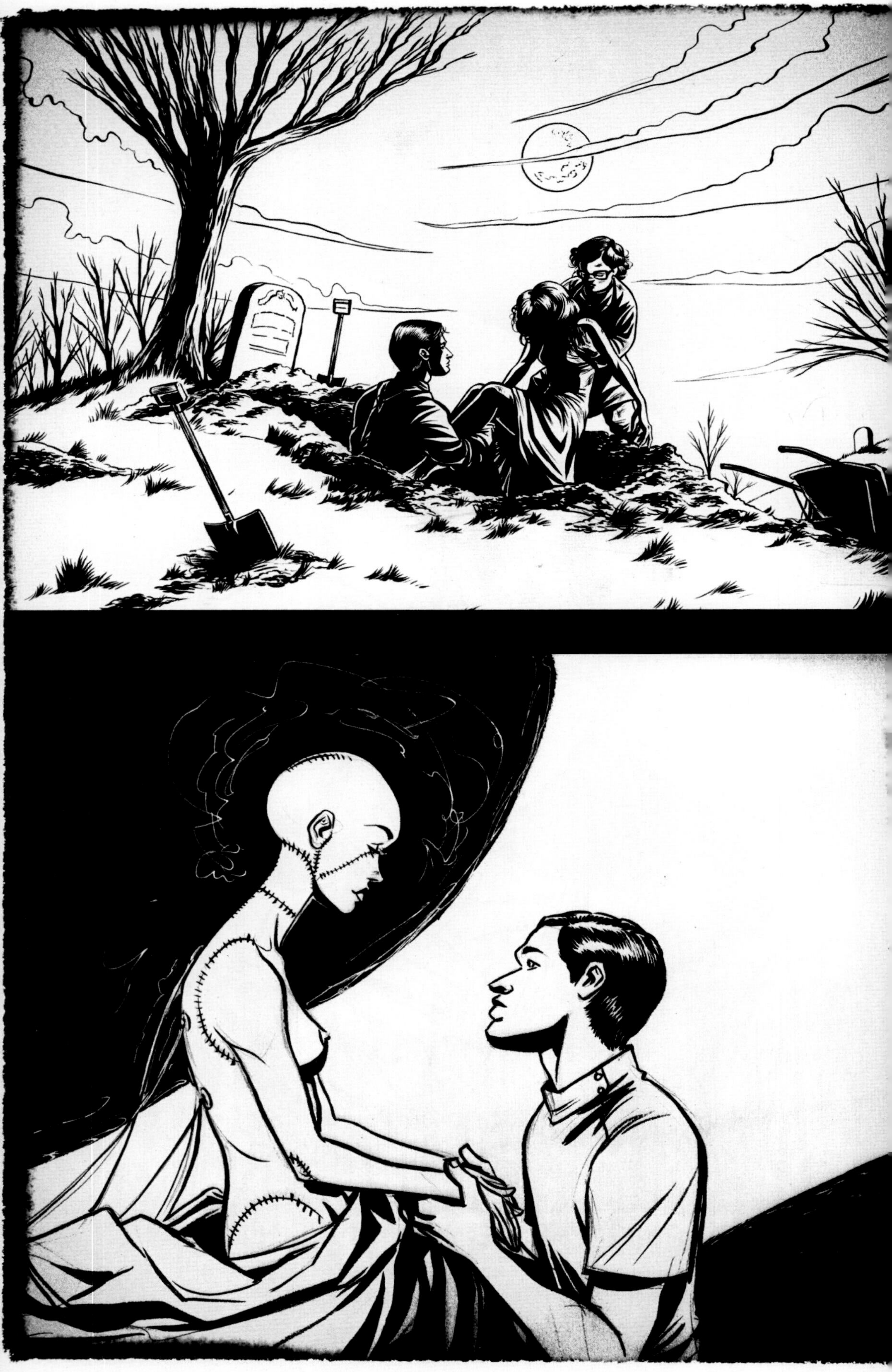

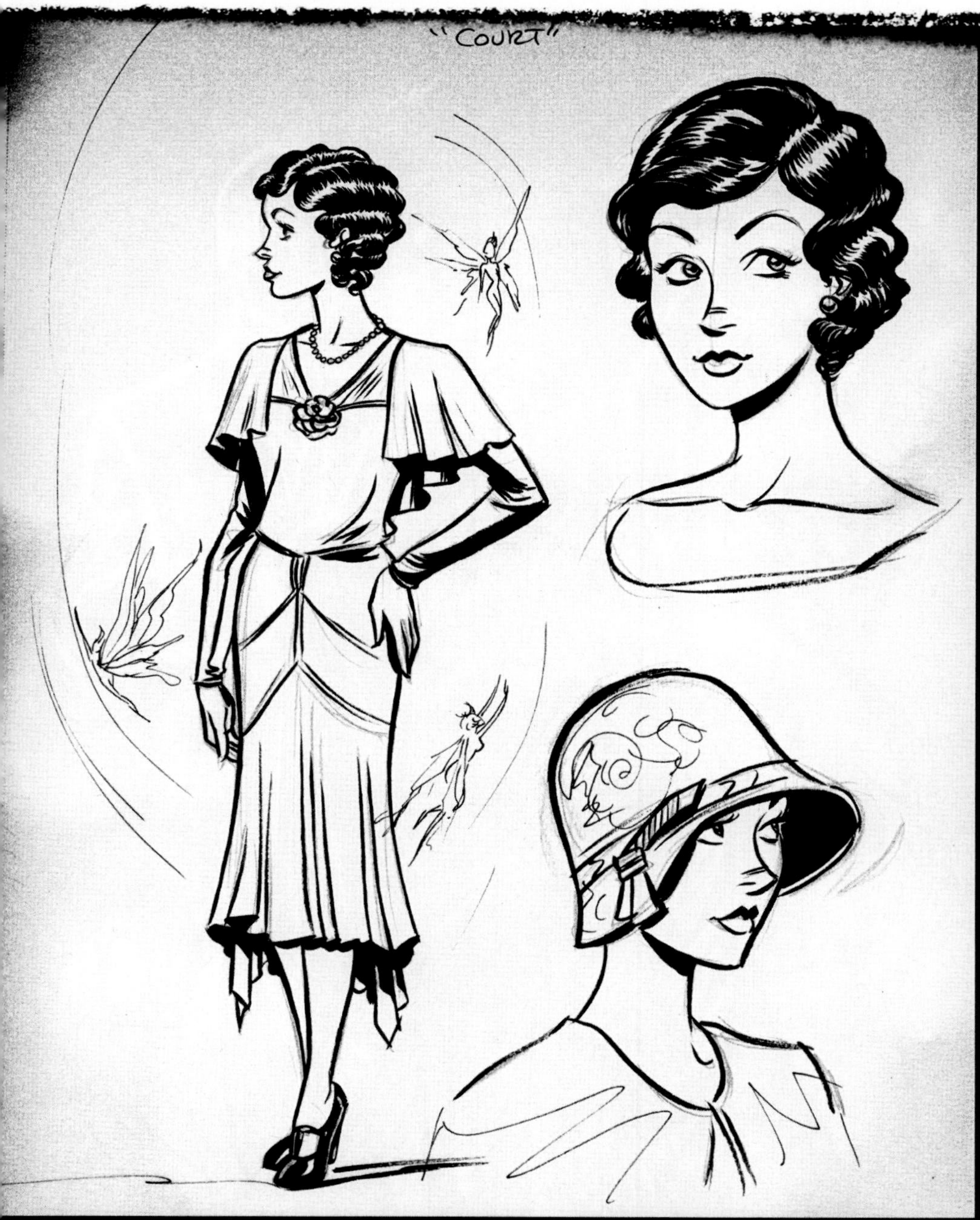
"COURT"

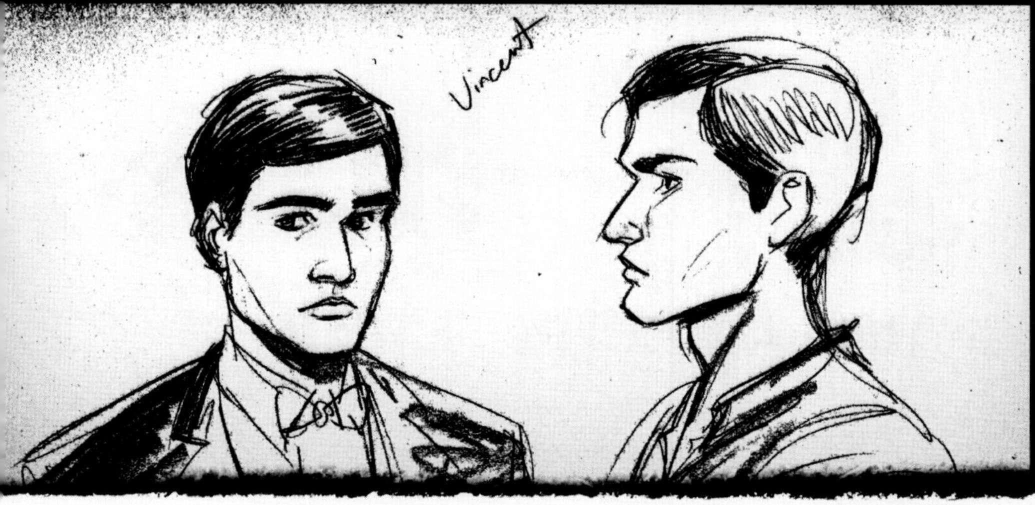
Vincent

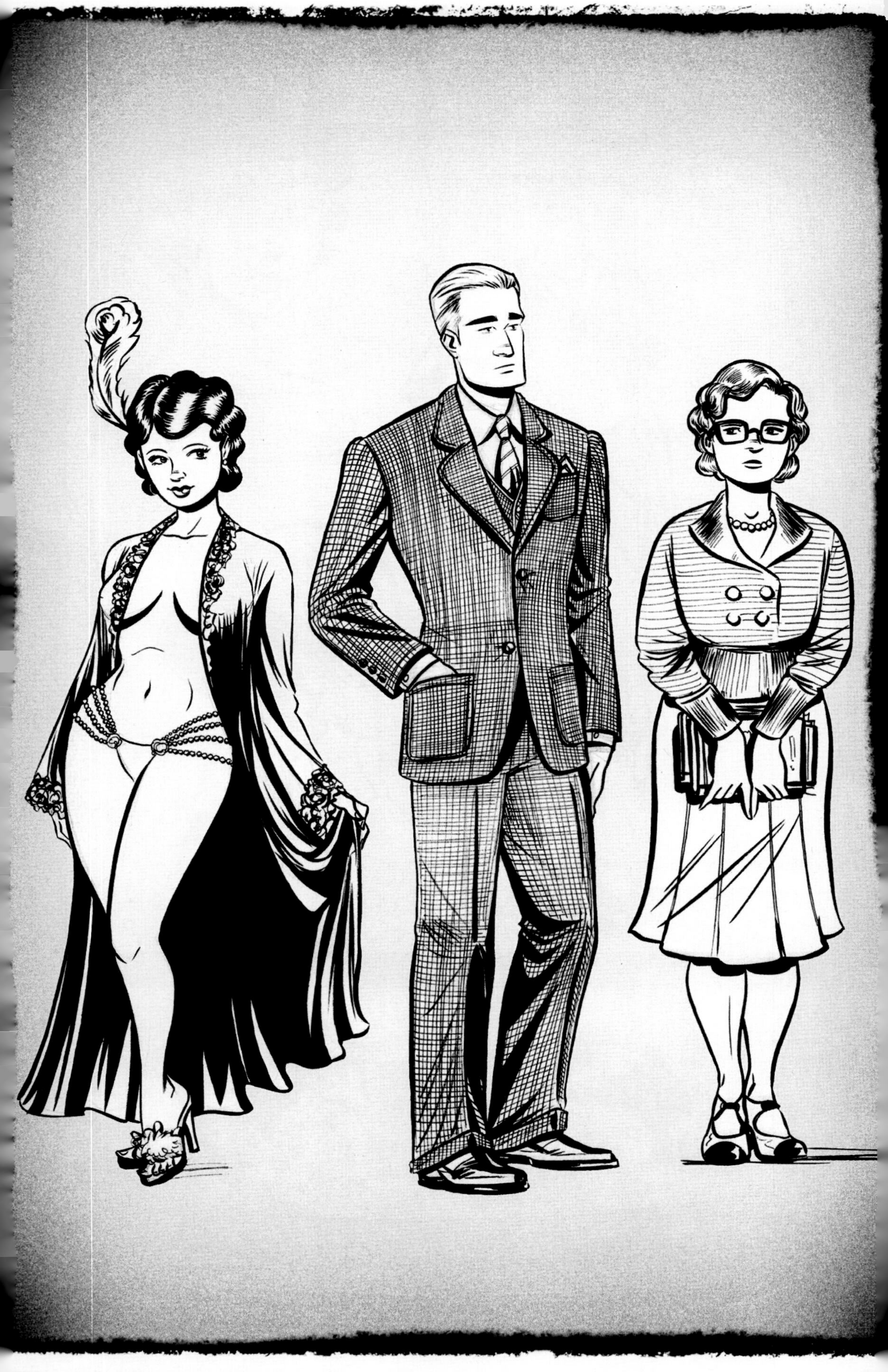

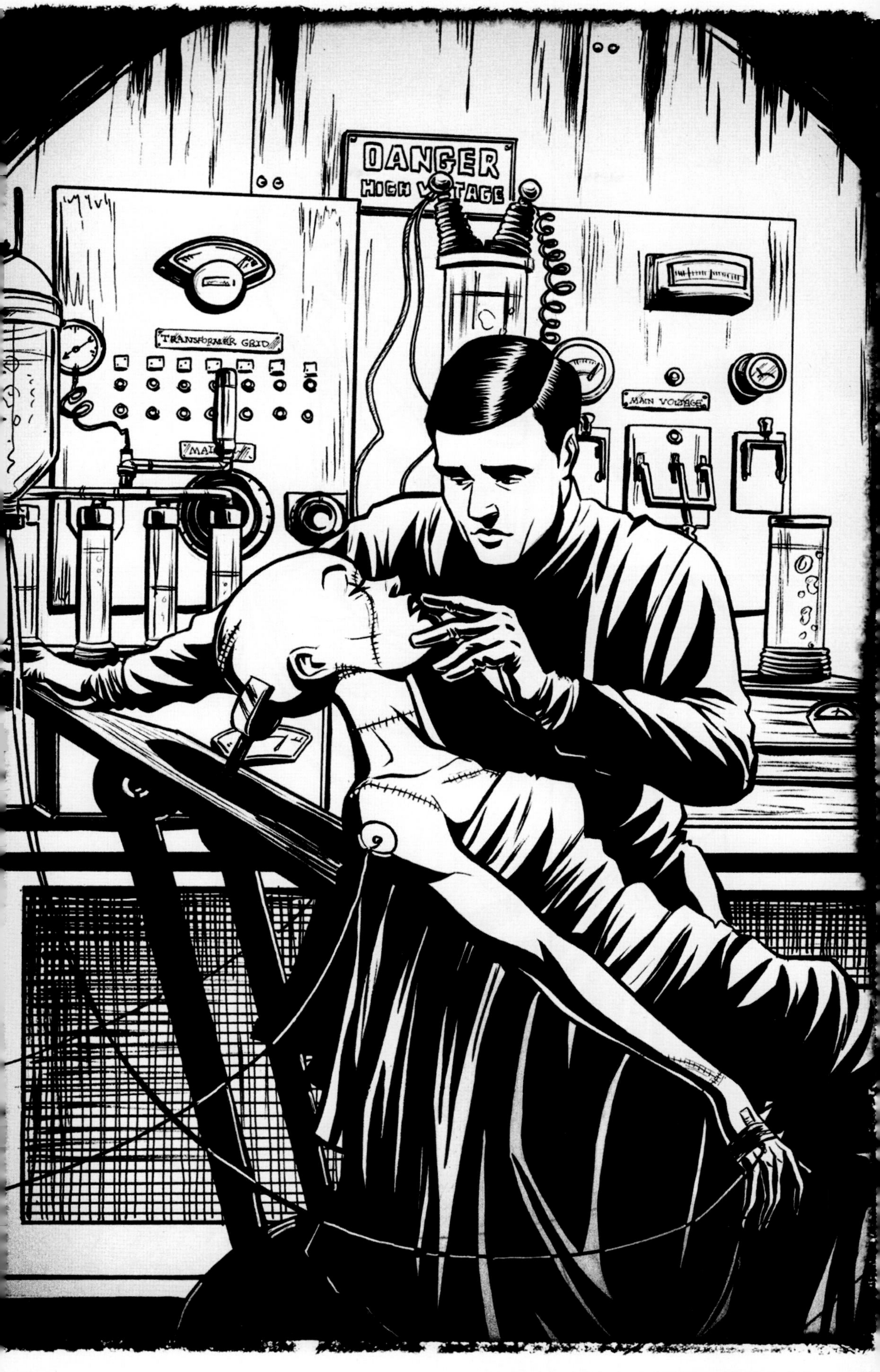
DANGER
TRANSFORMER GRID
MAIN VOLTAGE

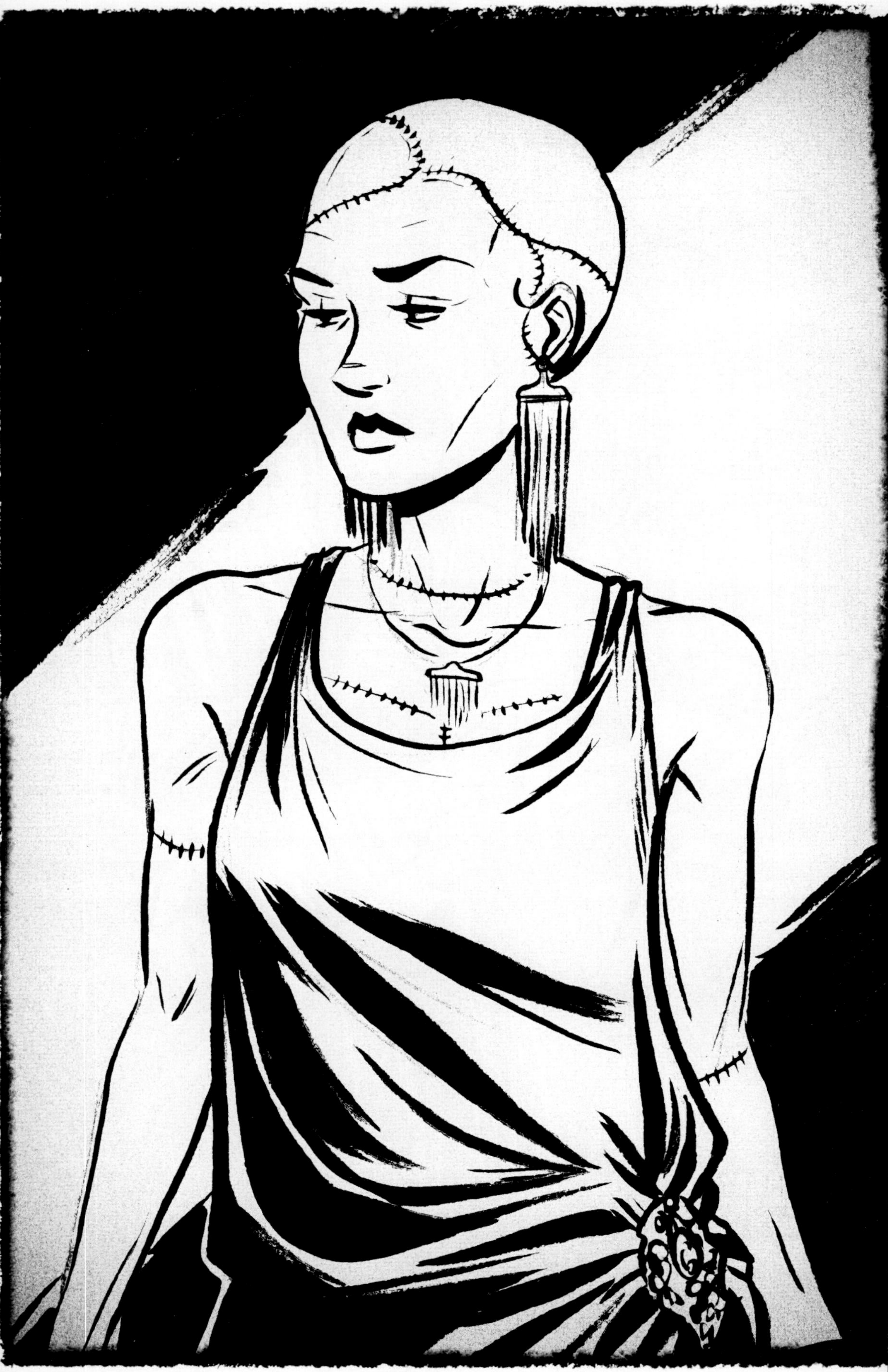

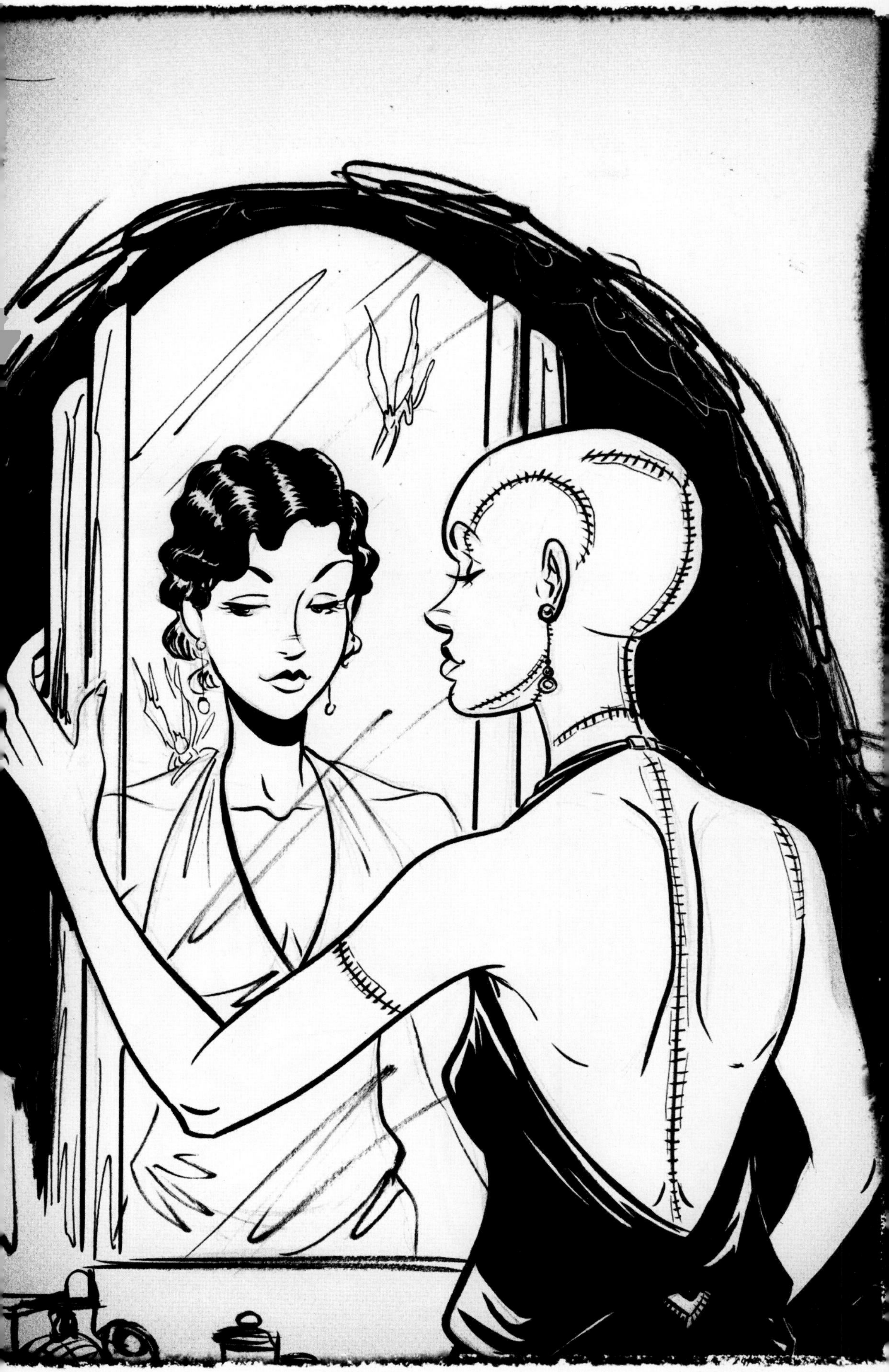

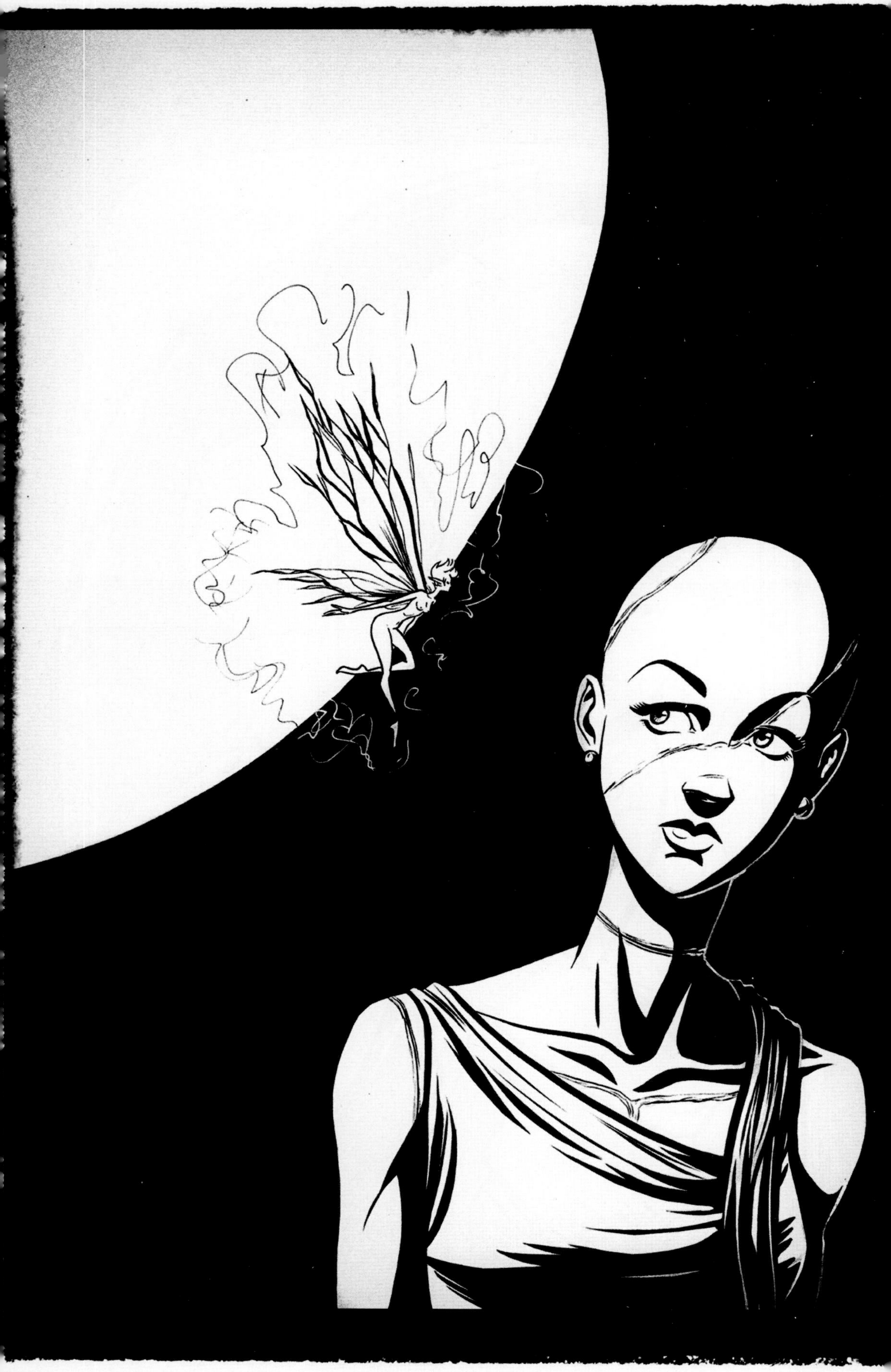

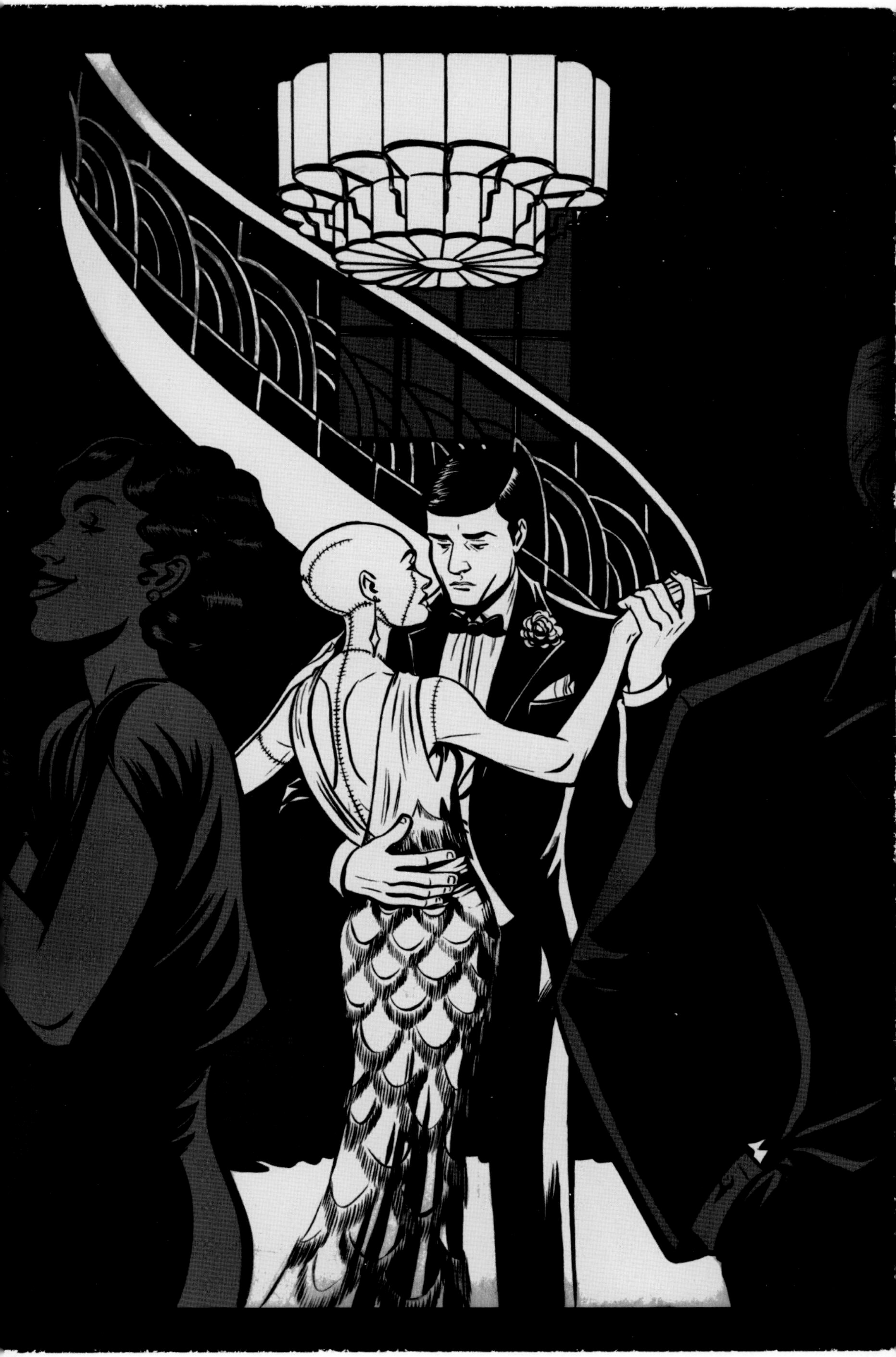

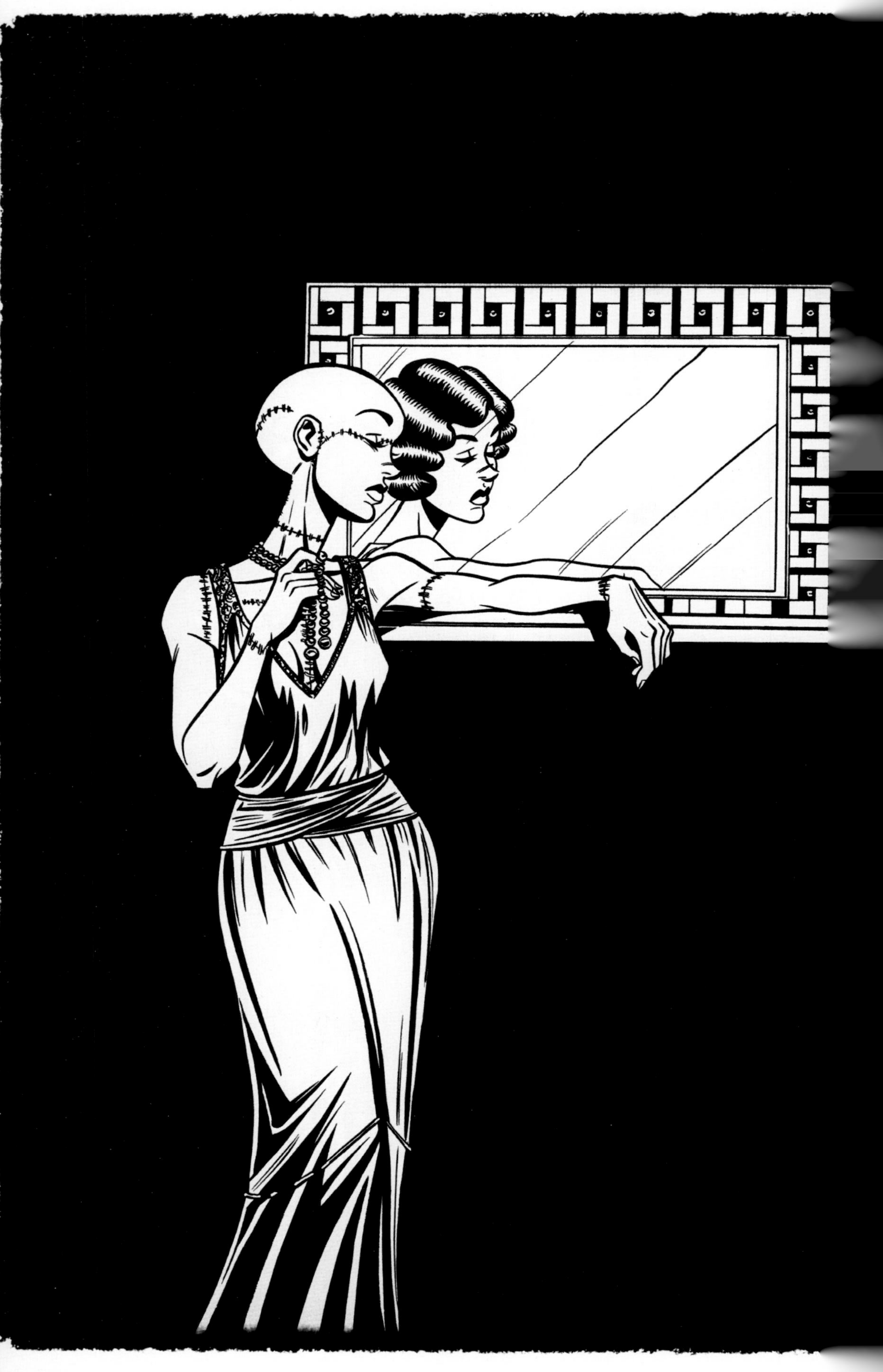

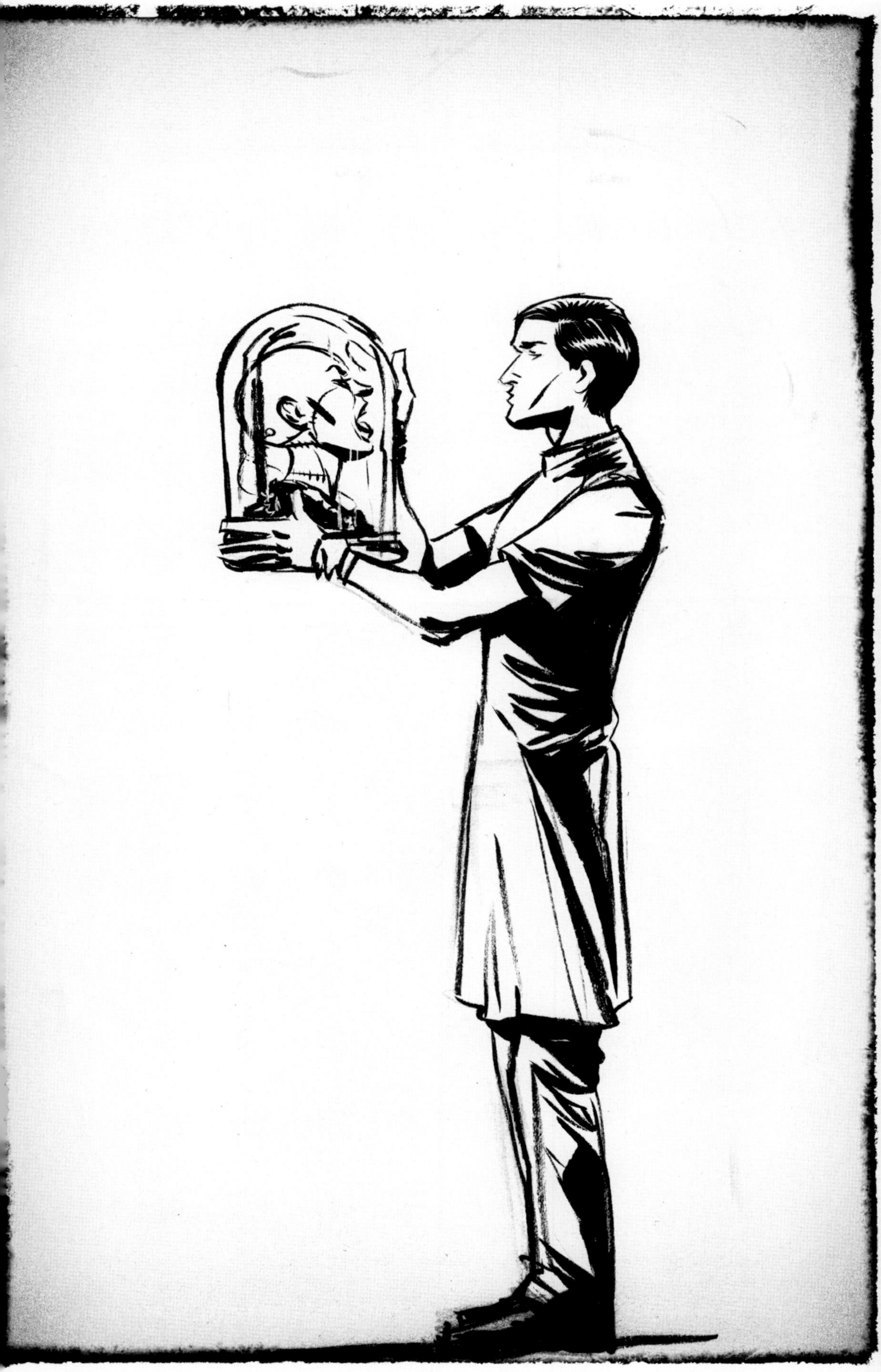

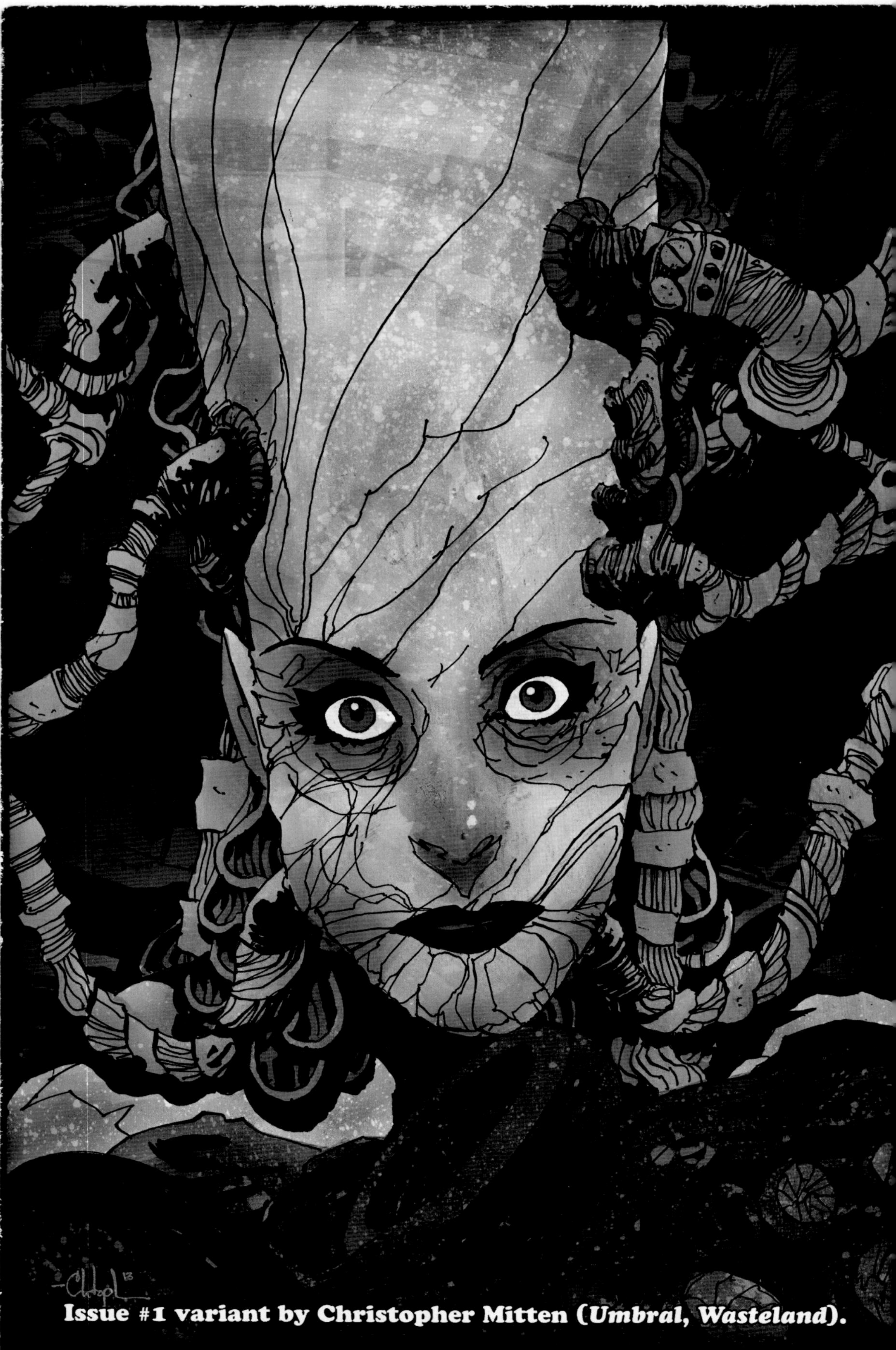

Issue #1 variant by Christopher Mitten (*Umbral*, *Wasteland*).

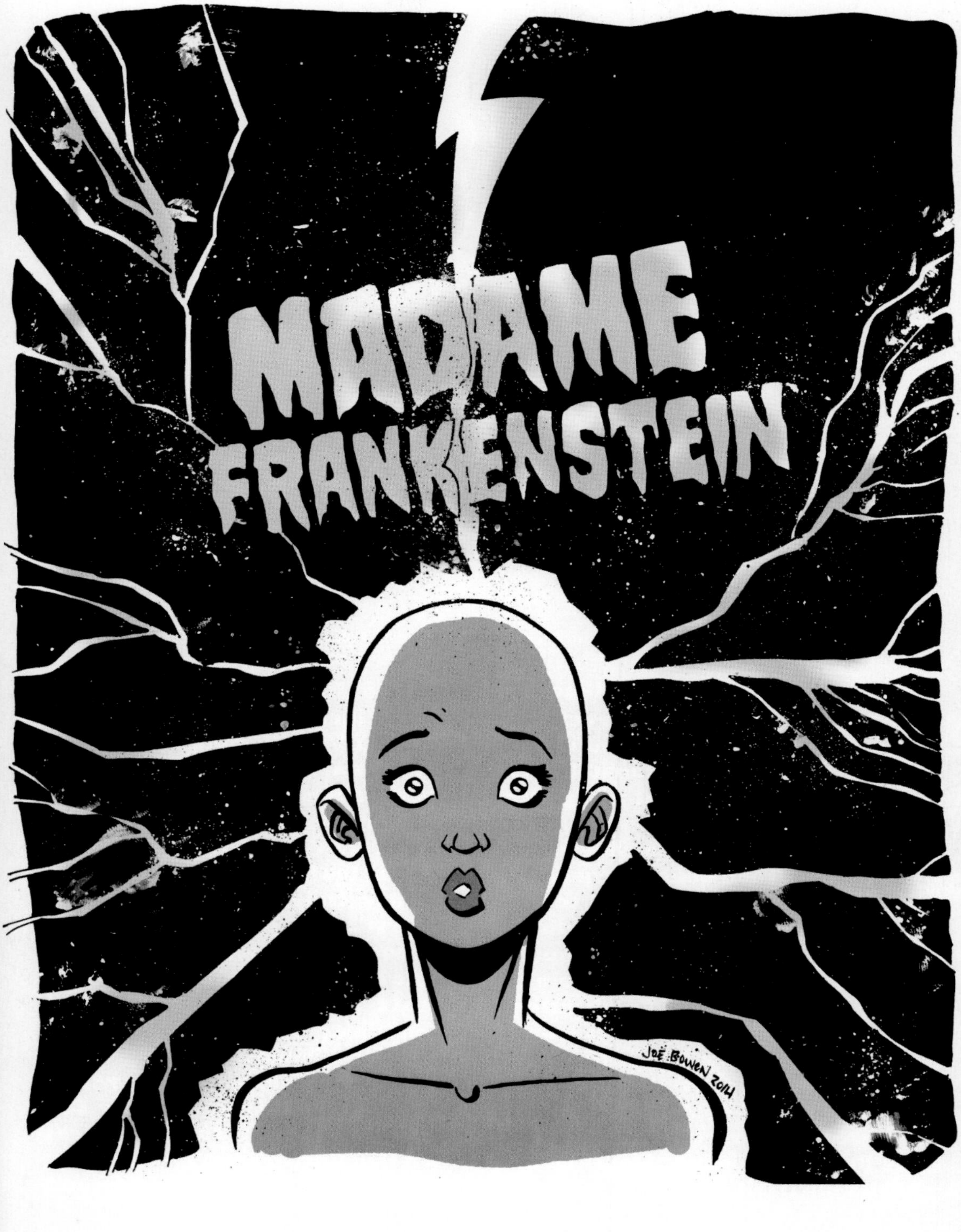
MADAME
FRANKENSTEIN
JOE BOWEN 2014

#7 back cover by Joe Bowen (*Model Student*).

Photo Credit: Aron Tiongco · Follow on Instagram @LoveAndComics

Born and raised in rural Missouri, *Megan Levens* began her art career as soon as she was old enough to draw on the walls. Fortunately, her parents never liked that wallpaper design very much anyway. After graduating from the Savannah College of Art and Design's sequential art program, Megan moved to Los Angeles to begin a career in advertising illustration, which helped support the pursuit of her lifelong dream to draw comics. *Madame Frankenstein* is her first published comics work, and second collaboration with writer Jamie S. Rich, after the Oni Press romance *Ares & Aphrodite: Love Wars*. She also recently worked on the *Buffy the Vampire Slayer* comic books for Dark Horse.

Jamie S. Rich is an author whose venues include Oni Press, Image Comics, DVDTalk.com, and various dive bars around Portland, OR. He is best known for his collaborations with artist Joëlle Jones on the graphic novels *12 Reasons Why I Love Her, You Have Killed Me*, and, most recently, *Lady Killer*. He published his first prose novel, *Cut My Hair*, in 2000, and his first superhero comic book, *It Girl and the Atomics*, in 2012. In between, he has worked on multiple projects in both mediums, including his most recent graphic novels, *A Boy and a Girl*, drawn by Natalie Nourigat, and *Archer Coe and the Thousand Natural Shocks* with Dan Christensen. He currently reviews film for the *Oregonian* and blogs at confessions123.com.

CHRIS CRANK: Hi! I go by crank! You might know my work from several recent Oni books like *The Sixth Gun, Brides of Helheim, Terrible Lizard,* etc. Or maybe you've seen my letters in *Revival, HACK/slash, God Hates Astronauts* or *Dark Engine* (Image). Or perhaps you've read *Lady Killer* or *Sundowners* (Dark Horse). Heck, you might even be reading the award-winning *Battlepug* (battlepug.com) right now! If you're weird you could have heard me online at crankcast.net where I talk with Mike Norton, Tim Seeley, Sean Dove and Jenny Frison weekly about things that are sometimes comics related. If you're super-obscure you've heard me play music with the Vladimirs or Sono Morti (sonomorti.bandcamp.com). Catch me on Twitter: @ccrank.

Probably you don't know who I am at all.

That's OK.

JOËLLE JONES is a comic book artist currently living in Portland, OR. She has worked on various projects with Graphic Universe, Vertigo, DC, and Marvel. Jones collaborated with Jamie S. Rich on the Oni Press graphic novels *12 Reasons Why I Love Her* and *You Have Killed Me,* and currently draws the *Helheim* series written by Cullen Bunn and colored by Nick Filardi.

She is also the co-creator, lead writer, and artist on *Lady Killer* from Dark Horse Comics. Visit her website at joellejones.com and on Twitter at @joelle_jones.

NICK FILARDI grew up in New London, Connecticut listening to Small Town Hero and watching *Batman: The Animated Series.* After graduating from Savannah College of Art and Design in 2004, he colored for Zylonol Studios under Lee Loughridge in Savannah, GA while maintaining the pretense of working an "office" job.
He is currently in Gainesville, Florida with his three-legged dog, DeNiro.

You can find his work in *Helheim, Powers, The Victories,* and *Atomic Robo.* He can be found on Twitter at @nick_fil.

MORE BOOKS FROM THE CREATORS OF
MADAME FRANKENSTEIN:

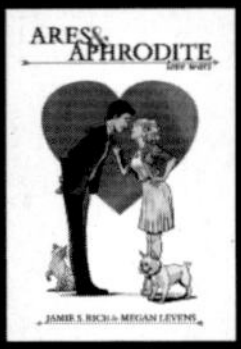
ARES & APHRODITE

ARES & APHRODITE: LOVE WARS
Jamie S. Rich & Megan Levens
168 pages * Softcover
Full Color Interiors
ISBN 978-1-62010-208-4

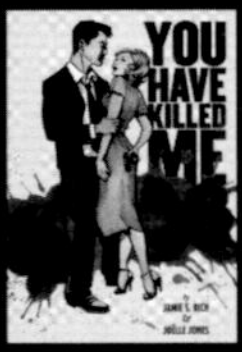
YOU HAVE KILLED ME

YOU HAVE KILLED ME
Jamie S. Rich & Joëlle Jones
192 Pages * Hardcover
Black & White Interiors
ISBN 978-1-932664-88-1

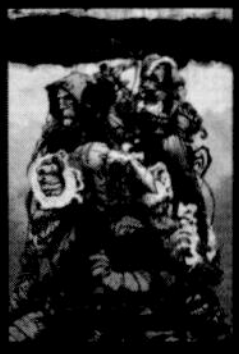

HELHEIM, VOL. 1
Cullen Bunn, Joëlle Jones, & Nick Filardi
160 Pages * Softcover
Full Color Interiors
ISBN 978-1-62010-014-1

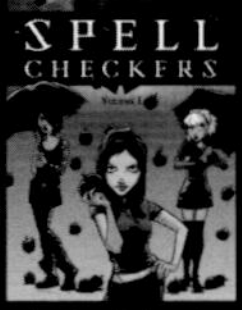
SPELL
CHECKERS

SPELL CHECKERS, VOL. 1
Jamie S. Rich, Joëlle Jones, & Nicolas Hitori de
152 Pages * Softcover
Black & White Interiors
ISBN 978-1-934964-32-3

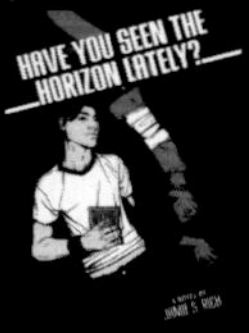
HAVE YOU SEEN THE HORIZON LATELY?

HAVE YOU SEEN THE HORIZON LATELY?
Jamie S. Rich * Cover by Joëlle Jones
264 pages * Softcover
Prose Novel
ISBN: 978-1-932664-73-7

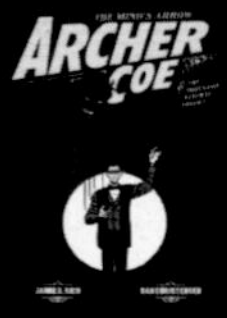
ARCHER COE

ARCHER COE & THE THOUSAND NATURAL SHOCKS
Jamie S. Rich & Dan Christensen
160 Pages * Softcover
Black & White Interiors
ISBN 978-1-62010-121-6

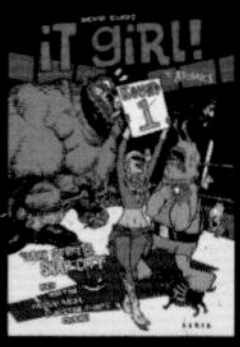
iT GiRL!

IT GIRL & THE ATOMICS, VOL. 1
Jamie S. Rich, Mike Norton, & Chynna Clugston Flores
168 Pages * Softcover
Full Color Interiors
ISBN 978-1-607067-25-5

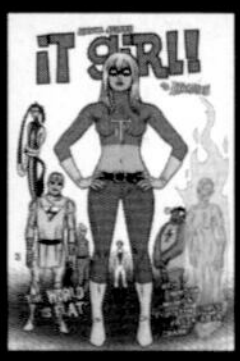
iT GiRL!

IT GIRL & THE ATOMICS, VOL. 2
Jamie S. Rich, Mike Norton, Natalie Nourigat,
& Chynna Clugston Flores
168 Pages * Softcover
Full Color Interiors
ISBN 978-1-607067-91-7

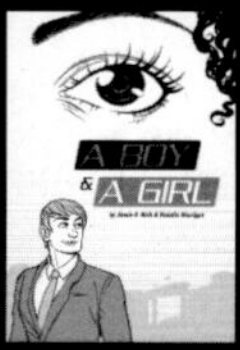
A BOY
& A GIRL

A BOY AND A GIRL
Jamie S. Rich & Natalie Nourigat
176 Pages * Softcover
Two Color Interiors
ISBN 978-1-62010-089-9

To find a comic specialty store in your area,
call 1-888-COMICBOOK or visit www.comicshops.us.